Dublin Pub Life
and Lore

An Oral History

7/20/20

By the same author

Georgian Dublin: Ireland's Imperilled Architectural Heritage
Dublin's Vanishing Craftsmen
Stoneybatter: Dublin's Inner Urban Village
Dublin Street Life and Lore: An Oral History
Dublin Tenement Life: An Oral History

Dublin Pub Life and Lore

AN ORAL HISTORY

Kevin C. Kearns

ROBERTS RINEHART PUBLISHERS

Published in the United States and Canada by
Roberts Rinehart Publishers
6309 Monarch Park Place
Niwot, Colorado 80503

Distributed to the trade by Publishers Group West

First published in Ireland by Gill and Macmillan Ltd.

International Standard Book Number 1-57098-164-7

Library of Congress Number 97-67692

Cover design: Ann W. Douden
Production: Pauline Brown

Manufactured in the United States of America

10 9 8 7 6 5 4 3 2 1

To my late father, Bernard Owen Kearns, who lifted a few jars in his time

PUB CRAWL

Maid of Erin, ere we part has the barman ere a heart?
Give, oh give me time to state I'd like three pints upon the slate!
Or since that might seem in vain, may I call "the same again?"
Or must I beat a quick retreat and take my custom down the street
To hie away and pocket pride, and try my luck at *Flowing Tide*?

Or wander to some other bar, the *Abbey Mooney*, the *Plough and
Star*
Or *Madigan's* house, snug and cosy, and gossip there with Moore St
Rosie?
Or cross the bridge with eager paces—*Scanlan's, Dwyer's* or then to
Grace's
With docker and with stevedore to enter through *The Twangman's*
door?
Or *Regan's* pub in Tara Street, where firemen oft are wont to meet
(Were porter freely to cascade it could not quench our Fire
Brigade!)

Or Poolbeg Street—that famous joint, where *Mulligan's* boast the
grandest pint
And students line the ancient bar and "Press" men down their
cutline jar—
For "cubs" and "comps" can quickly sink pints as black as printers
ink!
Or *Flynn's of Fleet*, and *Bowie's* nice, beside the *Pearl* of such great
price
Where drama buffs and theatre critics quietly sip their glass of
Smith'icks
While jotting down the various scenes just enacted in the Queens
Commenting on the actors' capers for tomorrow morning's papers—
With faintest praise quietly damning the histrionics and the
hamming.

Or in my quest for festive jar should I wander wide, and forage far?
To Harry Street, and thus, *McDaid*, where poet and playwright
often paid
A visit to this fine abode to recite their latest ode.
Or *Davy Byrne's*, so smart and trendy "Re-may Mar-tong and gless
of shendy!"
Or other houses that I know *Do'eny Nesbitt*, Merrion Row
Or *Toner's* where the balladeers will sing their songs and sink their
beers

(For Dubliners are all good sports—And there's pubs galore up near the courts
Like *Wig & Gown*, where lawyer with brief debates the law with petty thief,
Where bailiffs booze an 'ttornies tipple, and all engage in legal piffle!)

Or further still—the countryside! (Ah, God be with the bona fide!)
To step it out with marching feet to *Eugene's* or *The Sheaf of Wheat*,
Or thumb a lift from passing car out to the *Boot* or *Man-O'-War*
Or *Tolka House*, or *Cat & Cage*—where soccer talk is all the rage,
Or opposite end of Richmond Road *The Widow Meaghar's* and Gaelic Code
Or *Kelly's*, *Cole's* or other pubs where they all booh Kerry and cheer the Dubs!
Or further on the road to Howth—that other inn of happy note
Harry Byrne's of noble fame, and echoes of Bram Stoker's name. . . .

But I've gone too far in "bounds an' leps", and must, alas, retrace my steps
Past all the pubs of Ballybough, with visits brief, before the clock
Warns me that it's "closing time", and puts a finish to my rhyme.

So here I am, back at the start and musing if the barman's heart
Is made of substance hard as stone—he ignores my loud impassioned tone:
"Three pints of stout, for Goodness sake! I've hoorin' thirst that's hard to slake!"
(He's pretending that he cannot hear—perhaps he thinks I'd too much beer?)
Perhaps he's right—I'll call a halt "Aidan, please—a ball o' malt!"

(Courtesy of Vincent Caprani)

"All that is left of the old Dublin seems to concentrate itself in the old pubs, and sometimes, when you go out, you could almost expect to find the trams running outside."

Maurice Gorham, *Irish Pubs Of Character*, 1969

"The walls of so many Irish pubs have heard stories of great joy and celebration, also those of tragedy and great sadness. They have listened impassively as one might expect, taking neither side of any argument, like the same diplomatic barmen under whose cautious eyes all of humanity passes by."

Liam Blake, *Irish Pubs*, 1985

"The fame of some of Dublin's pubs has spread to the far corners of the world."

Living in the City, 1991

CONTENTS

Acknowledgments

To historically chronicle Dublin pub life and lore as it existed earlier in this century I had to find elderly publicans, barmen and "regulars" who possessed vivid recollections of the "old days". Since many of the city's famed pubs were long ago demolished for urban renewal it was a challenging task to track down individuals once intimately associated with them. This search could never have been successful without the generous assistance of many individuals to whom I am much indebted. I owe great thanks to Frank Fell, director, and Liz Byrne of the Dublin Licensed Vintners' Association for their efforts to locate a number of Dublin's famous publicans from a past era. Similarly, the staff of the Vintners' and Grocers' Union directed me to several prominent barmen who were leaders of their organisation during the turmoil and strike of four decades ago. Paula Howard, head librarian at Pearse Street Library, was extremely helpful in my archival research on the history and evolution of the public house. My research assistants Jamie Urban and Martha Emmanouilides worked tirelessly in our quest to find and tape record pub folk and have my lasting appreciation. Special gratitude is due to the late Paddy O'Brien, legendary barman at McDaid's, who in 1988 (only a few months before his passing) shared with me his long and colourful personal history in the public house trade. By telling of the rich, ebullient pub life which flourished in Dublin a half-century ago he unknowingly inspired me to write this book.

Introduction

"In the pub one can gather up stories and legends . . . and lore."

G. Ivan Morris, In Dublin's Fair City, 1947

"In its influence on public opinion, the pint has been as powerful a catalyst as the pulpit, and the pub is as worthy of serious discussion and consideration as the Church."

Liam Blake, Irish Pubs, 1985

In 1610 Englishman Barnaby Rich in *A New Description of Ireland* proclaimed with dismay that "in Dublin the whole profit of the towne stands upon alehouses . . . there are whole streets of taverns."[1] By the eighteenth century in some city parishes nearly one out of every four dwellings was a tippling house. So prevalent were public houses in James Joyce's day that in *Ulysses* the protagonist Stephen Dedalus muses how it would be a challenging game to try and get from one side of the city to the other without passing the doors of a pub. For centuries Dublin has been renowned for its profusion of pubs and exuberant pub life. Pubs have been the nucleus of social life for Dubliners of every ilk, from plebeian dockers and drovers to aristocrats and genius writers. The public house has providentially survived into the modern age as a vibrant social institution and the most ubiquitous feature of Dublin's cityscape. Venerable pubs are the quintessence of old Dublin, embodying local customs, traditions, folkways, wit and characters which give the city its unique ethos. No other city in the world is so famed for its rich pub culture. Indeed, public houses are so synonymous with Dublin that it is scarcely possible to envision the capital without them.

The traditional Dublin public house evolved from the dusky drinking dens of an earlier epoch. During the Middle Ages ale was the most common table beverage in Dublin and most brewing was done in the home by women. The good reputation of a house's ale undoubtedly led to the first public houses being set up for local folk. By the early 1600s an unbridled proliferation of alehouses led to blatant drunkenness and riotous behaviour. English visitors condemned it as a "swinish vice" and moral scandal.[2] In 1650 when the population of Dublin was reckoned to be about 4,000 families there were 1,180 drinking houses.[3] Along many streets half or more of all buildings were taverns. At the close of the seventeenth century Dublin had gained an "unenviable notoriety" for its multitude of public houses and insobriety.[4] Even the crypt in Christ Church Cathedral was converted into a tavern where "sepulchral boozing flourished".[5]

The eighteenth century saw a dramatic increase in the number of pubs and alcohol consumption. Ale, whiskey, wine and other drinks were so cheap that one could get quite drunk on tuppence. By 1760 there were 2,300 alehouses and taverns in the city.[6] Dublin was noted for its ebullient public houses and their often fascinating names like the "Old Sots Hole", "Bleeding Horse" and "Wandering Jew". They ran the gamut from squalid to splendid and became rendezvous points for various groups such as labourers, tradesmen, lawyers, businessmen, professionals, political party members and common rogues for all of whom the pub became their "local".

In 1791 the creation of the notorious spirit grocers markedly increased drunkenness among women as well as men. The sight of people staggering out of drinking houses in a pathetically sodden state alarmed "respectable" citizens. Insobriety permeated every social rank. By the end of the eighteenth century "compulsory drinking customs among all classes had firmly established a drunken tyranny".[7] Moralists, social reformers and medical men sermonised about the need to eradicate public houses and champion the cause of sobriety. In 1805 the Reverend James Whitelaw in his *Essay on the Population of Dublin* railed passionately against the abominable public houses and the human degeneration they caused:[8]

"Dram-shops are the most alarming of all nuisances . . . [they] vend raw spirits, a poison productive of vice, riot and disease, hostile to all habits of decency, honesty and industry and, in short, destructive to the souls and bodies of our fellow-creatures. These houses, open at all hours by day and night, are scenes of unceasing profaneness and intemperance."

The Temperance Movement, which began in Ireland in 1829, focused vigorously on the capital which claimed the highest concentration of public houses and most distressing rate of inebriety. Temperance groups such as the Dublin Total Abstinence Society held public rallies and parades, gave free lectures and introduced coffee houses as an alternative to pubs. By the time Father Theobald Mathew, Ireland's most famous temperance reformer, held his third public meeting in Dublin in the 1840s he had given the pledge to 173,000 citizens.[9] Despite the early successes, the calamitous Potato Famine struck the Temperance Movement a blow from which it never recovered and Dublin sadly returned to its wanton ways. By the 1870s the number of arrests in the city for drunkenness exceeded that of London which was ten times larger. One female drunkard had 264 convictions. Owing to excessive drinking the city was besieged by crime and riotous conduct.

Finally, in 1876 a Select Committee of the House of Lords on Intemperance was appointed to inquire into the problem of inebriation and the role of public houses. After gathering a plethora of testimony from experts and commoners alike, much enlightened sociological evidence was forthcoming. There clearly emerged a link between the poverty and hardship of the lower classes and their need to use the public house as an "escape" from their plight. The pub was recognised as an emotional and psychological "safety valve" and refuge for the impoverished masses. Sir Charles A. Cameron, Chief Health Officer in Dublin during the latter part of the nineteenth century, validated the justification for public houses in his sympathetic report on *How the Poor Live*:[10]

> "The workman is blamed for visiting the public house, but it is to him what the club is to the rich man. His home is rarely a comfortable one and in the winter the bright light, the warm fire and the gaiety of the public house are attractions which he finds it difficult to resist."

On the basis of such rationale, the Committee accepted the legitimacy of pubs as a beneficial social institution—but they strongly condemned the habit of customers drinking to excess. As a consequence, they favoured eradicating illicit drinking places, tightening the controls and limiting the number of legally licensed pubs and encouraging publicans to prohibit drunkenness on their premises.

After centuries of being cursed and condemned, "buffeted by storms of public controversy, assailed by the slings and arrows of temperance reformers", H. A. Monckton concludes that it is "remarkable that the public house has survived in so ubiquitous a way".[11] Its very survivability is unmistakable testimony to its enduring importance in Irish society. As Gorham affirms, the pub has evolved as a "living" social institution which plays a profound role in the daily lives of the populace.[12] Indeed, it has been calculated that "of the social institutions that mould men's lives" the pub has more buildings, holds more people, takes more of their time and money, than church, cinema, dance-hall and political organisations together.[13] As a consequence, pub goers develop a strong institutional identity with their local pub where they find communal solidarity with their mates. And perhaps more than any other social institution, the pub is founded on the principles of equality and democracy. In 1936 Burke praised the egalitarian nature of the public house, noting "It is the one place where a man may greet and talk with strangers on level terms. It is the common and open club."[14] Only the pub provides a climate for intimate social interaction in which persons of every social and economic class can share personal feelings. The pub thus becomes a true microcosm of local life, reflecting the socio-economic ethos of its host community. Furthermore, writes Smith in the *British Journal of Sociology*, the neighbourhood pub is the "locus of popular culture".[15] Every pub possesses its unique "cultural character" based upon distinctive lifeways, customs and values of the local people.

The most coveted social niche in the life of many Dubliners is their status as a "regular" in their local pub. It has traditionally been the epicentre of social life, local news, companionship and even entertainment since every neighbourhood pub is blessed with its own local talent of singers, musicians, dancers, comedians and story tellers. But the art of conversation has always been the very heart of pub life and here it survives as in no other forum. The pub setting is like a stage with a cast of characters each acting out his natural role. Be they philosopher, wag, wit, grouser, political pundit, buffoon or mere listener—all are welcome in the conversational circle. Gregarious cronies cluster in cliques to discuss and dissect sports, politics, literature, local happenings, world events and the general state of mankind. All are treated with equal solemnity or frivolity depending upon the prevailing mood of the moment. There may be hushed tones during a serious story, clamorous laughter at a good yarn or roaring oratory amidst political debate or literary analysis. The scene is not only orally stimulating but physically animated for amid the banter and badinage men pound the table to make a point, slap their knee in appreciation of a witty word and gesticulate wildly with their arm to beckon the barman for another pint. At peak moments a pub can crackle with human electricity.

Even more important than the entertainment they enjoy in their local pub is the deep friendship they cultivate. The social chemistry among regulars creates over time a "support group" environment in which they can openly share personal feelings about domestic life, work, health, finances and phobias. Based upon interdependence and mutual trust, strong fraternal bonds are forged. Men often confess to feeling closer to pub mates than some members of their own family. For some pub regulars, especially bachelors and widowers, their pub pals actually become a surrogate family. As they grow old together when a lifelong friend passes away it is regarded as a death in the immediate family.

The publican has always been one of the most essential ingredients in the composition of a public house. His role goes far beyond that of congenial host behind the bar. Historically, he has been a leading figure in the local community performing valuable services for people in times of need. Publicans lived above their shop, knew customers intimately, generously dispensed advice, guidance, financial assistance and even mediated family disputes. They customarily provided money and drink for life's great moments—births, christenings, first holy communion, weddings, wakes and burials. Such debts were routinely "put on the slate" to be paid off over months or years. Often, they were simply forgotten. Explains 75-year-old publican John O'Dwyer: "The publican was the man who [financially] *christened* them, *married* them, *buried* them. He was *the* man, he was there for them." He was also frequently called upon to read and write correspondence for persons with relatives abroad and to provide letters of reference for people seeking employment or buying a piece of furniture or a bicycle. There was no one else to serve as their financial benefactor and guarantor. Because of his indispensable role in Dublin's poor and working-class neighbourhoods 60-year-old Clara Gill, a publican's daughter, always felt that "a good publican was like the father of the community". Thus, in respect and status he was often at a level with the parish priest. Publican Jack Cusack, 76, of the Coombe, contends that some enjoyed an even more exalted pedestal —"Oh, those old publicans, they were the captains of us all . . . a publican years ago was *Jesus Christ*!"

Women have long been part of the Dublin pub scene, though as a sequestered and numerical minority. By long and sacred tradition, Dublin's public houses were exclusively a male domain or, as some flinty old regulars prefer to put it, the "holy ground". Neighbourhood pubs stood as an anachronistic bastion of male supremacy until recent decades. Back in the 1920s recalls 90-year-old May Hanaphy of the Liberties: "Oh, a woman'd be *murdered* if she was caught in a pub. It was a *disgrace* for a woman." There were, however, two conspicuous exceptions—revered grannies and hardy women street dealers. Owing to their longevity and difficult life they were excluded from the social mores which barred other women. For them it was perfectly acceptable to sit beshawled in a cloistered snug sipping a glass of porter and perhaps smoking a clay pipe. Some of the most amusing tales about old Dublin pub life focus on their behaviour. Their special place in the history and folklore of Dublin pubs is well preserved in the oral tradition, as evidenced by many of the personal narratives in this book.

Dublin has always been noted for its remarkable variety of pubs, from the most raunchy to elegant. Such posh, pedigreed pubs as the Scotch House and Palace Bar drew professionals and intelligentsia who "held court" over the finest whiskey and brandy. By contrast were the dingy matchbox-size locals in working-class neighbourhoods frequented by manual labourers and tough dockers who could put away pints of porter by the dozen. Then there were the truly wretched watering holes like Crilly's of Sarsfield Quay, packed with diseased prostitutes, pimps, thieves and hustlers of every sort. There was a pub for every human species.

Between the 1930s and 1950s Dublin was acclaimed for its singing pubs and literary pubs, both of which received international attention. Gala singing houses like Lalor's of Wexford Street were crowded nightly with visitors from Europe and America as well as every class of Dubliner. During their heyday they were touted as one of the city's greatest attractions. Equally heralded were Dublin's literary pubs, the likes of the Bailey, Davy Byrne's and McDaid's. Here Dublin's poets, novelists, journalists, artists and intellectuals congregated in a Bohemian atmosphere of stimulating conversation and social interaction. In its halcyon days McDaid's boasted the grandest galaxy of literary luminaries on the Dublin scene. Regulars included Brendan Behan, Patrick Kavanagh, Brian O'Nolan, Gainor Crist, Austin Clarke, Anthony Cronin, J. P. Donleavy and Liam O'Flaherty. Head barman Paddy O'Brien, who had to cope daily with this coterie of egotistical and temperamental writers, fondly remembers "*all* types of literary people, poets and writers. There was this *great* blend. And the conversation at McDaid's . . . *great*!" It is not likely that any Dublin pub will see their collective likes again.

Apart from the legitimate public houses in Dublin there was an underworld of illicit drinking dens known as shebeens, kips and speakeasies which did a flourishing business. Though illegal, these places *were* public drinking houses which played an important part in the lives of Dubliners. Hence, their story is told here as well. Indeed, much fascinating history surrounds these clandestine premises which were always risky and exciting by nature. The city's more famous madams, prostitutes, kip-keepers, shebeeners and speakeasy operators hold a special niche in the folklore of the public house.

Although the public house has for centuries played a significant role in the social, economic, political and literary life of Dublin it has been a woefully ignored topic of study by scholars. Blake outrightly declares the local pub a seriously "neglected part of our national heritage".[16] Monckton theorises about this scholarly omission:[17]

> "The very existence of the public house seems to have been rather taken for granted in much the same way as the air we breathe. It is perhaps this attitude which accounts for the dearth of literature about its historical connections with national life."

As a historical and contemporary social institution and locus of community culture it deserves serious attention. However, as Clinard discloses, "Despite the obvious importance of the public drinking house most publications about it have been popular articles or propaganda."[18] Typically, literary pieces are of a superficial, stereotypical nature, depicting the pub as a sort of comical set on the Abbey stage filled with contrived characters and dialogue. As a consequence, there has been "little attempt to make an objective appraisal of how the pub works out in *human* terms of everyday life".[19]

To chronicle the human dimension of pub life and lore as it existed in the early part of this century we must use the oral historical method of seeking out elderly publicans and regulars and tape recording their verbal testimonies for posterity. As "old-timers" from generations past, they are a rich repository of pub history and folklore. Local historian Vincent Caprani acknowledges the existence of this valuable "pub lore of our city", as does Gorham who identifies old Dublin public houses "around which a folklore has grown up".[20] But such accounts of pub life and lore have never been systematically gathered, recorded and preserved in written form. There is now an urgency to document this history before all the old publicans and pubmen pass from our scene, for they are a fast-vanishing breed. Most of the individuals whose oral narratives appear in this book are between 60 and 90 years of age. Their recollections of pub life a half-century and more ago are astonishingly vivid, filled with accounts which are variously humorous, raw, compassionate and brutal—but always fascinating and authentic. Through their collective oral testimonies the bygone world of old Dublin pubs comes to life once again in exuberant form.

Not only are the old publicans and regulars fading from the scene, but over the past fifty years the traditional Dublin public house has undergone dramatic social and physical transformation. Change began in the post-war 1940s with the gradual admission of women, the creation of lounges and the insidious intrusion of television. But the most ferocious assault upon old public houses began in the 1960s when Dublin was swept up in a mindless craze of modernisation and urban redevelopment. Vulnerable pubs were assailed by developers, demolitionists and greedy investors who had no sense of historical appreciation or heartfelt affection for them. As a consequence, hundreds of public houses of historic importance, architectural integrity and unique social character have been altered and adulterated beyond original recognition, or bulldozed into oblivion. Elegant Victorian interiors have been ruthlessly gutted of their lovely marble, mahogany and brass, replaced with gaudy plastic and formica. To traditionalists and preservationists it has been heartbreaking. Today, only about twenty of Dublin's 775 public houses retain an authentic Victorian interior and ambience.[21] Equally distressing, wealthy businessmen now buy pubs from elderly publicans for astronomical sums and install in their place accountants and professional business managers with no historical ties to the trade. The result is a sad and ridiculous paradox—pubs without publicans!

Having evolved from its primitive alehouse days many centuries ago, the Dublin public house enters the twenty-first century a providential survivor. It stands as a last tangible relic of a simpler, more romantic, genteel age. But many of the city's surviving venerable pubs are fragile and imperilled by economic and physical forces. With emotion, publican Larry Ryan, whose pub was on the Coombe forty years ago, expresses his sentiments about the passing of Dublin's old pubs and their regulars:

"I hope that all the old Dublin men die before the old pubs go . . . because pubs was a *tradition* in Dublin, a way of life."

1

HISTORY AND EVOLUTION OF DUBLIN PUBLIC HOUSES

"Public drinking houses have their origins in the foothills of time."

Peter Clark, The English Alehouse, *1983*

"The Irish have had a long and picturesque history with alcohol—a history in which the use of alcohol has penetrated deeply into nearly every aspect of their social life."

David J. Pittman, Society, Culture, and Drinking Patterns, *1962*

ORIGINS AND USES OF ALCOHOL

Alcohol probably dates back to the Stone Age when primitive man serendipitously discovered that grapes left to ferment produced a drink pleasing to the taste and intoxicating to the senses. It is not known when the art of distilling alcohol from a fermented mixture was perfected but it existed in the age of Aristotle. When exactly distilling was introduced into Ireland remains obscure. Beverages such as ale and mead had long been staple drinks among the Celtic peoples and Irish folk tales contain many references to great feats of drinking. Folklore has it that when St Patrick was travelling through Connaught he was visited by a king who appeared before him "sadly in liquor".[1] Displeased with this discourtesy, St Patrick foretold that all the king's descendants would be drunkards and come to a bad end. It is said that his prophecy came true. Although St Patrick could reprove a drunken king he had no compunction about retaining a brewer of his own. In those ancient days ale was the most common drink and was consumed daily in monasteries. Even St Brighid was praised for the excellence of the ale she brewed.

Uisge beatha, the Irish word for whiskey, means "water of life". Though it is not known when this *aqua vitae* first appeared in Ireland it is thought that whiskey was first distilled in the country by monks who had come in contact with spirit-making on missionary journeys through Europe. In Ireland the natives were producing a drinkable spirit when the soldiers of Henry II invaded the country in 1171.[2] Actual references to *uisge beatha* and *aqua vitae* began appearing in Irish sources in the fourteenth century. Throughout the Middle Ages whiskey was the staple alcoholic beverage of the Irish countryside. Conversely, in Dublin ale was the common table beverage and most of the brewing was done in the home by women. The good reputation of a house's ale undoubtedly led to the first public houses being set up for the local folk.

Ale, whiskey, wine and other alcoholic drinks were consumed for both medicinal and convivial purposes. There are indications that medicinal uses of alcohol, preventive, palliative and curative, were prominent in Irish culture from very early times. The appellation "water of life" is a clear tribute to whiskey's perceived medicinal qualities. It was used to treat illness, cure disease, revive fallen warriors and combat the damp climate. It is well documented that large quantities of brandy were used to fight the cholera epidemics of 1831 and 1849.[3] Copious amounts of both whiskey and beer have traditionally been consumed to dispel fatigue and instil bodily strength. Both have also long been seen as a purifying agent used to cleanse innards and kill germs. In fact, on the birth of a child it was "no uncommon thing to give the poor innocent babe itself a sort of baptism by sponging it over with whiskey directly after birth."[4]

Historically, convivial drinking in Ireland has been even more prevalent. Over the centuries the Irish have developed a strong tradition of social and circumstantial drinking in which virtually every "occasion" must be celebrated by sharing drink—births, christenings, marriages, indentures, fairs, business transactions, wakes and social gatherings of every sundried sort. Drinking has also long fostered a spirit of courage and rebelliousness among the Irish, especially in terms of arousing patriotic sentiments and opposing British rule. Over centuries the perceived powers of drink to engender health, strength, courage and friendship became deeply ingrained in Irish culture. Indeed, the drinking custom became so inculcated in Irish life that "from cradle to grave it accompanies almost every individual".[5]

A CITY OF TAVERNS AND ALEHOUSES

Dublin became the centre of heavy drinking in Ireland and gained an unsavoury reputation for its insobriety. By the early 1600s "Dublin was not clean, neither was it sober."[6] Entire streets were given over to drink houses while brewers' carts were wheeled creakily about the streets, creating great nuisance. Excessive drinking was commonly associated with bawdy conduct, prostitution and riotous behaviour. Critical commentaries on Irish drunkenness were common in the writings of English visitors who regarded it as a "swinish vice" and moral scandal.[7] In 1610 Barnaby Rich, an English pamphleteer and soldier who served a term of duty in Ireland, wrote caustically in his *New Description of Ireland* about the deplorable drinking habits of the Dublin "natives":[8]

"In Dublin the whole profit of the towne stands upon alehouses and the selling of ale . . . there are whole streets of taverns . . . young housewives that are both very loathesome, filthy, and abominable both in life and manners are called tavern-keepers, the most of them known harlots."

Rich's proclamation was no exaggeration for Dublin was indeed awash with drink, much of it, he certified, the quality of "hogge wash". The entire face of the city was pock-marked with watering holes every few paces. In Rich's time ale brewing was largely a domestic craft conducted by women who were generously called tavern keepers. Every dwelling was potentially a public house. In fact, some of the most active brewers in the city were wives of City Aldermen. By the mid-1600s when the population of Dublin was reckoned to be about 4,000 families there were 1,180 drinking houses.[9] Along many streets half or more of the houses were taverns. Winetavern Street, from which its name derived, was especially noted for its conglomeration of drinking places. Even Christ Church Cathedral was adulterated by drink when the crypt was converted into a tavern where the practice of "sepulchral boozing flourished".[10] It was alleged that even members of the clergy had fallen victim to drunkenness. In 1633 the Lord Deputy, Thomas Stafford, Earl of Wentworth, complained to Archbishop Laud in London that the entire crypt had been given over to the sale of drink and tobacco.[11] This situation gave rise to an irreverent distich:[12]

"Spirits above and spirits below
Spirits divine and spirits—of wine."

Concern over the spread of public drinking houses and drunkenness in Dublin led to the first statute governing the sale of intoxicating liquor in Ireland in 1635. This Act ordained that no one was to keep any tippling house or sell any alcoholic beverage unless licensed by commissioners. While this first licensing law was ostensibly aimed at limiting the number of public houses in the city and reducing insobriety, it had little effect. Virtually nothing was done to decrease the number of drinking houses because the financial benefits to be derived from regulating, rather than suppressing, the drink business were too great to be disregarded, particularly by a government much in need of revenue. As a consequence, according to the records of the Dublin Corporation, by 1667 the number of taverns and alehouses in Dublin had risen to over 1,500.[13] Toward the close of the seventeenth century Dublin had such an "unenviable notoriety" for drunkenness that an Irish priest dubbed his native city "Dublin of the wine bottles".[14]

The eighteenth century saw an increase in public houses and alcohol consumption. By 1750 there were 879 licensed stills and 930 breweries in Ireland.[15] Most of the breweries were very small operations in which the publican was producing his own supplies. Dublin was the dominant brewing centre producing about 65 per cent of Irish ale and beer.[16] Women still managed their alehouses and the quality of their drink remained quite poor. Commercially produced beer was very much a town drink at this time and being relatively expensive was restricted largely to the middle and wealthier classes while the working man's drink was the cheaper whiskey and home-brewed beer. Heavy drinking permeated all social classes as the number of alehouses and taverns swelled to 2,300 by 1749.[17]

In the 1750s the brewing of beer commenced on a larger scale, thereby increasing the supply. The most important date in the history of Irish brewing was 1 December 1759 when Arthur Guinness opened his brewery at St James's Gate on the banks of the River Liffey in Dublin. From this first small premises was to grow the great industrial empire that has become so entwined in Irish life and culture. The first beers that came from the Guinness brewery were simple ales but in 1770 a new beer of English origin was produced. It contained roasted barley which gave it its distinctive dark colour and since it was particularly popular with porters at London's Covent Garden it was commonly known as "porter". By the end of the eighteenth century Dublin was flowing with porter, ale, whiskey and wine as the "alarming number of dram shops" approximated 3,000.[18]

DUBLIN'S COLOURFUL PUBLIC HOUSES

The traditional Dublin public house evolved from the dusky drinking dens of an earlier epoch. The distinction between alehouse and tavern was always a bit vague but the latter was generally distinguished by the provision of wine and spirits in addition to beer. By the mid-1700s the term "public house" was commonly applied to both, and eventually shortened to "pub". During the seventeenth and eighteenth centuries Dublin was noted for its colourful, effervescent public houses and their often fascinating names. All had hanging wooden signs with both the name of the public house and its symbol boldly painted. These signs swung and creaked in the wind. In an age when many people were illiterate, pubs were readily identified by their bright symbols, such as the "Bull's Head", "Dog and Duck" or "Coach and Horses". Many of the old names of Dublin public houses from this period were quaint and curious:

House of Blazes—Aston Quay	The Flying Horse—Mountrath Street
The Blue Leg—High Street	The Sots Hole—Essex Street
The Holy Lamb—Corn Market	Three Candlesticks—King Street
Golden Sugar Loaf—Abbey Street	The Bleeding Horse—Camden Street
The Wandering Jew—Castle Street	Black Lion—Temple Bar
The Unicorn—Capel Street	

Dublin's pubs in this period ran the gamut from squalid to splendid. As John Gamble wrote in 1826 in his *Sketches of Dublin*, the "taverns of old Dublin are either so miserably low that a respectable person cannot be seen going into them, or they are equally extravagant with the most expensive London ones".[19] Every public house built up a regular clientele for whom it became their "local". Many pubs became regular rendezvous points for specific groups such as tradesmen, businessmen, lawyers, writers, political party members, unionists and even renegade cliques. At this time the public house was the most convenient venue for such gatherings. Publicans gladly provided separate space or a private room since a good amount of money would be spent on drink.

Many public houses gained historical and political significance for the groups they held. For example, the Rose Tavern in Castle Street was a favourite haunt of prominent lawyers during the 1700s. Likewise, the Castle was a regular meeting spot for Dublin city officials who daily discussed their affairs over drink. The Phoenix in Werburg Street, very fashionable in its day, was patronised by politicians, journalists and the Bar Society as well as the Grand Lodge of Freemasons. Dame Street boasted of several distinguished public houses like the Rose and Bottle which attracted important businessmen, and the Duke's Head which was favoured by the nobility during the reign of James II. Another tavern on the same street called the Robin Hood was a hangout for a political club known as the Robin Hood Society who opposed the government during the early period under the reign of George III. The Bleeding Horse in Camden Street was a meeting place for United Irishmen in 1798 and of the Fenians at a later time. The Brazen Head in Bridge Street, Dublin's oldest pub dating from the thirteenth century, was for centuries the site of much plotting and intrigue as revolutionaries of different eras found it a safe haven in which to conspire. Robert Emmet, Daniel O'Connell and Tim Healy, among a host of others, drank and planned within its ancient walls. Even the eminently respectable and charitable members of the Sick and Indigent Roomkeepers Society, prior to taking possession of their present office in Palace Street, held their weekly meetings at the Eagle pub in Eustace Street.[20]

One of Dublin's most famous surviving pubs, in existence as a hostelry since the seventeenth century, is the Bailey in Duke Street. The history of the Bailey is closely associated with the cultural and political happenings in Dublin over the centuries and has a strong nationalistic record. Parnell and the Irish Party, Isaac Butt, the Invincibles, the United Irishmen, the Fenians, the Irish Republican Brotherhood and Sinn Féin all used its premises, while Collins and Griffith met there continuously during the Troubled Period. It is even said that Parnell met Kitty O'Shea for the last time in the upstairs dining room.

But if some public houses deservedly enjoyed their good reputation, others were known for their raffish character. The Eagle tavern on Cork Hill, for example, regularly entertained profligate young aristocrats known as "bucks" who were notorious heavy drinkers, gamblers, duellists and womanisers. Here they would hold drunken orgies all night long. Similarly, in the latter part of the seventeenth century there was a rough and forbidding tavern in St John's Lane simply called "Hell" for its unbridled boozing and brawling. Nearby rowdy pubs were the Dragon Shipp, Red Stagg and the Half Moon. They became such a moral blight on the area that all were eventually suppressed after the Dean of Christ Church complained about the sounds of the revelry interfering with the services. Another pub noted for serving "gamblers and bad characters" was the Sun Ale House in Dame Street, while at the Black Lion alehouse on Sir

Rogerson's Quay it was said that the drink was cheaper than elsewhere only because the wines and brandies were smuggled in.[21] In 1807 a Dublin inn and tavern called the Coach and Horses was visited by highwaymen who robbed the owner and visitors, caroused and drank for about an hour, and upon leaving offered profuse apologies for their rude intrusion.

DRINKING CUSTOMS OF THE SOCIAL CLASSES

"Inebriety was not only a custom but a cult."

Dawson Burns, Temperance in the Victorian Age, *1879*

By the latter part of the eighteenth century "compulsory drinking customs among all classes had firmly established a drunken tyranny".[22] However, drunkenness among the lower classes was the most widespread and blatant. The Reverend James Whitelaw determined that two-thirds of the city's population of 172,000 were of the "lower class", most of whom lived in "truly wretched habitations . . . crowded together to a degree distressing to humanity".[23] These tenement dwellers lived in horrid conditions of congestion, hunger, poor health, disease and human frustration. The local public drinking house provided temporary relief from their daily suffering. Men worked sporadically at manual jobs such as dock work, carting and construction. It was their custom upon collecting their meagre wages to head directly to their neighbourhood pub seeking drink and companionship. Pubs were packed from morning to closing time. The lower classes mostly drank beer and cheap whiskey and a man could get "dead drunk for two pence".[24] The popular custom—or "curse"—of standing rounds with mates was a major cause of drunkenness in public houses as every man sought to show his good fellowship.[25]

At this period, whiskey consumption especially seemed to debilitate and "madden" men. In 1772 John Rutty, the Quaker doctor, in his *Natural History of Dublin* described the degenerating effects of hard whiskey drinking:[26]

> "Whiskey among the lower ranks has for some years so enormously prevailed, not only to the corrupting of morals and destroying of the constitutions of the drinkers, even of both sexes, but to the debasing and enfeebling of their progeny."

Dubliners took their whiskey drinking so seriously that in 1792 there was rioting among the common people of the city when Parliament discussed measures to curb whiskey consumption. When rumours circulated that it was to be made a felony to drink a dram, people paraded through the streets protesting while balled singers sang sorrowful lamentations about the demise of their good friend "whiskey".

Drunkenness among the poorer classes was an especially public exhibition. They were far more susceptible to intoxication than the upper classes because of their poor diet and weaker constitution. In fact, many virtually lived on drink. As a consequence, excessive imbibing led to spectacles of boisterous behaviour and brutal brawling. In 1836 G. C. Lewis in his *Observations of the Habits of the Labouring Classes in Ireland* commented on this conspicuous trait of the lower classes:[27]

"The Irish are not so dishonest as the English of the same class, but more riotous when drunk. They get drunk on Saturday evening and Sunday; having eaten little in the week a small quantity of spirits has much effect on them. They fight with one another in public houses and in the streets."

Members of the upper classes in Dublin may have been more discreet in their drinking habits but many were just as prone to drunkenness. In fact, in this period heavy drinking was actually fashionable among the higher social ranks. The leisured class spent much of their spare time "hunting and whoring, drinking and gambling".[28] They favoured fine whiskey, brandy and wine. Heavy drinking among the rich often led to duelling. It was said that "a gentleman's chief ambition was to be able to imbibe an enormous quantity of wine and use the small sword with dexterity" to dispatch in single combat any man who presumed to question or insult him.[29]

The upper classes devised their own rules for drinking. One was that no man was allowed to leave his company until he was highly intoxicated. If on any occasion a guest had to leave the room bits of paper were dropped into his glass indicating the number of rounds the bottle had gone in his absence. Upon his return, he was obliged to swallow a glass for each, under penalty of so many glasses of salt and water. There were many subterfuges invented to make one drunk. For example, it was a practice to have decanters with round bottoms so that everyone was obliged to keep filling up his glass as the bottle was passed around on peril of upsetting its contents on the table. Another common custom was to knock the stems off the glasses with a knife so that they had to be emptied as fast as they were filled since they couldn't stand. At some public houses where the "young bloods" revelled it was a rule that all boots and shoes be removed by the tavern boy and taken out of the room. Then broken glass was scattered around the door to prevent drinkers from leaving too early. Such drinking orgies were a regular custom of the wealthier classes. Insobriety infiltrated the most august bodies in Dublin as even the most distinguished members of society were given to habitual intemperance:[30]

"The Bar, the Church, the Senate, the Medical Profession, even the Bench itself, were alike subject to this degrading excess; and drunkenness was so common, especially among the higher classes of society, as to entail no censure whatsoever."

Indeed, even judges on the Bench were seen frightfully inebriated and utterly without shame.

DISREPUTABLE DRINKING DENS

Spirit grocers, cursed as the "greatest evil in Ireland", became one of Dublin's most notorious types of public drinking establishment for more than a century.[31] The spirit grocer's licence, which led to "untold mischief and damage", was introduced in 1791 and survived until 1910 when it was finally abolished.[32] Under this Act any grocer dealing in tea, sugar, pepper, chocolate and other basic commodities could acquire a liquor licence allowing him to sell any quantity of spirits not exceeding two quarts at a time for consumption *off* the premises. No certificate of "good character" was required, as for publicans, and it was said that many, indeed, were not of good character. Their licence was not even endorsable in the event of conviction for selling drink consumed in the shop. Since this licence was easy to obtain any person unable to acquire a legitimate publican's licence owing to the more stringent requirements and the reluctance of the magistrate to grant new ones, simply set themselves up as a spirit grocer.

At the outset it was naively reasoned that the Spirit Grocers Act would spare women the moral danger of having to enter public houses to purchase spirits. Instead, it lured scores into alcoholism. The lax laws invited abuse. Although the grocer was permitted to sell up to two quarts at a time the most frequently purchased amount was a "noggin", or two glasses. The grocer would supply this in a bottle, although many customers brought in their own bottle and proceeded to drink it on the spot. Women who would dare not risk being seen in a public house had no compunction about slipping into a spirit grocer's and sipping away contentedly behind high stacks of biscuit tins or partitions deliberately constructed as cover. For women it provided the ideal clandestine way to get drink. For countless numbers the temptation was too great. At many grocers it was common practice to provide full protection against discovery by stationing young boys outside the front entrance who would alert the grocer at the sight of a policeman. It became a common sight that women departing the shop after their "grocery shopping" were in noticeably good cheer, if not singing uproariously. Others, sadly, staggered down the street and clung to railings for stability. One dismayed observer alleged that many spirit grocers operated as illegal public houses catering to the weaknesses of women:[33]

"I attribute a great deal of the drinking habits among females to the spirit grocers which are about the very worst houses to which licences have been granted. At first, a female would not like to go into a public house, but would have no objection to go into a spirit grocer's house, either to buy groceries or otherwise, and there she becomes more or less tempted to take a drink. As long as the grocer is allowed to sell one glass of spirits, and keeps a watch upon his door, his shop is literally nothing better than a public house licensed for consumption on the premises."

Indeed, by the mid-1800s many proprietors were "simply spirit grocers in name and publicans in reality".[34] Clearly, the spirit grocers law had become a mockery. In 1867 the superintendent of the DMP contended that the *majority* of spirit grocers in Dublin violated their licence and freely got away with it. To prove this point, a member of a Dublin temperance society went around to fifteen spirit grocers' shops in one night and declared that he had been offered liquor for consumption on the premises in every one of them. He found men and women drinking openly at the counter, behind partitions or in a back room. In some cases police were standing on the pavement outside the shop with a clear view through the window at imbibing patrons. Because of the reluctance of licensing authorities to grant new public house licences there was a steady increase of spirit grocers. In 1877, of the 641 spirit grocers in Ireland 310 were in Dublin.[35] Because they were a source of considerable tax revenue there was little political will to shut them down.

Shebeens were the lowest form of drinking den on the Dublin scene. They were illegal drinking quarters usually located in a squalid tenement room or huxter shop. Every sort of alcohol was served at all hours of the day and night. Untold hundreds of shebeens were scattered through the maze of tenements doing a thriving business. Shebeen operators commonly placed a piece of turf or an oil bottle in the window as a sign of identification for customers. Scouts, usually young lads, were posted outside in the street to keep a vigilant watch for policemen. When a policeman was spotted the scout would let forth with a mighty whistle alerting those inside to scatter. Shebeens did their biggest business on Sundays when the pubs were open only for a few hours. There were endless complaints against the "degrading shebeens where they can get drink, as much as they ever choose to drink, from petroleum champagne to bad whiskey".[36] The often poor quality of drink commonly led to drunkenness and civil disorder.

Critics charged: "The police in Dublin could put their hands in a morning upon nearly every shebeen in the city; those places are very well known."[37] Police rebutted that while they did indeed know the location of many shebeens they were unable to collect solid evidence against them because of the early-warning system which allowed operators and patrons to carry off the drink and go their merry way. In 1877 when there were 117 well-documented shebeens in operation a police magistrate explained the difficulties in shutting them down:[38]

"In the low, squalid districts are miles of filthy streets with lanes off them where there are houses known to the police carrying on illicit trade where crowds of people congregated and got drunk—but there was no getting legal evidence of this fact. As many as 50 or 60 people, labourers, common people, upon a Sunday morning would be seen going along whistling and chatting in groups and gradually disappear into a house. But by signals and otherwise communicating rapidly from one end of the street to the other it was utterly impossible for the police to reach that house in time to get evidence."

One Sunday the police observed 168 people entering a shebeen between the hours of ten and two and yet they were "unable to establish a case against the house" because of the operator's advance warning system.[39]

The problem was exacerbated by the fact that the modest £2 fine for arrest was so small that it was no deterrent to the crafty "shebeeners". Certified one policeman: "The profits are so large upon the sale of this liquor that they can afford to pay the £2 every week."[40] However, it was also well known that the laxity of many police was due to bribes they were receiving for turning a blind eye. In Belfast, Cork and Limerick the police were often dispatched in plain clothes to hunt down and close the illegal shebeens. However, in Dublin this tactic was strongly rejected by the police who feared that plain clothes officers would be regarded as detested "informers" by the local people. Thus, Dublin policemen preferred to carry out their duties openly in uniform because they were more respected for it. Owing to their elusive nature shebeens survived all the way into the 1950s.

PROUD AND PROSPEROUS PUBLICANS

Relations between Dublin's respectable publicans and the disreputable spirit grocers and shebeen operators were far from amicable. Legitimate publicans, most of whom were honourable and law abiding, resented the reckless and illegal conduct of their bogus brethren. They were also angry over losing business to these renegade traders. Dublin's publicans, or tavern keepers as they were originally known, took great pride in their heritage, having belonged to the old Cooks and Vintners' Guild which survived for nearly four hundred years. After the guild fell into desuetude there were several feeble attempts among publicans to form a trade association but they faltered after a few years. In 1817 publican James Lube of Ship Street called the tavern owners of Dublin together to discuss the protection of their interests.[41] In that year the Grocers Bill was going through Parliament and the publicans felt that if they joined forces with the grocers their combined influence would be better able to protect their livelihoods. This linking of the grocery trade with the vintner's trade produced a public house with long counters with brass scales hanging down at one end where the grocery items were weighed out. Most publicans, in addition to dispensing drink, did a brisk business selling such basic commodities as tea, sugar, biscuits, tobacco, meal and other items. Publicans lived above their shop, took great pride in their work and were noted for their neat attire and gleaming brass and glass:[42]

"Everything shone, the windows, the register, the pumps, the glasses, the barman's boots, his artificial cuffs and collar and his hat. No barman would go behind the counter without his hat. The boss would wear a waistcoat complete with watch and chain and whatever medals he had honestly come by. It was said that no one would get a foreman's job until he had a walrus moustache."

Around the middle of the nineteenth century Dublin's pubs became increasingly valuable properties. Sir Fredrick Shaw, the Recorder of Dublin for forty years, decided in the 1850s that the city had a sufficient number of public houses for its needs. He thereafter became very reluctant to grant certificates for new ones. This policy, as intended, stabilised the number of public houses but it also had the effect of substantially increasing their value. It was estimated that between 1858 and 1878 the marketable value of public houses in Dublin soared over 500 per cent.[43] Owing to their valuable property and booming business, publicans became a very prosperous class. When the Liquor Licensing Law of 1872 tightened the requirements for obtaining a public house licence, a publican's good reputation became an indispensable asset. Licences were issued only upon the production of a certificate granted by the Recorder or the magistrates which attested to the unblemished "good character" of the prospective publican. To obtain such a cherished certificate six householders had to attest to the applicant's honourable reputation and record. Licences were then renewed each year based upon the publican's continuing good character and the orderly conduct of his house during the preceding twelve months.

There were specific rules governing the orderly conduct of a public house. It was against the law for a publican to permit drunkenness or riotous conduct on his premises, to knowingly permit prostitutes to frequent his house, or to allow unlawful gaming. Illegal gaming was determined to be any games played for money. Billiards, bagatelle, cards, dominoes, chess and draughts were not unlawful unless played for money. Publicans also had to adhere strictly to closing hours and were not to be open on Good Friday and Christmas. If a publican was found guilty of violating any of these laws he was liable to a fine of £10 but, far worse, he could have his licence refused when it came due for renewal. Because few publicans were so foolish as to break the law and risk losing their lucrative licence they were regarded as a very "respectable and law abiding body of men".[44] In 1878 the good reputation enjoyed by the publicans was verified in the *Report From the Select Committee of the House of Lords on Intemperance*:[45]

"In Dublin a public house licence is so valuable that publicans are most careful in no way to contravene the law; as a rule, they are a very respectful body of traders, and the value of the licence makes them most watchful, so that the offences against publicans are very rare indeed."

By the last quarter of the nineteenth century Dublin publicans, represented by the Licensed Grocers' and Vintners' Association, were regarded as successful businessmen and prominent members of the community. Many were financially quite wealthy. Their living quarters above the pub were spacious and well furnished, they employed maids to do the cooking and cleaning, their family were well dressed and children highly educated. Their sons often went into the priesthood or medical profession. Many publicans delighted in showing off their horse and trap and seating their family in a prominent pew in church. They became quite active in civic affairs and charitable causes and were known for their generosity. As they became increasingly prosperous and socially respected, they also sought political influence. Publicans became well represented on various corporations and by the 1890s twenty of the sixty Aldermen and Councillors on the Dublin Corporation were publicans. Some even ascended to become MPs. Thus, by the turn of the century they wielded, as a group, considerable political clout.

Dublin Temperance Movement

Toward the end of the eighteenth century when there were about 2,300 taverns and alehouses flourishing in Dublin, drunken men and women were strewn about the streets to the horror of "respectable" citizens. The Surgeon General for Ireland testified that nearly one-fourth of all deaths of persons in Dublin 20 years of age or above were caused prematurely by excessive drinking.[46] Moralists, social reformers and medical men began sermonising about the need to eradicate public houses and champion the cause of sobriety. As a consequence, in 1798 the Dublin Committee Against Drunkenness was formed. They expressed particular concern over the increase in drunkenness among women, asserting: "If whiskey produces brutish rebels among men, among women it destroys all feminine modesty, producing viragos and sluts."[47] In 1805 the Reverend James Whitelaw in his *Essay on the Population of Dublin* railed passionately against the abominable public houses and the human misery they wrought, exclaiming "Dram-shops are the most alarming of all nuisances . . . destructive to the souls and bodies of our fellow-creatures."[48]

By the 1820s there was a concerted effort in Dublin by members of the Catholic clergy to reduce the number of public houses and drunkenness. Father Henry Young, one of the most vigorous opponents of drink, wrote a piece in 1823 entitled *A Short Essay on the Grievous Crime of Drunkenness* in which he vilified drink:[49]

"A witch to the senses, a demon to the soul, a thief to the purse, the wife's woe, the husband's misery, the parent's disgrace, the children's sorrow, and the beggar's companion."

He had particular condemnation for unscrupulous publicans and spirit grocers who, he warned, "have a most dreadful account to render in the divine tribunal of our Sovereign Judge after death" for selling corruptive spirits to the vulnerable masses.[50] As an alternative to the detested public houses he set up in the city several stalls selling coffee and buttermilk but they were not financially profitable and were soon discontinued.

The actual Temperance Movement in Ireland is generally considered to have begun in 1829 with the establishment of anti-spirits societies in New Ross, Belfast and Dublin. One of the most energetic was the Dublin Total Abstinence

Society which was the first to introduce coffee taverns in the city as a rational substitute for public houses. For obvious psychological reasons, these early coffee houses were often called coffee "taverns" and the man behind the bar was the "barman". Some of the coffee taverns had a lecture hall and reading room and became quite popular, like Lucas's coffee house on Cork Hill and the Globe in Essex Street which was frequented by merchants, physicians and lawyers. The most opulent was the Coffee Palace at 6 Townsend Street which boasted a magnificent thirteen foot long marble-topped bar, huge polished copper urns, gold fish tank, reading room with all the current newspapers and magazines, club room with games such as chess and draughts, smoke room, library and elegant temperance hall in which free lectures were given on health, science and temperance. For the first few years these alternative establishments did a brisk business, perhaps as a novelty as much as anything. It was impossible to gauge how many patrons were actually being drawn away from public houses.

As Dublin stumbled through what O'Brien calls its "besotted Victorian years" the temperance movement was led by Father Theobald Mathew, the Capuchin friar from Cork who, by his dynamic zeal, turned the tide within a few years with his total abstinence campaign.[51] He stormed the country preaching against "those pestiferous erections, public houses".[52] In concert with other temperance groups he held massive rallies and put on spectacular parades. For Dubliners, the lively temperance processions and public meetings were great street theatre. Bands, floats and colourful pageantry usually accompanied a procession. Huge crowds gathered and men even flocked out of the pubs, drink in hand, to witness the gala event. A good illustration was the grand procession put on by the Irish Total Abstinence Society in Dublin on St Patrick's Day, 1839:[53]

"The officials were riding in a carriage preceded by the society's banner, then following a carriage drawn by four horses in which sat the Rev. Dr Spratt and Rev. Mr McClure; then a third carriage containing a band of musicians, followed by John Smith, the king of reformed drunkards on a white charger, and the rear being brought up by a body of mounted police. The shops of the streets were all closed and every balcony and window was filled with spectators. The whole affair was imposing, interesting and instructive."

Some of the marching teetotallers became too exuberant, having their bands blare loudly outside churches on Sunday. Groused one policeman:[54]

"The teetotal societies with their band nuisances is very great. We have great difficulty in making them stop when they come near a church where divine worship is going on and assaults have arisen out of them."

In one case, the drum major attacked a policeman who was trying to quell the disturbance. Other band members immediately joined the fray, physically assaulting the police who were interfering with their holy crusade.

By the early 1840s, when Father Mathew held his third public meeting in Dublin, he had given the pledge to 173,000 Dubliners. But then the calamitous potato famine occurred and "struck the temperance movement a blow from which it never recovered".[55] Temperance reformers turned to relief work as temperance halls and coffee houses closed down and alcoholism went on the rise again. By the late 1850s there was a modest revival of the temperance movement in Dublin and the reopening of a few coffee taverns. But the main thrust of reformers in this period was to close down the public houses on Sundays. In 1865 the Irish Sunday Closing Association was founded and their prime target was Dublin. The opponents, known as the Anti-Sunday Closing Movement, were those who would not countenance any interference with the sociability of enjoying a drink on Sundays. Naturally, the city's publicans were very generous in their financial support of this group. The two groups held open meetings in the Phoenix Park in which "divergent views were simultaneously expressed on different platforms, fortunately with no more serious consequences than occasional heckling, bad language and clod throwing".[56]

By the 1870s the proposal to close public houses on Sundays was being bitterly debated in Parliament as persuasive arguments were heard on both sides. Proclaimed one man in favour of keeping the pubs open: "On Sundays the working man gets the best dinner of the week and cannot possibly enjoy it unless he sends down to the public house for a pot of freshly drawn beer to wash it down."[57] In rebuttal, it was reasoned that there was a simple solution:[58]

"Publicans supply the working man with bottles of beer and if he will send down his bottle to the public house on Saturday night and get it filled fresh from the barrel and get it corked up till Sunday dinner time it will be just as good as if brought fresh from the public house. Of course, the difficulty is, as some suppose, that the working men would not keep the cork in the bottle till dinner time."

One of the strongest arguments put forward, even by police, for keeping licensed public houses open on Sundays was that if they were closed down it would inevitably result in hordes of thirsty men being driven to shebeens where they generally drank more, got bad whiskey and became rebellious. Thus, keeping the pubs open was considered by many as the lesser of two evils. In order to determine the volume of business on Sundays the police were dispatched to watch 210 public houses on the Sunday of 9 January 1876. They counted 46,257 people entering them between the hours of 2:00 and 8:30. They concluded that on this day of the week "people who used the public houses in the city are lower-class and middle-class" while the higher ranks, it was reasoned, go to clubs, hotels and on excursions.[59] As a result of this sociological revelation, it was argued that closing the public house would be clearly perceived as a discriminatory act against the lower classes of the city:[60]

"People might feel sore if they observed that their public houses were shut down on Sundays while the club houses and hotels remained open . . . there would be jealousy. They would feel that they were worse treated than the upper classes where a gentleman can go and get a glass of sherry."

Authorities did, in fact, express concern that it could lead to rioting in some of the poorer parts of the city. Eventually, owing to passionately expressed public opinion and the powerful influence of publicans, the efforts to close Dublin's pubs on Sundays failed. The revered custom of Sunday drinking in the city was simply too popular for the government to dare abolish it. Thus, the publicans and Sunday tipplers won the day.

GOVERNMENT INQUIRY INTO INTEMPERANCE AND THE ROLE OF PUBLIC HOUSES

"Dublin is saturated with drink, it is flooded with drink, it is the staple manufacture. Every kind of drink which the people care to consume is manufactured in unlimited quantities in Dublin; every third or fourth house deals in drink."

(Report from the Select Committee of the House of Lords on Intemperance, *1878*)

So testified one frustrated magistrate in 1877. Marlborough Street alone had sixteen public houses. Widespread intemperance bred crime and civil disturbances. It was the opinion of one medical doctor that nearly 90 per cent of all crime in the city was induced by drink.[61] In 1875 arrests for drunkenness in Dublin exceeded that of London which was ten times larger. One female drunkard with 264 convictions wound up in Grangegorman Prison on fifty-two occasions in one year. On Saturdays, especially, men brawled wildly in pubs and out in the open streets. In some of the poorer and rougher districts such as Corporation Street, Queen Street and parts of the Liberties the DMP had to travel in squads and baton charges were almost nightly occurrences to quell drunken mobs. Men and women addicted to drink would satiate their thirst by any means necessary, as evidenced by the great whiskey fire of 1875. On that occasion a malt house and bonded warehouse in the Liberties went up in flames and sent an intoxicating stream of burning malt and Irish whiskey down Ardee Street. Scores of people had to be dragged off the street insensible, having lain in the gutter to lap up the free booze.

Finally, in 1876, a Select Committee of the House of Lords on Intemperance was appointed to inquire into the problem of insobriety and the role of public houses in Dublin. Testimony was gathered from temperance reformers, clergy, medical doctors, police, judges and common folk as well. Much enlightened sociological evidence and theory were forthcoming. There clearly emerged a "connection between intoxication and the poverty, dirt, ignorance and want of amusement" of the lower classes.[62] There were over 100,000 impoverished Dubliners living in squalid one-room tenements with virtually no diversions from the drudgery and suffering of the slums. Conversely, the higher classes had their comfortable homes, clubs, hotels and excursions. For the underprivileged masses the local public house with its warmth, drink and social camaraderie provided an "escape" from bleak tenement life. The poor and lower-income classes relied psychologically and emotionally on the public house as a sort of "safety valve" and refuge in a world of deprivation and hardship. As one witness before the Select Committee sincerely contended:[63]

"Public houses are chiefly established, I think, for the use of those who have no private houses, and two-thirds of the population of Dublin have literally no dwellings, no private houses; they have simply a place to sleep in, and if you consider a man with a wife and children and perhaps the children a little cross occasionally . . . what are they to do? They cannot go and sit on the flags in the open street . . . the accommodation that they have in a well-conducted public house in proportion to their circumstances is as good as gentlemen have in a club."

In their local pub men could drink, play games, socialise with their mates and at least temporarily forget their woes. Certainly it seemed that the less fortunate of the city were entitled to such small enjoyment in their lives. One sympathetic upper-class gentleman eloquently put forth his candid view of the plight of the poor and their right to a bit of pleasure:[64]

"Thousands upon thousands of the multitudes in this city live and die in places whence a humane sportsman would be ashamed to whistle forth his spaniels. Surely it is vain that I, or such as I, should bid them, steeped in squalor and besieged by disease, joyless, hopeless, Godless, not seek the light and warmth of the gin-palace, and the oblivion, however temporary and baneful, they can purchase therein."

To be sure, some witnesses condemned public houses outright and argued passionately in favour of their eradication. But there was much support for the concept of the local pub as the "poor man's club". Properly conducted public houses had a valid *raison d'être* on the Dublin scene since they served the social and psychological needs of the less-privileged classes. Thus, in terms of social function, comparing the local neighbourhood pub to the gentleman's club seemed a fair perspective. Even Sir Charles A. Cameron, Chief Health Officer of Dublin in the latter part of the nineteenth century, agreed with this premise in his compassionate report on *How the Poor Live*:[65]

"The workman is blamed for visiting the public house, but it is to him what the club is to the rich man. If he spends a reasonable proportion of his earnings in the public house is he more to be condemned than the prosperous shopkeeper or professional man who drinks expensive wines at the club or restaurant?"

Many witnesses also expressed the belief that the habit of excessive drinking was due in great part to the inherent social nature of the Irish people. Pronounced one observer: "Men in Ireland do not take drink for the sake of drinking, but for the sake of companionship."[66] This strong trait of sociability in the Irish character could scarcely be denied. That it centred on the local public house seemed quite natural. Furthermore, by the Victorian period the custom of "rounds" in pubs was deeply entrenched as the lower classes seemed especially gregarious when it came to sharing drink with their mates. Reasoned another witness: "Where a man has the example of a number of persons drinking around him, and where his vanity as a good fellow is tickled, he is induced to go on drinking by the persons around him."[67] Some of the most compelling testimony regarding the sociability factor was proffered by a parish priest from the Liberties who concluded that the drunkenness he so commonly saw around him was due in large part to social pressures and simple camaraderie:[68]

"Our people are exceedingly sociable and I think that I could scarcely venture to say that I have met a dozen men in my life who got drunk for the pleasure of drinking; they go into the public house without any intention of excess; there they are joined perhaps by a friend and are naturally hospitable and they are impelled to ask their friend to drink with them; then their friend being hospitable himself must return the compliment, and then three or four more coming in, the circle is enlarged; and every man must be as good as his neighbour and the consequence is, perhaps, that they all get drunk, not through the love of drink but through the love of society."

Based upon volumes of interesting testimony from a multitude of witnesses, the *Report from the Select Committee of the House of Lords on Intemperance* was issued in 1878. In essence, the Committee accepted the rationale that the public house was a legitimate and beneficial social institution when well conducted—but they strongly condemned the habit of customers drinking to excess. As a consequence, they favoured eradicating illicit drinking places, tightening the controls and limiting the number of legally licensed pubs, and encouraging publicans to prohibit drunkenness on their premises. As Monckton concludes, after centuries of being cursed and condemned, the beleaguered Dublin public house proved to be a resilient survivor:[69]

"It is indeed by uneasy steps that the pub has wandered through the paths of history, buffeted by storms of public controversy, assailed by the slings and arrows of temperance reformers, sometimes harassed and sometimes supported by instruments of legislation. That it has survived in so ubiquitous a way is remarkable."

ORAL HISTORY AND PUB LORE

"Using an oral tradition, as old as human memory, we are reconstructing our own past."

Sherna Gluck, Oral History: An Interdisciplinary Anthology, *1984*

Oral history may be defined as a "process of collecting, usually by means of tape-recorded interview, reminiscences, accounts and personal interpretations" of past places, conditions, events, people and human experiences.[70] Simply put, oral history is a data collection technique which can be applied to any topic that is "within living memory" of the people.[71] With the advent of oral history in the 1940s scholars began focusing attention on the lives and work of common people, generally in the rural setting. By the 1960s American pioneering oral historians were collecting testimony for *city* folk such as merchants, tradesmen and factory workers. Dorson professes that "city folk possess a culture and a history well worthy of study".[72] He implored oral historians to concentrate on specific urban neighbourhoods to learn about people's relationship to their workplace, church, schools, shops and drinking houses where they gather, socialise and share life's experiences. This is what Morrissey terms "grass roots" history, proudly asserting that the new breed of oral historians is a fresh vanguard of scholars practising their craft in the "real world".[73] As Thompson explains, by recording the life experiences of ordinary city folk we truly *democratise* history.[74] As a consequence, a new genre of literature appeared which historians and folklorists call "urban folklore". Recording urban folklore via the oral historical method makes possible the "preservation of the life experiences of persons who do not have the literary talent or leisure to write their own memories".[75] It thus creates a new kind of history, the history of common people.

In Ireland oral history and folklore are still strongly associated with rural life and customs. People do not ordinarily think of the city as a repository of old customs, traditions and folkways as they do the countryside and village. Actually, Dublin is fertile ground for the gathering of oral urban lore because of its surviving inner city neighbourhoods, shops, public houses and large elderly population. In recent years the concept of collecting Dublin's folklore via the oral historical method has gained both credibility and support. In part, this is due to *Comhairle Bhealoideas* (the Folklore Council of Ireland) which came to recognise the "similarity between traditional customs and social attitudes of Gaeltacht people and those of native Dubliners".[76] Coincidentally, in the early 1980s Professor Seamus O'Cathain, lamenting that "ordinary people have been largely written out of history" in the city, launched the Dublin Folklore Project in which students were dispatched to collect the recollections of elderly residents.[77] A few years later the North Inner City Folklore Project was initiated with modest government financial support to record the life experiences of ordinary city dwellers.

There could be no truer "grass roots" or "real world" history to be extracted from Dublin neighbourhoods than that of the local public house, the very centre of social life and conversation. Dublin's pubs are the richest oral repositories of local history and folklore. For centuries they have been the central gathering places for Dubliners of every socio-economic type—the poor, working class, professionals, politicians, intellectuals, writers, even pariahs. Seventy-five-year-old publican John O'Dwyer, who served as a barman in his early days in a "rough and tumble" pub in York Street, recalls how the public house functioned as the core of all local life:

> "In my time the local pub was *the* thing, very important in people's lives. *Everything* that happened was all discussed in a pub. *That* was the place to be. Drink and *conversation*! *Whatever* happened would always drift back down into the pub. It was like a confession box."

As a consequence, long-established public houses have accumulated their own unique history and lore built up over generations and even centuries. Since this information is not recorded in written form it can only be extracted through the oral historical method from publicans, barmen and regulars who possess an invaluable memory bank of information about bygone days.

Over the course of three summers in Dublin I tracked down over fifty public house "old-timers", most of whom are now between 60 and 93 years of age. Many of the pubs with which they were associated have long since disappeared from the cityscape. However, through their remarkably vivid memories such vanished pubs and pub life can be authentically reconstructed. Because most old publicans, barmen and pub regulars were good conversationalists and learned to be keenly observant of life about them, they possess a gift for recall and detail which enrich their oral historical testimonies. All expressed a historical appreciation for the role of the public house in Dublin. They were unfailingly eager to share pub life and lore as they experienced it over several generations. Taping sessions typically lasted from one to three hours, though some extended to twice that. A number of individuals were revisited and taped again to better distil some relevant points or to elaborate on a dangling theme. Tapings were normally conducted in the respondent's home or local pub, the settings in which they were the most comfortable. Final transcriptions were condensed and arranged to create literary cohesion and natural flow. But their words, expressions and intonations were not tampered with in any manner. Their oral narratives are variously humorous, raw, compassionate, and brutal— but always fascinating and authentic. Through their collective oral testimonies the bygone world of old Dublin pubs comes to life once again in exuberant form.

2

DUBLIN PUB CULTURE
AND SOCIAL LIFE

"True pubs are the microcosm of Dublin life."

Desmond Clarke, Dublin, *1977*

*"Whether you love it or loathe it the pub is at the hub of Irish life and to ignore its
existence is tantamount to losing sight of the heart of the people."*

Liam Blake, Irish Pubs, *1985*

THE PUB AS A LIVING SOCIAL INSTITUTION

The remarkable survivability of the public house is unmistakable testimony to
its importance in Irish society. As Gorham affirms, the pub has evolved as a
"living" social institution which plays a profoundly important role in the daily
lives of the populace.[1] Indeed, it has been calculated that "of the social
institutions that mould men's lives" the pub has more buildings, holds more
people, takes more of their time and money, than church, cinema, dance-hall,
and political organisations together.[2] In analysing the social importance of the
pub a research group in 1943 determined in their publication *The Pub and the
People* that "there is a close relationship between the pub and the drinker—-a
state of affairs in which they are part of an institution to which they *belong*", like
members of a political organisation to their party or a congregation to its church.[3]
Thus, pub-goers develop a strong sense of institutional identity and membership.
As a social institution, the pub provides an environment in which "you are living
among your fellow men . . . the issues of life are not solitary but communal".[4]
This feeling of community solidarity is the heart of pub life.

The pub, perhaps more than any other social institution, is founded on the
principles of equality and democracy. Thomas Burke in 1936 praised the
egalitarian nature of the public house:[5]

"It is the one place where a man may greet and talk with strangers on level
terms. It is the common and open club, with no rules or formalities of entry

save those of decent behaviour and mutual respect. On the floor of the bar your clothes, your position, your income, go for nothing. Only in the bar can you see, in one easy gathering, rich man, poor man, poet, merchant, soldier, squire, scholar, tailor, and—perhaps—thief."

Also distinctive is the fact that the pub is the only type of public building used by large numbers of ordinary people where their thoughts and actions are not arranged for them. In other kinds of public structures they are the audience, watchers of political, religious, dramatic, cinematic, instructional or athletic spectacles. But within the four walls of the pub once a man has his pint in hand he enters a social environment in which he is a *participant* rather than a mere spectator. This generates intimate social interaction in which men of all social and economic ranks share personal feelings about life, love, work, religion, politics and world affairs. As a result, the pub becomes a true microcosm of local life, reflecting the socio-economic ethos of its host community. Declares Jim Higgins, 70, a regular at O'Dowd's pub in Stoneybatter for the past thirty years: "A local pub like here, it's like the *pulse* of the neighbourhood. You can gauge how the area is going."

Michael Smith, writing in the *British Journal of Sociology*, concludes that the neighbourhood pub is not only a vital social institution but the "locus of popular culture".[6] He defines this as an "earthy culture" consisting of the basic lifeways, customs, values and traditions of the local folk. Furthermore, states Selley, the public house is the "home of native philosophy".[7] Consequently, every pub possesses its unique "cultural character" which has evolved over time and from its own distinctive history of multigenerational publicans, barmen, regulars, renowned characters, codes of conduct, entertainment types, dramatic or humorous incidents and famous episodes of drinking and brawling. All combine over time to create a pub's particular cultural heritage. In pubs where the oral tradition has survived, local folklore has been passed down from generation to generation and thus preserved. Publican John O'Dwyer who worked in many pubs in his time vouches that every one had a "culture in its own right". It is precisely this social and cultural variety that makes the Dublin pub scene so fascinating and exhilarating.

As social institutions vital to the local community, the parish church and public houses are without rival. In recent decades the number of church-goers has declined while attendance at the pub has increased. Because of their relative status the church and pub naturally invite comparisons, some of which are sociologically interesting. Each has its authority figure, devout patrons, rituals and spatial patterns. Both offer their own solace to bedraggled souls weary of the outside world. Parallels even exist between priest and publican. Both enjoy exalted status of respect and power and hear confessions, one dispensing advice and the other absolution. And one cannot ignore the religious symbolisms associated with the public house—the barman was long known as the "curate"; afternoon closing time was the "holy hour"; snugs were termed "confession boxes"; a black pint of Guinness with its white collar is called the "parish priest"; regulars are the "faithful"; persons barred feel "excommunicated"; pubs closed to women were the "holy ground"; privileged bar space was the "inner sanctum"; and when notorious pubman Brendan Behan would crawl from pub to pub he proclaimed he was "doing the stations of the cross". Which of these two revered institutions, the church or the pub, is more indispensable to modern life is open to lively philosophical debate. Publican Thomas O'Dowd, 70, who has spent more than half a century behind the bar, speculates that if pubs were abolished it would give rise to another type of social institution. "If you did away with the neighbourhood pubs in Dublin you'd just have to build mental *asylums* all over the place."

THE PUBLICAN'S ROLE AND STATUS

"From behind the counter the pub is controlled as a ship is from its bridge."

Mass-Observation Study Group, The Pub and the People, *1943*

"Oh, back then they had great respect for publicans. Ah, he was next to the parish priest."

John O'Dwyer, publican, age 75

From earliest times the publican has been one of the most essential ingredients in the composition of a good public house. Even centuries ago, writes Clark, "A vital factor in the success of an alehouse remained the strength of the landlord's personality."[8] His character and demeanour set the tone for his establishment. He needed to attract customers, blend socially with them and keep order. As Burke contended in 1936, this demands certain human qualities:[9]

"None but a man of genial temper can keep a tavern or an inn. It is a job that calls for patience, tact, understanding, wide interests and that love of mankind in its bright or sorry aspects which these qualities imply."

No ordinary man, a publican must "know something of everything and be something of a psychologist", able to understand human nature, judge character and resolve conflict.[10] Or, as *Irish Licensing World* more poetically put it, "A publican must be a democrat, an autocrat, an acrobat and a doormat."[11] Customers *expect* him to possess wit and wisdom as they seek his advice. A gifted chatter full of flavourful small talk, he must also be capable of conducting lofty conversations on serious topics of the day. But being an empathetic listener is equally important. As Higgins believes, "A good publican is a man who will listen, not pry, sympathise, not pity." Always the consummate diplomat, a publican should be able to entertain prime ministers and TDs and be on both sides of the political fence."[12] Thus, like a social and political contortionist, he must adapt naturally to every situation he faces. McNamara's apt description of "The Ideal Publican" penned nearly forty-five years ago still holds true:[13]

"A good publican should be a man to take his place in any company. He should have the welcoming grace of a good private host and be able to talk on every subject under the sun . . . but he would know when to talk and when to possess his soul in silence. He should have a proper pride in what he does behind the bar and regard it as a calling rather than a trade. He should be a man well fit to be put into a book or a play—as he has been—by many an Irish writer. A publican should be full of history and legends, of athletics, of hurling and football and well versed in horses and dogs. There would be no use in having a training college for publicans; your good publican is always a self-made man."

The publican's role extends far beyond his duties as congenial host behind the bar. Historically, he has been a leading figure in the community performing many valuable services for the local folk in times of need. When crisis struck, people often found their publican more approachable and understanding than their parish priest. Because of mutual familiarity it was easy to confide in him without fear of chastisement. Like a doctor on call, the publican who lived above his pub could be beckoned at any hour of the night for advice, comfort or a "sup" of whiskey to revive the sick. Clara Gill's father, publican James Gill, was so skilled as a mediator in resolving local family disputes that "they said he should have been a judge because he was so good at weighing up the sides of a story". Publicans also customarily provided money and drink for life's great moments—births, christenings, first holy communions, weddings, wakes and burials. Exclaims O'Dwyer: "The publican was the man who [financially] *christened* them, *married* them and *buried* them. He was *the* man, he was there for them." Debts were routinely put on the slate to be paid off over months and even years. Often they were simply forgotten. Publicans were also regularly called upon to read and write correspondence for persons with relatives abroad and to provide letters of reference for people seeking employment or buying an item of furniture or a bicycle. There was no one else to assist them financially. Owing to his indispensable role in the local working-class neighbourhoods years ago, Gill feels that "a good publican was like the father of the community".

Because of their important role, publicans enjoyed elevated status. Frank Fell, Director of the Dublin Licensed Vintners' Association, confirms that historically the "status of publicans has always been very high in working-class areas of Dublin, always great respect for publicans". Lar Redmond divulges that "in the social hierarchy of the Liberties the publicans were at the top", followed by shopkeepers, tradesmen, bakers, carpenters and bricklayers.[14] Mairin Johnston, 60, of Pimlico, recalls how publicans stood out socially:

"They were looked upon as the pillars of the community. Publicans had a better lifestyle and they had a prominent place in the church. And they always had sons who were priests or bishops."

As a powerful patriarchal figure in the daily lives of the poor and working classes, the publican's status was often at a level with the parish priest, or slightly below it. Sometimes, blurts publican Jack Cusack, he was held on an even higher level—"Oh, those old publicans, they were the captains of us all . . . a publican years ago was *Jesus Christ!*"

Within the walls of his public house the publican has always been the king of his tiny fiefdom. "The publican was lord and master and what he said was the *law*", declares policeman Paddy Casey, 68, who walked the beat in the toughest northside neighbourhoods back in the 1940s. Conscientious publicans felt a strong sense of social responsibility not only to patrons but to their families as well. They knew which men when drunk could be abusive to their wives and children. It was their moral duty not to turn such a drunkard loose on society. In John B. Keane's *Letters of an Irish Publican* publican Martin MacMeer, the model of social responsibility, forcefully espouses his philosophy:[15]

"Dirty braggarts will drink, drink, drink till they can hold no more and then stumble home like cattle to abuse and manhandle their innocent families. It is the Judases amongst us who betray all humanity when they serve drink to sated monsters like these. Any decent publican will always stand up to those defilers of home and family. I will not tolerate the presence of these men under my roof. I will serve drink to no man who will not show respect to me, to my house and to my customers. When a man comes into my pub he comes into a sanctuary and he is entitled to drink in peace. A good pub is entitled to the same respect as a good home."

The concept that the public house is entitled to the same respect and control as one's private home is the basis of the Licensing Law of 1872 which gives the publican the absolute right to refuse service to any customer and bar him at will without having to cite any reason. Wielding this ultimate power, a publican may be "as choosy and selective as he wishes".[16] Acting as judge and jury, he alone determines the sentence for violations. A man may be barred temporarily or for life. For a man to be barred from his local pub is a disgrace which can also carry the social stigma of pariah. Therefore, the decision to bar a man is never lightly made. In practical financial terms the publican also realises that by barring one individual he might also lose the business of his family and friends.

Sometimes, however, a publican actually seeks to expel a whole crowd. When Eugene O'Reilly, 84, bought a bonafide pub in Santry in the 1940s he discovered that it was inhabited by a bad bunch of "bowsies and prostitutes". To build up a respectable trade, "I cleaned it out completely, barred them and wouldn't let them in." Sometimes this demands physical force, as Larry Ryan, 61, found when he bought the disreputable Deer's Head pub in Parnell Street:

"I barred the whole crowd. I had to, to raise standards. *Physically*, basically by myself. It often went to fisticuffs. Oh, yeah. The real bowsie, he'd look for trouble. They would challenge me. You had to *earn* their respect. Little by little then you started to build up trade and a good name."

The decision to bar a man for life is so serious that it has been the custom in

Dublin for a new publican to honour the word of his predecessor. This decree can be transferred verbally or in the form of a written statement left to the new owner. Christy "Diller" Delaney, 68, an old cattle drover, was barred from a pub around Smithfield years ago for fighting. When a new publican bought the house Diller and his fellow combatant found that they were still not welcome on the premises:

"We got barred for life. Never got served in there. Even with *new owners*. A note would be left on the shelf. And it's still carried out in pubs."

Despite the financial benefits and social rewards, the publican's lot has never been an easy one. Over a lifetime of standing on his feet, pulling countless pints, commiserating, advising, settling disputes and listening to woeful tales, he understandably becomes weary of the human condition. A bit of verse, anonymously scribed, which was found in a pub tells of the publican's burden:[17]

> "A publican arrived at Heaven's gate,
> His head was bent and low,
> He asked the keeper of the gate
> the way he ought to go.
> What have you done below, he asked
> To seek admission here?
> I've kept a public house, My Lord
> For many a weary year.
> Peter took him by the hand
> and gently pressed the bell,
> Come, my man, and choose your harp,
> You've had your share of hell."

Though publicans may grow weary, they are noted for resisting retirement. Theirs is a "way of life" not easily relinquished. The pub has been such a socially stimulating environment that many find they are addicted to it after all the years. "I've been active for fifty-five years behind this counter and I know nothing else", confides Cusack, "it's a religion with me." Similarly, O'Dowd faces a real quandary as his family is trying to coax him into retirement:

"I'm going through a terrible time trying to make up my mind whether to retire. There are an awful lot of publicans who have tried to retire and they've all come back to the trade. I would miss it terribly. *I just can't!*"

PUB REGULARS AND THEIR LOCAL

"All pubs have one thing in common. Every one is somebody's local. Every one has its regular customers."

Maurice Gorham, The Local, *1939*

The most coveted social niche in the life of many Dubliners is their status as a "regular" in their local pub. It is a position gained by trial and time. Pub regulars can be very clannish and do not casually admit newcomers. One must be "accepted" into the tribe. Pete St John describes this achievement:[18]

"Your acceptance in the local was in Dublin a saviour. A sanctuary. Beyond explaining. Here men knew their place in life. Their value as human beings. So the great limbo of the knowing descended. Inchoate. Priceless."

Old neighbourhood pubs around the Liberties, Smithfield, Ringsend and Stoneybatter have the highest percentages of regulars. As publican O'Dowd proudly pronounces: "Regulars here would be as high as 85 per cent. We get three generations of customers in here . . . possibly *four*." In such traditional pubs it has been customary that when a lad comes of age his father will bring him in for his first pint. It is a rite of passage into manhood, often as memorable as one's first holy communion. Of course, every person is entitled to eventually choose their own local. Pub selection is determined by such factors as family tradition, character of the staff, hospitality of regular customers, quality of drink, and general ambience. As John-Joe Kennedy, 75, of the Liberties avows, once a man decided upon his local he was loyal for life. "You made one pub your local and you were part of the furniture then, you *stuck* to your local." Some discriminating Dubliners, like Tom Corkery, are very specific in identifying criteria which constitute their "ideal" local pub.[19]

"A good cellar, insulated from extremes of heat and cold; a dedicated landlord; a regular and knowing clientele; an absence of ale-quaffers, gin-sippers, whiskey suppers or wine-bibblers; a seemly and decorous interior in shades of brown and mahogany, relieved only by the glitter of glass; a counter of marble or mahogany, sufficiently high to permit that a man, resting his left foot upon the foot-rail and his elbow on the top of the counter, should be almost at eye level with his pint; sawdust and framed enlargements of hurlers, footballers, horses or dogs. Partitions are useful, protecting the superior pint man from the intrusions of more vulgar drinkers; and there should be an absence of carpets, fancy little tables, women, piped music, or anybody under the age of 21."

Regulars are the privileged pub elite. They form an inner social circle as secondary groups defer to them in seating and conversational status. They have *earned* their acceptance and superior position over many years by proving their worth as decent, trusted and loyal pub mates. Many become entitled to their own seat and it is reverentially given over to them when they enter—without a word being spoken. Real regulars develop a daily visitation pattern that is like a sacred ritual. "You'd know they'd be in at a certain time", avers publican Liam Hynes, 47, "and you could nearly put their drink on the counter." Tony Morris, 52, over thirty years at O'Dowd's pub in Stoneybatter, typifies the habitual regular:

"I come in normally twice a day, fourteen times a week. It would be fair to say that I spend a good portion of my life here. Some days there could be fifteen of us together. We discuss our problems."

There develops a kind of social "chemistry" among regulars in which they can share all life's issues. They get to know one another's good and bad qualities, habits, moods, quirks. A man becomes accepted for his weaknesses as well as his strengths. A "support group" environment is created in which they openly discuss problems relating to domestic life, job, health, finances and phobias. Over time there develops a strong interdependence and mutual trust. Recounts Tommy Murray, 75, who was a regular in Walsh's pub on City Quay in the 1930s:

"We were neighbours, very local, grew up with one another and we knew one another's complaints. You might as well be living under the one roof, no secrets. You couldn't *hide* a secret if you tried to."

Within the social dynamics of the pub each regular becomes valued for his distinctive personality and contributions to the group. One seasoned observer of the pub scene uses the term "pubmanship" to describe the manner in which pub regulars come to play out their familiar parts.[20] The pub setting is like a stage with a cast of characters, each acting out his expected role. Every man develops his own natural persona and no script is necessary. Be they philosopher, wag, wit, grouser, fool, sportsman, political pundit, buffoon or mere listener—all have their original role in the cast. It is this variety of personalities that allows a group of pub regulars to enjoy one another's company day after day throughout their lives.

Regulars develop great loyalty not only to pub mates but to their local pub as well. They exhibit a strong sense of territoriality and possession. It is quite common for regulars to psychologically and emotionally regard the local pub as *theirs*. Larry Ryan found that when he bought an old neighbourhood pub in the Coombe some forty years ago the regulars treated him as an "outsider" for nearly a year until they accepted him on their terms:

"The pub is the centre of their life and *every* day they were there as regular as clockwork. Oh, the local is *their* pub. In their mind it *is* their pub and you daren't interfere with it. Oh, you're very much an intruder for the first twelve months until they get to know you."

Because of their sense of shared ownership, pub regulars often assume the responsibility for defending the peace and integrity of their local, sparing the publican the trouble. Such violations as fighting, foul language, drunken behaviour and mooching are regarded as personal effrontery and the perpetrators promptly ejected. Higgins tells how his local was invaded by several thugs and the regulars instinctively came to the rescue:

"This pub was raided some time ago by two young hoodlums and the customers beat the hell out of them. They came in to rob it. They had a bar and a stick. And a number of men here physically hammered them. Ah, you have to stand up and be counted. Ah, those two hoodlums, they won't come back here any more. No way."

Men who belong to the same clique of regulars for decades develop a strong fraternal bond. Ninety-year-old May Hanaphy who grew up around the turn of the century in Golden Lane, known as the "four corners of hell" for its pubs, drinking and brawling, observed how local menfolk, including her brothers, found not only friendship but brotherly love in their local pub:

"The pub was a way of life for them, their friendship. It was their *whole* world. In the pub they could have love, in a fashion, among the men themselves."

As a result of this closeness, contends Gorham, "The real regular is one of the family."[21] Men often confess to feeling closer to their pub mates than some family members. For many bachelors and widowers their pub pals actually become their surrogate family. They grow old together and when a lifelong pub mate passes away it is regarded as a death in the immediate family. The regulars have lost one of their "own" and the circle is never quite the same again. Over drink, pub mates extol his virtues, reminisce about old times, and mourn the loss of his companionship. One of Dublin's most famous pubmen, J. P. Donleavy, author of *The Ginger Man*, lamented that he would one day himself have to depart the pub scene and thus devised a most glorious way to go in which he could share himself with old mates even after death. "When I die", he is reputed to have requested, "I want to decompose in a barrel of porter and have it served in all the pubs in Dublin."

PORTERS, APPRENTICES AND BARMEN

"The ideal barman is a man with three hands, a set of extra eyes, and a telepathic mind."

Irish Licensing World, *1953*

A publican's staff normally consisted of a porter, an apprentice and barmen. Porters held the lowest position and did the "slaving" work. They washed out filthy spittoons in the perilous age of TB, mopped up when men became sick, cleaned bathrooms and did the dirty cellar work. It is said that sometimes porters were lads with lower than average intelligence but hard workers. Some served for over fifty years until they grew old. John-Joe Kennedy from the Liberties got a job as a pub porter when he was 18 and found it gruelling work:

"I got thirty bob a week and worked from 10.00 in the morning till nearly

1.00 in the morning. I worked in the cellar and you had a fire but it was always very damp and alive with rats. Washing bottles was desperate. Only an ordinary wooden tub and cold water. We used wire brushes inside each bottle. Your hands were like ice and as red as a cherry. I used to get sick of it. The only thing I liked was bottling the beer cause you used to have to suck the taps to get the beer going."

Another rigorous task that fell to the lowly porter was delivering and collecting hundreds of stout bottles for weddings, wakes and rousing hooleys held in the old tenement buildings. He would precariously peddle his heavy bike with a big wicker basket laden with several dozen bottles of stout through the streets and then haul his cargo up long flights of rickety stairs. But this chore sometimes had its benefits as appreciative recipients might reward him with a bottle for himself. Mary Corbally, 75, recalls that around the Monto it was a custom at Christmas to share a drink with the weary porter as "he'd stand at the door and you'd open one of the bottles for him. He'd drink it on the spot there and you'd wish him a merry Christmas and off he'd go." By the end of the day the porter, full of good cheer and light of head, could be seen zigzagging through the holiday pedestrian and horse traffic. Oftentimes when loyal porters grew old and arthritic they were looked after by the kindly publican since they had become one of the "family".

Apprentices were always carefully chosen by publicans since they were their future barmen. Almost all were from the country and it was long the tradition for a publican to select only young lads from his home county. Fifty years ago the trade was dominated by publicans from Counties Tipperary, Cavan and Limerick. "Tipperary men were probably 50 per cent of the Dublin trade at that time", speculates Michael Gill, 66, "and Cavan was next." Apprentices tended to be relatives or sons of friends who showed a strong country work ethic and were regarded as honest and friendly. Typically 14 or 15 years of age, they were put on a bus or train by their parents and sent off to Dublin for the first time in their lives to begin their apprenticeship.

Most apprenticeships lasted from three to five years as the young novice was required to live-in with the publican's family above the shop. They normally worked ten or more hours a day and received meagre, if any, wages at first. When Tom Bourke, at age 86 the oldest publican in Dublin still behind the bar, began his apprenticeship at 14 in a pub in Parnell Street back in the 1920s, "my wages . . . I had *nothing at all* the first year! Only my food. But I was glad to have the job". Apprentices got one half-day off a week and one Sunday each month. On days off there was a curfew of 11.00. Each morning the publican or head barman would inspect them for scrubbed face, combed hair, clean nails, brushed teeth and polished shoes. They had to learn the trade from the bottom up, meaning they were promptly put to cellar work learning how to tap casks and do the tedious bottling. Once put behind the counter they were taught how to pull a proper pint, serve whiskey and deal socially with customers. Additionally, they were responsible daily for polishing brasses, windows and mirrors. The reason most apprentices were willing to "suffer on" was because it led to a lifetime job as a barman and possibly even that of a publican one day. Though most publicans were tough taskmasters many adopted a paternal attitude toward their young wards. Gill describes how Patrick Conway, one of the "great characters" among old Dublin publicans, would personally escort his staff of apprentices and barmen up the street like a row of ducklings to Sunday morning Mass:

"When they'd get up on a Sunday morning they were polished and brushed out and shined and everything else and they'd march up to Mass, the staff, and he handed each one of them a penny on the way up to put on the plate."

Upon graduating from apprenticeship one became a junior barman for two years. Earlier in the century barmen were called "curates". Like apprentices, most had to live-in, endure curfews and were often forbidden to marry. Barmen needed to possess most of the same skills and social traits as a publican. According to Jack Cagney, 70, who worked behind the counter at the Oval pub in Abbey Street, a good barman was measured by two major factors. "Oh, a barman had to have a reputation for drawing a good pint", and second was his personality. It was common practice that barmen started out at small "backstreet" pubs in working-class neighbourhoods and gradually worked their way up to the prestigious central city houses like Mooney's or Madigan's. Eighty-three-year-old Frank O'Donnell who is proud to have worked at the elegant Scotch House for most of his career, confides that most barmen aspired to one day become publicans, though he personally did not achieve it:

"Your aim all the time was to go on to be a publican. *That* was the reason most fellas went into the trade, to become the *owner* of a public house himself, and many of them did. If you were quite a few years with a publican and he liked you, well, you could ask him to go security for you."

Bosses were usually willing to financially support a loyal barman in buying his own pub. However, the publican expected him to first save up a hefty down payment on his own. Most barmen, who were scrupulously honest, stashed away every pound possible toward their own pub purchase. That many were bachelors helped their cause. However, local lore has it that a good many barmen routinely siphoned money from the cash register in building their savings. In the local vernacular this was known as "fiddling the till". Old-timers *swear* that they personally witnessed this going on all the time. Back in the 1940s Billy Sullivan, 80, commonly observed barmen in the pubs around the Dublin markets fiddling away:

"Some of these barmen opened up their own public houses in a few years. Oh, it was on the fiddle. *Definitely.* They'd be lifting money out of the cash register. They *did* that."

Kennedy concurs that in his local in the Liberties it was just common knowledge. "Oh, yeah, fiddling the till. *All* barmen, every *one* of them done it." Though local men may exaggerate the numbers, many former barmen and publicans confirmed that lifting a few bob from the register on a regular basis was indeed a common practice passed down over the generations.

PUBS AS IRA MEETING PLACES

"For men in the Movement, for meetings, we'd go into a certain pub where we had support, like a curate there was in the Movement and they'd make arrangements to hold the snug private for so many hours."

Frank Wearan, age 93, former IRA member

Earlier in the century, during the troubled times and even thereafter, there was a network of "safe pubs" in Dublin where IRA activists regularly met to exchange information, plan missions and stash weapons. Historically, these public houses played a significant role in the political life of the city. Oral testimony from surviving IRA members, publicans and regulars who personally participated in or observed these manoeuvres in old pubs confirm their value to the Movement. Most such public houses were in the poor tenement neighbourhoods around the northside, Monto and Liberties. Among the lower classes there was much anti-British sentiment and support for the "cause". Here, in the local pubs, IRA men felt safe in their dealings. Noel Hughes, 60, a repository of local history on the northside, has gathered information on political pub life via the oral tradition over the past half-century. Some of the safest IRA pubs, he reveals, were the following: Kirwan's, the Seven Stars, and Phil Ennis's pubs in Parnell Street, Backhand pub in Coleraine Street, Macken's in Church Street, "Big Macken's" pub in North King Street, McGowan's in Francis Street in the Liberties and Walsh's pub in Stoneybatter which was a "notorious" house for harbouring IRA men on the run. Other well-known safe pubs back in the 1920s and 1930s were O'Hagan's in Cumberland Street, the Barrel in Benburb Street and Leach's on Drumcondra Road. All had pub staff who were active in the Movement which gave them their "safe" status.

Hughes testifies: "Pubs were the most important places of IRA men, a lot of information was passed on there." Clandestine meetings were usually held in a pub corner, private snug or back room. Participants spoke in hushed tones and kept a vigilant eye on those around them. Even the highest ranking, most recognised members of the Movement carried out their affairs within pub walls. Tom Bourke, born in 1908, began his apprenticeship at the tender age of 14 in James Kirwan's public house in Parnell Street, one of the major IRA pubs of its day. Here he observed history in the making as he served drink to the likes of Michael Collins and Dan Breen as they planned operations:

"Now Kirwan's was a very important public house during the troubled period. Oh, Mr Kirwan was a very big noise in the Movement. And the barmen in Kirwan's were very high up as well. Kirwan's was where everything was discussed. A lot of the 'boys' would come in. Michael Collins would come in and have a drink of a small sherry. See, Michael Collins, he was a great friend of my boss's. I very often saw him. Oh, a very nice man he was. And Dan Breen, he was there in the pub as well. Mr Kirwan was always in on the conversations. See, there'd be men in there passing on information. There was secret meetings there *all night*. After hours there was three knocks for to get in for the meeting in the pub. And you were supposed to not see anything or hear anything or know anything. Your instinct would tell you to ask no questions."

Men met under the careful aegis of the pub staff. Publican and barmen knew every local regular by face and name and were instantly aware of any unfamiliar outsider who walked through the door. British soldiers and Black and Tans were, of course, immediately identified. Pub staff relied upon a system of signals for alerting IRA men to the presence of persons who might be "earwigging". Frank Wearen, now 93, joined the IRA as a young man, carried a revolver, participated in actions and was imprisoned. He and his compatriots regularly held their meetings in safe pubs under the protective watch of the publicans and curates who were themselves in the Movement:

"We'd go into a pub where we had support. You always had certain pubs you could go into and leave information. But you had to *whisper*. They'd get to know you and could *trust* you. The curates knew everyone going in and had their own signals. Like if there might be an ex-British Tommy that was living on wounds disability they'd be able to make a sign like that [eye wink] or maybe tap their right shoulder or take off their cap, put it on again . . . so you'd know to keep away from him. It was giving you information whether you were safe or not in the pub. And if you left a message on paper for the curate if there was any danger he was to put it in his mouth and *swallow* it. It'd be a small note only that size. They had to do it because if that was captured you were gone!"

Pubs also provided a perfect hiding place for weapons, ammunition and explosives. Their cavernous cellars were pock-marked with nooks and crannies where weapons could be secreted. Some publicans even devised what Hughes calls "secret barrels broken into sections and they'd stuff ammunition and dynamite in the middle". Sometimes weapons were kept closer at hand. As a young lad behind the counter at Kirwan's, Bourke found that "there were revolvers in the drawer and we used to have rifles stored down in the cellar" which were regularly used by his barmen who would be "off during the night raiding". Wearen and his mates used certain pubs to store their weapons.

"Guns were always hid away in pubs where they wouldn't corrode or get rusty and when the IRA wanted them they could get them. The curate

would go down to the cellar and roll them up in paper and come up behind
the counter and say 'There's a parcel that was left for you' and that'd be two
guns."

Some suspected pubs were regularly raided by British soldiers and Black and
Tans. Pubs known to harbour wanted men were the prime targets. Two such pubs
in the old Monto were Phil Shanahan's and Paddy Clare's. A raid by the detested
Black and Tans was most feared since they would sometimes physically abuse
pub patrons. Wearen held a deep hatred of them:

"The Black and Tans did often come into the pub and raid. Could be six or
seven of them and they'd *rush* right in with their guns and *'Hands up!'*
They'd give you a battering and clattering on the face—for *nothing*. Oh,
everyone was afraid of the Black and Tans."

Shanahan's and Clare's not only had cellars for hiding men in the Movement but
contained secret tunnels which allowed them to escape. Timmy Kirwan, 75, a
docker born and reared in the Monto in the 1920s, observed firsthand how these
tunnels were used as escape hatches:

"Phil Shanahan was a great leader of the IRA at that time. In the cellar of
his pub and Paddy Clare's pub across the road there was tunnels used to lead
for *miles* underground . . . right down to the Liffey River. The lads were able
to do business and hide from the British soldiers in them cellars. When the
British army would come to raid them the lads would get down there and
they were *gone*. All underneath the ground."

Those pubs which were IRA strongholds have become an important part of
Dublin's history and urban folklore and when old-timers congregate they delight
in recounting the action and excitement they experienced within their walls.

WOMEN ON THE "HOLY GROUND"

"It was a sort of religion among the men that a woman wouldn't be seen in the bar."

John Greenhalgh, age 82

By long and sacred tradition Dublin's public houses were an exclusively male
domain or, as some crusty old regulars prefer to put it, the "holy ground".
Inviolable. Especially in the working-class neighbourhoods of the inner city,
where old ways die hard, the local pub was the last true bastion of male
supremacy. Here in their private sanctuary a man could shut out domestic life
and womanhood and "be himself" in the company of like-minded mates. Here

men were free to drink, smoke, spit, curse, brag, laugh uproariously without worry of chastisement from the more refined sex. In short, it was a male utopia. "The bar is a man's refuge", spouts Higgins, "it was almost unknown for a woman to go into a pub, it was *verboten*."

However, because many pubs were also grocers in those days women did have to enter the respectable part of the premises to buy provisions. This allowed them a glance into the hallowed den of manhood just beyond the brass weighing scales. To Mairin Johnston, the pubs around the Liberties back then were so dirty and dismal that most women wouldn't even *want* to enter them.

"Your first impression was that pubs were *horrible* and there was sawdust all over the place and the men just spit everywhere and they'd urinate everywhere. There was no hygiene at all. And the *smell* of the smoke and tobacco! They chewed tobacco so when they weren't drinking they were spitting. And TB was rampant then. I mean it was *disgusting*. I used to be horrified with it."

Although women as a general species were prohibited from entering a public house, there were two conspicuous exceptions—revered grannies and hardy women street dealers. Owing to their longevity and difficult life they were excluded from the social mores which barred other women. As Johnston deftly explains, "Grannies could go in because they were beyond sin." Cloistered in their shawls, cloaks and bonnets, they could sit at the back wall of the pub on a hard wooden bench. Many grannies, like Mary Corbally's, preferred to settle into "little snugs that'd hold about three people, *confession boxes* we'd call them, and they'd have their gill". During their "little sessions", as they were called, grannies usually had a "GP", a glass of plain porter. A Liberties lad, Kennedy was fascinated how grannies could combine drinking and pipe smoking:

"All the older women went into the snug. They'd have a glass of plain, all porter. And you'd see them puffing a small little clay pipe, a 'scutch' they called them. It'd be underneath their shawl. You'd never see them smoking *openly*."

Women street market dealers were the most notorious female drinkers. They were a tough breed, accustomed to the raw life of the streets, able to drink, curse and brawl with the best of the men. They wore shawls and generally frequented the pubs around the market areas of the city. These women dealers, endearingly known to Dubliners as "shawlies", are depicted in Vincent Caprani's affectionate poem "The Shawlie":[22]

"You can see her beyond in the snug,
Wrapped in her ould black shawl,
Whisperin' softly to herself
And mindin' no one a-all.

> She'll sip at her glass of porter
> Prolongin' the dark delight
> And tastin' the stored-up mem'ries
> That must last her through the night.
>
> So let's buy her a bottle o' Guinness
> Or a glass of the warmer stuff
> A drop of the 'how's-yor-father?'
> To go with her pinch of snuff."

The dealers' capacity for drink sometimes astounded observers. It was said that many women could hold their own against the best of men. Publican Ryan who knew all the dealers around the Dublin markets maintains, "I knew several of them that could *outdrink* a man any time. Oh, yes." And, like men, if they had too much booze they could become combative. Charlie Dillon, 75, witnessed many a bloody brawl between bellicose women dealers outside the Blue Lion pub in Parnell Street:

"If the women dealers went on the beer there might be jealousy and then there'd be a row between them. Oh, there was always a row on a Saturday night. Me mother was a dealer and she'd be fighting two or three of them. Pulling the hair out of one another! Women'd get a grip, like a dead person's grip, and it was very hard to get out of it. Kicking and all. The women was *better* than the men. Oh, the language!"

The most practical problem facing women in pubs back in the prehistoric days was the lack of a ladies' toilet. Undeterred, they devised a natural alternative. Kennedy laughs when describing how women handled this predicament:

"No toilets for women—they'd have to go out in the street. Yes, in the open street. Out in the street over the railings [grates] by the pub. They wore skirts down to their ankles and they didn't wear any underwear."

When Ryan served his apprenticeship at Slattery's of Pearse Street women customarily used the grate directly over the cellar as their toilet, which posed a hazard for staff. He remembers well the day he and the porter were working directly beneath the grate when the "storm" came. "Two ladies came out and standing right over the grate and down on yer man! I remember his swearing and grabbing a hose as he passed me." Eventually, publicans realised that they had to share the men's toilet with women. Normally, a trusted male regular would be posted as guard at the door as women were hurriedly ushered in for their "turn". John Greenhalgh, 82, of Ringsend, claims that the first *real* women's toilet in Dublin can be attributed to the ingenuity of the publican in his own local pub:

"It was a terrible thing, all right, no toilets for women. But this publican in Ringsend, he had the first toilet for ladies. How did he manage it? Well, I'll tell you. He got a Jacob's biscuit tin, half filled it with sawdust, and put it in the snug for the ladies. Half filled with saw dust, that was the silencer. Niagara Falls! That's true."

Women other than privileged grannies and dealers had several means of obtaining drink from their local pub without actually entering. It was acceptable for them to linger at the pub doorway with a delft jug or billy can in hand waiting to catch the eye of the publican or a man they knew to have the vessel filled with porter for them. Sometimes they even dared to peer in and call a man out. It was equally common for tenement women to simply dispatch children to the pub with the jug or can. Once a woman got her "gill" of porter home she often liked to mull it by sticking a red hot poker into the liquid believing this put in iron vitamins and warded off sickness. Similarly, many women preferred getting baby Power's whiskies, convinced that it gave them energy and strength. They could put it in their tea or drink it straight. One legendary old woman named Maggie who rambled around the Dublin fruit and vegetable markets some fifty years ago concocted her own scam for extracting drink from the local pubs, as Sullivan recounts with obvious amusement:

"Maggie, she'd faint, playing possum. And a crowd would congregate around her and she'd say, 'Ah, me poor old heart!' Always outside a public house she'd do this and someone who didn't know the act would go in and get a half of whiskey. Pretend she was sick and there was nothing wrong with her at all. It was an *act*. Cause she'd get a half a whiskey! Always done this outside the boozer . . . and then Maggie'd do her act again."

On the occasion of a funeral women were granted a sort of dispensation, allowed into the pub with the funeral party to drink. Burial days were actually anticipated with glee by the tenement poor since it gave women a break from rigorous domestic chores and provided an opportunity for drink, socialising and merriment. No sooner was the corpse placed in the ground than they headed directly for the pub and made a real "excursion" of it, often remaining there until the establishment closed that night. Perhaps because women were not accustomed to regular drinking, they often over-indulged and came home jolly and singing. Dublin's women dealers were especially noted for "putting on" a good funeral for one of their own. One memorable case was that of a dealer named Maggie in Moore Street who was fond of her beer at O'Neill's pub at the lower end. It was her wish that upon death she be buried in Glasnevin Cemetery with a couple of large bottles of Guinness stout placed beside her in the casket. The other dealers honoured her wish and on her funeral day the hearse pulled up outside O'Neill's, the hearseman went inside and brought out the bottles, and off they all went to bury old Maggie. Bernie Shea, 60, who sold next to Maggie for forty years, describes the scene:

"The hole was dug and Maggie's coffin was put down into the hole and two large bottles of Guinness was put down on top of her in the coffin cause she said, 'Let me go out with a bang.' That's the way she wanted it. So Maggie was buried and all the crowd came back here [to pub] and they danced and sung. She's nine years dead now and if you was to dig up Maggie's grave them two bottles would still be down there . . . unless she got up and drank them—which I wouldn't be a bit surprised if she did because she loved the bottle. She's entitled to it!"

The male pub used to be so inviolable that wives dared not enter even when seeking out their husbands. She had to wait by the entrance and ask another man to call him out for her. To approach her husband in his local pub was to belittle him in front of his mates. The man would feel shamed and it could result in a social stigma being attached to him. Also, back in the hard tenement days when men could be brutally abusive to women, a wife could fear her husband's wrath for such a violation. "Oh, she daren't go near the pub for him", swears Greenhalgh. "Oh, it'd be *murder.*" Publican O'Dowd translates this strict code of pub life:

"It's just one of these things that's been accepted over the generations that a wife *doesn't* call her husband out of a pub. She can do what she likes with him when she gets him home, she can hammer hell out of him—but she doesn't let him down in a pub. It's just one of these taboos. She won't cross that threshold and make a fool out of him in front of his mates."

In the post World War II period the barriers of male exclusivity began to be dismantled. It was a period of social enlightenment as women were gradually liberated from their domestic confinements. They began to speak out forcefully about equal rights and opportunities, including entry into pubs if they so wished. Ethel Mannin was an outspoken critic of the old male-dominated pub system and condemned the "prejudice against women drinking in public".[23] In 1947 she wrote a provocative article entitled "Women in Bars?" in *Irish Licensing World* which reflected the view of many modern women of the day:[24]

"In Ireland where once no decent woman could be seen in a public bar, now perfectly decent women are to be seen in bars and lounges. What is the difference, morally, between a man taking a drink in a bar and a woman doing likewise? To say that bars are all right for men but not for women is illogicality of the most sentimental kind. If women are banned in bars they will drink at home and it is much easier to drink too much at home."

Apart from the rationale that women simply deserved equality, she argued that "decent well-behaved women" would serve to soften or "civilise" the "ribaldry and coarseness in a purely masculine bar".

During the following decades her predictions were conspicuously borne out. Husbands began taking their wives out with them more often in the evening for entertainment and for most this included a visit to their local pub. Recognising the social changes, publicans began to install attractive lounges with comfortable furniture where couples could drink together. After wives became accepted in pubs, single women gradually appeared on the scene. During the 1960s and 1970s segregated pubs toppled like dominoes. Those local neighbourhood pubs which continued to bar women were condemned, and sometimes even picketed, by feminist groups as dark dens of male chauvinism as the regulars were viewed as a mean pack of sexist Neanderthals. Walsh's public house in Stoneybatter was probably the last truly segregated pub in Dublin. Tom Ryan, head barman at Walsh's for fifty years, still refused to seat women at the bar in 1988 when he confidently proclaimed, "It's a male preserve. Men prefer to be on their own. I know this from experience. Women just wouldn't fit in." Ironically, a woman owned the pub. In 1990 she sold the public house to new owners who opened the establishment to women on an equal basis—and Ryan decided the time had finally come to retire.

THE PINTMAN AND HIS PINT

"The true pintman always approaches his pint with reverence in a contemplative fashion, and a tranquil state of mind."

Tom Corkery, Tom Corkery's Dublin, *1980*

"When things go wrong and will not come right,
Though you do the best you can,
When life looks black as the hour of night—
A pint of plain is your only man."

Flann O'Brien, "A Pint of Plain"

The "pintman" is one of Dublin's great legendary figures. His origins are as deep as those of the drinking house itself. It has been theorised that "great pintmen are born, not made", a sort of gift of the genes.[25] Famous pintmen are a part of every pub's folklore. They are esteemed by pub mates as the "expert" pint drinkers, set apart from the plebeians by their discerning manner and technique. To Tom Corkery, bonafide pintmen are a special breed distinguishable by their cerebral approach to the pint:[26]

"The true pintman knows that the pint is to be contemplated as well as to be drunk. He does not even need to be in company, for his pint is his company. If you study the good pintman in a pub you will observe how he can stand [no pukka pintman ever sits] staring into his glass for long periods, thinking deep thoughts. This is because he knows that truth lies at the bottom of his glass. It is rewarding to the body, soothing to the soul, and leads one into long, pleasant and philosophic conversations. This, then, is pintmanship in the true sense."

Upon closer scrutiny, pintmen exude a sort of spiritual aura when in union with their pint. An ethereal look can be seen in their eyes as they are transported beyond spatial and temporal bounds. Over forty years ago John D. Sheridan penned an insightful psychological profile of the pintman as a unique human species:[27]

"The man behind the bar knows the pintman when he sees one. It is not a matter of dress, or age, or social status; it is a sort of spiritual look. The pintman takes up the tumbler with ritualistic care. Nothing can touch him then. The clock ticks for you and me, but the pintman is on an island in time. He is no longer old or young, rich or poor, married or single. He is beyond the numbing grip of circumstance—a devotee at a solemn rite, a poet with an unfrenzied eye, a man with a pint. There is a restful, mesmeric quality about the whole business."

As the quintessential connoisseur, the pintman demands no less than a *good* pint. Perfection is an ideal always sought. As only Pete St John can put it, to the dedicated pintman, "the jar was King. Regal. Supreme. Bacchus."[28] Tributes to the pint are legion. It is regarded as a magic elixir by its devotees. James Joyce called it the "wine of the country". Others have hailed it as the "nectar of the gods" and the "mother's milk of the Irish". "The common pint is one of man's great allies", feels John B. Keane. "Apart from its curative and body-building properties, its appearance is a work of art."[29] Certain pubs are renowned for serving an especially good pint. Famed pint houses have always possessed ideal cellars in terms of temperatures. Tommy Murray nearly salivates when describing the fantastic pints he used to get at Dooley's pub on the quays back in the 1930s:

"*That* pint, I'll tell you, it was always perfect. Oh, what a drink! They had one of the best cellars in Dublin and it kept a certain temperature. They had the thermometer in the front of the shop—it was like a tube going down—and the first thing you'd do, you'd look at it and you'd know the pint was going to be all right. Oh, they was *noted* for their pint. And *no rush*. It might take ten minutes to bring it to a head, the creme. It was so strong that you could *feel* the substance of it. Oh, lovely. You could drink about twenty of them in a night and the next morning you'd be like a two year old, there'd be no hangover. Yes, sir."

Old-timers swear that the porter and stout from the wooden casks before the introduction of the metal barrels, called "iron lungs", were far superior to that of the present day. It is believed that the ingredients were purer and richer, that there was a natural harmony between the wood and the beer, and a longer ageing process produced perfection. John Preston, 67, who did his drinking around Sean McDermott Street, disdains the chemicals and artificial techniques now used in making beer, claiming that today "You're not getting the real

McCoy!" Virtually every pint drinker over the age of 60 will testify to the same—so therein must lie some truth.

Pulling a proper pint has always been regarded as an "art" in the trade. Its mastery was much respected. Real regulars have always known which barmen had perfected the art. In what has been glorified as a "solemn rite" the skilled barman goes through the ritualistic process of pumping, re-pumping, scraping, topping, and settling.[30] Working the pump requires a delicate touch to produce the right pressure for creating the best froth. The mature pintman never minds waiting, for these minutes are filled with heightened anticipation. Indeed, it would be the "very apogee of impertinence to betray impatience during the ceremony".[31] Con Murray, 62, who started pulling pints in his father's pub in Sean McDermott Street as a young lad, agrees that there is a definite talent for pulling a good pint:

> "Now I was pulling a pint when I was 13. But there was certain barmen that never got the art of it right. You had to have a *feeling* for what you were doing. See, when you were using the pumps you had to know how to nip the tap to produce the pressure and this produced the froth. And when I started pulling a pint you had to learn how to blow the froth off it. The sign of a good pint was that it hung to the side of the glass and by counting the rings on the glass you'd see whether he was drinking fast or sipping his pint."

If a good pint is a godly gift, a bad pint is an abomination, an affront to humanity. It is, regrettably, a reality of life—*it happens*. To the purist drinker it is a woeful experience, seldom forgotten and never forgiven. One feels a "victim" of a bad pint, and the guilty barman is regarded as the "perpetrator" of the crime. So grievous an act is this that Corkery proclaims: "The very walls of a pint house would fall down if a poor pint was served . . . if there is any taint of sourness the barman should be assaulted forthwith."[32] Serving a bad pint can be an accidental or intentional act. Sometimes it is due to the pumps not being properly cleaned out or a fluctuation in the cellar temperature. But quite often bad pints are attributed to unscrupulous publicans or barmen who cunningly serve up what is known as the "slops" or "old man" to unsuspecting customers. This is left-over, stale beer that was either left in glasses or had been spilled behind the counter in a metal pan beneath the taps. When Paddy Mooney, 75, was duped in this manner, it affected not only his sensibilities but his system:

> "Slops . . . now that was supposed to be thrown out. But some publicans have got it down to a fine art and all those slops are given up as drink and, of course, they're saving on that. I got bad pints and, my God, my stomach would be in an awful state."

By reputation, the greatest pint drinkers in Dublin, in terms of sheer capacity, were the dockers, drovers and jarveys. Their drinking feats were mammoth, and seldom exaggerated. Manual labourers needed drink to replenish bodily fluids lost through perspiration. It also gave them strength and energy. Back in the impoverished tenement days men went without sufficient food and a decent diet which made them very susceptible to the effects of alcohol. Publican O'Dwyer was always troubled by the dockers' reliance on beer for their daily sustenance:

"For dockers drink was their main diet. Dockers *lived* on that. They *lived for pints*. It was *food*—they used to call the pint the 'liquid food'."

Years ago a number of public houses around the docks and markets had a 7.00 early morning licence which allowed dockers and others to get a fast start on their daily drinking. And since many labourers used to be paid in pubs it encouraged them to remain and squander their wages on drink. Decades ago there were even pint drinking competitions. There was always great rivalry among dockers, drovers and jarveys. Each group claimed supremacy as Dublin's greatest drinkers. "Jarveys were the best drinkers of the whole lot", boasts old jarvey Tommy O'Neill, aged 68. Jarveys purposely established their ranks outside pubs so they had easy access throughout the day. Many a jarvey used to be seen meandering through traffic in a completely sodden state being dutifully led home by his trusty horse. Drovers were always noted for their incredible binge drinking on the one or two days of the week when they found work driving cattle, horses and sheep to the quays for shipment. Old drover Diller Delaney confesses with sadness that "drovers were all heavy drinkers", noting that many died from the affliction. Without a hint of braggadocio he relates that when he was a young man, "one time I drank forty-two pints of Guinness. That's no lie!" And it was done *before witnesses*.

Dockers were indisputably the most gargantuan pint drinkers on the Dublin scene. They possessed the strongest physiques and greatest endurance. They heaved mightily and sweated profusely. Alfred Millar, 70, head barman at North's pub in Ringsend, knew their habits well:

"They were the toughest men in all Dublin. They had to work *hard* on the coal boats. They had a tremendous capacity for drinking. They'd drink pints all day. Their whole life seemed to be bent around Guinness."

They would start off drinking around seven in the morning and take a "beero" break every few hours, and then spend the entire evening in their local. Accounts of dockers consuming twenty pints in a single session are commonplace—and well documented. Preston was always fascinated by a burly docker named "Sherlock" who was known around the pubs in Sean McDermott Street not only for his capacity but unusual drinking technique:

"That fella could drink. He was a huge man. He put his pint out of sight in one gulp. That's the way he drank. One sip! That's the gospel truth. I'd say he could put away at least thirty in a day. At *least* thirty. And still be standing on his own two feet."

Great drinkers might be admired locally for their "heroic" feats but they have contributed unwittingly to Ireland's national character image. Consequently, Cleeve contends: "The drunken Irishman is as firmly outlined a stereotype as exists in world mythology."[33] Yet, it is not cause for national shame. As Gray explains, "in Ireland drunkenness is regarded as a good man's fault" and thus there is much toleration, little censure, and even sympathy.[34] The Irish have come to cushion the drinking problem by treating it with gentle humour. John B. Keane tells of an "impecunious old gentleman of my acquaintance" who confessed with utter sincerity, "I spent most of my money on porter, and the rest of it foolishly."[35] Through long experience, the Irish are notably creative in devising terms and expressions about drinking. Popular phrases about inveterate boozers are "He'd sell his soul for a pint of stout" or "He'd drink it out of an old shoe." Surely one of the most graphic descriptions is "If he was caught by cannibals and boiled in a pot, the soup of his bones would have his children drunk for generations."[36] Nearly a half-century ago Sheridan postulated that the Irish have a "weird fascination about the condition" of drunkenness and have created a "luxuriant litany of synonyms" for the state of being drunk, as evidenced by the following examples:[37]

scuppered	stewed	scuttled
squiffy	tipsy	flattened
primed	plastered	blotto
paralytic	hog-eyed	crocked
blithero	stocious	jarred
muzzy	canned	mouldy
well-oiled	maggoty	well-cocked
mellow	pie-eyed	fluthered
liquor logged	lock-jawed	spiflicated
boozed	pickled	drunk as a skunk
cock-eyed	drunk as an owl	plowed
under the weather	creased	three sheets to the wind

Such terms can make the state of being intoxicated sound quite interesting and amusing. It may not be very nice to be "drunk"—but to be "muzzy", "fluthered" or "spiflicated" sounds perfectly socially acceptable. Even the common expression about a reformed alcoholic that he is "on the wagon" can be attributed to Irishman W. A. McIntire who, as New York City Sanitation Commissioner in 1910, went around in a municipal water wagon collecting inebriated New Yorkers who had over-celebrated.[38] The Irish, indeed, have a wonderful "way with words".

PUB CUSTOMS AND TRADITIONS

"The Holy Hour was a play in itself. Quiet. A man's time. You could think. Going home would be unholy."

Pete St John, Jaysus Wept!, *1984*

THE HOLY HOUR

Closing for the "holy hour" was a venerable tradition in public houses. Publicans were required by law to close their doors between 2.30 and 3.30 so that the staff could air the place out, tidy up, sweep out soiled sawdust and sprinkle a fresh covering. Busy publicans and barmen were certainly entitled to a break. It also expelled drinkers who would hopefully head home for some tea and food. Most publicans gently coaxed their customers out the door at the designated time and enjoyed their bit of respite. Others, however, perfected the practice of concealing an elite fraternity of regulars inside after patrons had departed. The annointed few felt themselves part of a wonderful conspiratorial fraternity:[39]

"Now it was indeed the Holy Hour. The great daily drama of clearing the house had begun. Full of nods and winks and whispers. Credentials were checked in that secret, timeless way known only to the selected few. The hard core. The privileged ones. They would stay behind. All else were banished to the grim city streets. Soon the shutters went into place and the doors were locked. The inner sanctum brotherhood of drinkers reigned incarnate. To the drink. To thinking."

In most neighbourhoods local police knew perfectly well which publicans carried out the clandestine caper. But "the guards didn't mind", intimates publican Liam Hynes, "They turned a blind eye." It is well known that it was customary for publicans to reward such guards with a few pints after hours. No harm was done to anyone. However, on occasion the police were given orders to conduct a raid. Such an order might come down from an ambitious superintendent or as a result of another law-abiding publican in the area filing a complaint about his competitor who did not honour the holy hour. The ensuing scene could well be something out of an old Keystone Kops film, filled with drama, excitement and chaos. It began as a sort of tactical cat-and-mouse game, the police creeping toward their huddled quarry. Sometimes it even demanded breaking the secret door-knock code in order to gain lightning-quick entry. Guard Senan Finucane, 75, delights in recounting the frenzied scene when he raided pubs in the Liberties:

"Certain places didn't keep the holy hour. But people could be *sneaky* in keeping out of sight and there could be thirty or forty people inside. It's

1

*Winetavern Street which derived its name from all the taverns
situated there.*

2

Patrick Lane's pub in Watling Street. He sold an excellent pint of Guinness but his chimney also proclaims he bottled his own whiskey.

3

Davy's pub in Portobello.

4

McNally's pub on the South Circular Road.

5

Thomas Delaney's pub in Commons Street was conveniently situated next to the National Sailors and Firemen's Union.

6
The Winter Garden Palace in Cuffe Street.

7
Barney Kiernan's pub in Little Britain Street
below the Court of Appeal.
(Chandler Collection)

8

*Denis Hayes's pub in Lower Abbey Street proudly advertised its
"creamy pint". Today it is the Flowing Tide.*

9

One of Dublin's notorious spirit grocers which enticed women as well as men to drink illegally on the premises.

10

Women publicans and barmaids were an unusual sight in Dublin. They were almost always the widow or daughter of a publican. (Chandler Collection)

11

J. Maguire's pub, "Late of the Stag's Head", in Marino House.

12

*The elegant
Irish House
with its
magnificent
figurines.*

13
Two little girls carrying a jug, possibly to be filled with porter for their mother or granny. This was a common custom into the 1940s.

14
Huge pyramids of casks at Guinness's Brewery.

15

Loading floats at Guinness's Brewery.

16

Cask filling department at Guinness's Brewery.

17

Scald bank (unloading empty casks) at Guinness's Brewery.

18

Bleeding Horse pub in Camden Street, 1930s.

19

In the old days the bar was a man's refuge and no women were allowed.
(Courtesy of Bord Fáilte)

20

Mick's Bar in Parnell Street, 1950s. (Courtesy of Bord Fáilte)

21

Two mates sharing a pint at Mulligan's pub in Poolbeg Street.
(Courtesy of Bord Fáilte)

22

Segregated sign of the
times in Dublin's pubs.
(Courtesy of Bord Fáilte)

23

From the late 1930s to the 1950s Dublin was famed for its singing pubs such as Lalor's of Wexford Street. (Courtesy of Bord Fáilte)

24

Dublin's singing pubs were always jam-packed, especially during summer months when tourists were lured as well. (Courtesy of Bord Fáilte)

25

At Dublin's top singing pubs competition among volunteer vocalists was keen and a two-song limit was strictly enforced. (Courtesy of Bord Fáilte)

amazing how quiet they could be. Couldn't hear a *thing* outside until we knocked on the door. See, they'd always have a code knock for the door or the window or so many rings on the bell. But we used to break the code! Oh, yes. One time we went in there with the right code and to their *great surprise*. There were *sixty* in there. All drinking and not a *word*—'hush up!' But when we went in they were *jumping* all over the place, out the back door and over the wall. Oh, yes, maybe a dozen of them made an escape. Great excitement!"

"Putting it on the Slate"

Another age-old custom enjoyed by pub regulars was "putting it on the slate". This form of credit became a way of life in small neighbourhood pubs where the local men worked sporadically and seemed always short of money in advance of receiving their meagre weekly wages. Originally, there was a real slate and a piece of chalk kept behind the counter to record how many drinks a man received on credit. Later a small book and pencil were used. The system was based on a bond of trust between patron and publican. Giving a man drink on credit was illegal but it was so common—and deemed necessary to the times— that the law was rarely enforced. It was simply left to the discretion of the publican who knew his clientele as well as his own family members. The slate system worked practicably for centuries. Most publicans would carry a customer for a week or two, but seldom beyond. Many men lived their entire life drinking on credit and if they died a week short of payment their descendants would honour the debt—though the publican often abolished it out of respect for the deceased. To save pride, a regular at his local pub often did not even need to ask for credit when ordering a pint. As Greenhalgh discloses, in Ringsend pubs a man relied upon non-verbal communication to express his wishes to the barman:

"There was 'put it on the slate' for regulars. If you died for a couple of pints you'd go in and you'd just give him a nod or wink and he'd pull up the pints. He was very, very rarely let down. Because you *knew* [if you didn't pay] that you were only hurting yourself and losing your mates because you couldn't go into that shop anymore."

Any man who gained a reputation for the non-payment of credit was disrespected by publican and mates alike. It was a violation of their collective honour code. As 80-year-old Tom Byrne stresses: "You had better pay it back or you were finished in other pubs as well. Yeah, your record went ahead of you if you were a 'bad pay'." By hook or by crook—even if it meant going without food —most men somehow found the few bob required to keep their slate clean and remain in the good graces of their publican and pub mates. But owing to illiteracy or senility, men sometimes had difficulty keeping track of just how many pints they had put on the slate. Michael Gill recalls how some of the elderly men at his father's pub on the North Circular Road back in the 1920s devised their own system of economics to keep their account straight:

> "We got these old fellas and they were largely illiterate and they'd get a pint on the slate. The old chaps, they'd just have this string on their belt and every time they got a pint on the slate they'd put a knot on the string, to keep track."

"GOING ROUNDS"

The old custom of "going rounds" was cited by temperance reformers of the nineteenth century as one of the greatest evils leading to insobriety in Dublin. When drink was cheap the system of rounds thrived. According to the custom, each man in turn would call for a round of drinks for his mates. One was simply duty bound by long and honourable tradition to "stand one's round". Even men who took a pledge to limit their drinking commonly found themselves entrapped in the rounds custom, as deplored by Michael Geoghegan nearly a century ago in an article in the *Irish Ecclesiastical Record*:[40]

> "It is Saturday evening. The week's work is done. Five or six men who have toiled together during the week, find themselves near a tavern. They go in. After a few rounds of drink a man finds he has got to the limit of his pledge allowance. What is he to do? Stand up and walk out, after having drunk at his workmate's expense? Far be from him such unpardonable meanness. If a dozen pledges stood in his way, he breaks them all, in order to stand his round like a man. On then, the drinking goes, until it reaches the tenth or eleventh round."

Publicans had conflicting feelings about the custom of rounds: it was good for business but led to drunkenness on their premises and depletion of their patron's finances, often causing hardship for their families. None the less, the custom prevailed well into the middle of the twentieth century. When Paddy O'Brien began as a young barman in McDaid's in the 1930s everybody participated in buying rounds:

> "Oh, buying rounds was in then, in a *big way*. If you had the money you spent it! Cause when you hadn't got it someone else bought it for you. So you could come into the shop without any money and sit up there and say your piece and be put on the round. Cause somebody'd say, 'What are you having?' So you'd be on the rounds."

Back in the 1940s when a pint of stout was eight pence buying rounds was a viable custom but it finally fell victim to economics when the price of drink began to soar in the 1960s. Buying one's own drink was difficult enough; paying for friends as well became financially prohibitive. "It used to be that when somebody came in we'd buy rounds for the whole company", pledges Morris. "Now we stopped buying rounds, we just buy our own drink."

FUNERALS

It used to be customary that when a regular died his "pub family" assumed a central place at his wake and funeral. The publican commonly provided drink for the wake, money for the funeral, and sometimes even took over the arrangements for the grieving family. The man's pub mates rallied to the financial assistance of the family by taking up a collection. According to Mairin Johnston this was standard practice in pubs around the Liberties:

> "There'd be a collection in the pub. They'd all go into the pub the night of the funeral and there'd be a 'whip around' for the wife and kids. 'Whip around' means you'd go around with a cap, pass it around."

It was equally common to pass around a brown sugar bag into which people would toss coins. Alfred Millar, barman at North's pub in Ringsend forty years ago, observes, "they were like a clan" as pub mates came together in time of loss of one of their members. The publican would *always* attend the funeral, usually standing directly beside the family of the deceased. In some tenement districts it was a custom for the hearse to draw up outside the door of the man's local pub and pause for a few moments before the same would happen in front of his home. After his pub mates had attended the funeral all would adjourn back to their local. As Joe Murphy, 66, one of Dublin's last shipwrights, puts it, "They'd go back to the pub after the funeral and 'sympathise', they used to call it, and get *scutted drunk*." It often ended up with lofty tributes to their departed friend and a great sing-song. There was no more fitting way for loyal pub mates to send one of their own on his last journey.

"GOING BONAFIDING"

"Going bonafiding" was a cry that brings vividly nostalgic memories to many an old Dubliner. Bonafides were public houses on the outskirts of Dublin whose original function as an inn and tavern was to serve weary travellers with food, drink and rest. As publican Fergus Newman, 81, explains, according to the law a "bonafide traveller came at least three miles by the shortest route from wherever he slept the night before". Bonafides had a special licence and remained open until the wee hours of the morning, and some all night. When Dublin pubs closed hordes of thirsty men headed out to the bonafides on foot, by bicycle, jarvey car or automobile if they were fortunate to have access to one. On Sunday nights the stream of men along the roads leading out to the major bonafides looked like an exodus of refugees fleeing some war-torn village. There was always a mood of high merriment as John Ryan describes in his memoir *Remembering*

How We Stood:[41]

"As soon as the town pubs closed the night people took to their cars and struck out for the mountainy bonafeed where a merry hour or so was put in by all. There was that carnival atmosphere that so often attends the accomplishment of a deed standing somewhat up to the letter of the law. There would be periodic checks to test the authenticity of our *bona fides*. When the guards would raid the pubs and quiz us on our origins the atmosphere would become electric with subterfuge and intrigue. Most people learnt to lie fluently."

Bonafides on the Naas Road, Lucan Road and around Santry did a booming business. Sometimes a crowd of 400 or more spilled out of the pub along the road and into adjacent fields. In some of these "roadhouses", as some bonafides were called, there was a rough element characterised by prostitution, drunkenness and fighting. Conversely, well-managed houses drew a respectable crowd. By law, local people could not be served. However, they often made up about half the clientele. Eugene O'Reilly bought the most famous bonafide in Santry in the 1940s and after cleaning out an unruly crowd of boozers and brawlers ran a proper house:

"I was open *every* night of the week. And we had no holy hour at all. It was a hard job. I could not serve local people. No. But I knew damn well that many *were* local. But I ran the house well and the guards gave me no trouble—and they were getting no backhands or anything."

Many guards, however, in the locality of a bonafide did freely accept bribes to turn a blind eye. But every so often a highly conscientious guard decided that he was duty bound to uphold the letter of the law regarding the three mile provision. In 1961 there was a famous case in County Kildare court where a garda measured with a chain the distance from the man's house to the licensed premises in order to prove a breach of the licensing law. The garda found that the distance was *twenty-two yards* short of the three mile limit. In jestful fashion, the *Irish Licensing World* commented on the case:[42]

"We can picture the big, fine hulk of a man dragging his measure along the highway, stooping down to mark off each length—for the whole 5,258 yards! We get offended then when foreigners sometimes refer to the comical situations as being very 'Irish'. Too bad the defendant did not demand a re-check of the distance."

When their pockets were empty bonafiders began straggling back toward the city, many in a stuporous state. Fortunate were those who had some form of transportation. Crowds of pedestrians meandered their way home along the roads as dawn was breaking. Diller Delaney used to make a pilgrimage out to the "Dead Man" Murray's bonafide on the Lucan Road every Sunday night with his chums from around Smithfield:

"Then we'd walk the road from Lucan back into Dublin. Singing! No fighting. We tried to walk along the tram tracks and we'd be drunk, fall off it, and get back up on it. Ah, we'd get home at maybe four or five in the morning—daylight."

In 1960 the bonafide law was abolished as another colourful chapter in the history of old Dublin pub life was committed to memory and folklore.

PUB ENTERTAINMENT

"In the old days we used to make our own entertainment. We had fellas come in here and we'd be in stitches laughing. Oh, the Dublin wit is famous all over the world. And I've seen the finest of singers in here."

Jack Cusack, publican, age 75

THE ART OF CONVERSATION

From the ancient alehouse days onwards, conversation has been the very essence of public house life. And here the art of conversation survives and thrives as in no other social setting in Ireland. The old saying that pubmen lift a jar to loosen their tongues is an absolute verity. St John marvels at how men are transformed by drink into inveterate babblers:[43]

"Amazing how people can rattle on in public bars. Silent at union meetings. Struck dumb at a pay claim clash. But voices of wonder, wit and reason over a jar. Dublin talkers wound up like watch springs."

It is indeed as if a special social chemistry is activated in a pub by the mixing of drink and myriad personalities. Men meek and reticent in other social circumstances wondrously "bloom" when sipping their pint amidst their mates. Utterly inexplicable.

In 1948 Eric Whelpton recommended in *The Book of Dublin* that for some of the best entertainment one need simply "go to a tavern in a working-class district and listen to the conversation of the locals".[44] His advice holds just as true today as the pub scene is still highly socially invigorating. Gregarious cronies cluster in tight cliques to discuss and dissect sports, weather, local happenings and the state of mankind in general. All are treated with equal solemnity or frivolity depending upon the prevailing mood of the moment. There may be hushed tones during a serious story, clamorous laughter at a good yarn, or roaring oratory amidst political debate or literary analysis. The scene is not only orally stimulating but physically animated for amid the banter and badinage men pound the table to make a point, slap their knee in appreciation of a witty word, and thrust their arm wildly in the air to beckon the barman for another pint. At peak moments a pub can crackle with human electricity.

One of the factors that accounts for the stimulating conversation in a public house is the egalitarian setting in which all sorts of individuals mix together in open discussion. Intellectuals, manual labourers, professionals, shop clerks, civil servants and office workers share freedom of expression in which an uncommonly wide range of ideas and attitudes are exchanged. In probably no other social setting in Dublin could one find such a variety of socio-economic types rubbing elbows in spirited chat. It is an unwritten code of the public house to respectfully hear another person's opinions, be they brilliant or bizarre. This is why publican Cusack opines, "Oh, no university in the world could give me the education that I've had here. It's just from over the years of listening to people." Indeed, it is well known that many of Dublin's great writers gathered rich literary fodder from simply *listening* attentively to conversations around them in pubs. Many characters and much dialogue in the works of James Joyce, Sean O'Casey and Brendan Behan were doubtless extracted from Dublin pubs. In her father's pub, Clara Gill often observed Behan as he culled material for his writings:

"He had a great ear for conversation, a great love of humanity. Brendan used to come in a lot and he wrote lovely short pieces often about the customers here."

Topics of pub conversation have remained standard—and timeless. "Conversation in a pub has never varied", finds publican O'Dowd, "it's simple —politics, religion, the price of drink, cost of living, work and football and hurling matches." The *quality* of conversation, however, ranges from pure blather on the most mundane subjects to eloquent, enlightened discourses on world events or a Yeats poem. Most publicans enforce their own rules regarding delicate subjects, vile or abusive language, and the vocal level. Buffoons spouting gibberish are usually tolerated so long as they keep a civil tongue. However, most publicans overtly discourage—if not prohibit outright—heated discussions on religion and politics owing to their inherent volatility. O'Dwyer always enforced a tough policy:

"Anywhere I worked there was a rule that if conversations turned to politics or religion we could intervene and say, 'Listen, we don't entertain politics and religion here.' Cause it always led to trouble. It was impossible! It was a big powder keg! The whole thing could explode."

By general consensus among conversational purists, the invasion of television into public houses took a heavy toll on the simple art of talking. Many revile it as the worst "curse" ever put on the pub. Few would deny that the quality of pub conversation was vastly superior in the old days before the blaring picture box stared out at defenceless customers. There are still those few traditionalist publicans in Dublin who have managed to repel "modernisation" by prohibiting disruptive electrical contraptions on their premises. As Eugene Kavanagh, 55, sixth generation publican of the Gravedigger pub beside Glasnevin Cemetery, proudly proclaims, "We've no TV, no noise box, no phone, and people really talk to one another." Likewise, publican Tommy Smith, 54, has kept his Grogan's pub free from television and radio which is one reason why it has survived into the present day as Dublin's last genuine literary pub.

MUSIC, SONG, DANCE AND COMEDY

Neighbourhood pubs have always been blessed with their own local talent, a colourful cast of singers, musicians, dancers, comedians, story tellers, mimes, jugglers, acrobats and the inevitable "court jester". Some, of course, were decidedly more talented than others. None the less, on Saturday nights some pubs were converted into a theatrical stage as various entertainers did their "piece". Some men had to be coaxed into action while others were always primed to give an impromptu performance. The local pub was a small, intimate forum in which to perform and there could be no more appreciative an audience. Good performances were always rewarded with thunderous applause, hearty pats on the back and a string of pints. Only a few pubs were fortunate enough to have a piano but all had customers who could play a fiddle, melodeon, mouth organ, tin whistle, or even spoons. They provided the music for sing-songs which were a Saturday night custom in many local pubs. A favoured regular would be called upon by the publican or barman to serve as MC, for which he was given a few pints. It was an honour and responsibility seriously taken as he would fairly call forth each individual performer in his proper turn. Greenhalgh depicts the scene in his local pub in Ringsend in the forties on a Saturday night:

"They'd have an MC and, well, you know the old mop they'd use for mopping up the pub, he'd get a cigarette pack and put it on the top of the mop handle and use it as a microphone. Then every fella would sing in his turn and a fella with an old melodeon that'd play for the night, he'd go around with his old hat and they'd throw a few coppers into it. That made *him* happy."

Some men were truly gifted with great voices and could enrapture their audience. Apart from the aspiring John McCormacks were those dancers who featured themselves to be up-and-coming Fred Astaires, always eager to patter about the rough wooden floor once a small space had been cleared. Tommy "Lyrics" Murphy, 83, always especially enjoyed watching one man:

"We used to have a great old character, a great man with the tap dancing.

He worked in the coalyards and Terry Lynch was his name, a *great* dancer. Ah, you'd want to see him, great with the reels and jigs. And he was a lovely singer. Terry'd hold the floor for nearly an hour. How he used to keep going with the dancing and singing I do not know—he got a few pints!"

Comedians had their special niche in pub life, always ready with an amusing story, witty word or new joke. Their mates actually came to count upon them for entertainment and, in turn, they then had to live up to their reputation. They played an important role by cheering people up and making them laugh during life's hard times. A naturally clever or amusing man was always a welcome asset in any pub. When their routines became stale they were expected to get new material. Pub regulars would daily anticipate their arrival to put a bit of zest and humour into the mood. John Preston remembers a local comedian in the Sligo Bar in Parnell Street fifty years ago who even dressed for the part:

"There was this fella named 'Hustler', a great character in the pub, a great sense of humour he had. He was like Charlie Chaplin. He had the moustache and a trilby hat and all. And he had a stick and he used to *walk* like him and all. Great crack and jokes and he'd really make you laugh."

Cusack's Cozy Bar on the Coombe is a matchbox-size pub, probably the smallest in all Dublin. Yet, a half-century ago it was known for the great talent from around the Liberties that used to congregate there. It was the extraordinary *blend* of talent, variety, spontaneity and innovation that made this pub so special on a Saturday night. As he fondly recalls, he probably could have sold tickets if he had had the extra space:

"On a Saturday night we created our own amusement. A fella used to come in here with a pair of horn-rimmed glasses as thick as two jam jars and he was a trained opera singer and he'd give out with a song. My God Almighty, he had a magnificent voice! Another woman used to come in here and she'd sing the arias from different operas. Then there'd be an old gentleman, Mick—the 'Guxter' we used to call him—and he'd know about the old Vaudeville days and he'd start to whistle and then the old soft shoe. Then another chap would take out two pieces of ordinary sandpaper and go [rubbing], like he was the 'effects' man. Then another fella might come in with a big pair of spoons or maybe two bones off an animal that he'd been skinning down and he'd have them in his fingers and he'd rap them and he'd sing a song. Or a fella came in with a mouth organ. Then another fella came in here and he was an acrobat and he'd come in walking on his hands. That was part and parcel of the old days."

GAMES AND GAMBLING

Gambling on games in public houses was illegal but it probably took place in every pub in Dublin back in the 1930s and 1940s. Men could bet for money or for pints. Rings was the most popular game in the first half of the century. Most every neighbourhood pub had a ring board and perhaps a ring room. Many pubs even had their own ring team that travelled around the city competing with other houses. Publicans usually scheduled competitions on a slow weekday night knowing that the match would fill his house with a crowd of locals and followers from the other pub. An MC was designated to handle the rings, make certain the participants toed the line, and keep the crowd back. Big ring matches could not have been taken more seriously had they taken place in Croke Park. Wagering was widespread as the money was entrusted to the publican or barman. Apart from team competition, individual ring champions, who sometimes became hustlers, would make the rounds of pubs seeking challengers who wanted to make a few pounds and a reputation for themselves. Paddy Coffey, 83, was a barman at Murphy's pub on City Quay in the thirties when rings was at its peak of popularity:

"We had a great ring team down there. There was always wagering on it, ten shillings or a pound note would be the most because they hadn't *got* it at that time. The money would be handed inside the counter and put on the shelf. Oh, it was a very serious effort. Then some men that were champions going around Dublin would come into the pub and see was there anybody capable of taking them on for a pound. Oh, yes, a hustler like. They'd be well known. I remember one chap named Greene, a hustler, and I think he was the best in Dublin and he had a style of his own. Anybody that fancied himself wanted to have a go at him, challenge him."

Betting on card games was also commonplace. It was mostly small stakes just to pass the time. Players huddled in a corner like bandits crouched over a small table on which their money was openly displayed. Visiting guards seldom batted an eye. A good session could last eight hours during which players would usually call for more drink rather than leave the group. Betting in pubs on horses and sports matches could involve considerably higher stakes. Early in the century bookies were common figures in public houses. Though illegal, bookies were not expelled by publicans because they were good for business and fulfilled a necessary role at the time. Bookies were seen daily scurrying in and out of pubs taking bets and paying off. They cultivated their own clientele and became men of money and power. Frank Wearen saw bookies at work in pubs way back in 1916:

"There was always a bookie in a busy pub. There was no such thing as bookie shops at that time, so if you wanted a bookie you patronised a certain pub. You always knew the bookie, they were dressed in the *best* of style. Some of them'd wear big gold watches and chain and big rings on their fingers."

Bookies usually followed a pattern of setting up for business in certain pubs at regular hours. In this sense, the first bookie shops were actually established in pubs. Men would gather around and wait their turn to wager. Those bookies with the best reputation always did the most business. Coffey always treated bookies with respect when they entered his pub:

"Oh, he was a very important man, the bookie. He dressed spectacular, like a man of prominence, a big white hat and a big heavy coat. Oh, he always had about a hundred quid on him. Maybe that evening he'd come into the pub with the results and he paid off. But he wouldn't drink at all, he was on business."

Some publicans provided their loyal regulars with extracurricular activities for entertainment. For instance, most pubs in Ringsend had their own rowing clubs and competitions, sponsored by the publican. In this village of seamen and dockers competition was keen and the winning team reflected pride upon the entire public house. "Lyrics" Murphy was honoured when he was selected to row for Fitzharris's pub in the big race of 1940 and was thrilled to win it:

"We had skip clubs down here. Each pub had their own rowing crew. Maybe seven or eight pubs would be rowing against one another. It was a public house race. I rowed for Fitzharris's. And we won it. And there was a hooley going on for a whole week in the pub. Drink on the house for a whole week!"

Other publicans provided outings for their preferred patrons. These were sometimes called "buck excursions". Tommy Murray recalls with delight his days back in the thirties as a regular at Walsh's pub on City Quay when the boss would escort the select "gang" on their annual buck excursion held on the first Sunday in August. *Every* year. Mr Walsh would hire a coach and take about thirty men and as many cases of beer and head into the countryside for a fine summer's day of drinking and merrymaking. It was an all-day excursion in a pioneer bus rambling along rough, dusty roads—enough to make a man thirsty. Tommy and his pals anticipated the event all year long:

"It was called a 'buck excursion', only men'd go. To Arklow. Anything from twenty-five to thirty men. I'd say it went on for over twenty years. Mr Walsh, he'd supply all the beer free. And you'd want to see the beer *before* we'd go! Cause he'd open the pub early and you'd have a few pints and he'd always have a 'watcher' in case there was a policeman. So you went to Arklow and went out into a field and sat down and had your drinks, cases of stout. Could be out there for four or five hours. And then you'd drink it coming home on the bus. Come home about three in the morning. But you'd always have a cure for the morning, about four or five bottles in your pocket."

Singing Pubs

"The singing pub is one of the last outposts of the common man. The singers are real, they have dignity and their hearts are in the right place."

John D. Sheridan, Irish Licensing World, *1962*

From the 1930s to the 1960s Dublin was renowned for its gala singing pubs which "evolved from the old-fashioned music hall".[45] However, in Dublin the tradition was solo singing rather than group participation. Dublin's most famous singing pub was Lalor's of Wexford Street which began in 1938. Ted McGovern, 65, who came from County Cavan to serve his apprenticeship at Lalor's recalls, "it started accidentally on a Sunday night" when Mr Lalor invited about a dozen friends after hours up to his private quarters with piano for a bit of a sing-song. It was eventually decided to turn this private gathering into a public offering and the room was converted into a formal singing lounge holding about 130 people. From the outset, its popularity and reputation soared. By the 1940s there were about a dozen authentic singing pubs around the city, including Lambert's of Green Street, Donnelly's of Camden Street and the Regal Bar in Benburb Street. The best singing pubs became internationally known, drawing tourists from a host of countries for, as one devotee professed, "When you find a well-run Dublin singing house you are in for a night's entertainment that will leave your Munich beer cellar or your Blackpool tavern way behind."[46]

Singing pubs did their best business during the summer months on weekend nights. At the better houses a crowd started gathering an hour in advance. A doorman screened patrons for proper dress, general appearance and sobriety before admitting them—respectability was required. There was no cover charge but drink was more expensive than that served in the bar. People were packed in and seated at tables. Most singing pubs did not allow standing customers. People liked to attend with other family members or friends and make a festive evening of it. All social ranks were in evidence, from working class to professionals. Great numbers of tourists, especially British and American, were drawn to the singing pubs. Indeed, Bord Fáilte literature promoted the singing houses, heralding them as one of Dublin's major entertainment attractions. The phenomenal success of Dublin's singing pubs was best exemplified by Lalor's where barman McGovern worked at a frenzied pace:

"Lalor's was the *first* singing house in Dublin which became world famous. Anybody who was here in Dublin, it was a *must* to go to Lalor's. We got people from *all* areas and from all walks of life. From plumbers to foreign dignitaries and professional people—the lot. And everybody was dressed up as if they were going to the cinema or a hotel. People came from all over the world. We got a *huge* amount of English tourists. It was as important to go to Lalor's at that time as it would be to go to the Wax Museum in London."

Once everyone was seated and served the anticipation mounted. It was the responsibility of the master of ceremonies to quiet the crowd, select singers, and to maintain what was known as "proper order". Usually the MC was a member of the publican's family, a barman, or a trusted patron who possessed the necessary social skills to conduct the show. In the absence of a microphone he ruled by a strong voice and personality. All singing pubs employed a piano player and occasionally a violinist as well for accompaniment. The "proper order" system meant that each singer was formally called in turn by the MC and allowed two songs. A singer who really dazzled the crowd could be called back for an encore by popular demand and find his table laden with gratis drinks. As Sheridan describes, the proceedings were taken most seriously:[47]

> "Singing pubs take themselves seriously, and properly so. They know their worth. There is no rowdiness, no interruptions. The hubbub of talk ceases, the glasses go down, the waiters stand immobile. The world is waiting for Mr X's song. He sings 'Roses are Blooming in Piccardy', or 'Shannon River', or 'Lullaby of Broadway', sings it dreamily, happily, confidently. When he finishes there is a glow about him. He is a bigger and better man than he was ten minutes ago."

Owing to the great number of customers eager to sing and the highly competitive environment, the MC had to conduct affairs in a very diplomatic manner. As the evening progressed and drinks were consumed, prospective performers could become impatient and demanding. Oftentimes a one-song rule might be enforced in order to accommodate more people. The crowd, too, could become agitated if they felt that their favourites were being ignored or slighted. Since each participant, of course, regarded himself or herself as a gifted vocalist, the competition for recognition and applause was fierce. There were indeed some extremely talented pub singers who could well have performed on the stage at the Theatre Royal or the Gaiety given the opportunity. Some actually became personalities in their own right on the singing pub scene. McGovern was often called upon by his boss to serve as MC:

> "Oh, fantastic competition. There was a lot of jealousy because they were *proud* of their singing and very conscious of what people thought of it. Very competitive. The songs were from opera to comedy. *Any* type of song . . . Frankie Lane, Frank Sinatra, John McCormack, you name it. They were all Frankie Lanes in their own mind! Or John McCormack. Some of them were absolutely great and you wouldn't hear a sound. The applause, that *made* their life."

Apart from the highly respectable singing pubs there were those which catered to a rough and unruly element where one would encounter a "cacophonous horde of howlers, brawlers, messers, hooters, moaners and flat-voiced bleaters who constantly threaten at the gates".[48] Such customers regularly arrived at the door well jarred and in a troublesome mood. Rowdies often came in clans which would rival one another for attention, causing a competitive situation to become combative. Billy Sullivan used to act as the MC in some of the tougher singing pubs around in the forties in return for a few bob and a few pints—which were *hard* earned. He was routinely bribed and bullied and once found himself in the midst of a real Donnybrook:

"The singing houses were rough. I used to do the MC in one and you'd name a fella to come up. Then a fella might give you a pint for to let him sing. But maybe there'd be three or four fellas and they'd say '*I'm* next, or else!' And you had better call them up next or they'd give you a bang with a bottle on their way out. There'd be murder cause you'd get different types and a fella'd get a few drinks and he'd want to sing and then there'd be some other fella coming up and *he'd* want to sing. They were messers. I seen a pub wrecked from fighting. It was Lalor's singing house on the quay. The fight come up and must have been sixty or eighty fighting. Could have been a hundred in it. Oh, everything was flying. The place was *wrecked!*"

LITERARY PUBS

"There is a unique and lasting relationship between the city's poets, novelists and dramatists and her pubs."

Liam Blake, Irish Pubs, *1985*

What exactly constitutes a true "literary" pub is open to some interpretation and debate. In general terms it has come to mean a public house where a significant number of known writers and intellectuals congregate on a regular basis to discuss matters of literature as well as every other subject under the sun. Over the centuries certain pubs served as gathering places for Dublin's novelists, poets and journalists who found the social environment fertile ground for observing the human condition and exchanging thoughts and ideas. Historically, a number of Dublin pubs took on a literary patronage and ambience as a result of their proximity to bookshops and publishers' offices:[49]

"The literary tradition of the pub may date from the time when many of the best-known publishers had their bookshops and printing offices in a building which was also a tavern. Many of the news-sheets, ballads, lampoons, pamphlets, political tracts—libellous, vituperative and abusive—were issued from offices in taverns. It was also a custom in the middle of the eighteenth century to conduct book auctions in taverns or coffee houses."

The literati naturally gravitated toward those establishments where they found their intellectual peers. In this century the most acclaimed literary pubs include the Bailey, Dolphin, Pearl, Palace Bar, Neary's, McDaid's, and Davy Byrne's where James Joyce drank. Each gained a reputation in its time for being intellectually stimulating and socially vibrant.

Literary pubs drew not only writers but artists, professors and amateur philosophers which created a Bohemian atmosphere. Typical of this genre was "an obscure public house" in the 1920s known as "The Old Bull and Bush" in Duke Street which played a significant part in the "artistic life of Dublin".[50] Here writers and artists would meet at lunch time, drawn by its sumptuous bread and cheese sandwiches and "most excellent black brock". As Dickinson records in *The Dublin of Yesterday*: "During these lunches a sort of habit or custom grew up that no serious subject matter must be introduced into the conversation."[51] This little group became known as "Euphagists"—those who refused to discuss serious topics at lunch time. They instead delighted in writing witty and outright silly verse, of which the following is an example:[52]

> "In a quiet little side street off the City's foaming flood,
> There's a charming little spot to sit one down in.
> Where the intellect and talent hie them, be it understood,
> Quite regardless if proprieties are frownin';
> Where the solar rays in summer shining from the brassy skies
> Are reflected in a manner hotly shocking.
> There the amateur Bohemians all are wont to 'Euphagise'
> And to spend an hour bread-and-cheese-and-brocking."

Writers in the early part of the century such as James Joyce and Sean O'Casey, as well as most Irish Revivalist writers, "went into pubs, learned from watching people, and better practised their profession from having done so", contends Dwyer.[53] Even Synge, who apparently drank very little, would purposely go into a pub to observe the social dynamics and conversation.[54] Joyce drew liberally, depicting pub scenes in *Ulysses* and writing "Counterparts" in *Dubliners* which is the story of a pub crawl. To Joyce, the pub was a theatre of the ordinary folk:[55]

"James Joyce cast a colder eye than either Synge or O'Casey on the democracy, the wisdom, and the amoral vitality of the public house and on those who frequent it. Although he recognised the pub as a place of release, he did not mistake it for an asylum from the exacting demands of the church and state in Ireland. Rather, he viewed it as a theatre where the common people had the freedom to be themselves, and to act out what their spirits wished they might do in the outside world."

By contrast, it was said that W. B. Yeats had an inability to appreciate the society of the pub. It is purported that Toner's in Lower Baggot Street is the only public house in Dublin ever to be visited by Yeats who, like his contemporaries A. E., George Moore and most of the literary set of the pre-Behan age, did most of their entertaining in private. It is well known that Yeats "spurned the informality" of pubs and more particularly their boasters.[56] When Yeats returned from Oxford in 1922 to assume a political career in the Free State Senate he purchased 82 Merrion Square which was located directly behind the buildings opposite Toner's. As the story goes, Yeats was one day persuaded by Gogarty to rectify his pub deficiency and taken to Toner's. He slipped unobtrusively into a snug close to the door and ordered a sherry. Upon finishing it, he rose stiffly to his feet, proclaimed "I have seen a pub. Will you kindly take me home", and departed in obvious relief.

In the 1940s many of Dublin's literary figures habitually convened in their favourite public houses. John Ryan, 76, then publisher of *Envoy* literary magazine and later publican at the Bailey, confirms that writers "used those pubs like the Dolphin and the Pearl for ambience. The Dolphin seemed to catch the spirit of the times. There'd be intellectuals and writers . . . it was ideas and arguments. Oh, free political expression." The Palace Bar in Fleet Street was a watering hole for journalists, most notably R. M. Smyllie, editor of *The Irish Times*, who held court there from 5.00 every evening. The judicial Smyllie's corner was dubbed by wags the "intensive care unit". But writers and poets of the day could be heard pontificating in a number of literary pubs:[57]

"Patrick Kavanagh could be heard discoursing in McDaid's on such esoteric subjects as professional boxing, the beauty of Ginger Rogers, or the dire state of Gaelic football in Ulster. Flann O'Brien could be heard in Neary's or the Scotch House on any subject known to man."

The archetypal Dublin literary pub was McDaid's of Harry Street, just a few paces removed from bustling Grafton Street. In its halcyon days of the 1940s and 1950s McDaid's boasted the grandest galaxy of literary luminaries on the Dublin scene. Regulars included Brendan Behan, Patrick Kavanagh, Brian O'Nolan, Gainor Crist, Austin Clarke, Anthony Cronin, Brian Donleavy, Liam O'Flaherty and others—the collective likes of which Dublin will likely never again see within the walls of one pub. However, McDaid's was originally a most unlikely candidate for Dublin's premier literary pub. Ryan recalls that in the 1930s "McDaid's was a dowdy little pub. Oh, the *plainest* possible pub, that was one of the things I liked. And 90 per cent of the people in it were working class." Paddy O'Brien, head barman at McDaid's for nearly thirty-five years—whom Anthony Cronin called "one of the greatest barmen of all time"—found the pub dark and dreary when he first came to work there in 1937:

"The only literary pub that was alive then was Davy Byrne's. That was the 'in' place where you'd find St John Gogarty and those of his generation. They all drank there and made it a literary pub. But McDaid's was nothing at all. It was a *dreadful* place. Just an ordinary pub with snugs and little partitions and sawdust and spittoons and you'd have elderly men in little groups spitting and all this sort of filth. And TB was rampant but you had to wash out those spittoons. I was saying to myself, 'I won't be here long.'"

O'Brien found the elderly, conservative Mr McDaid to be a "very shy man, very nice, quiet" who would periodically "go on the booze" and neglect the management of the establishment. Finally, after about a year on the job, at the ripe age of 23, he summoned the nerve to suggest to his boss that he "tear out the whole place", dismantle the partitions to open up the space and improve the lighting to brighten it up. To his surprise, McDaid followed his suggestion and made enough changes to noticeably improve the atmosphere. Gradually it began drawing a more diverse clientele. But, according to O'Brien, the most significant single force of social change in the history of McDaid's was the arrival upon the scene of John Ryan in the late 1930s. As the publisher of *Envoy*, one of the most important literary journals of its day, Ryan established the habit of ensconcing himself daily in McDaid's which he found perfect for meeting with prospective and established writers. In effect, the unpretentious little pub became his editorial "office" where he conducted most of his literary dealings. A highly respected writer and intellectual himself, he befriended all of the major Dublin literary figures of the period and often mediated disputes between egotistical and temperamental personalities. In an unmistakably wistful tone, he recounts those times he so dearly loved:

"In those days I published *Envoy* and people would come into McDaid's who were seeking me out. And at McDaid's they could fill the stage with characters. There'd be Behan, who was a marvellous stage filler and Kavanagh and O'Nolan and Donleavy and Tony Cronin. And Liam O'Flaherty was there quite a lot. Quite regularly you'd see five of them together there. And they'd converse with their friends, their coevals, as it were. In their pub conversations they'd endlessly be talking about Katherine Mansfield and Joyce was never off their minds. He was the subject of *continuous* correction, in very critical ways. And Yeats would often come up. I remember Kavanagh saying once that he could 'do without Yeats'. And imminent fights were always on the horizon. *Tensions*, really, with Behan and Kavanagh and O'Nolan and Donleavy. Behan and Kavanagh would stir it up at times. They could be critical of one another. Small irritations that would mount to a crescendo. Verbal abuse was their main weapon. But they were notably kind hearted . . . I loved that period."

Anthony Cronin, a charter member of the original McDaidian club, records in his book *Dead as Doornails* that "McDaid's was never merely a literary pub. Its strength was always in variety, of talent, class, caste and estate. The division between writer and non-writer, Bohemian and artist, informer and revolutionary were never rigorously enforced. The atmosphere could have been described as Bohemian-revolutionary."[58] From behind the bar, O'Brien witnessed the gradual evolution of McDaid's from a sleepy backwater drinking house to Dublin's most renowned literary pub over a period of more than three decades. He clearly credits Ryan with being the catalyst in this transformation:

"John Ryan is a *founder member* of that public house. He's the man who made it a literary pub. It just *happened*. He got this thing called *Envoy* going and he'd come over to McDaid's and have a drink. And then, bit by bit, it all came into a circle, all types of literary people, poets and story writers and you name it. From that on it just mushroomed. Then McDaid's became the 'in' place if you wanted to *find* somebody. When the literary people took over there was always something happening. You had Behan, Paddy Kavanagh, Brian O'Nolan and Gainor Crist. There was this *great* blend. They all seemed to live in the *one time*. And the conversation at McDaid's . . . *great*! To know them they were *lovely* people. I loved me life at that stage."

No other pub in the city held such a volatile mixture of characters. Egos were gargantuan and sensibilities fragile. Heated conversation often sparked fussing and feuding. Sometimes serious rows erupted in what Ryan regarded as "potentially the most explosive pub situation" in all Ireland. Miraculously, physical confrontations were avoided, often just in the nick of time. Observers of the scene claim that only under the gentle diplomacy of O'Brien were such social squalls becalmed. Behan and Kavanagh, particularly, were famous for stirring up trouble. "Kavanagh and Behan didn't get on well at all", discloses O'Brien. "Behan was big and robust, real rough, and he *couldn't* hold his drink." Rather than bar the gladiators for verbal abuse or shouting matches, O'Brien preferred to put them on "probation" once they were stone sober. He knew their nature and deftly handled their temperamental behaviour. No barman in Dublin was so respected and loved by all with whom he came in contact.

Behan, the most flamboyant pubman of his day, deserves special mention. He was commonly called "a lovable rogue", always entertaining and craving attention. O'Brien, who should know better than anyone, debunks the myth that Behan was a drinker with great capacity—he simply couldn't hold his beer well. By all accounts, he possessed the most foul mouth in all Dublin, even inventing wonderful obscenities which he flung about with wild abandon, obviously for effect many times. He loved playing the role and it became *expected* of him. The moment he would plod through the pub door the environment seemed to change. He relished provoking a spirited argument—on any subject. Behan lived in Russell Street directly across from Noel Gill's father's pub which he regularly visited. When Noel was a young barman he knew Brendan had entered the pub without having to look up because his thunderous voice announced his presence:

"His voice would be head and shoulders over everybody and his f——-ing would be *twice* as loud and that'd be the way he emphasised a point whether it was politics or football. And he'd give a *thump*, stamp his authority on the subject. We treated him as a character but he could be tricky and boisterous. But he was quite lovable. Brendan would get excitable quite quick and he'd get into hectic arguments. Anyone who picked an argument with him got the worst of it cause he was quick at putting them down."

Many of the pub regulars at Gill's who had known him since he was a child romping about the street "adjourned here when Brendan died" to pay their last respects and share stories about their encounters with him. He was indisputably one of Dublin's most storied pubmen of all time and many regard his passing as the end of a special chapter in the city's pub history.

It had always been Paddy O'Brien's dream to one day own his own pub, so when McDaid's was put up for sale in 1972 he acted swiftly. With a financial partner he presented the full asking price of £78,000, confident that the offer would be summarily accepted. At the last moment a wealthy woman from London who was "determined to buy herself a literary pub" substantially outbid them. In desperation, they matched her bid several times but had to drop out of the competition when the price reached £87,000. Despondent over the defeat, Paddy considered retiring. By an extraordinary coincidence—or act of fate—the same day that McDaid's was sold a friend of O'Brien's, Tommy Smith, bought Grogan's pub in South William Street only a few blocks away. As a young man, Tommy had been a regular at McDaid's, loved the literary atmosphere, and came to know the head barman well. Having heard about O'Brien's misfortune, Smith had a brilliant idea—he and his partner invited Paddy to become manager at Grogan's. Tommy, who was an experienced barman, was delighted to become a publican and now he was given the opportunity to install his good friend and Dublin's most loved barman behind the counter. For both parties it was a Godsend. When O'Brien enthusiastically accepted the offer and took up residence in Grogan's it changed the course of Dublin's literary pub history. Smith documents the consequences:

"Up to the time McDaid's was sold it was still a literary pub. And we bought Grogan's at the very same time that McDaid's was sold. That was in 1972. Would you believe that the two houses changed hands on the same day! *Purely* a coincidence. And Paddy came over as manager and most of the people from McDaid's, they all shifted to Grogan's. He took the literary pub with him. Ah, there was a lot of literary and artistic people still around at that stage. You had an array, like Hayden Murphy, Michael Hartnett, Tony Cronin, Macdara Woods and John Ryan and Ben Kiely and Liam O'Flaherty. They *all* shifted to Grogan's."

This extraordinary flight of the faithful was the ultimate tribute to O'Brien as Grogan's immediately took on a literary flavour. Apart from "inheriting" the writing fraternity, the unpretentious pub drew a loyal core of artists, musicians and intellectuals. Today it enjoys the undisputed status of Dublin's only surviving authentic literary pub. Because Smith prohibits radio, TV and piped music, the setting is conducive to intimate human interaction and thoughtful conversation. Conversely, McDaid's has become a trendy "yuppie hangout" devoid of soul and character. Even the old ghosts hovering in its high ceiling must occasionally cringe when overhearing some of the witless and inane chatter. What a lovely irony, some say. Only a few months before his death in

1989 Paddy was sitting before the tape recorder reminiscing nostalgically about the glory days of McDaid's. In ending, he mused, with the slightest of smiles, "Yes . . . *all the McDaid's* people come right across! . . . so she never got her literary pub."

NOTABLE PUB CHARACTERS

"Characters make a pub."

Noel Gill, publican, age 60

"Think of all the characters who have walked straight out of pubs into our novels and plays."

Brinsley MacNamara, Irish Licensing World, *1950*

A pub without characters? Inconceivable. Every pub has had its characters. Indeed, the local pub is the very *breeding ground* for Dublin's characters. Legendary for their idiosyncratic personalities or bizarre antics, they became part of their pub's folklore. Many an old publican sighs, "Ah, I could write a book about the great characters we've had in here." Their buffoonery entertained generations of pub mates before they disappeared from the scene. Regrettably, most of Dublin's quirky and colourful pub characters over the ages have gone unrecorded, living on only in the memory of those who knew them or were told about them via the oral tradition.

Pub characters have come from all walks of life. Many of the aforementioned literary figures were, of course, genuine pub characters in their own right, as exemplified by the Behan caricature. It is often claimed that many of the city's old jarveys and *all* the women street dealers were unique characters. But a pub character could just as well be a tailor, docker, tradesman, tram driver, chimney sweep, lamplighter, journalist or eccentric professional. There was never a single mould, they came in impressive variety. The stereotypical Dublin pub character so widely recognised around the world in literature, the theatre and in film is of real, not mythical, origin. Joyce, O'Casey and Behan did not need to invent their characters, they merely extracted them life-size from their local pub—and seldom was embellishment necessary. Dublin's fascinating pub characters, past and present, are far too numerous to be satisfactorily documented in this book but brief coverage of a selected few will hopefully provide a sense of their special role in Dublin pub history and folklore.

Publicans and regulars have a sort of perverse pride in having some delightfully daffy and deviant types around for diversion and comic relief. They affectionately refer to them as our "head cases", "local looneys", "resident lunatics", "outpatients", or "quare fellas". It may even be argued that possessing genuine characters is one measure of a pub's uniqueness. Of course, one of the most pleasing features of many such characters is that they are usually serenely oblivious to their annointed status. As John Ryan put it, the "essence of the Dublin character is complete unawareness of the fact that he is one himself".[59] To illustrate this point, he relates the story of three men some forty-five years ago being overheard outside a Dublin pub deploring in a "genuinely aggrieved" manner the sad absence from the Dublin scene of any real remaining characters —they were Myles na gCopaleen, Sean O'Sullivan and Brendan Behan![60]

Fortunately, some famed pub characters have actually been recorded. One notable example is Fluther Good, fondly recalled by Bernard Neary in *North of the Liffey*. A curmudgeonly fellow, but affectionately treated, Fluther became part of "north Dublin folklore" for his escapades early in the century.[61] He used to plant himself daily on a butter box on the Ballybough Road and Sean O'Casey gave him fame when he included him in his *The Plough and the Stars.* He had a steel plate in his head as the result of being hit with a bottle over the skull in a pub which probably caused a good deal of his unorthodox behaviour. Stories about Fluther around the northside abound. One deals with Archdeacon Brady who was building the church in East Wall and asked Fluther to get some sand for the construction. When the job was completed Fluther called into the Archdeacon for his payment, whereupon the good reverend placed in his open palm a beautiful picture of the Sacred Heart. The next day Fluther went into Noctor and McCann's, his local pub, and ordered a pint and a small one. When the barman asked for one shilling and two pence Fluther put the holy picture on the counter and uttered, "This is what Jesus Christ paid me—and you can have it in payment for me gargle."

In those days a slate was kept in Noctor and McCann's allowing regulars to get drink on credit. The amount owed was written in chalk on the slate. The story goes that following a break-in at the pub one night the only thing discovered amiss the next morning was that the slate had been tampered with— only one name had been rubbed off—Fluther's. Another evening a customer came into the pub and began to "touch" people for money. With great indignation, Fluther promptly approached the man informing him, "There is only one toucher in here and that's me. Now get out!" The intruder quickly exited. Fluther died in 1940 at the age of 75 and in his honour a pub on the Ballybough Road was named the Fluther Good.

Bill Kelly documents another interesting pub personality in *Me Darlin' Dublin's Dead & Gone* whose name was Dingers. He was a bruising bully and the scourge of all the pubs around his neighbourhood. It is said that when Dingers got into a brawl it took six hefty DMP men to haul him off. There was no tougher or meaner pubman around his parts, as Kelly tells it:[62]

"'Twas said that when he had no money and needed a drink he'd walk into the pub and spit into the nearest pint on the counter. If the owner objected he'd get a punch that would fell him, and Dingers would drink the pint. If the owner didn't object Dingers drank the pint and left him alone."

Many a meek and prudent patron went home thirsty but intact.

Dublin's old jarveys always had a reputation for being great pub characters. They were known for their heavy drinking, earthy wit and quirky nicknames. Many strategically located their hazards outside a pub so that they could drink and socialise with their brethren all day. "Wherever there was a hazard there was a pub", declares 70-year-old jarvey Mickey Sheridan, "and the publican got plenty of money." Tommy O'Neill worked as a jarvey during the 1940s with mates nicknamed "Lousy Cushion", "Kissing the Bottle", "Blue Nose", "Redpole", "Run away with the Hearse" and "Banker":

> "Jarveys were the best drinkers of the whole lot and terrible witty. The old jarveys were all great characters and there were *all* nicknames for the jarveys. My uncle, Corny O'Neill, was crowned king of the jarveys in Dublin. Oh, my God, all he could do was drink, drink, drink. He drank himself into the grave."

There was a notorious jarvey from Queen Street who would go on the drink, "get religion", and in his missionary zeal would terrify church-goers on Sunday morning after he had been boozing in a shebeen. Billy Ennis, 76, saw him in action many times:

> "He was a big man about six foot four. A big lump of a man he was. A *character*. And he got religious mad, he did. One Sunday morning on Blackhall Street all the people were going to Mass. Well, he got the horse whip and the rosary beads and the people were coming down to Mass and he made them all kneel down and say the rosary. Big whip and beads in his hands! Frightened the life out of them, he did."

Some of the most hilarious characters on the pub scene were known as "hoggers", men who would hang around the dockside pubs in search of discharged Guinness barrels still containing a few precious sups of porter or stout. Such casks would be stacked outside the pub or along the quay after being unloaded from a Guinness vessel returning from London or Liverpool. Hoggers usually worked as a team of two or three, examining each barrel with the precision of a surgeon. Tops of the casks were painted with bright red raddle which would stain their faces as they pressed to sip the liquid which had been poured onto the surface. After one of their successful excursions hoggers often returned to their local pub looking like a parade of clowns, much to the amusement of their mates. John Greenhalgh still chuckles when describing their technique:

> "The hoggers'd come along and pick one hogshead and there might be a pint in that and they'd tip that and say 'time to have a sup'. But they'd clean the top first, make sure its nice and clean. Then they'd put the peak of their cap to one side of their head and sup it up. And then they had the red raddle on their nose and on their forehead. Oh, there was no need to have a circus —no Hollywood make-up!"

Pubs in the Liberties seemed to have a special profusion of pub characters. In Cusack's Cozy Bar back in the forties Granny Roche, an 84-year-old tinker woman, would come in wearing her little straw hat with imitation cherries, her black shawl in which she always kept a tiny pet mouse, and she'd sit and sip her porter while smoking a clay pipe. She looked like a comic figure on the Abbey stage. On any given day she could be followed by another customer who used to bring his pet monkey into the pub. When waggish regulars would ply the beast with booze it could have dire consequences, moans Jack:

"He'd bring the monkey in here, and it'd sit on an old seat over there. And we'd give him a sup of stout and get him half-drunk. There was a chain on him and he'd get very vicious then and you had to be very careful. Oh, he'd scratch the face off you. Oh, he'd tear you to bits! Now one day the man went off and his monkey got a bit vicious and we were afraid of our lives."

Just across the River Liffey in Stoneybatter there was a pub character named "Baby" Nugent who could match any in the Liberties. He was forever going on the gargle, mounting his horse and creating havoc in the neighbourhood. Noel Hughes was an eye-witness to many of his drunken antics:

"One time 'Baby' Nugent, he painted his horse *pink* and he got on his back and rode him into the pub. Opened the door of the pub and come in with the horse. *Rode* that horse into the pub. Just for devilment!"

He rightfully became regarded as a public terror when riding his horse drunk on the open street. But even worse, sometimes he would go on a binge and decide to ride his horse up the steps into the local picture house. Ninety-two-year-old Robert Hartney, who was the usher at the Manor Street picture house back in the 1920s era of silent films remembers all too vividly the shock of seeing Nugent burst into the cinema astride his horse during a matinee. It was more dramatic than the action on the screen:

"He was a character, a bit mental, you know. Not dangerous or anything. Used to take a drink. He had a horse that was blind in one eye. One time he went into the public house and called for two pints. And the barman says, 'Where's the other man?' 'Ah,' says he, 'he's outside.' And so you know what he done? He went outside and put the pint glass down and the horse drank the pint. Drank the beer! Well, he come down to the cinema and, would you believe, he brought the horse up the steps into the hall. And the manageress says, 'Oh, don't attempt to go in there, you'll have the whole place upset.' You know, the people would be running in panic. So he backed the horse down the steps and went off. Anyway, in the end, unfortunately, one day he made a bet with somebody that he could cross the bridge on the Liffey [walking the stone wall]. He got halfway across and he fell in and was drowned. That was the unfortunate end of him."

In contrast to characters who could be a menace to society were the completely innocuous ones. It was their very simplicity and innocence that endeared them to their mates, as Paddy Mooney reflects:

"There were great characters in a public house, they were simple characters. Like 'Professor' Murphy, for instance. Now Professor Murphy was as thick as a bus. He knew nothing. He *lived* at the pub. And it didn't matter *what* you were talking about—politics, art, science, music, literature, drama—he was an *authority* on it. And he knew *nothing*! But he was the last word."

Years ago a similarly benign fellow by the name of Huey was to be found every day in Gill's pub on the North Circular Road. Though simple minded, he was never derided by other customers. They even felt protective toward him. In his gentle, unknowing way he brought endless amusement to the local crowd, as Noel observes:

"Huey, he was a great character. He was a *profound* village idiot. He'd be standing at the corner waiting for someone to call him in for a drink. And in the summer time his wellington boots used to stink to high heaven. And when there was a match on in Croke Park he'd buy *two* colours and for the Mayo crowd he'd have their colours and he'd be congratulating them and that'd be a sure pint for him. And if the other side won he'd have *their* colours up. But sometimes he'd get half-drunk and get so mixed up that he'd have the wrong score."

Tommy Murray can match that story with his account of "Jingle Bells", a favourite character in Walsh's pub on City Quay fifty years ago. Jingle Bells was the name bestowed upon a newspaper seller who could have the regulars at Walsh's in absolute stitches of laughter. Customers would entice him into one song after another as the barman rewarded him with what he thought to be small whiskies:

"And here's the *best part* of it—he'd be singing and do you know what it was all the time? It was lemonade with water in it! And he'd start staggering. He *really thought* he was drunk. We used to look forward to it, that was the greatest laugh."

One of the most legendary characters around Dublin was Father John Edward Kavanagh, born in 1909. He was known to everyone around the northside as "Flash" Kavanagh because of the speed with which he celebrated Mass—ten to twelve minutes. Local lore has it that he raced through Mass so that he could be down to his local pub when it opened and there is much oral evidence that this was so. He was unabashedly fond of the jar and established a daily pub routine like any other man. In fact, sometimes he would dart directly from the altar to his favourite snug in full religious attire, as John Preston witnessed many times:

"Father Flash Kavanagh, he'd drink in the pub called the Deer's Head in Parnell Street. Used to drink in there in the mornings and you'd see him locked [drunk]. You'd see him in there with his red vestments and he'd go in right through the bar to a little back snug there and that's where he used to be and that was his berth. Nearly every day he was there. He used to do 10.00 Mass because the pubs opened at half ten and he'd be in there at half ten—in a *flash*. He'd drink pints and small ones—all according to the collection that morning!"

ECCENTRIC PUBLICANS AND NOTORIOUS PUBS

"All sorts of characters among the publicans. There was one that'd go on the beer and he'd be stark naked behind the counter with a bowler hat, nothing else on. Another publican, very religious, used to walk around with a cross."

Clara Gill, publican's daughter, age 60

"There was always terrible rows in pubs, dirty rows. Always blood-spilling in the pub at that time. Always."

John-Joe Kennedy, age 75

Some of the most fascinating characters on the Dublin pub scene were eccentric or loony publicans noted for their unorthodox or bizarre mannerisms and practices. In the old days many publicans lived a sheltered bachelor's existence above their pub and became reputed for their peculiar ways. Dublin pub lore abounds with stories of idiosyncratic publicans who enlivened their houses. One of the great publican eccentrics around the 1940s was "Daddy" Egan whose pub was in cobblestoned Smithfield Market, a hive of cattle men, horse dealers, drovers and tinkers. As a young man he entered the priesthood but didn't succeed. He later became a finicky bachelor, religious fanatic and a bit of a rogue. Using his place behind the counter as a sort of altar, he sermonised to customers and prohibited foul language. Yet, he routinely served roughnecks turned away by other publicans and even allowed horses into the pub for a few gulps of porter, confirms Diller Delaney:

"He'd give you a holy medal when you'd go in. Oh, he had bags of medals. And in Daddy Egan's you didn't curse. Couldn't even raise your voice. Now the tinkers drank at Daddy Egan's and they drove *horses* in. Oh, Daddy Egan, he let the horses in. Bring the horses into the pub and give the horses a pint! Give the horse a full bucket of porter."

The older he grew the more religious and tyrannical he became, even imposing obligatory prayer upon his patrons. When the noonday bells rang for the

Angelus everyone had to participate. O'Neill dropped to his knees in prayer many a time to remain in Daddy's good graces:

"He was religious mad. He went to be a priest and failed. Now at noontime he'd walk out with a rosary beads and you had to join in with the Angelus. That's true, inside the pub. Oh, you'd have to kneel down and you'd be saying 'Hail Mary' and he'd be saying 'Our Father'. Every day. He was a lovely little man. But a rogue in every way. He'd rob your change and everything. Oh, but you had to say the rosary! And he'd keep people in during the holy hour and there was police raids into the pub."

He is equally remembered for the two unusual bouncers he employed. Both were ex-soldiers who had lost a hand in the war and had an "iron hand" installed in their place. As O'Neill saw on many occasions, they could knock a man cold with one solid blow:

"One was 'Fisty' Carney and the other was 'Stealer' Gagan. One had an iron right hand and the other had an iron left hand. Gagan, he could screw it off. And he always had a glove on it. It was just like the iron hall door knocker and when you got a belt of that!"

Women publicans were a rare sight in Dublin. They were usually the widow or daughter of a deceased publican. The few who did exist were often known for their unusual ways. For example, publican Kate McCauley of the Liberties was xenophobic by nature and allowed in only a small coterie of familiar faces. Her pub in New Street was probably the most "closed" pub in Dublin. When Iveagh Market dealer Tess Ryan, 65, was a young girl her father was one of Kate's "chosen few":

"She was never married. Always dressed in a navy serge costume. She lived above the pub and was very wary of people, always very protective. She never let strangers in, they were always the one regular crowd from the local area. And you had to knock at the window for her to open . . . and then the people were there till all hours of the morning."

By far the most famed woman publican of her time was Kate Gilligan, better known as the Widow Reilly, who originally had a pub in Thomas Street and later another in Phibsborough. Larry Ryan who worked for her as a barman in the forties calls her a "legend in her own lifetime", known for her manly dress, tough manner, selling black market tea and sugar during the war years, and for running a speakeasy and a match-making operation in her pub. She weighed twenty stone, tied her grey hair in a tight bun, wore dark colours and always appeared to Ryan as, "Oh, very stern looking." She would not hesitate to personally drag a troublesome customer to the door by the scruff of the neck and boot him out. Even burly men feared inviting her wrath. Mickey Guy, 70, of the Liberties knew she was not a woman to be trifled with:

"She was a big heavy woman and dressed as a man with a shirt and collar and tie. She was a very tough woman, real rough and ready. And she run a speakeasy, closed the doors at 10.00 but as long as you had the money she'd keep you inside. And she had friends in the police."

It was her role as a match-maker that most distinguished her from all other Dublin publicans. Match-making pubs were common in small country towns, but not in urban Dublin. Hence, her pub in Phibsborough which brought couples together was unique. O'Neill frequently went to her match-making pub which did a thriving business and was always fascinated by the proceedings:

"I knew the Widow Reilly well. She ran a marriage bureau out there in the pub. Yeah, a marriage bureau. Match-making! You'd go in there and you had to pay her a fee. She had a special compartment of her own and she'd take all the particulars. Oh, she'd write it all down. And you'd meet them [women] then in the bar. It was like going to the cattle market and buying a cow. That's true. Oh, it'd be *packed* with women and she'd make a match. She'd get you fixed up, get you married. And then she'd give you a wedding present."

Her legend was enhanced by the strange relationship she had with her husband who had his own separate pub in James's Street. He was a noted dandy and dapper dresser always in pinstripe suit with a fresh red rose on his lapel and wearing spiffy spats. It is widely said that they detested one another and never spoke. Exactly how this curious condition came to exist no one knows, but it certainly added to the Widow's mystique. However, O'Neill noticed that when her husband passed away the Widow exhibited unusual good spirits and generosity—"She *hated* him! And he never spoke to her. And when he died everyone [in her pub] got free drink for three days."

A good many Dublin publicans kept behind their counter as a weapon a wooden mallet used to tap beer casks. Some were known for wielding it too freely. Publican Matt Lynch of Church Street, for example, was noted for his strict discipline and custom of giving a belligerent man a bang on the skull with his handy mallet before dragging him outside. Two other Dublin proprietors were known as "battling publicans" who actually relished participating in a wild brawl in their house. One was Dan Griffith whose pub in North Anne Street often erupted in rows. As a regular in the pub, Hughes never tired of watching Griffith in action:

"Dan Griffith was an old terrier, an IRA man. He was around 60 but he could fight like a young fella. He was strong and boney, cauliflower ears and he had a broken nose. And if there was a fight with customers he'd take his apron off and come outside the counter and fight himself as well. Old Dan Griffith loved to fight."

His counterpart was a publican named Humphrey down by the Five Lamps who dressed impeccably but delighted in taking part in bloody fights when they broke out in his pub. Tom Byrne regarded Humphrey as a curious contradiction of gentleman and brawler:

"Mr Humphrey was a lovely man, a lovely looking man. He used to wear steel grey suits and a white apron tied on him and a red flower in his buttonhole. But when a row would start he'd *bolt* the doors and keep everybody in. And he'd jump out and go around and 'ding, ding, ding', he knocked 'em cold! And there'd be about six or eight fellas lying on the floor. He used to *love* it!"

There were always a number of Dublin pubs, mostly along the quays, notorious for catering to gurriers, prostitutes, thieves and social outcasts of every sort. Such Dublin "dives" were well known by their unsavoury reputations. By most accounts, Crilly's on Sarsfield Quay was the lowest and meanest of the lot. He had the reputation for harbouring prostitutes and thieves, drugging customers with spiked wines, and sharing in the profits from the illicit activities. William Mullally, 76, who worked as a barman in another pub in the neighbourhood, alleges that Crilly's deserved its wretched reputation:

"That was considered to be a public house of ill repute. All these women, prostitutes, used to frequent his pub. A man could meet them, pick them up there. And you'd go in there and he'd always give you some of this wine and fellas used to end up getting drunk in his pub."

As a curious young man, Hughes liked to spend evenings in Crilly's watching the sordid social dynamics as randy sailors would negotiate with beyond-prime prostitutes in smokey snugs, then depart for the back alley for their sexual activity. Though never using their services, he befriended some of the prostitutes over the years and came to feel great compassion for them and their plight in what he regards as the most depraved of all Dublin pubs:

"Crilly's pub, that was the *lowest* of all the public houses, where there was down-and-out prostitutes who had gone *beyond* the age and who were diseased. Crilly's was a well known pub throughout the world where there was sailors. It was a house of prostitution. I knew a lot of the women and they were old and haggard. It was maybe five shillings, ten shillings they got. And there was more fellas got a dose of the 'pox' out of it than any other place. Gonorrhoea! And syphilis. And strangers, he'd give them a sup of this wine and it was more of a drug and it would make you drowsy. And there was a lot of fellas mugged in Crilly's and he held a lot of the money that was robbed."

There was always lively argument over which public houses in Dublin were

the "roughest and toughest". A good many qualified. Johnny Curran's pub in
Engine Alley in the Liberties was indisputably a dangerous place to enter. Back
in the 1940s it was filled with heavy drinking tinkers and animal gang members
always spoiling for a good fight. Many Liberties folk had the habit of walking on
the opposite side of the street, never knowing when beer bottles or brawling men
might fly out the door. "It was a *rough* place, *really* rough", says Stephen
Mooney, 68. "There were fights between the tinkers and they'd be all sprawled
outside the pub, *really* drunk." This is verified by John-Joe Kennedy, a member
of one of the toughest animal gangs which claimed Curran's as their local:

"I was in the local animal gang and we hung out at Johnny Curran's. There
was about twenty-five of us together. There was always blood flowing in the
pub. An argument and there'd be digs and lashing and 'bang' in the pub.
The tinkers used to mix with us, have a bit of crack. We used to love to see
them fight. And it was all bare-knuckle. Sometimes it was two families. The
women, they'd start a row with another woman and you'd see blood flow
then! They fought like men."

The Railway Bar near Connolly train station was equally noted for its violence.
Fifty years ago it became a bloody battleground for rival dockers and drovers.
Feuding between the two factions began when dockers were allowed to come up
to the cattle market in Stoneybatter and do a day's work driving cattle and sheep
down to the docks, but drovers were not allowed to go down to the quays and
load animals onto the boats. On Thursdays both groups worked at loading and
unloading cattle in the railway yards and later clashed in local pubs where they
fought with fists, bottles, shovels and ashplants. Old drover Diller Delaney knew
the inside of every mean pub in Dublin but claims that the Railway Bar was the
most explosive:

"Between the dockers and drovers there was jealousy. Bitter. We loaded cattle
at the trains at Amiens Street and then at the Railway Bar there'd be
slaughters! Cause the drovers'd go over into it for a drink and the dockers'd
be in it. Oh, there'd be *murder* . . . through the windows and all they'd go.
Oh, the frames of the windows and all would go out into the street. The
Railway Bar became the *worst*, it did. It was eventually closed up over
fighting."

In contrast to Dublin pubs noted for their immoral or violent environment is
Kavanagh's beside Glasnevin Cemetery, better known as the "Gravedigger's"
pub, which is renowned in its own right. It has been held in the same family for
six generations and is reputed to be haunted by a benign ghost actually seen on
occasion by reliable customers. One wall of the pub is within inches of the
cemetery railing and for more than a century it was the custom for dehydrated
gravediggers to reach their arm through and knock on the wall indicating what
drink they wished. Though it was against the rules and they could be sacked,

most of the sixty or more gravediggers who used to be employed were willing to take the risk. They devised a precise knock code to indicate to the barman which drinks to bring out. Current proprietor Eugene Kavanagh reveals how the gravedigger system worked:

"There would be knocks on the wall which would echo inside the bar and you'd know *exactly* what drink was needed to go out. It was usually pints of porter or a small whiskey. Just passed it through the railing and they'd consume it and they'd leave the empty glasses down beside the railing. It was *hard work* . . . so maybe they'd have a few pints when they weren't supposed to. But it was a *tradition*. If you were left money you'd take it and if you weren't you just took in the empty glasses. You'd always be paid."

The Gravedigger's still stands today as one of Dublin's truly unique pubs, sought out by curious tourists and used by television and film companies for its perfectly preserved turn-of-the-century architecture and ambience.

UNDERWORLD OF SHEBEENS, KIPS AND SPEAKEASIES

"I knew all the madams in the Monto. They had kips, red light houses, there in the tenements. Madams had seven or eight girls, lovely girls. And they were selling porter and whiskey after hours and hiding the drink in the manholes, in the sewers."

Timmy "Duckegg" Kirwan, age 75

Apart from the legal public houses in Dublin there existed an underworld of illicit shebeens, kips and speakeasies which did a flourishing business. Though unlawful, these places *were* public drinking houses and therefore warrant inclusion in this book. As previously defined, shebeens were places where drink was illegally sold, mostly in shadowy tenement rooms or huxter shops. Kip houses, or brothels, also functioned as shebeens since they sold drink to clients and oftentimes others as well. The shebeens and kip houses which were cursed by temperance reformers and government inquiry boards back in the 1870s survived and thrived throughout the first half of the twentieth century. As evidenced by the oral histories of this book, they are well remembered by Dubliners and hold a special place in the folklore and history of public houses because of their clandestine and risky character.

Anyone who could afford to buy a few bottles of porter or whiskey could set up a shebeen in a dark tenement room. After selling them for a few pence profit their "business" was under way. Initially, they might place some artifact, such as a bottle, in the window to advertise. In time the shebeen became known by reputation and drew a regular crowd. In the 1930s and 1940s there were hundreds of shebeens scattered through the tenement maze. Going "shebeening" was a way of life for local men. Shebeens did a great business on

Sunday mornings when many men had hangovers from the night before and were seeking a "cure" to hold them over until the pubs opened later. As Charlie Dillon divulges, sometimes the most unlikely persons operated a shebeen:

"Me own granny done a shebeen. Just around the corner here she used to sell cabbages and potatoes and for a Sunday morning she'd get a few crates of beer in and people'd go in and buy the stout off her. See, the pubs would all be shut and she'd sell it for about tuppence dearer—and then you had to buy the cabbage and potatoes and walk out. She'd make a few bob."

The combination kip house-shebeens also did a brisk business serving hard liquor as well as beer. The Monto was the most famous red light district in Dublin drawing, as Kirwan observed, "well-off people, sailor men, gentlemen, 'big shots', Lords and everything else". In addition to sexual services, they were plied with drink at an inflated price. Frank Wearen nightly plodded the streets of the Monto in the early part of the century when the kip houses were in full swing:

"There was thirty or forty of them kip houses. Now 'brass nails', that was the name the girls had on them, instead of calling them prostitutes. Always nice young girls dressed up clean and spotless, attractive. The owner of the kip house, she'd always have a bottle of whiskey or two hid and you paid the highest price for it. I often remember seeing this madam in Gloucester Street go to the grate and opening it and taking out the large bottles of stout. She'd have them hid in the grate outside the path, under the grill."

Clients often drank heavily and gladly paid the premium price as the madams made a handsome profit off their hidden booze. Mary Corbally knew all the madams around Corporation Street and marvelled at their ingenuity in secreting away precious bottles of whiskey:

"I knew the madams by name. These kip houses sold beer. And they used to hide bottles of whiskey. Cause the police would raid the place and if they found the drink they were summonsed. So the kip keepers used to hide it. Do you know the gramophones with the big horns on them? Well, I remember them putting their bottles down the horn of the gramophone!"

Police often turned a blind eye towards the kips and were nicely compensated for their visual affliction. When actually given an order to raid, they were required to issue a summons and either smash the bottles or take them as evidence. Oftentimes this "evidence" mysteriously disappeared.

Dolly Fawcett was one of Dublin's most famous and endearing madams and a genuine legend in her own time some fifty years ago. She ran the Cozy Kitchen in North King Street and the Cafe Continental in Bolton Street. Ostensibly they were restaurants but in actuality functioned as a kip and shebeen. As Hughes certifies: "They were brothels. The whole of *Dublin* knew about it. You got your whiskey in a cup and there were prostitutes." When the pubs closed a stream of men, many highly respectable, headed for Dolly's door where they were admitted to drink into the early hours of morning. Dolly housed her girls, dressed them well, and even escorted them to Sunday Mass on occasion. But her establishments were more of a "pick-up" spot where men met the women and then took them elsewhere for sexual favours, commonly in the back lane. Tommy O'Neill's family had a piggery in the same lane directly behind the Cozy Kitchen and "when they'd be finished with the condoms they used to throw 'em into our pig yard. And the sows was eating the condoms—and the little pigs was born with rubber coats on them!"

Although everyone knew Dolly as a madam, she was well liked and respected as a kind and charitable woman. She assisted the poor and would have her girls take a covered tray of food to widows or sick neighbours. Sometimes she would even pay their doctor's bill. James Slein, 65, a distinguished Dublin physician, grew up in the living quarters above his father's pub directly across from the Cafe Continental. As a young lad he got to know Dolly and her husband well when they came across the street to have a drink. At night he enjoyed peering out of his bedroom window at all the men going in and out of Dolly's at all hours. He developed a genuine fondness for Dolly whom he always saw in a very sympathetic light:

> "She was a *notorious* person because she ran a brothel. And both were shebeens, they served watered down whiskey in cups. Some nights I'd just sit at the window, gaze across, seeing the chaps going in until two or three or four in the morning. The men were lawyers, politicians, businessmen. The girls were in their twenties. The local police turned a blind eye and some of them even patronised her. Even though it was a brothel I can't remember anybody speaking badly about Dolly. She was part of the community. She was very lady-like, educated by the world itself. Dolly was regarded as a neighbour. Dolly was an attractive, *very intelligent* lady and certainly well dressed for her time. She was an *extraordinary* person . . . a *big-minded* person. Oh, she was an extremely charitable lady."

He last saw Dolly on the street only a short time before her death when she was dying of throat cancer. He was touched by her personal parting words and request for prayers, confessing: "I *wept* at the bus stop. That was the very last time I said goodbye to her. Poor Dolly, she was a good soul . . . she was one of us."

Dublin's speakeasies provided high excitement and drama, like a film scene about Al Capone in the "Roaring Twenties" prohibition era. Speakeasies were public houses that illegally served drink behind closed doors after hours. Cloistered patrons were warned to "speak easy" so they wouldn't be overheard by policemen outside. It was a clandestine gathering of the chosen few who scrunched low in their seat to avoid having any seeping street light cast upon them. Men sat quietly, spoke in hushed tones, and tended to wink and nod knowingly as they sipped their most coveted pints of the day. Drink always seemed to taste better if it was ill-gotten. After hours, men could be admitted if they knew the secret code knocks on the window or door. Resourceful publicans concocted ingenious devices for serving customers in the dark, using candles, matches, and screens placed around single light bulbs directing a small shaft of light directly down. As with kips and shebeens, many local guards found it to their benefit to ignore speakeasies. Police were even known to frequent their local speakeasy when they finished night duty, sometimes still in uniform. On occasion the police were ordered to conduct a lightning raid as they broke the code knock, barged in scattering frenzied customers, and handed summonses to the publicans and trapped men.

One of the best-known speakeasies around the Liberties in the forties was "The Yank" Reynolds's in Marrowbone Lane. Paddy Mooney tells how when closing time approached "the barman'd say, 'We're closing now, anybody want to get out? Last chance . . . OK, you're locked in." He would then bolt the door, pull the shades and douse the lights. After that, anyone wanting in had to know the secret knock but "if you were boisterous in any way *out* you'd go". Another noted speakeasy of that period was Sorohan's in Corporation Street. Sorohan's not only served drink after hours but sneaked men in *before* opening time, especially on Sunday mornings. John Preston, who began drinking there as a teenager, would fly out the rear door with his mates when there was a police raid, clamber over the wall and dart for his tenement house to hide:

"I used to drink in Sorohan's at 17 years of age. I used to get in the side door and pay sixpence for a stout and we used to drink it out of a jam jar. A fella named 'Ski Heaps' was the doorman. I don't know how he got his nickname cause there's not much snow here! It was three knocks to get in. Ah, he'd get twenty fellas in. But the police, they'd raid occasionally and they [customers] used to jump over the wall and some of them'd even bring their drink with them. You know, destroy the evidence! And they'd run in their house and get under their mother's bed. That's the truth now."

Since speakeasies conducted business in the dark the publican had to discreetly use matches and candles when exchanging money with customers. And in Paddy Reilly's pub at the corner of Henrietta Street "let the pint buyer beware" because he was famous for watering his whiskey and short-changing people in the darkness. And he did it under the very noses of policemen who drank there. To Hughes he was a real rogue:

"Paddy Reilly's pub was a *really* well-known speakeasy. You got your change in candle light or by match, cause the lights were blacked out. And you had to keep the noise down . . . you might say '*Speak easy*, there's a policeman outside.' So he'd be pulling your pint and he struck a match while giving you change. But you had to watch him cause he'd fiddle you. And he was a bugger for watering the whiskey. There was even policemen drinking in that speakeasy."

Perhaps the most unique and adventurous speakeasy in Dublin in the 1930s was the Killarney House pub in Oriel Street, owned by a Kerry publican named Donoghue. It did a booming after-hours business and Donoghue always managed to stay just one step ahead of the law by being more clever than the police who periodically raided. He devised a hidden escape passage through which his frantic customers scrambled when police were spotted by a watcher. Tom Byrne depicts the scene like that in an old Keystone Kops episode:

"The Killarney House, that was a speakeasy. I have vivid memories of it. The pub closed and the blinds came down and men'd be sitting around on barrels and talking in the dark and it was 'Shhh . . . be quiet!' So the police, they'd have an odd raid and come around in the open cars like what you see in some of those early gangster pictures like Al Capone. Nearly all had trench coats on them, plain clothes, and soft hats. And they'd *whiz* down, four or five or six of them, in these cars and they'd *pile* out and 'bang, bang, bang' on the door and then they'd run in. But he [Donoghue] had a tenement house next to his pub and he had a big wardrobe in the living accommodation above the pub along the wall there and another big wardrobe in the tenement next door along the wall. And they backed one another. And there was a door broke open in it [through the wall] and he was hanging clothes in it. And when there was going to be a raid it was, 'Everybody *upstairs*!' So they went upstairs through the wardrobe and the door closed and he slides the clothes back on the rack. The police came in and raided the place—nobody there! Most ingenious it was."

The ploy worked perfectly for years until a disgruntled former employee of the pub went to the police and "spilled the beans", thus ending one of Dublin's most exciting speakeasy operations.

FAMOUS BARMEN'S STRIKES

"This was a bitter strike. Emotions were very high. If you passed the picket you were called a scab."

Jack Cagney, barman, age 70

"After the five-week strike we won, we got some more money and better hours."

Danny Gleeson, age 83, President of the Barman's Union during the 1955 strike

The 1955 Barmen's strike was an important event in the history of the public house trade in Dublin. It established their union as a powerful force and significantly improved wages, hours and working conditions for its 3,000 members. The strike broke the tyrannical control some publicans had over their staff and created an atmosphere of reasonable negotiation for the benefit of all. There had been previous strikes in 1919, 1922 and 1927 but as Jack Cagney, an old barman and union man, declares, "In previous strikes the bosses always won. Oh, the barmen lost and had to come back and eat humble pie." But after the 1955 stand-off, barmen enjoyed greater power, stature and self-esteem.

In the mid-1950s Dublin's barmen were experiencing real hardship in terms of poor wages and working conditions. As Cagney explains: "Wages were poor, you couldn't exist, couldn't rear a family . . . and your unsocial hours." As members of the Irish National Union of Vintners, Grocers and Allied Trade Assistants, the barmen engaged in bargaining negotiations with their publican bosses who belonged to the Licensed Grocers' and Vintners' Association. The weekly average wage for a barman at that time was £7.3s. They were working a fifty-six hour week, far more than other shop assistants, and received only a half-day off a week and one Sunday off in four. Under such conditions many men found it impossible to have a normal social life or to marry. Those who did marry and had children endured great financial hardship. Barmen felt exploited and deprived relative to other comparable working groups. By 1955 the situation had become intolerable and they asked for a wage increase of twenty-five shillings per week, every second Sunday off and an allowance of one and a half hours for each meal. In response, the publicans grudgingly offered an increase of eight shillings per week and a vague promise of "certain improvements" in working conditions.[63] After negotiations twice broke down and barmen questioned the good faith of their employers, they formally commenced a strike on Saturday, 9 July.

Of the 650 public houses in Dublin, 220 were open as usual the first day of the strike, nearly 100 having signed provisional agreements with the Barman's Union and the remainder being family-run or non-union pubs. All others were picketed. On the whole, the drinking public did not patronise the picketed premises. Yet, as confirmed in the *Irish Licensing World*, they were "suffering no severe hardship" since they could always find an open pub.[64] None the less, drinkers were irritated at the inconvenience of not being able to use their local pub and drink shortages at those which were open. To exacerbate matters for drinkers and picketers, Dublin was sweltering through one of the hottest summers on record, causing nerves to fray and tempers to flare. From the outset, barmen received overwhelming support from Dubliners showing their union loyalties. William Mullally was a barman at Donoghue's pub in Mary Street doing his picket duty and appreciated his customers' support:

"I was on picket duty and we done it in shifts. The doors were open and the boss himself was inside but there were no people in it, they wouldn't go in. Any man that was a trade union man, he wouldn't pass your picket. You had loyalty to one another. They *honoured* the barman's picket. Oh, the Dublin people were fantastic. They *gave* us their support, stayed out of the pubs."

There were several eruptions of violence where scabs were called in or customers dared to cross the picket lines. "Oh, there was hellish murder cause people crossed the pickets", exclaims Alfred Millar. "There was a place in Cathedral Street and there was punching going on." For the most part, however, it was a peaceable five weeks of protest.

If the barmen were grateful to Dubliners for their support, they were equally furious at Guinness's for their perceived betrayal. Since over a hundred publicans had signed agreements with the Barman's Union and others were moving in that direction, the strikers were confident that they were succeeding. These "settled" houses found themselves doing several times their normal business volume but Guinness's refused to provide them with sufficient additional supply of drink. Barmen were enraged, feeling that Guinness's were clearly taking the side of publicans and, by doing so, were endeavouring to break their strike. Cagney, who was working as a barman at the Big Tree pub in Lower Dorset Street at the time explains the predicament:

"Guinness's took an extraordinary line. See, Guinness's were your main suppliers, about 80 per cent. And the employers that settled, that had no dispute, Guinness's only offered them the quota of the previous year plus 5 per cent. But these houses were doing *at least three times* their normal trade and would be quickly *sold out*. So there weren't sufficient supplies to keep the customers happy. In other words, Guinness's were backing the publicans. Guinness's policy of not supplying the 'settled' houses with all the stout they wanted angered the barmen. They felt that Guinness's policy was aimed at favouring the publicans and trying to break the strike."

In retaliation, barmen decided to mount a massive protest march against Guinness's to show their solidarity and determination. Warned by their union officers to be orderly, they marched from Parnell Square through the heart of the city toward Guinness's. For Dubliners, it was quite a spectacle to see 3,000 barmen marching eight deep down O'Connell Street chanting "Guinness, the strike breakers!" Having been notified of the angry mood of the marchers, Guinness's management secured gates and windows in advance of their arrival. When the barmen reached the brewery they began to parade around the block shouting "strike breakers!" at a heightened pitch. Some thrust their clenched fists upwards towards the hundreds of faces peering down at them from the windows. It was a very unnerving sight to the Guinness staff. Mullally believes that some Guinness officers were genuinely fearful:

"We marched on Guinness's shouting 'strike breakers!'; and it was a sunny day and you'd want to see them running and closing windows and doors. When you see a couple of thousand men outside you don't know what! Yeah, they got terrified up there. They thought we were going to wreck the place."

The strikers' much-publicised march proved a brilliant strategy because it exposed Guinness's unfair favouritism towards the publicans, demonstrated the strength and unity of the Barman's Union, and persuaded brewery management to help negotiate a settlement. "After the demonstration Guinness's realised the strength of the union and our solidarity and agreed to help mediate the strike", vouches Cagney, "and then after five weeks it was settled." President Gleeson was pleased with the terms, noting that they received "a definite improvement, more money and time off and better hours". For the most part, publicans and their barmen made peace and returned to work with no ill feelings. Cagney appreciated the conciliatory mood at the Big Tree his first day back on the job:

> "Now my boss at the Big Tree, I'll never forget his face when all his customers walked in. *All* the customers that were traditionally there, they all filled up the place that night. And the number of customers that had passed the picket was only four—out of a possible thousand. They all came in that night and shook hands with the boss and the staff. It was 'let bygones be bygones'."

A far less significant barman's strike, but one which gained international interest, took place at Downey's public house in Upper George's Street in Dun Laoghaire. It went on for more than *fourteen years* and was hailed as the "world's longest strike". The dispute arose when Mr Downey sacked a barman, Patrick Young, in February 1939. There was no good reason for his dismissal. When the publican rejected the union's demand to reinstate him they called a strike against him on 6 March. Union members were prohibited from working on his premises but, as one publication reported, "He couldn't care less."[65] Indeed, he advertised to recruit four new barmen and received over 400 applications. The picketers outside his pub did not make a dent in his business as the house was always packed. As the years passed, the story of this prolonged strike against an Irish pub was picked up by the media as a human interest feature and disseminated around the globe. Tourists even began seeking out the pub. Downey actually came to enjoy his celebrity status as he steadfastly refused to settle with the union. For more than fourteen years dutiful picketers shuffled back and forth in front of the pub during opening hours seven days a week, nearly etching their path in the pavement. When Downey finally passed away in June of 1953 the *Irish Licensing World* paid him this tribute:[66]

> "This fine old warrior died at age 79. His story had been featured in publications all over the world. Mr Downey was never given a respite. It was a sorry spectacle for Irish trade unionism at work. He once declared, 'For all I care the picketers can stay here until I die, and I hope they will march at my funeral.' They did!"

The new owner, Mr Neville, promptly reached an agreement with the Barman's Union to employ union men and the strike finally ended. The end of the strike was celebrated in cheerful fashion in the pub on 27 November 1953 by hundreds of patrons and "excitement seekers" who packed in and drank a "farewell" toast—while outside the last picketer paced his final steps.

TRANSFORMATION AND DESECRATION OF VENERABLE PUBS

"When a favourite pub is 'done up' it's rather like a friend having a nose altered—the personality is never quite the same again."

Daniel Farson, The Pub—A Celebration, *1969*

"The Irish pub is unique in the drinking world . . . it would be a sad day for Ireland if the traditional pub was to disappear."

Irish Licensing World, *1973*

Over the past half-century the traditional Dublin public house has undergone profound social and physical transformation. Changes began in the post-war forties when women were gradually admitted, lounges created and comfortable furniture installed. These were healthy changes which served to "civilise" the social setting without destroying the original character of the bar area. But in the 1950s the insidious incursion of television not only inhibited the natural flow of conversation but glaringly brought the problems and complexities of the outside world into the simplicity and quietude of the neighbourhood pub, thus diminishing its role as peaceful retreat.[67] Next, the pub was assailed by developers, demolitionists and greedy investors who had no sense of history or heartfelt affection for the venerable institution. As a consequence, hundreds of public houses of historical importance, architectural integrity and unique social character have been altered and adulterated beyond original recognition, or bulldozed into oblivion. It has been one of the saddest sagas on Dublin's cityscape.

The most ferocious assault upon public houses began in the 1960s when Dublin was swept up in a craze of modernisation and urban redevelopment. The new "progressive" philosophy meant discarding things viewed as "old fashioned". Dignified Georgian houses and Victorian pubs were destroyed with impunity by ruthless developers and demolitionists who made huge profits by building modern structures on the sites. Such elegant pubs as the Scotch House and Irish House were smashed to smithereens to make way for sterile office buildings. Laments elderly Frank O'Donnell, who spent most of his life as a barman in the Scotch House: "Developers bought it and it's a block of offices now. It was a pity to see it go . . . but there was money to be made." Similarly, small centuries-old neighbourhood pubs were turned into a rubble heap of brick, wood and dust clouds in a matter of minutes. It was a heartbreaking sight which literally brought tears to the eyes of many regulars.

Old pubs left standing often met a fate just as cruel as their rich interiors and façades were stripped bare for modernistic refurbishment. To be sure, some changes were clearly for the better, such as modern toilets, sanitary facilities, central heating and improved lighting. What was horrifying was the gutting—or "rape"—of beautifully ornate Victorian decor as magnificent marble counters, old gilt mirrors, screens, lamps, mahogany and brass fittings were torn out and trashed. Installed in their place were formica, plastic, stainless steel, aluminium, glitzy carpets and harsh lighting. To traditionalists and preservationists it was a hideous "plague" of historic destruction. Publican Tommy Smith expresses with sadness and anger his feelings about the desecration of stately old pubs:

"You had a period in the trade in the sixties which was the 'formica age'. I have personally seen a pub where I worked, McCauley's, where the *finest* of mahogany fittings, the *finest* of marble tops and beautiful ornate counters were taken out and replaced with formica. Oh, what a sin! What a *disaster*! It made me *mad*, I couldn't believe it. That was alien to me . . . it was a hatred of the old."

By 1968 even the trade publication *Irish Licensing World* felt compelled to sound a clarion alarm:[68]

"Practically every pub in the country is being redecorated. Most of them are just factories for drinking in. It's a great pity the way some of the old pubs are being gutted. A pub with atmosphere should preserve it. We'll be sorry in a few years time that we have destroyed all the old places. Marble counters, old mirrors, mahogany, it's a sin to throw them all out. You're up against vulgarity all the time now. We're vandals as regards history."

The drastic transformation of pubs also had great social impact upon the regulars who found it depressing and disorienting. Asserted one sympathetic observer: "It is the regulars who suffer. Like fish out of water they try to adapt themselves to the new environment and fail."[69] Many long-time pub patrons confess that when their local was demolished or radically changed it adversely affected the very quality of their lives, a personal blow from which many never recovered.

The 1970s and 1980s brought further social change to the Dublin pub scene. As the value of public houses soared, many older publicans began selling out to a new breed of investor and businessman. The traditional publicans had been part of the long tradition in the trade, serving an apprenticeship, living above the pub, knowing regulars intimately, assisting their families, and being a highly respected member of the local community. By stark contrast, new owners were outside businessmen with no historic ties to the trade who hired a professional manager to operate their economic asset. Frank Fell, Director of the Dublin Licensed Vintners Association, explains the consequences of this transition:

"A great sense of tradition—but it's dying. The older publicans saw the pub trade as a *way of life*. Nowadays it's changed because the *value* of pub property has escalated beyond all recognition. And that has changed the whole way of seeing pubs. Pubs now in very many cases are just seen as simple business assets to be bought and sold. So there was an exodus of older publicans and people investing in the trade from the outside. That was the *real* change. You might have a professional manager, an accountant and a couple of business people and they wouldn't even *declare* themselves to be publicans. They were *not* publicans—and therefore it's non-traditional. So the traditional aspect of the trade is dying. Only about half the publicans in Dublin now would be traditional publicans who served their time in the trade."

This development has produced a sadly ridiculous paradox—pubs without publicans! To old-timers long accustomed to an intimate personal relationship with their local publican, such modern drinking establishments have no heart, no soul.

Perhaps by divine providence, a number of authentic old Dublin public houses have survived and been preserved. In some cases this was an inadvertent act based on the publican's lack of funds to modernise. Other times it was an enlightened decision to eschew the fad of plastic-formica modernisation and retain the historic ambience. Some of these are small unpretentious neighbourhood pubs which still boast a simple turn-of-the-century atmosphere, such as Kavanagh's "Gravedigger's" pub next to Glasnevin Cemetery and Jack Cusack's Cozy Bar in the Coombe. Both publicans still live above the pub, carrying on the old tradition. There are also some exquisite Victorian pubs glorifying Dublin's cityscape. According to a calculation by the Licensed Vintners Association, out of the total of 775 Dublin pubs "there are now less than twenty pubs that have *authentic* Victorian interiors, about 3 per cent, that's all". Ryan's of Parkgate Street is a splendid example. After a few hours thoughtfully spent in one of Dublin's Victorian pubs one can almost imagine walking out the front door into a world of cobblestones, horse-drawn vehicles and trams.

Having evolved from its primitive alehouse days centuries ago, the Dublin pub is about to enter the twenty-first century. To many, it stands as a last tangible link to a simpler, more romantic, genteel age. Publican Larry Ryan, who had a pub in the Coombe forty years ago, expresses the sentiments of many old Liberties folk:

"I hope that all the old Dublin men die before the old pubs go, replaced with modern things that are not pubs at all. Because pubs was a *tradition* in Dublin, a way of life. They weren't just a watering hole, the family's life was built around the pub."

Fortunately, many of the city's surviving historic pubs have been placed on the preservation list. They should—at all costs—be protected by law for future generations, for Dublin without its venerable pubs would be unimaginable.

"A world without pubs. Well, I don't know. A world without pubs . . . not yet, thank God."[70]

3

Oral Testimony of Publicans and Barmen

Tom Bourke—Age 86

At the age of 86 he is the oldest publican in Dublin still pulling pints. He first came to the city from Tipperary at 14 to do his apprenticeship in James Kirwan's pub in Parnell Street which was a major IRA meeting place. Young Tom served drink to Michael Collins, Dan Breen and other Movement notables who met to converse privately in dark snugs. He was always told to hear and say nothing. Knowing that revolvers and rifles were hidden in the pub, he was scared when the dreaded Black and Tans raided with guns drawn. Having spent more than seventy years behind pub counters, he has been an eye-witness to real history. Today he owns the posh Blue Haven pub in Templeogue, a far cry from his old Parnell Street pub days.

66 I'm from Tipperary and we were farmers. I had seven brothers and five sisters and with that size family you had to get out and do something to make a living. No matter how big the farm is at the end of the day it's only for one person. So I came to Dublin at 14 and I had two brothers in the pub trade here. I got up on the train and there was a group of people in the car playing cards and my father says, 'Will you look after this young fella?' I didn't mind because I knew that my brother was meeting me at the station. Never been to Dublin before. *Never before.* When I saw the sea and the trams I said, 'What is this?' I did my apprenticeship at 49 Parnell Street. It was James Kirwan's public house and he was a neighbour of ours in the country and he was looking for an apprentice. So I was an apprentice for two years. 'Grocer's assistants' we were called. That was our title. Oh, and I had to live-in above the premises with two other assistants. There was a maid and we were very well looked after. Now you'll feel sorry for me when I tell you my wages—I had *nothing at all* for the first year! Only my food. But my boss would give me five shillings now and again and I'd say 'thanks'. I used that to have my collar washed and done in the laundry. I had to pay for that myself and it cost a penny ha'penny in English money. And a shirt was sixpence to have washed and ironed in the laundry and a handkerchief or maybe two handkerchiefs every week. Oh, you had to pay for that yourself out of the five shillings. But I was glad to have the job, very glad.

"Kirwan's was a very good, high-class house for a working-class area. There were a lot of tenements around there at that time and around Dominick Street. Living was very poor then. There was one house with twenty-seven families in it. It was a very rough and tumble sort of area and then you were near the market in Moore Street with all the stalls. There was an old woman trader outside our premises, a nice poor old woman who'd wear a shawl over her head. Ellen Oglesby was her name and it was a very long time ago. She sold apples and oranges and bananas and things for a penny each. Women didn't drink much in those days but the dealers from Moore Street, they'd come into the snug and drink a glass of porter or a small whiskey hot in the winter time cold. They were very amusing and a lovely type of people and there'd be children in their arms. They shouldn't have had the children there in the pub but you'd take a chance with the law. They came in and held their children in their arms and [breast] fed them even.

"Now Kirwan's was a very important public house during the troubled period. Oh, Mr Kirwan was a very big noise in the Movement. And the barmen in Kirwan's were high up as well. And there was another public house further up, number 68, it was William Devlin's and that public house was almost as prominent [an IRA meeting house] as James Kirwan's, not quite. Kirwan's was where everything was discussed and all the Irish secret service men would be in there as well. And Mr Kirwan was always in on the discussions. And you were supposed to not see anything or hear anything or know anything. Your instincts would tell you to ask no questions. See, there'd be men in there passing on information. And there were too many ear-wiggers. What I mean by ear-wiggers is that there were people sitting over there and maybe listening to your conversation here. So someone could pick it up and it'd be used against you later. Oh, you had to be very careful. And Mr Kirwan was a very decent man in the sense that all his business nearly went haywire for the fact that he was in the Troubles himself and the business was being neglected. And he was able to give support financially to the cause as well.

"Now Michael Collins would come in and have a drink of a small sherry. See, Michael Collins, he was a great friend of my boss's at the time. He was a man around six foot high and very good looking. I very often saw him. Oh, a nice man he was . . . a little hasty but a very nice man. Oh, that was a terrible tragedy when he was shot. And Dan Breen, he was another very big noise and he was there in the pub and a very nice man. Oh, he came in as well. A lot of the 'boys' would come in. But they mostly came not when the ordinary hours of business was on, they always came more or less when the place was clear. And there was a kind of secret place in the shop where they met and I don't know whether it was ever discovered during the secrecy period, unless they discovered it after I was gone. But during the troubled times there was secret meetings there at night, all during the night. *All night*, after hours. See, a lot of them would be in before closing time and then later there was three knocks for to get in for the meeting in the pub. And there were revolvers there in the drawer and we used to have rifles stored down in the cellar. Because, see, the staff who were in the

Movement might have to use them. The barmen, Jack Kennedy was one of the staff and Ned O'Connor was the other one, they were in the Volunteers and they'd be off during the night raiding. Oh, yes. And I remember when I was a young lad there was four of the 'boys', as we used to call them, there sleeping in the bed and I was in *between* them. You can imagine four big men in a double bed and I couldn't *move*, left or right. I just didn't know what to do. We had another man there that slept on the premises, D. P. Walsh, and he was afterwards on the sentence of death in Mountjoy and when the Truce came about then he was reprieved. When you were young then you'd see no danger, it was only after you got older and then you'd see the danger.

"Oh, it was a desperate time, a terrible time it was. And the Black and Tans were around at that time, very much so, with their revolvers. You didn't know exactly what was going to happen. You were living in a sort of fear so to speak. You were scared, naturally. When the Tans raided they were fine looking men in fact. The Black and Tans came into Kirwan's one day and I was there just a few months and they went to search and said, 'Put up your hands!' And they walked down to a big snug at the end of the room and there was a private meeting going on there between the late Michael Collins and others. So the Tans spent a couple of hours there drinking. Oh, the Tans had drinks galore. Then Michael Collins excused himself to go into the toilets and he didn't return. So that was one narrow escape he had.

"I served two years in Kirwan's and there was great wit in the Dublin people along Parnell Street. And if an old person was getting buried they had the cabs and horses and when they'd be coming back from the burial they'd go into their local pub, particularly in Parnell Street, and there'd be a sing-song for the rest of the evening. Absolutely. They were hard-working, honest people. But after Kirwan's I went into Davis's pub in Leeson Street and I found it very hard to settle in because the people were the real high class, all doctors and barristers and solicitors. All professional people. It was not near as interesting as Parnell Street. But it was always my ambition in the back of me mind to get my own public house. So my two brothers and myself saved as much as we could and in 1937 we bought a public house for £3,025 on Lower Canal Street. It was a good house but the wrong people were allowed to go into it. It wasn't well managed and it took a while to clean it up. We had to assert our authority. We lost some of them and that was what we called the 'clean up'."

Jack Cusack—Age 75

An old-fashioned publican, he still lives above his Cozy Bar in the Coombe. For fifty-six years he has been pulling pints behind the same counter. A gifted conversationalist, he likes to philosophise about all aspects of life. In the old days his regulars made their own entertainment on Saturday nights with a melodeon, spoons, animal bones, singing and sprightly dancing. He feels that no university could have provided him with the education he has gained as a publican.

"I was born in Aungier Street in 1920. There was ten of us children and I was the first boy after four girls. My father had no education and he was a tram driver for fifty years. The 'Reverend' Pat they called him, a very gentle man and I could *never* fill his boots. He was a lovely man and I loved him. My father bought this pub in 1939, more or less off a friend of his. When my father was applying for a licence he had to have a reference from the superintendent saying you were of high character. Oh, yes, and then you got a letter from the parish priest and then you'd go to the bank manager and present your case. Because at this time a publican was the bee's knees! Like a man of *repute*, a man above the ordinary standard. But the bank manager said: 'Well, you're a man of very good character and good standing, *but* you've no experience. I'll give you the money providing you get a foreman to look after it and let your son go in there and work under him.'

"So I come in here in 1940 and worked under Christy Delaney and he was trained in Galway. He was trained in the weighing of tea and sugar which was a portion of our trade at that time. As an apprentice I scrubbed the floor and then sprinkled white sawdust—couldn't be brown cause that wouldn't look well—all over the floor. And we used to bottle our own ale and stout, label it and cork it. And you had to wash hundreds of bottles in cold water. And when I first came here we had some pewter mugs with glass in the bottom and they say that in the old days that was so that in taverns you could see your enemy when you'd look through this. So I learned the trade from Christy and he left then in 1947 and I took over. But when I first came to the Coombe I didn't know what the hell the Coombe was. They didn't sort of adopt me for a while. They called me a 'buffer' and I didn't know their language, their lingo or their method of living. It was all tenement people and they had to share to exist. Things here were very, very poor.

"Now the famous publican who was here before us was Tom Flanagan. He was famous around the district. As a matter of fact, I remember an old hard ticket that'd come up the Coombe and he'd rub my windows outside, caressing the window, saying, 'No, no, no, I wouldn't break *that* window. That's Master Thomas's window.' But he broke every *other* window in the Coombe! Master Thomas had a porter who was the knockabout man that did the odd jobs and he'd have to clean the boss's boots on a Saturday night. And back then they had what was called beggin' cans. See, the old workmen on the streets used to boil their tea on an open fire in these cans. But the old ladies used to send down these cans on a Sunday in the old days for a half a pint or a pint of porter. And the porter here had a light bamboo cane that he used to hold in his mouth and he would carry so many cans at the one time on the bamboo cane to Mrs so-and-so. And then some of the old ladies was a little bit better off and they'd have these lovely old jugs that were hand painted, like delft china. I wish to God I had a few of them now. So the old ladies would send down these jugs in the early days and they'd say [to the child carrying it], 'Go to the fella with the bald head, he'll give you a little "tilly".' A tilly was when you'd give them a half-pint and then you'd jerk the pump a couple of times and you got that bit extra, that was a tilly. And that would be brought back to the house for them.

"A publican at that time was a very, very powerful man. A publican years ago was *Jesus Christ*! Oh, those old publicans, they were the captains of all of us. Like Mr Joseph O'Connor across the road from me, God rest his soul, he was a fine big man, a huge man, with a pair of shoulders and as strong as a bull. Big hands that reached down past his knees. He was a fine big man with a big white moustache and he used to wear this little gold chain and his gold watch. Oh, fabulous. And then maybe the old black armlets and he used to always wear his cap behind the counter. A lovely old gentleman. Of course, I looked up to him and called him 'sir'. And if he was alive I still would! When I was starting out I went across the road to Master Joe for advice. Cause publicans were very powerful men and we'd fix family quarrels and we had to attend all the funerals. And years ago you'd write a reference for a person if you knew his character. You'd just say, 'I've known so-and-so for a number of years and he's quite sober and I've found him quite trustworthy and honest', and then you'd sign it. And then *your* reputation was on the line for him.

"There used to be small snugs in here and you had access from the street from a small door and if a woman wanted to have a little nip she slipped in there. She didn't come in here to the public bar because there was a rule that this was the man's section. Young women didn't drink in here, it was mostly grannies and they wore shawls. Maybe just an old woman might come in here with a small clay pipe they used to buy in Francis Street for a penny. And they used to break the shank off it and order a pint of plain and they'd throw the clay pipe into the pint of plain and they'd moisten the pipe and then they'd take it out. She'd throw the whole lot into the porter. She called it a 'dugeen', a jaw warmer. And then she'd smoke it under the shawl cause she didn't want people to see her smoking. And then she'd have a little bit of snuff and it was up her nose. Now when we used to have O'Keefe's the knackers up here, it was a skin yard that was for dead old horses, and the ladies who worked in there used to come in here and you'd *hate* it cause their clothes would *smell*. But they'd only be on the premises for a few minutes and you'd leave the doors open after they'd be gone. And another thing, in the old days there was no such thing as a ladies' toilet. So they used to go out in the street. Now a gentleman across the road there had a car, a Morris Minor, and the old ladies used to go to the toilet behind it and his *wheels rotted*. So then we became 'modernised' and we used to put a man at the toilet door here, Billy, who helped out here. He used to stand at the door and say, 'Now, ladies, *quick*!' And they'd all run in and if fellas'd come along toward the door Billy'd say, 'Sorry, you'll have to wait for all the ladies.' They were marvellous old ladies and one of them is actually still alive and comes in to see me.

"Now years ago the Roches, they were travelling people, and they came mostly from Galway and they used to come here for the races in Punchestown by pony and trap. Well, before the races they'd have a few drinks in here. And Granny Roche had a little stall [at the races] selling little knick-knacks. And she'd be wearing a shawl and she'd have a straw hat with imitation cherries and fruit on top of it. Oh, she'd have been 83 or 84. And she had permission to sit where she *liked*. Cause, see, we had to respect her for her age. And as an attraction she used to keep a little pet mouse inside her shawl on her chest and she'd drink porter and she'd smoke a clay pipe. And Granny and the other women like her sat outside the door here on a fine summer's night and have maybe a bottle of stout or wine about 1.00 in the morning. And the policeman would come down the street after maybe summonsing them that day for dealing on the street, what's called a 'hawker', and might fine them a half-crown. And they'd be giving out to him. But then eventually they'd sit him down and give him a cup of tea or a bottle of stout and then they'd be all palsy-walsy.

"It takes you *years* to make a [good] reputation for a public house—and it'll take one month to destroy it. The police used to come in and inspect to see if you might be hiding people after hours, illegal trading. Of course I knew them all. And huge big men they were at that time. Oh, big six footers, fourteen or fifteen stone weight and no education. And back then the bye-laws of the city of Dublin said you *must* have your premises swept in the morning before 9.00 and swept into the [street] channel. After 9.00 you could be prosecuted. And a clock facing the public must be correct. Because it can be misleading if it's not correct. And in the old days the Guinness traveller used to come in and say 'Good morning' and he thought he was Jesus Christ or God Almighty! He was a commercial traveller and he tapped his silver cigarette case, but he never offered you a cigarette. No. Then he'd say, 'Give me a glass of plain and a bottle of stout.' And then he'd get out his little book and his thermometer, put the thermometer down inside each one and check the temperature and write it in the book and then he'd say, 'A little warm, the stout.'

"Then the excise man used to come in and we didn't know who he was. He'd be from the Corporation. He was coming around to examine your spirits. So what happened was the publican down the street, he'd ring me up and say to me, 'The excise man is here, look out!' What happened was he'd point to any whiskey bottle and then he'd put a glassfull in his little bottle and that was sealed. He'd seal it and put it in his case and he'd take it away and analyse it. And if you heard from him within fourteen days you were in trouble but if it went over fourteen days you were OK. Actually, some publicans *did* water it down, it was scandalous. But the average publican was proud of his whiskey.

"When the trams finished running [1949] we had tram seats in here. Oh, they were magnificent. You had the springs and the canvas and hair and then a sheet again and then covered with a *beautiful* top sheet. A lovely top layer of velvet. I had them in here. Oh, you could sit on it forever. And in the old days we used to make our own entertainment. Oh, the Dublin wit, it was famous all over the world. We had fellas come in here and we'd be in stitches laughing.

"On a Saturday night we created our own amusement and there was no such things as mikes [microphones] or sound system. I've seen the finest of singers here. A fella used to come in here with a pair of horn-rimmed glasses as thick as two jam jars and he was a trained opera singer and he'd give out with a song and God, he had a mighty voice! My God Almighty, he had a magnificent voice! And another woman used to come in here and she'd sing the arias from different operas and, my God, what a voice would come out. And then people'd give them a pint. And then there used to be an old gentleman across the road here, Mick—the 'Guxter' we used to call him—and he'd know about the old Vaudeville days and he'd start to whistle and then the old soft shoe. Then another chap would take out two pieces of ordinary sandpaper and go [rubbing], like he was the effects man. So one fella'd be dancing and another fella'd be whistling. Then another fella might come in with a big pair of spoons or maybe two bones off an animal that he'd been skinning down. Two bones or huge spoons and he'd have them in his fingers and he'd rap them and he'd sing a song. Or a fella came in with a mouth organ. That was part and parcel of the old days. And they'd say, 'That was very good, give him a pint.' Just to reward him. Then another fella came in here and he was an acrobat and he'd come in walking on his hands. He'd do this for devilment, you see.

"And we had a monkey in here. Now this fella, Joe Thompson, was his owner. He used to take the monkey out to the race meetings and he had a little game which was called 'take a pick'. There was little objects rolled in brown paper and you could pay him a penny or a shilling or whatever and the monkey'd pick one of these and you'd take the paper off and you might win a pound. And when the police would be coming the monkey'd jump back into the box. And when the crowd wasn't coming around, if the monkey wasn't performing, that man used to get a big blob of mustard and put in on the monkey's bare backside and the monkey'd be jumping around and it'd excite the monkey and then everybody'd gather around. And he'd bring the monkey in *here* and it'd sit on an old seat over there. And we'd give him a sup of stout and get him half-drunk. There was a chain on him and he'd get very vicious then and you had to be very careful. Oh, he'd scratch the face off you. Oh, he'd tear you to bits! Now one day the man went off and his monkey got a bit vicious and we were all afraid for our lives.

"I have no guarantee who's going to walk in that door. How the hell can I? Anybody could be coming in here. It could be a genius, could be a clergyman, could be a bishop, could be a rogue, could be a murderer. Could be *anybody*. I don't give a damn if a man is a Buddhist or a Jew or whatever, so long as he has some religion . . . as long as you have *something* to look up to. *Then* a man can be controlled. But a man without something to obey, he's an animal. But the old Dublin saying is 'a public house angel and a rogue at home', the man that'd come in and treat all his friends and then he'd go home and maybe kick his wife and give her no money. Years ago the man *was* the lord and master at that time, he was the *boss*, no doubt about that. But most fellas today like to just come in here and have their pint for the *conversation*, for the talking. Pubs, they're the greatest confession boxes in the world.

"I've slaved here till 2.00 or 3.00 in the morning to rear my family and educate them and my wife did too. I did the work and she had most of the brains. She's a very clever woman and she could have been a doctor, she could have been a lawyer . . . the only mistake she made was marrying me! As a matter of fact, my wife hates this place. Let's be honest, she never did like it. My wife wants me to retire, she's never liked this place and I don't blame her because it's not a life, it's a sentence. Now I've been active for fifty-five years behind this counter and I know nothing else and unfortunately it's a religion with me, I've married it. But the fact remains that if I retire tomorrow, sell this place tomorrow, what's going to happen to me when I walk the streets of Dublin? Oh, no university in the world could give me the education that I've had here. It's just from over a period of years *listening* to people. I've known prostitutes and pimps and three-card trick men and millionaires, gougers . . . *everything*. You can learn a certain amount out of books but experience is a wonderful thing."

Thomas O'Dowd—Age 68

His pub in the old Dublin neighbourhood of Stoneybatter is known for being properly run and immaculately clean. Having served behind the counter for over a half-century, he has gained great insight to human nature. His regulars praise him as a kind and diplomatic publican. He disdains social distinctions and in his pub treats the street cleaner just the same as the bank manager.

"My mother's people were publicans. They were over 100 years in the business so it's in the family. I've never worked at anything else in my life. I started in 1944 and served my time with my uncle in Christ Church Place. It's known now as the Lord Edward House. I was 16 and I served a four-year apprenticeship. An apprentice had a tremendous amount of brasswork to clean. I was sick and tired of brass for years. And we used to have to soak each glass back then individually in hot water, soap them with a brush, washed, dried, polished and put away. And customers in those days used to have their own pewter mugs and they were identified by names. Then you had your cellar duties and we did all our own bottling. Guinness had a plain porter which we called 'Single X' and they had a 'Double X' which was stout. The porter was eight pence a pint and the stout was eleven pence. Everybody drank porter then but it's gone off the market altogether. And the stout was much better then when it was in wooden barrels. There was much more grain used then. Today, with the metal containers, they use a lot more chemicals. The other was natural, it was yeast and barley and grain and it came up as God meant it to come up, not any pushing or shoving or putting gas into it.

"Now I bought this pub in 1959. This is really an old Dublin neighbourhood pub. Regulars here would be as high as 85 per cent. It's as local as that. We get three generations of customers in here . . . possibly *four*. And customers not only have their own patterns but their own seats. Especially in the old days you didn't sit on *that* seat, that was Mr C's seat. See, back then you would *never, never* refer to a man by his name. If your name was Kelly I'd always refer to you as Mr K. In those days you had divisions all around the counter and if I said 'Hello, Mr Kelly' to a man in one section the man in the next section might think that was his boss, or somebody he didn't want to see. So he was just Mr K. to me. You just didn't give people away. Confidence in a pub is a tremendous thing, you know.

"And conversation in a pub has never varied. It's simple—politics, religion, the price of drink, the cost of living, work, and football matches and hurling matches and such. We had no television in those days and conversation was much better, much more interesting. Because, I'll tell you, you had people *discuss* things. They discussed their jobs and I found it very interesting myself. Cause you go down to the local pub and you've got fellas there of all different trades and professions. So you could learn an awful lot in a pub. Any person who doesn't go into a pub is missing an awful lot of life, whether you drink or not. Like I learned a lot about different trades that you would never have heard anywhere else. Where I used to work was near Guinness's and Jacob's Biscuit company and I learned all about how they made biscuits just from listening to the men talking.

"There's no subject that's not acceptable for conversation but if it gets into a big argument and spreads around the pub, especially about religion, I try to hold it back because you can argue about religion for a million years and still not settle it. Religion, it's personal . . . it can get sticky with religion. Religion is one thing I'm nervous of because religion can be very hot headed. It's something you can argue over for years and find no solution to. I mean, being a Catholic country we're based on mysteries and how can you *prove* anything if you believe in mysteries? Now in the last ten or twelve years priests even come in and they can stand at the counter, have a pint and tell a joke and I like to see it. Now ten years ago that would have been unheard of.

"Now why does a fella go into this pub rather than that pub? It's not the drink. It's the people in it and the people behind the counter that makes the difference. A fella walks in and feels that he can relax in a place and that's what it's all about. It's about the atmosphere of the place that brings them in. And what makes a good publican? I wrote a poem about that one time, 'You're a doorman, a diplomat . . .' Anyone can serve a whiskey, serve a pint, but it's *handling* the different individuals that is the important thing. Learning to handle people. You have to know about human nature. And you never stop learning because we meet different characters every day, that's what makes it so interesting. You wouldn't become bored in a pub! Basically, you have to remember that people are good at heart and you appeal to their good nature at first and if you don't get anywhere then, well then, you just run up your sleeves and let fly at them. For instance, if some fella comes in here and he's noisy, he's rowdy, or he's the type of character who wants to butt in, it's my job to see that he doesn't butt into your company. Now I *can't* tell him that he can't butt in but I've got to be able to steer him away from your company. There are people who just don't mix. So you listen for any kind of a row whether it's political related or football or whatever it may be. Your ear is trained to know when the pitch goes a little high, then you move in and say, 'Cool it down, boys.'

"The reputation of pubs is important. 'What you are, your house will be'—

that's what I've often thought. If you're strict, if you run a place properly, people will respect it. If you're lazy, if you're a bad character yourself, it just seems like bad characters follow bad characters. It just seems to go that way. Like when you walk into a pub you can *sense* discipline, or you can sense untidiness. I can't put my finger on *why* you can do it but you *can*. I've done it myself. You say, 'this is a well run pub', or you just *feel* it. Atmosphere is terribly important to a pub. That's something you can create on both sides of the counter. It's not something you can buy or see but it's *there* and people recognise it. They recognise a pub that's badly run, they recognise a house that's well run. The rough character will walk into a pub and if he feels that it's disciplined and well run he'll conduct himself properly. But if he feels that it's not well run he'll let fly. I'm over thirty-five years here now and I've never had a physical row in this place. We've had some very close ones. They respect your house. But there are pubs around town where there are fights every night of the week, in houses that are very badly managed. They're known for that.

"There are people who when they get a few drinks in them can change and you've got to watch those things. Drink affects people differently. Some of them will get boisterous, some people get funny, some people get very morose. You just couldn't believe it, drink changes people completely. But women's personalities don't change nearly as much as men's when they drink. And they can hold a lot more. Definitely. I don't know what their make-up is but they can drink a hell of a lot more. But it varies how much a man can drink. If he has food he can drink more. But an average man coming in here can drink six or seven pints and no trouble. And our friend here [Tony Morris, featured in a later chapter] can put down a bottle of whiskey before dinner and still walk out. But with some men you have a responsibility to them, as well as to yourself, to see that they don't get too drunk. You have a responsibility to stop someone if they're drinking too much. I'll just say, 'c'mon over here in the corner and sit down and have a sleep' and they'll do that. And some customers, they'll leave their car keys here with me and drive home with a friend.

"Now there have been some very prominent characters in here either going up to the hospital [St Brendan's] to be 'dried out' or coming back. Funny, but an alcoholic when he'd be going into the hospital they have this thing that they just love that last drink before they go in. And I've actually seen them come in that door on their *hands and knees* and we know he's looking for that last drink. And if he doesn't get that drink he'll go berserk and give terrible trouble to the person that's taking him in, his brother, his father, his mother, his wife, the taximan. But if he just gets that *one* drink, nine times out of ten he'll walk back into that taxi and go up with no trouble. It's psychological. He just *has* to get it. And if you don't give it to him it's wrong. I usually go to the person he's with and say, 'Look, if I give him this he'll go easier', and they say, 'Whatever you say', and we give him the drink.

"In the old days it was unheard of for a woman to come into a bar. The bar was reserved for men only and women just weren't allowed in. You wouldn't *serve* them, the men wouldn't accept it. See, it was referred to in those days as the 'one place to get away from the wife'. Because a wife will very rarely come into a pub to get her husband home. It's very rarely done, just one of these things that's been accepted over the generations that a wife *doesn't* call her husband out of a pub. She can do what she likes with him when she gets him home, she can hammer hell out of him, but she doesn't let him down in a pub. It's just one of those taboos. Really, she can kill him when he goes home if she wants to, she can beat him up on the road if she wants to, but she won't cross that threshold and make a fool out of him in front of his mates.

"Now for a while I had another pub, on the south side. They had more money than the people around here and I didn't like their attitude of looking down on other people. I don't believe in class at all. I meet a man and I make my own judgments. I've seen judges, labourers, doctors, every profession mixing together here at the counter and no one minds who everyone else is. But in the other pub if a doctor came in or a solicitor came in everyone looked up to them. I don't like that. But there are publicans who won't serve working-class people if they're in working-class clothes. Oh, very much so in several parts of Dublin —you don't come in in your working clothes. I don't go for that myself at all. I don't know if they're trying to lift themselves or their pub to a higher standard. What the higher standard is I don't know because people are people as far as I'm concerned. I don't give a damn as long as they behave themselves and have a few jars and enjoy themselves, that's all I'm interested in. Who they are, what they are, makes no difference to me. There is *no class distinction* whatsoever here.

"There are an awful lot of publicans who have tried to retire or semi-retire and they've all come back to the trade. I don't know what's in it because it's a long day's work and tiring work. My family is trying to get me to retire now and I'm going through a terrible time trying to make up my mind whether to retire. But I *just can't!* I would miss it terribly. To the local people the pub is still the *centre* of the whole *neighbourhood*. If you did away with the neighbourhood pubs in Dublin where the man comes in after a day's work for a few drinks you'd just have to build *mental asylums* all over the place."

Eugene Kavanagh—Age 55

As the sixth generation publican in the same family public house he can claim the longest lineage in Dublin. His famous pub known as the "Gravedigger's" next to Glasnevin Cemetery has been in the family for over 160 years. In traditional fashion, he still lives above the pub which retains authentic Victorian fittings and ambience. It is even haunted by a benign ghost seen on several occasions by reliable witnesses.

"I'm sixth generation in the trade. From 1833 this was opened as a pub and it never changed hands. It's unique. John Kavanagh's name was on it and they had something like twenty-five children. His children were scattered all over the world. Three of his sons went to America and fought in the American Civil War.

One was Joseph who took over the pub. After about ten years in America he came back here and succeeded his father. And he put in a shooting range and a skittle alley down at the back. Big timber skittles that were eighteen inches high and you bowled down this round piece of timber to knock these skittles and they were set in a diamond. This was for his pub customers. Then he was succeeded by his son John who was a bit of a character, an oddball, who was fond of drink. He was more interested in drinking and socialising than he was in his work. *Fortunately*, his wife came from a similar type of background, the McKennas from Howth, who were involved in the pub trade. He died as a young man and she fortunately held it together. Then the pub was referred to as 'Josie's' cause her name was Josephine. This would be my grandmother. She was 74 when she died. She was the boss and she ran it and she had five sons. She was a very strong woman and a *big* woman, big in stature. She lived here and worked here behind the counter. Oh, she was out front. Somebody had to do it!

"I was born in 1939 and my first impressions here were of my grandmother as a woman in *black* with a big bandaged foot because she had varicose ulcers. And she always had an Alsatian dog here for security. And it was always a sort of half semi-ghost house in the sense that it always seemed to be dark and no electricity came into this premises until 1943. Prior to that it was all gas lit. And it was a grocer's and mostly credit transactions and you had a book and you got paid at the end of the week. Basically it was bread, tea, butter, maybe some cheese and biscuits. And in the front part of the pub you'd see the drawers and the vats, like a ball of blue to put in the washing, and boot laces, snuff, spices, and that sort of thing. And that time ladies used the snug and they were referred to as 'shawlies' because they wore black shawls. And women who liked a drop of the black stuff, they'd come in with a can and there'd be a couple of pints put in the can and they brought it home. But the number of ladies who'd frequent the pub would be very few because they were sort of tarnished—rightly or wrongly—and they didn't carry a good name.

"Josephine left the pub to her son, John. And my mother married Michael [his brother] who died—and she then married John. My father, Michael, died a young man of 43 years of age and my mother married his brother, John, who was a bachelor. So John was my uncle and my stepfather and he took on the wife and five children. The reason that I liked to come here as a boy was to work with him and go down in the cellar and bottle stout and ale. And they had hens roaming out in the garden and the kitchen had an open range. And you were looking across a very high timber counter at all these people outside the counter laughing and talking and smoking. As a child that was all something new. So when you're doing something as a child it's second nature to you. It's bred in me.

"I left school at 13 years of age and when I was 15 I started to work in Guinness's. So the amount of schooling I got was very little. I started work at Guinness's as a boy labourer and I worked there for nineteen years. I came back into the pub here around 1965 assisting my sick stepfather and the place was going very badly. So I capitalised on my stepfather's lack of business drive and took it over in 1973. The pub was structurally sound but in a sad state of dilapidation and money had to be spent on it. We moved on from there and things went very well. I inherited a few good *loyal* people. And then you had newer customers. Like my stepfather used to say, 'Some of *your* customers were in last night.' And he had *his* customers. He was born and died in this house so you can appreciate that he had his certain crew of people. So anyone 'new' was referred to as *my* customers. And it went on from there and the business snowballed.

"Now the 'Gravedigger's' tag obviously comes because we're beside the cemetery [Glasnevin]. In fact, it's a communal wall between the cemetery and ourselves. And this gate here beside us closed in 1879. At that time funerals would have been horse-drawn hearses and mourning coaches. And there was body snatchers and they used to rob the bodies for medical science. Used to dig up bodies and sell them to science. So they had watch towers and dogs in that time. But at one time there was about sixty gravediggers in the cemetery, way up to the 1960s. And they were a great bunch of men and they had great principles. At that time you could give credit and you wouldn't be let down. They would honour their debts and they were paid once a week and they'd come in and pay what they'd owe. So there would be an amount of gravediggers drinking here. But if they were caught drinking *during* working hours they'd be *sacked*. But going back over the years and in my stepfather's time there would be knocks on the wall which would echo inside the bar and my stepfather would know *exactly* what drink was needed to go out. Now people thought it [drink] went through the wall [via an opening] but it didn't, it went out through the front door and was passed through the railings to the gravediggers. So after a few burials they'd hot-foot it down and knock on the wall.

"These were hard-working men. I mean today they have these machines and they just scoop out the dirt but these men had to *get in* [the grave] and use a pickaxe and shovel and they had to go through the roots of trees and everything —it was *hard* work. They were hard men but principled men, you wouldn't meet more decent men. And their social life was a few pints. So maybe they'd have a few pints when they weren't supposed to. But it was a *tradition. Don't forget,* they should not have been at the railing drinking! It was usually pints of porter then or a small whiskey. Just passed it through the railing and they'd consume it and they'd leave the empty glasses down beside the railing. And my stepfather knew the characters by a heavy knock or a light knock and he knew what the person would be requiring. You just took it out and if you were left money you'd take it and if you weren't you just took in the empty glasses. You'd always be paid. And they might be short of cigarettes and they might come down and knock and it might be ten Woodbines and I would take them out. But if the men were caught they'd be sacked. And it was a tradition that the gravediggers would get a *tip* when there was a burial and it would be shared among them and at the end of the day they'd come here and drink whatever money they had. *Strong,* hard men and very good people.

"And there were stories about ghosts here. My brother has had experiences and I've spoken to people who claim certain things. Just to give you a couple of instances: my brother was here one night and everybody gone, all the rooms were secured and locked up, and bearing in mind that we always had an Alsatian indoors. He was doing the cash and the dog was between him and the door. Now this door was a door that stuck and you had to give it a good push to open it. And he heard the door opening and the dog stood up and the hair stood on the dog's back and he was snarling and growling. And my brother could see nothing. And the dog continued to snarl and growl and my brother was getting a little bit uneasy with this because he *knew* everywhere was closed. So eventually the dog calmed down and settled and as soon as he did he closed up everything and *out* the front door. They say that a dog senses these things.

"Now in the corner of the bar there's a door that led down to the old toilet which was also the way down to where the skittle alley and shooting range was. And there was this regular customer here who was in with a companion, a stranger friend. And this regular customer was watching the ring board with his companion and so on the way home the stranger says, 'Who was the little gentleman with the butterfly collar and the waistcoat with the gold watch chain and the little white beard drinking the glass of Guinness?' So the regular customer says, 'What are you talking about? There was nobody there.' 'Yes, the little man with the white beard.' And he described him. And the regular customer says, 'There's *no* such thing.' So some months had passed and a friend of my brother's, he was talking to this other [different] guy down at the front of the shop at what was formerly the grocery end. And he came up after having been in the toilet and he says, 'Who's the fella down at the back drinking a bottle of Guinness?' And he described the man with the butterfly collar and waistcoat and the watch chain. *Identical!* Now these people didn't know each other.

"When I took over in 1973 it came natural to me. There was so many generations that there was a lot bred in me, I accepted it as normal. And we were the last pub in Dublin with the corked bottles of stout. Ours was all hand done and we used to have to wash the corks and steam the corks and do the hand corking and label all our own bottles by hand. I did that myself. In 1971 was the last we sold of them. And here we've no TV, no phone, no noise box and people really talk to each other. The art of communication is talking to each other. I like to meet people as they are and if you have a noise box up in the corner then you're competing with the noise. I think the television is for your home.

"In the bar we have a lot of characters. And you'd get to know these people and their *habits* and their *fears* and their *phobias* and everything else. They'd come in here in the morning suffering from the over-indulgence of alcohol the previous night and they're in the 'horrors' as they say. Well, they'd come to assemble themselves to get their shattered brain and thoughts together. Great characters and expressions. I often regretted that I hadn't a tape recorder in this pub. I mean I had 70-year-old men down there who had never married and the *stories* about being deported from America during the McCarthy era because they were supposed to be communists. And expressions like, 'The last time I was in church they poured water on me head, they called me names, and I haven't been back since.' These sort of expressions. Or two fellas with some drink consumed and one looking at the other and saying, 'You know as much about opera as a pig knows about a bank holiday!' In a serious vein! The *real* Dublin wit, it was just *there*.

"Since time began everything happened in a pub from start to finish, whether a rebellion or revolution or whatever, whether it's forming football teams or cricket teams or drama classes, ninety-nine out of a hundred would start in a pub over a drink. Oh, everything is sorted out in a pub. People can sort out the world's problems and very *convincingly*. Sort out everyone's problems and sort out the world's problems and, do you know, they can't sort out their own! But it's their *meeting* place. I have about 80 per cent regular trade and they would call this place their local. And now it's become the 'in' place, the place to go. There's lots of reasons for that. It's an old original type of pub. They've made all sorts of films and serials in here. It became an attraction. Now someone hears about it or visitors have been told about it and they're taken here. It amuses me sometimes because I can remember when it was referred to as a 'dirty kip'."

PADDY COFFEY—AGE 83

At the tender age of 13 he came to Dublin from County Limerick to serve his apprenticeship in Murphy's pub on City Quay. He befriended a rough but decent bunch of dockers, seamen and coal porters. The pub also drew a motley assortment of bookies, prostitutes and ring players who were hustlers. They were exciting times, but today he finds the docks as silent as a graveyard.

"I'm from Limerick, my father was a farmer. I had four brothers and no sisters and I had no option. An older brother was to go [to Dublin as an apprentice] and he refused that morning, so my mother just put me on the train. He refused to budge so I was put in his place. I was 13 years old when I came to Dublin first in 1924. My mother came up with me and dropped me down at this public house on the quays. It was Murphy's on City Quay down on the docks. Jobs were very scarce in the twenties don't forget and anything you got, you *took* it.

"It was a different world completely. No taxis at that time. It was a side-car, a jaunting car, like you'll find in Killarney still. I always remember that it was a half-crown from Kingsbridge railway station to City Quay where I was 'dumped'. The terms were arranged, all you got was your food and five shillings a week. You had to live-in whether you liked it or not. That was the rule then. And if you got married you were out of a job! They wouldn't keep you if you were a married man because they'd have to pay you living accommodations *out* and they didn't want to do that. But I lived with a nice family and I had a room to myself. There was only myself and the boss, George Murphy, and his wife but they had no children. I'd eat with them and they were very social. They made you feel at home. And on a Sunday he'd bring me out for a walk when I was off, around Dublin.

"I done three years there at Murphy's as an apprentice. I worked about seventy or eighty hours a week, at least. You'd have only one half-day off from half past one and every fourth Sunday. So you were there all the bloody time. It wasn't what you'd call a very up-to-date house. It was a small little backstreet pub. They were all dockers, all very tough men, *real* locals. But it was a clean and tidy pub. Oh, we sold tea and sugar and everything else as you came in the door. We'd spend half the day when we were weighing up tea in ounces and two ounces at that time in small little paper bags. There was sawdust a foot or two out from the bar and spittoons were there too. Wooden stools and we didn't have *any* heating. I wore a big black apron and, oh, a collar and tie and shoes shined. Anything inside the counter, that was my job and I started with bottling stout and ales. Now for the cellar work we had a porter as well. He was a young lad too, about 17 or 18, a lower class shall we say. I was senior to him because I was an assistant. He was a very nice chap and we got on very well the two of us. He was great company for me.

"The Guinness man was very important then, a big-shot that'd come in and buy a bottle of stout and take a sup and then put a thermometer down to test the temperature. They were called Guinness's 'travellers'. Oh, you nearly had to take your hat off he was such an important man. Oh, they were very important fellas then. He dressed very well. Guinness's men were the big snobs at that time, they had a complete hold on things. Oh, Guinness's men were really uppity, put a bit of fear into you. They paid for the bottle of stout and he'd drink a drop of it and the big-shot would walk out again then. Their word was law. See, they could refuse to supply you with their own labels and you'd have to get your own labels made and once you had your own labels people'd say, 'Oh, that's not Guinness.' See, they'd sell you the stout but you wouldn't get their official label, you had to print it yourself by hand . . . second rate.

"There was never a dull moment in that public house. It was mostly dockers, seamen and coal porters, they were a rough bunch as well. There were snugs for ladies and they wouldn't be allowed to be served with the men in the bar. Most of them down along the quays wore shawls at that time, in the twenties. They'd get a glass of stout, or a gill of stout. Had to be in a glass. You wouldn't serve a woman at that time with a pint. And the locals would send a kid around for stout in a can. Come up to the bar and I'd fill that for them. It wasn't *legal*, you had to watch that a policeman wasn't around the corner. And the slate, that was against the law. But I remember every Saturday you'd have the little book out there with all the credit accounts and some would owe you fifteen bob and he might give you ten. And the boss himself would be there checking that. And then a fella wouldn't pay at all and you wouldn't see him *any more*—he'd disappear. Oh, it happened. And if a man didn't pay he'd be barred. But most dockers were *decent* men, decent hard-working men. Dockers were badly paid at the time and when I came into the pub it was after the big strike of 1916 and they were badly beaten. When I came in 1924 some of them were practically starving to death. Scabs took their jobs. I remember these scabs from 1916 and eight years later they never forgot it. Some of the scabs were afraid to come into our pub. They'd go where they congregated among themselves. But I saw real hunger. I saw two men commit suicide on the docks. They were barred [from work] since 1916 and this one man, he jumped into the Liffey on a cold winter's day. I saw it myself, I was doing nothing standing at the window of the pub looking out. It was hunger and idleness. Depression. Hopelessness. Lost his job in 1916 and he couldn't get a job. He gave up the will to live.

"The dockers always stuck together, they were very loyal. And in the pub tradesmen kept their distance. We had carpenters and *they* were socially above dockers. And a docker if he wanted a job he'd have to bribe the stevedore. Oh, a man didn't get a job unless he done it. See, dockers were paid *in the pub* so the stevedore, he came in *looking* for it. And the docker'd leave five shillings in a matchbox for the stevedore in the pub and he gave it to me. Five shillings at that time was a lot of money. Oh, and the stevedore didn't drink with the dockers, he kept his distance. *Socially*, he was above the docker. And he looked the part. Big leather jacket on him and he drank the rawest whiskey around, they liked the bite in it. But dockers drank pints of porter. And when they were paid in the pub the dockers drank their wages, drink the whole bloody lot, and the wife'd get nothing from him. It was a bad system and they were paid each day and that was a problem as well. Their poor children would go hungry.

"There was one fella down there and he was a bookie. He started off as a docker and he took little bets and then he finally became a fully fledged bookie. He was up and down the street and he'd be going from one pub to another where the lads with the money would be. It was illegal but nobody'd stop the man. Mostly horses. Oh, he was a very important man, the bookie. He dressed well, dressed spectacular at that time, a big white hat, like a man of prominence, and a big heavy coat and it looked well. Oh, he always had about a hundred quid on him. He was very well known on the docks. That evening he'd come into the pub with the results and he paid off. But he wouldn't drink at all, he was on business.

"And there were prostitutes around there on the docks. Oh, yes. They came in with a man. It'd be the sailors that'd always pick them up. Some public houses had a reputation for fighting and prostitution. Prostitutes came into our pub but he wouldn't serve them unless they were with a man. Any unfortunate woman that was 'on the town', I found them all decent. A lot of them were from the country and 'in a family way' and had to get out. At that time in the country if a girl was in a family way they'd throw her out the door and she'd have to come to Dublin. They hadn't much charity then. I'll always remember one good fight I saw down there. It was a sailor who apparently didn't pay her and I happened to be standing out on the North Wall and he came along and one of the prostitutes gave him a kick in the balls and the other gave him a kick in the head. I never saw a man getting done in as quick as the two of them done it. He was laying on the ground. It was really a classic knock-out by the two women!

"We had a great ring team in the pub down there. As a matter of fact, I was one of the champion ring players myself. Cause you'd nothing else to do, only practice. There was always wagering on it, ten shillings or a pound would be the most because they hadn't *got* it at that time. The money would be handed inside the counter and I'd put it up on the shelf. Oh, it was a very serious effort. Then some men that were champions going around Dublin would come into the pub and see was there anybody capable of taking them on for a pound. Oh, yes, a hustler like. They'd be well known. I remember one chap named Greene, a hustler, and I think he was the best in Dublin and then everybody wanted to have a go at him, you see. He had a style of his own and he'd go around the board. See, anybody that fancied himself wanted to have a go at him, challenge him for ten shillings or a pound.

"And then there'd be a card game, about eight or nine playing at a table by themselves. It'd be about a shilling a game bet at that time, to pass the time away. And we had singing there in the pub on a Sunday. There was one fella that would bring in a violin and he'd play. Everybody had their crack at singing. Oh, there were great characters there. Very humorous. I found them very, very nice people and I got on with them. The old pub, 'twas the social gathering place for the locals down on the quays. There'd be three, four, five generations. There was life down there at that time. There's no *life* down there now. They put those people out, those unfortunate people, out in the flats in Ballymun and all these bloody places. I think it's sad. They were a grand old people, you know, a grand old people."

NOEL GILL—AGE 60

It is his experienced belief that local characters make a pub. He has known a good few in his pub on the North Circular Road. Blusterous Brendan Behan was a regular customer and source of wit and controversy. There were other colourful characters as well, such as "Chuckles", Huey and Mr Lynch, an old shoemaker who didn't drink regularly but would go "on the tear" once a month.

"I think characters make a pub. Brendan Behan lived here on Russell Street and this was his uncle's local, Paddy English. Now *he* was a character. He was a character in that he was kind of aloof, had a superiority complex in one sense. He kept himself spic and span. He always dressed well, white collar every day, tie and cap, the cap on all the time, not to cover his baldy head but to look the part. Now Paddy wouldn't get the cap off him. Even when he was in *bed* he wouldn't take it off, it was unlucky. He'd always come in for the heat cause there was a little electric fire down at the end of the bar and he'd be crouched up against it and he'd always start with a drop of whiskey. He was always a moaner. He'd be saying that he couldn't stand his relations and all this and be 'f—-ing'. But he was a moaner that you'd like, not a moaner that you'd shove off.

"Now Chuckles, we used to get great sport out of ribbing him. Chuckles was a hard man in his late fifties. Chuckles had a very peculiar laugh, a whining sort of laugh. You couldn't describe it now. He had a three-decibel laugh. It may start out at the bottom and end up soprano—or vice versa! But different to any other laugh. He was raised in Artane Reform School, a notorious place out there with the Christian Brothers, and he learned to be handy like an electrician and a bit of carpentry. But he wasn't gifted to continuous work. He'd take a job here and a job there . . . but he'd mainly stand on the corner. Chuckles and Paddy English and a group of them characters, they seemed to be doing nothing all day. Only standing on the corner all day long or playing cards or waiting on bookies' results. In the summer Chuckles would be down there at the canal in the morning and the evening and any youngster he'd throw them in and let them swim out of it and that's how you learned swimming. That's why all the kids were good swimmers around here. Now Chuckles was famous for lying on the bottom of the canal with a stone brick on his chest and they reckoned that he could last for three minutes. People used to time it. It was a bit of show. He had marvellous breathing but he was never short of a cigarette.

"Then there was this fella Huey, he was a great character that used to come in the pub here. He was a *profound* village idiot. He'd be standing at the corner waiting for someone to call him in for a drink. And in the summer time his wellington boots used to stink to high heaven. Now Huey had the capacity to keep saying the wrong things in the right context or the right things in the wrong context. The village idiot. And when there was a match on in Croke Park he'd buy *two* colours and for the Mayo crowd he'd have their colours and he'd be congratulating them and that'd be a sure pint for him. And if the other side won he'd have *their* colours up. But sometimes he'd be half-drunk and get so mixed up that he'd have the wrong score.

"Now Huey began to have trouble with his bronchials—he called them the 'veronicals'—and he went up to the hospital and the doctor'd say, 'I think you're too fond of the drink. Tell me, what do you do in the middle of the day?' 'Well, doctor', says he, 'I go over to Jimmy Gill's pub and have a pint of plain and I smoke a package of Woodbines.' 'Ah', says he, 'now, Huey, from now on you're going to cut that game out, you're not to go over there and have your pint of plain—and come back to me in a month.' So, right, Huey came back in and, 'Ah, me good man, Huey, now you haven't gone over there?' 'No', he says, 'I go up to the Big Tree [pub] and have a pint of stout and ten plains.' He was *always* saying the wrong thing. But he was genuine. And fellas here would be getting him going, getting him to say things, and used to leave drink down for him just to get him going. He wasn't offensive to anybody.

"Now cattle used to come down the [North Circular] road at that time on the hoof to be exported. Oh, every couple of minutes. And the *flies*, right in the window. Straight in the windows and into the fellas' pints. The flies off the cattle they'd swarm in during the summer time and we'd have these stickers hanging from the ceiling to catch them. And there was a case where a bullock saw its reflection in the glass outside the pub and made a mad rush and went through our front window. And there was a character here, Mr Lynch, an old shoemaker, and he used to go 'on the tear' once a month. Now he didn't drink regular, it was just once a month for a few days and then they'd be taking him home. And he had a pipe and a moustache and a mortar board hat down over his ears. And this day he was on the whiskey and everybody stood back when the bullock came through the window. But old Lynch was there puffing his pipe and he looked around laconically and philosophically and says to the bullock, 'What are you having, mate?' Oh, it didn't bother him.

"And the cattle dealers were great drinkers. They were all double whiskey men. They wouldn't be drinking with the ordinary pintman, like the drover or jobber. He'd be drinking double whiskies, he was an upper-class drinker. There was a certain class distinction in drinking. There was partitions in the bars and the crowd at the front were usually the whiskey men, whiskey, wine and sherry men. They'd be professionals or tradesmen, civil servants and that. And some wanted to go into the snug for privacy. And then halfway down you'd have the pint of stout men and then at the back of the shop you had the pint of plain men. That's usually the way it was. See, there was a beer that Guinness's used to put out that was a pint of plain. It was like cheap stout, 'Single X' we used to call it, weak stuff. It was light stuff and you could be drinking ten pints before it'd really make you merry. But if he had a few extra shillings he'd go for the 'fifty' and that was half-stout. You'd fill it halfway up [with porter] and put the stout on the top of it and there was a kick in that. But the pint of stout man was usually a collar and tie man, well-to-do . . . or after winning at the bookies! So the whiskey man or the pint of stout man would be up at the front of the bar and the ordinary Joe would be at the back. And the whiskey men wouldn't be loud about emphasising a point but the ordinary labouring man like the docker or horse driver, he'd be emphasising a point and have to let go with a string of language and the language was choice.

"Now Behan, in the fifties, he'd sooner be with the boys down at the back and his voice would be head and shoulders over everybody and his 'f——-ing would be *twice* as loud as everybody and that'd be the way he'd emphasise a point whether it was politics or football or whatever he'd be worked up about. And he'd give a *thump*, stamp his authority on the subject. And it was amazing about him that he varied his pubs. If he was after doing a play or writing a story and it had been accepted [for money] he'd then go on a binge and he'd start maybe in Grafton Street or Baggot Street, like McDaid's or the Bailey and Ryan's of Baggot Street and the Palace Bar, that'd be the route. Then he'd get the guys and he'd go on a sentimental tour down here cause he was reared here. The money would burn a hole in his pocket, he had to throw it away. He'd say, 'Have you had a drink?' and he'd throw a fiver down and say, 'Give that man a drink, he must be dying of thirst.' And anywhere he'd go people'd be coming up and congratulating him about how his book would be doing. We treated him as a character from a respectable family but he could be tricky and boisterous. But he was quite lovable. Brendan would get excitable very quick and he'd get into hectic arguments. Anyone who picked an argument with him got the worst of it cause he was quick at putting him down.

"Quite a lot of men adjourned here when Brendan died. See, he had been in about three weeks before that and he come in stone sober although the camp followers, as we call them, were very well oiled. But he was drinking soda water.

And he had shrunk so you wouldn't even recognise him. He was like an old grandmother, you know, hunched in like that and his tummy gone. He came in to tell us that he was the only Irishman that got an invitation to President Kennedy's inauguration. He was proud as punch and he showed me the official invitation here behind the counter. And it was all folded up—it was the cleanest thing you ever saw him with.

LARRY RYAN—AGE 61

As a Tipperary lad of 14 he came to Dublin to serve his apprenticeship at Slattery's pub in Pearse Street. He next worked at the famous Widow Reilly's pub and found her a strict disciplinarian. In 1958 he bought a pub in the Coombe where it took nearly a year for the local Liberties men to accept him in their pub.

"I'm from Tipperary. Now when you say 'Tipperary publicans' it's from *one* area of Tipperary. It's from *north* Tipperary. It was like the west of Ireland people going to America, if one went others would follow. It's a tradition. I would safely say that in my parish at home almost everybody there has some relations in the bar trade in Dublin. It's as simple as that. It's just a way of life, it just happened. I came to Dublin because my uncles before me came and my school chums came. Now my uncles came to Dublin in 1913, about six of them, and they pooled their money together and had a draw and [if you won] you got a deposit for a pub. And you worked very hard. And then after a year or so you put the money back in the pool again and that was a draw and another got *his* pub. Eventually everyone got to buy a public house. See, they worked that way in communities.

"I was 14 when I came. I got an apprenticeship. The pub was Billy Slattery's of Pearse Street. I had to have a letter from my local parish priest, schoolteacher, and from a local sergeant. At that period of time it was a *very much* sought after job because you always had a good chance of progressing to your own pub. That was the plan at that time. Back then they all came from the country and served their time. Dublin men were just not prepared to work during the social hours. I got five shillings a week and it was compulsory for an apprentice to live-in. You stayed upstairs and your meals were provided. Ninety-nine per cent of the publicans lived upstairs then. You had to have two aprons, white for the shop and blue for the cellar. Mr Slattery was a strict man but a good man. Even on your day off you'd have to be in by half ten at night time. The first three months you wouldn't see the light of day. You'd be down in the cellar bottling and labelling and washing the bottles. I suppose the old publican was very wise to put you down in the cellar for two or three months and he'd be learning whether you were fit to look after people or not.

"Now there was ladies that wasn't supposed to be using pubs in them days and there was no ladies' toilets. And when you were in the cellars you'd wash tanks out near the grating. And I remember being down there one time and I remember a porter working there and the tanks were out under the grate. And I remember him swearing and grabbing a hose as he passed me to another section of the cellar. Apparently there was a couple of ladies and at that time they used to wear long skirts and, of course, when they had a few drinks there'd be no toilets and the two of them come out and they were talking away and standing right over the grate and down on yer man!

"It was strictly a pint house, no frills attached. It was just all Guinness and whiskey. Mostly working class at that period we got in. You'd get a lot of workers out of CIE and men from the dockland and coalyards. At that time the rounds system was in being. Like if I was a regular in the pub drinking and you'd come in I'd say, 'Good evening, what are you having?' And eventually you could end up with nine or ten in the company. And you got class distinctions. The crane driver wouldn't drink with the docker, wouldn't even say hello to the docker. Dockers were absolutely tough men, but very fair, and by today's standards they were gentlemen. Paid by the day. A stevedore or foreman, they were very definitely a notch above because they had the 'read' in the morning and if you weren't nice to them your name wouldn't be called out in the read the following morning. You had to buy him a few drinks.

"Then I worked in the Widow Reilly's. She was known locally as the 'Widow Reilly' but I always knew her as Kate Gilligan. She had a pub in Phibsborough Road and her husband had a pub himself over in Thomas Street. Her husband, oh, a very dapper man, always a pinstripe suit and a red rose. He ran his own business separate from hers. He'd come in and I didn't know for *years* that was her husband. But she was a legend in her own lifetime. To me, she was very old, I'd say about 70. For a woman to have a pub was unusual—but she was an unusual lady. She worked behind the bar, she'd come out and pull pints. She was from the west of Ireland originally. She was grey haired and a bun tied in the back. And she always wore dark colours. Always. Oh, very stern looking. She was a very strict woman, very cross. She watched everything and knew everything. Oh, she would give out to you, like if you were too long in the cellar bottling. But she was friendly to customers, *knew* every one of them. She was a hell of a business lady.

"In 1958 I bought a pub in the Coombe. It was O'Connor's. And O'Connor was reputed to have left a thousand pounds in *cash* for every year of his life. A niece got it. There was *never* anything spent on the pub. He lived in a big tenement house over the shop and had no way of cooking, only an open fire, and there was an electric bulb in the kitchen. Never spent a penny on it. But Mr O'Connor, he was a god. Oh, very high respect for him there. He was a lifetime there. O'Connor was a very strict man and ran a very good premises. Ninety per cent of the customers were regulars. Once I came in I kept the standard high. I wanted to keep it as old fashioned as possible, as little change as possible. We sold tea and snuff and it was loose, in paper, and there'd be scales.

"That was really history in the Coombe. The pub is the *centre* of that community . . . the centre of their life. I had grandfathers, fathers, sons and great grandchildren, it was a whole family that'd come in. Men very much had their one local pub then and their own *spot* in the pub. It takes a while for them to get to know you. It'll take you six to twelve months to get established so the people get to know you and to know what standards you're going to keep. Oh, the local pub is *their* pub. In their mind it *is* their pub and you daren't interfere with it! Oh, you're very much an intruder for the first twelve months until they get to know you. But then you were very close to the people in the Coombe. A good publican, he would know every customer in the shop by name in them years. He would know *where* they worked, he would know their wife and how many kids they had. And you'd find that these men would be in the same spot at the counter. *Every day*, they were as regular as clockwork. And in the Coombe if a person was in bad circumstances somebody would tip you off about it and there would be a collection made for them. They'd take it in a stout bag. Moral standards in the Coombe were very, very high with the working class. And they still had wakes and I've been to *hundreds* of weddings and christenings and funerals.

"Now in the Coombe there was no way there'd be singing in the pub there. Oh, no. Oh, maybe Christmas Eve. But I remember one time we had this one man and he had a very bad stammer. So one time they said, 'No one can sing here except him, he's the only one that can sing here', knowing that no way could he sing. Jesus, if he didn't stand up and he was the finest singer I ever heard! But after a funeral, that was *one* day you allowed a sing-song. And usually it was the widow or widower that'd start it. Could be anything . . . ballads. It would be a typical Dublin funeral. I mean, they wouldn't continue with the sadness, especially if the person was very old. The Dublin person is basically a very, very happy person. Very positive outlook and generous. But it was rather funny during Lent in them times. They would [claim to] give up the drink—but invariably they'd go to another pub! They wouldn't want you to know that they'd broke their pledge, so they'd sneak away to some other pub. But I'd often catch them cause they'd drop some hint.

"Now there was a bacon factory here and they killed pigs and cured them and made sausages and there'd be a big barrel outside where he'd cut off the backbones and the crubeens and he was very kind to the Coombe people. They could actually take away that bone free of charge. So there was a system at that period in the pub where it was your turn this Saturday night and you'd go down and get the backbone and the pig's feet and cook it and you'd bring it into the pub. And another'd bring it the next Saturday night. They'd bring it in a basket and it would be handed around to anyone who wanted it and just hold it on the newspaper there and eat away. And the bones just throwed there in the corner. Then on Sunday pubs used to close at 7.00 and the older people'd have a 'bottle party'. It was 'bring your own'. You'd go to *your* house this Sunday and *your* house next Sunday. You'd bring your own half dozen or dozen bottles. We would get the stuff ready in paper bags and they'd go off and have a sing-song. And then we'd come along the following Monday morning and have to go to the house and pick up these bottles. We had a bike with a carrier basket in front. It'd be a tenement house, maybe thirty people. Oh, God, we often brought back *forty dozen*!

"There was a snug in the front of the pub. That goes back to the old days when very old women didn't want to be seen in the pub drinking, they'd slip into the snug. And the door had a little spring lock and a little chain so the door closed so you couldn't open it from the outside then. I knew a few old ladies there on the Coombe and they had actually *never* been into O'Connell Street. Never been as far as O'Connell Street. It was just their life. They'd meet in the morning and go up to Meath Street and do their shopping and come back and have a few glasses of porter, it was a GP, a glass of plain. Oh, and if it was cold they'd have a hot whiskey and sugar. The women dealers, they were very good drinkers. I knew several of them that could outdrink a man anytime. Oh, yes.

"Then I had a pub in Parnell Street for years. It was the Deer's Head. I built it up from nothing. It was dilapidated. It had the worst reputation you could possibly get. Sailors used to use it and that kind of stuff. Actually, there was a sailor killed outside. An English fella had it and the house got a very bad reputation. It had no standards. Parnell Street when I came there was very tough. I had to raise the standards. So when I opened the Parnell Street pub one month after opening I didn't have *one* customer that was there opening day. I had them barred. I barred the whole crowd. I *had* to, to raise the standards. They were very troublesome, they were not my type of people. I just told them that they wouldn't be served any more. Little by little then you started to build up a trade and you got a good name. But you had to *earn* their respect. From day one! Until they knew what you were made of, that you weren't going to tolerate any nonsense. You always had to mean exactly what you say. If you say, 'He's barred', he *is* barred, doesn't matter who he is. I never had to get the police, even once, to clear my house for me. I always took care of that myself. *Physically* if you had to, basically by myself. The real bowsie, he'd look for trouble. So you'd get a grip of his arm and get him out that way. Or it often went to fisticuffs. Oh, yeah. They would challenge me, back before they got to know me, in the earlier years. If he has a reputation to keep as a troublemaker and he thinks you're going to give him a hiding that will destroy his reputation then he'd give you a wide berth, he won't bother you. So if you made an example of one or two of them then you have no more problems. So I done it up and I made a very good shop out of it and built a very good reputation.

"Dublin would be a very poor place to be in if that local pub tradition died out. I'll give you a 'for instance' now. Now we done very well in soccer in this World Cup. Well, Jack Charlton come over to manage our national team here and when they were making the draw out he was watching it over at the Burlington Hotel and he was mobbed by the media asking about it. But Jack is not a fella that's mad about giving statements to the press. So he couldn't even have a drink in the Burlington, so he left. And he tried a couple of more places and the press was following him all the time. So as he was driving back out to Dublin Airport to get back to England he was driving up along Gardiner Street and his driver and his minder was with him and there is a little broken down pub on the top of Gardiner Street called Hill 16, it's a typical old Dublin pub. So he decided to go in there. And they're soccer *mad* in that area. And when they seen Jack it was 'Ooooh!' So the minder says, 'Ah, give him a chance, he's only going in for a pint.' If you're only going in for a drink they respect that. I mean, they always respect a drink.

"So Jack got his pint and the next thing the press was in to have him make a statement. And he says 'No, no statement at all, I told you no statements.' So the next thing was some of the boys there says to the press, 'He don't bleeding want you here and neither do we. *Out!*' So they threw the press out. And Jack settled down and nobody interfered and he was just one of themselves then. So he had several drinks there. And so next time he was passing doesn't Jack put in again. So when we played the last soccer match didn't Jack on the way back from the airport pull up the coach and brought the *whole team* into Hill 16. Took the whole team in there! And Jack knows now that nobody will say a *thing* to him and he doesn't *need* a minder, nobody'll touch his car and he'll give a few signatures for the kids. He'll have his drinks there and that's it. *They* mind him, in a big way. That wouldn't happen in a big pub, no way. But he has total privacy there. Absolutely. So, recently the locals got together and they made a little plaque and presented it to Jack and Jack was very touched by it.

"I hope that all the old Dublin men die before the old pubs go . . . and eventually they will be replaced with modern things that are not pubs at all. Because pubs was a *tradition* in Dublin, a way of life. They weren't just a watering hole, the family's life was built around the pub. They were part of the community."

TED McGOVERN—AGE 65

In the 1940s he served his apprenticeship in Lalor's of Wexford Street which was Dublin's most famous singing pub. An exciting place to work, it drew international visitors as well as devoted Dubliners. Apart from his barman duties, he had to help control the huge crowds queuing up at the door and even served as MC of the entertainment. In 1958 he realised a dream and bought Lalor's when it was in decline. Through hard work he was able to restore the singing pub to its former popularity.

"I'm Cavan. My father was in farming and we had no connection with the trade. In fact, I'd say we were more 'anti-pub' and my mother thought it was a terrible job to work in a pub washing up after people's drink and all. But I had worked a little while down in the country in a public house and grocery and as a young fella I worked behind the counter. I was 14. But that didn't have any bearing on the Dublin scene because it didn't count. Oh, no, you had to do your apprenticeship in Dublin at that time and you had to do four years. I came to Dublin when I was 19 and on a Monday I went up to the [Barman's] Union and

26

The Brazen Head, dating back some seven centuries, is Dublin's oldest pub.
(Courtesy of Bord Fáilte)

27

Lively conversation has always been the heart of Dublin pub life.
(Courtesy of Bord Fáilte)

28

Mulligan's pub in Poolbeg Street, 1965. (Courtesy of Bord Fáilte)

29

*Legendary barman Paddy O'Brien (left) serving up a pint in
McDaid's, 1965. (Courtesy of Bord Fáilte)*

30

*Dwyer's pub of Moore Street in 1958 when women were beginning to be
accepted in the bar. (Courtesy of Bord Fáilte)*

31

The famed Davy Byrne's pub in 1958 with its modern decor.
(Courtesy of Bord Fáilte)

32

Around 1950 Doran's of Marlborough Street was the sleekest pub in the city,
boasting one of the first lounges for women.

33

The Airway House pub in Findlater Street got its name back in the 1940s from being located just across the street from the Aer Lingus office.

34

Roger's pub in Thomas Street draws many thirsty women street dealers who sell their produce just outside the front door.

35
Old cattleman Luke Nugent lifting a pint in Walsh's pub in Stoneybatter.

36

The elegant façade of Davy Byrne's "Moral Pub" in Duke Street.

37

Men and women sharing space at the bar in 1960 at Davy Byrne's pub.

38
Perusing the morning paper in the International Bar.
(Courtesy of John Woodfull)

39

The Blue Lion in Parnell Street, once frequented by Sean O'Casey.

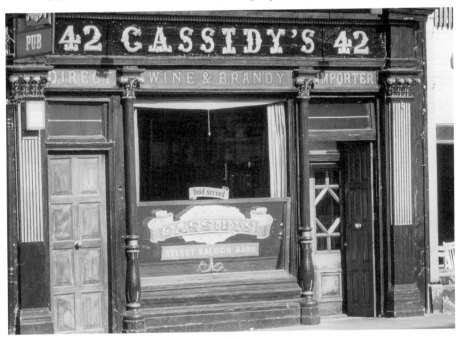

40

Cassidy's Victorian pub in Camden Street still retains its old world charm.

41
Kavanagh's pub in Aughrim Street boasts classical red-brick Victorian architecture.

42
The Norseman pub in Temple Bar.

43

*The Palace Bar where journalists, writers and intellectuals
traditionally held court.*

44
*Publican
Jack Cusack of
the Cozy Bar in
the Coombe
proudly showing
off his new clock.*

45
*John O'Dwyer's pub in
Aungier Street is the
quintessential small,
unpretentious
neighbourhood local.*

46

*Doheny and Nesbitt's pub in Baggot Street is admired for its
Victorian ambience.*

47

Kelly's Bar at the corner of Talbot and Corporation streets in the 1970s. Note the "open 7 a.m." sign.

48

Passing the time in good company. (Courtesy of John Woodfull)

49

Molloy's of Talbot Street does brisk business with railway passengers.

50

Slattery's pub in Capel Street.

51

Walsh's pub of Stoneybatter served as an important IRA meeting place and refuge early in the century.

the following Saturday I started working in Lalor's pub of Wexford Street.

"At that time Lalor's was a famous singing house. It was the *first* singing house in Dublin which became world famous. It started accidentally in 1938 on Sunday evenings. At that time the Sunday hours was from 5.00 to 7.00. So, naturally, a few people would stay back, maybe a dozen, and you couldn't have them in the bar so they brought them upstairs and there was a piano and obviously a sing-song started. That was a private party. Then with the war coming on they got the idea of opening what they called a private lounge. It *wasn't* private as such but that was their way of keeping it fairly selective. So you'd be privileged to get up there. So it really started accidentally. And then they saw some potential and so they started this singing house and it became world famous.

"It was a four-storey building. The bar was downstairs and the lounge was upstairs and there were two big rooms, like big living rooms. It held about 130 people and everybody had to be seated, nobody would be allowed standing. Up above, that was Lalor's private living quarters. So down below you had an ordinary bar and there was no singing down there. In the lounge they didn't have a bar as such, they had a little hatch under the stairs, enough for one person to work it. Then you had about three people on the floor serving. People sat around tables and in chairs and everything was packed. Now people didn't have to pay to get in but they paid extra for their drink. Say a pint of Guinness would be a shilling, they'd have to pay one shilling and three pence. It opened at half past seven and was full at eight. It did a good business, especially in the summer time you would bottle about eight hogsheads, five Guinness's and three ales, in a *week* in July and August. And there were roughly seventy-two dozen bottles in each of those, so you're talking about 570 dozen of bottled stout or bottled beer that was sold *per week*.

"Anybody who was here in Dublin, if they took a drink, it was a *must* to go to Lalor's. We got people from Cabra on the northside, from Dun Laoghaire, from Crumlin. See, six or seven buses passed the door and so you got them from *all* areas and from all walks of life, from plumbers to foreign dignitaries and professional people, the lot. And everybody was dressed up as if they were going to the cinema or a hotel. Everyone wore a suit then. But people came from all over the world. We got a *huge* amount of English tourists. They might stay out in Bray but they came into Wexford Street every night. Oh, people were in there every night for two weeks while they came on their holiday. Oh, *every* night. Yeah. For people who were travelling and came to Ireland it was a *must*. It was as important to go to Lalor's at that time as it would be to go to the Wax Museum in London. They were queuing up to get in. You had to wait and if two people left you got two more in. And then you had to sit, there wasn't room to move around—it was civilised.

"On a Saturday night you had to screen the people and you had a doorman for the first half-hour. And after that you closed the door. But you screened them because they mightn't be the *right* type and they might have too much drink on them. You can *read* people. So you took them as they came and if they weren't right at the door they didn't get in. Then a fella comes in and he's very prim and proper and a few drinks then and he's a totally different person. And they come out *obnoxious* sometimes. They could be the nicest person and give them two whiskies and the whole personality changes, they just become arrogant and aggressive and everything goes wrong. Now Brendan Behan used to go in there but he wasn't encouraged. He had a rough, tough reputation at that time. He was pretty fond of drink and he was liable to do and say anything. I wouldn't give him a whiskey because he was a trouble-maker. You didn't have to give a reason, that was the law. And Jack Doyle, the famous boxer, he used to come in here. This particular woman had a fancy for him and he'd come in with her and he'd always try to get the money. You know, he'd order a whiskey but he'd say, 'Just give me a bit of ginger wine' and then you'd take the money from her but he'd want you to hand it back to *him*, which you wouldn't do. See, at that time women were paying him to go to parties and giving him money to go to a function with them, to be seen with him.

"The son, Tony Lalor, he did the MC, master of ceremonies. He called up the singers. Oh, I did it myself. Had to. The son at that time was about 21 and his job was to call the singers and keep order. To keep order was very important. See, at that stage they didn't have any amplification, so when you got up there was no microphone. And you needed to keep people quiet. And if people didn't keep quiet they didn't get any more drink. The people would object *themselves* because they wanted to hear a good singer. From time to time you would have to bar somebody for talking. It's a terrible slight on somebody if they're barred in a pub. It's the worst thing that can happen to them, it's a terrible slur.

"So you had an MC and a pianist. The first pianist I knew was named Busher. He was a brilliant pianist, an older man, and he used to write music. He used to work with variety shows around the country as a pianist and he could write music and sing. He'd compose songs and all that. Then the next fella that came was Ricky Taylor and he was a blind pianist and he played on the BBC at one time. One of the things he loved was when you asked him the time and he had a pocket watch and he'd open it and he was able to read the time by the feel. He just felt the hands and would tell you the exact time. But the MC'd call the singers. People got up and they were allowed two songs. Anyone, provided they were good singers. Oh, you wouldn't have any chance of getting up to sing unless you were a good singer. You might get up *once* but there wouldn't be a second time! Oh, fantastic competition. So each singer was allowed two songs and that'd be about eight minutes but in a lot of cases you had so many singers that you couldn't get them all in. If you had an awful lot of singers you'd break it down to one song. And that would be continuous.

"There was a lot of jealousy because they were *proud* of their singing and very conscious of what the people thought of it. Very competitive. People would send up a note on a bit of paper but the problem was that you wouldn't have enough time to get them all in. The songs were from opera to comedy. *Any* type of song . . . Frankie Lane, Frank Sinatra, John McCormack, you name it. They were all Frankie Lanes in their own mind! Or John McCormack. Some of them were absolutely great and you wouldn't hear a sound. They had the pianist and then one fella used to bring his own violin. The applause, that made their life, that *made* their life. And sometimes a customer might buy the singer a drink. I liked the singing. And there was one comedian or two that were outstanding. There was one particular fella and you always held him for the part of the night when people'd be getting a little bit noisy. You held him for that time because there was always complete silence when he was on. He could stay up there for ten or fifteen minutes telling jokes and singing.

"I spent five years there in Lalor's. Then from there I went to Ballsbridge and then to New York. Then I came back home and in October 1958 bought the Wexford Street pub where I had worked. Now while I was in America Lalor's business went down, down, down. I think the old man's health wasn't good and his son had no interest. And things then, in the fifties, were generally pretty bad. So we bought it and the first night we opened there was no crowd. It was that bad. And I wondered, 'Have I gone mad in the head buying this?' The first week's turnover was £199. I still have the records. So we decided to do it up and put a bar upstairs and new seating. Oh, it was still a singing pub. We put in draft Guinness upstairs and then it really got popular. See, you couldn't get a pint upstairs in Lalor's time, he wouldn't let you. It was just served down below but you could *not* bring a pint upstairs. Just bottles upstairs. That was his rule. So when we got in the bar upstairs business went *way* up. I remember taking in £110 on Saturday night and that was a great night, that was an achievement. And when I bought the pub we put in toilets for women. We had three huge rooms on the third floor and from 1958 to 1965 we lived above the pub.

"I never even dreamt that I could own a pub. I didn't even know how to approach going to the bank. But you're always dreaming of owning *something*, but a pub seemed to be *way* beyond your means. But being a barman, that was the stepping stone. Starting off you had to pay your first [Guinness] order. And after about two or three months then if your credit rating was good enough you were put on a month's credit. But you could only sell Guinness. Couldn't sell any other stout. You had to put it on the label, 'Bottled by so-and-so who sells no other brown stout in bottles.' Guinness printed that on the labels. But like at that time there was also Beamish. And it was unfair because it was a *monopoly*! They had a monopoly and they used it. And when the Guinness traveller or inspector came in, no matter what other representative was sitting at the counter, they had to stand by and let him come in. He might be a cigarette representative or anybody but when the Guinness man came he had to step aside. And if he *didn't* get that respect you got a letter from the company complaining that their rep *didn't* receive the courtesy from you. Oh, when the Guinness man walked in it would be the equivalent of a tax inspector walking in today, the same fear, 'What's going to happen now?' And they *used* that power too. And now if you were *caught* selling any stout other than Guinness's—like Beamish—well, you had to put an apology in the papers that would read something like, 'We, the undersigned, apologise to Arthur Guinness and Company for selling a product other than theirs.' It would appear in the three daily papers where you'd see legal notices. It would have to be in a prominent position. And if you didn't apologise you wouldn't get any more Guinness. It was unfair because it was a monopoly. That lasted until about 1959 or maybe a little later.

"Then you had whiskey inspectors that'd come in and he'd say, 'I'll have two glasses of that whiskey' and he'd put a half of that into a little bottle and half into another bottle and seal them. And he left one with you and he took the other one away to be analysed. And if the strength of that was under 30 UP [underproof]—that was the recognised strength—you'd go to court and *no* court would listen to you. *You* were responsible—even though it might *come in* like that. You'd get the full headlines in the paper. This is one offence you could never quash, selling whiskey under strength. Very serious. That was very detrimental to your business cause if you were caught that appeared in the paper. And in a very simple way you could be caught because at night somebody might buy a whiskey and ginger ale or soda and the pub'd close and he'd say, 'Look, I didn't touch that, leave it down for me until tomorrow night.' And a young apprentice might pour it back into the bottle and suddenly there goes your strength. Oh, a genuine mistake. So the advice that everybody'd get is when somebody gives back whiskey put it into the measure and if it's *more* than the measure, well then, don't put it back into the bottle because it could be ice, water, lemonade. That's a thing you learned as you go along.

"Looking back on it all, I think the publican's life at that time was probably better and he got more enjoyment. There wasn't so much of this high-powered professional stuff that's crept into it. At that time you didn't have all the laws and the security regulations. It's a *very* tough business now, very competitive. The *money's* gone so big. To give you an idea, we bought the Wexford Street pub for £4,750. And we sold it for £30,000. Now you're talking about a million and a half! That's big money to pay back to the bank."

JOHN RYAN—AGE 76

A half-century ago he was publisher of the literary magazine Envoy *and publican of the famed Bailey. J. P. Donleavy called him 'your true Dubliner . . . if this city were ever thought to have had a king he was John Ryan".*
Barman Paddy O'Brien credits Ryan with being the catalyst in transforming McDaid's into a great literary pub. Ryan would daily ensconce himself in McDaid's where he was a magnet for the literati of his day—Brendan Behan, Patrick Kavanagh, Gainor Crist, Brian O'Nolan, Austin Clarke and myriad others. Commonly he had to play the role of peacemaker when rows arose among the egotistical writers. His following recollections of those halcyon days were orally recorded a few months before his death in 1992.

"In the post-World War II period there was a new spirit. We were aware that there was a big change happening in our lives and to our environment. It was a feeling that we were getting somewhere. At this time Davy Byrne's was still the most celebrated pub, and the Palace and the Pearl with probably more journalists than anything else. But the Dolphin Hotel, which had a lovely old bar and accommodated everybody, it seemed to catch the spirit of the times better than any other place I knew in the late forties. There'd be intellectuals and writers at the Dolphin. Oh, free political expression. It was ideas and arguments. We were very tolerant and very fair people. We used those pubs like the Dolphin and the Pearl for ambience.

"I had the Bailey in the late forties, early fifties. It was rather declining and I shot a bit of adrenalin into the corpse of it. There's nothing like reviving a place that has been up and is now gone down. I thought it was a great challenge, a delightful challenge. I began working on the pub itself and got down to the nitty-gritty. Each day brought its own problems and every day I'd think out answers. For example, we were the first to make it a mandatory law that a pub could serve anything it wanted. The Bailey was the first to do that. I proved that I could serve full meals but I didn't necessarily do it every day at the drop of a hat. But we did a dinner in the evening and that brought a very good crowd. Food and drink made it very popular. I thoroughly enjoyed my ten years in the Bailey. An extraordinary thing about it in all the years—and some of them were tumultuous years—no one was ever *barred* in the Bailey. I managed a pub without having to bar people, never had to bar a single person, including Patrick Kavanagh and Myles na gCopaleen. To me, that was the most stunning thing of all—because they could be difficult! There were people saying, 'God, it must have been a nightmare for you' and I've always said 'No, on the contrary, I've always enjoyed it. I liked the publican business.'

"I started going to McDaid's about 1945. McDaid's was then a dowdy little pub in a forgotten part of the city really. Oh, McDaid's was the plainest possible pub you could ever think of, that was one of the things that I liked, the very plainness of it. And 90 per cent of the people in it were working class. In those days I published *Envoy* and people would come in who were seeking me out and I could help them getting to meet anyone they wanted to meet. And at McDaid's they could fill the stage with characters. There'd be Behan, principally, who was a marvellous stage filler, and Kavanagh and O'Nolan and Donleavy, and Tony Cronin was one of the great intellectuals of the period. And Liam O'Flaherty was one man you'd see there quite a lot. Quite regularly you'd see five of them together there. And they'd converse with their friends, their coevals as it were. In their pub conversations they'd endlessly be talking about Katherine Mansfield and Joyce was never off their minds. He was the subject of *continuous* correction, in very critical ways. And Yeats would often come up. Yes, continuously come up. They could be critical enough. I remember Kavanagh saying once that he could 'do without Yeats'.

"Paddy O'Brien was there and I remember him as a very young man. Paddy was a very good stage manager. He was very diplomatic. He would have made a great bank president or a great publican. It was not an easy job to run a pub that was the most popular and potentially the most explosive pub situation in the country of Ireland. But he kept his cool and kept his nerves. Generally the humour was good but conversations could get a little bit hectic. Paddy did once or twice actually bar Kavanagh but it would be very rare to happen when you took into account the hundreds of times it *could* have happened. And Behan was probably the most barred one of all.

"Imminent fights were always on the horizon. *Tensions*, really, with Behan and Kavanagh and O'Nolan and Donleavy. Brendan Behan'd come in and then Kavanagh would drift in and you could nearly plot where they'd be in the pub. And they'd keep the statutory two paces or three paces away from each other. They were totally different. Behan was erratic and had shafts of genius. It was his *wit* really. But Behan felt an insecurity which manifested itself in very many ways and he could be *deliberately* difficult. But Behan had a good kind heart. But I considered Kavanagh to have the best mind of the whole lot of them. That was my considered belief. It was based on my personal knowledge and also the work he was doing at the time. I had great admiration for him, and still have. He was a wonderfully good writer, he was very amusing. I think it was Cronin who said that he was 'mordantly funny'. And to Kavanagh, his work had to be praised by the right people, above all praised by the people whom he admired. Like Myles na gCopaleen, he admired him *very* much. Kavanagh was very literate and the printed word meant a lot to him. And Kavanagh often advised other people to never even *attempt* to write poetry. He'd say, 'There are very, very few people in the world that can do it and *I'm one* of them and therefore I know what I'm talking about.'

"Behan and Kavanagh would stir it up at times. They could be critical of one another. It could be a series of small irritations that would mount to a crescendo. Behan in his natural behaviour was a more aggressive man. Kavanagh was a cowardly man by comparison. I don't think they did any harm to each other—but I don't think they did any *good* either. I never heard Brendan ever express any admiration for Kavanagh. Verbal abuse was the actual ammunition. Oh, yes, verbal abuse was the main weapon. Brendan was the rogue. But I don't think it was that genuine, all that animosity between them. There was a lot of publicity-seeking in it. But to keep pace with Brendan it took some doing. You had to be very firm and adamant about it with all of them so that no one pushed anyone else around, either intellectually or verbally. You had to see to it that no one got an easy victory over anybody. Once or twice I couldn't keep out of it because I was so near the centre of it. I was at the fulcrum of the thing and I felt that it was very hard to keep away from it. I'm not saying that any of them didn't have kind hearts. They were notably kind hearted. I think about those times often and it seems like another era. I loved that period."

PADDY O'BRIEN—AGE 74

Anthony Cronin called him "one of the greatest barmen of all time". Paddy was probably the best-known and most loved Dublin barman of his day. For nearly forty years at

McDaid's pub he diplomatically presided over the city's literary luminaries.
He had to cope daily with the antics and eccentricities of Behan, Kavanagh,
O'Nolan and a host of other gifted but temperamental writers. In 1972 when
McDaid's was sold Paddy moved over to Grogan's pub as manager—but the
remaining literary set faithfully followed him. He passed away in 1989, just
seven months after this taped oral history was recorded.

"I'm Dublin, though my people are from Meath. We lived off the North Circular
Road and I went to school at Brunswick Street till I done my leaving at about 17.
Actually, I went into the pub trade by accident because I used to go on holidays
every summer to the country and in Navan there was a job going in the local pub-
grocery. It was *the* shop in town, a big grocery and pub and grain store, they done
everything. So I started out and done an apprenticeship. I done everything. I
swept floors, filled sacks with grain, helping out at the bar, washing down
mirrors, polishing brass first thing every morning. And you'd have to wash the
front of the shop with a bucket and brush in the morning.

"Then I went to Foxrock which was one of the poshest golf clubs at that time
and I took over the bar. That was some hard chore because weekends you *never*
seen daylight from Friday till Monday because all the concentration was on playing
golf on the weekend. All barristers and solicitors and business people from the city
and they'd play poker at night and you had the bells in the bar for the rooms that
would be looking for service and you'd have to dash up to them and take their
orders and this would be going till 4.00 in the morning. So I gave that a year.

"Anyhow, I answered an ad for a pub job and it happened to be McDaid's. I
got an interview with a little old lady and I seen Mr McDaid himself. I was about
22 at the time. And I was told I'd be given a fortnight [trial] and if I passed I'd
be brought in for another interview. So I got the job but it was a *dreadful* place.
It was in a backstreet and you wouldn't see a soul after about 8.00 or 9.00 at
night. The only literary pub that was alive then was Davy Byrne's. That was the
'in' place where you'd find St John Gogarty and those of his generation. They all
drank there and made it a literary pub. But McDaid's was nothing at all. It was
incredible, just an ordinary pub with snugs and spittoons and you'd have elderly
men in little groups spitting and all this sort of filth. And TB became rampant
but you had to wash out those spittoons and hose them out. Anyway, I was saying
to myself, 'I won't be here long.' And Mr McDaid, he was a very, very shy man,
very nice, quiet, shy man. But he'd be on the dry for maybe six months and then
he'd go on the booze. And then he'd be away to dry out and you'd have to run
the place yourself. I don't know how he ever come to be a publican at all. But
there was another barman there, much older than I was, and I got on very well
with him.

"So one day I said to Mr McDaid, 'The only way this pub is going to take off
is if you *tear out* the whole place. It's a small pub and you want more space.
Open it up.' So it took off from that. And John Ryan, who is a *founder member*
of that public house, he's the man who made it a literary pub. It just *happened*.
John, his people were wealthy people property-wise and business-wise and John

could have the luxury of doing his own thing. He went to college and he went to university and he come out and was a very literary-minded man and had the resources to start up his own magazine. So he got this thing called *Envoy* going and he'd come over to McDaid's and have a drink. And then, bit by bit, anybody who'd want to meet him to get a story in *Envoy*, they all came to McDaid's. He might just say, 'I'll be in McDaid's at 1.00, so hop over there.' So then, bit by bit, it all come into a circle, all types of literary people. You know, poets and story writers and you name it. From that on it just mushroomed.

"Then McDaid's was the 'in' place if you wanted to *find* somebody. It used to be that once it came 5.00 the people that worked in the area were gone and you had an empty shop. But when the artists took over, the literary people, it was 'go, go' all day long. There was always something happening. You had Paddy Kavanagh, Behan and Brian O'Nolan and Gainor Crist, and Donleavy. And you had people coming back from England and they'd buy for all their friends. Then you had Americans coming along, going to college, and they'd be wanting to get in on the act, on the literary scene. There was always a bit of crack going on. There was this *great blend*.

"Like you'd have this house painter and you'd ask, 'Now how does he fit in with these literary people?' Well, he'd just blend in with them, voice his own opinion. I had a window cleaner and his whole hobby was to go in and sit amongst them and listen. Sit, blend in, *voice* his opinion. Cause he read books too! He might say, 'Kavanagh, that's not right!' This is how the thing blended so well. No one ever showed anybody down. I just treated people the same. Ah, there was no fussing over him cause he was Paddy Kavanagh or Myles na gCopaleen . . . they were all just ordinary to me. And [later] people would ask me, 'How do you make this place tick?' and I'd say, 'I don't make it tick, it just happened.' It was a *great blend*.

"And now the conversation at McDaid's . . . *great*! I can't tell you of any other pubs that'd be in the same category. Actually, most pubs wouldn't put up with it, the type of people in the shop and all the conversation and all the arguments about things of the day from the paper that was happening and in London and it'd all be going on and on. See, others [publicans], they were used to a straight-laced pub and just serving drink and fellas talking about a football match or horse racing which is the biggest topic of conversation in the city pub. So this was too lively for other publicans. Other publicans weren't inclined to go for literary people, they were just in it for the money. But I grew up with it. But other fellas might come in here and say, 'They must be all mad here.' To other people it might have been a nut house. Like there'd be fellas that are argumentative after a few drinks or might want to tell you stories and so you'd hear stories about people's lives. It's like you were in a confession box. But to me it was normal practice and I *loved* going to work.

"Oh, buying rounds was in then in a *big way*. And if you had money you spent it! Cause when you hadn't got it someone else bought for you. So you could come into the shop without any money and sit up there and say your piece and be put on the round. Cause somebody'd say, 'What are you having?' So you'd be on the rounds. See, money was very scarce. The literary fellas had plenty of talent but were short on money in those days. But they could write a nice story and might get £5 for it. Now £5 in a pub, you could get eight pints for a pound in those days. But you had £5 and you had ten other people too to supply with booze. Now Brian O'Nolan, Myles na gCopaleen, he used to write an article for *The Irish Times* every morning and he was a *most extraordinary man*. And he would be drunk every day at least by 2.00. And I'd often read his article in the *Times* at lunch hour the next day and it'd be *powerful* stuff. And I'd wonder *where* did he get time to do it? He must have been home and slept till about midnight and then got up to the typewriter and banged away. It would have to be.

"I first met Brendan Behan when he was a very young man and I didn't even know who he was because he was an apprentice as a painter. There was this young lad in McDaid's on a Saturday morning and the lads he was with went away and left him. He was only a kid about 17 and he was really *gone* [drunk]. It was a lovely summer day and we had a back entrance where we used to stack our crates and what have you. So I put Brendan out there sitting on a box so he'd be all right there and could go to sleep. And I said I'd have a look at him about 4.00. Anyway, it came to evening and I got out to have a look at him and here now he's *lying on the ground*. And out of the side of his mouth a trickle of porter and a pool of porter going down the alley. So, anyway, I straightened him up, took him in and washed him up and off he went. And I said to someone, 'Who was that young man?' and he said, 'His name is Behan.' And he had no literary talents *in those days*. But he was full of devilment, dancing and singing and talking and making up bits of songs and generally 'messing'. Then [some years later] Brendan and a whole lot of guys that were IRA men who were interned in Britain during the war started using McDaid's. They had IRA connections and Sinn Féin connections. They had been involved in putting bombs in letter boxes—which is a most despicable thing—but that was war. So they'd be hanging around. So we had political *and* literary types. They'd spend the whole day. I'd say by 11.00 in the morning it'd be a fairly full pub, all reading their papers. I never barred them. I put them out now maybe for today, for getting obnoxious or shouting. Brendan was the only one now that used to use a four-letter word. And I'd say to Brendan, 'Brendan, would you *ever stop* using that four-letter word?' 'Oh, Paddy, I'm sorry, I'm sorry.' He didn't even know he was doing it. And then he'd go back again telling another story and it's out with the four-letter word.

"Brendan was big and robust. And an open-necked shirt and never wore a tie and the shirt would always be hanging out. All pulled out and maybe not buttoned. And a big head of curly hair—real rough. That was the image of Brendan. A very lively guy and full of fun. And very good natured. I always remember that this one man had a wife and two little children and they'd always be coming in looking for him. They'd be living here and there and wouldn't be paying their way and somebody'd have to help them out to pay their landlord. But one morning Brendan says to me, 'Paddy, give me five bob.' He wanted to go somewhere to meet somebody so I gave him the five bob. And who comes in the door but the children, about 7 or 8 years old, looking for their daddy. And he gives them a half-crown each. So the money I gave him he gave away again. That was the *nature* of the man. A lovely man like that. *Flowing* with nature.

"But it was just the image that people had of him, saying he's a louse and a foul-mouth because he used four-letter words and he'd sing these old bawdy songs. But, see, four or five pints in Brendan Behan and he'd be falling around the place. He *couldn't* drink. He had the image of being a big drinker but he just couldn't *hold* it. But he never put on an act. He was always himself. Now he was a bit of a showman all right and he'd like to be in the middle of things if there was a party going on. But Kavanagh and Behan didn't get on well at all. Because he was afraid of Behan. He looked on him as rough. And I'd always try to explain to him 'Brendan Behan is a nice guy. Just try and be nice to him.' 'No, *never*, he's just a bowsie.' Brendan used to try and be friendly with him but Brendan could never get through to him. He'd always push Brendan away.

"I was very fond of Paddy Kavanagh. People would say he was an old grouch, but he was anything but. He was a very alive, simple-minded man. And a genius. I didn't realise it at the time. No, I just saw him as a country man. But behind all that you had all this beautiful stuff. Do you know this poem 'Raglan Road'? Well, he wrote that for a woman. Her husband at the time was Minister for Education and his wife was a tall raven-haired lady and Kavanagh fell in love with her. And that ballad, 'Raglan Road', is to her. Now when you read that it's so *full of passion* and so full of *Kavanagh*. And I'd say to meself, 'Jesus, how the hell could he flow out with that sort of stuff?', the man that was always in here telling jokes and this sort of stuff. Where did he get the *time* for poetry, to put it down? And I remember lads that'd be leaving college and they'd be writing stuff and I'd say, 'We'll ask Paddy to read that, see what he thinks of it.' And he'd read it and say, 'Oh, now let me tell you about that.' And he'd just tell them that they'd want to be far better than that, so they wouldn't pursue that type of life because they weren't going to do well at it. Not to belittle their stuff but because his stuff was far better and *he* was making no money on it. Cause here was Paddy Kavanagh's lovely verses of poems and *no money* coming out of it and here was these young fellas coming into McDaid's with ambitions of being poets and writers. It was his way of telling them. Paddy was very blunt.

"Kavanagh'd be sitting back there behind a big marble table at the back. And he'd get in there and pore over the papers and he had an *amazing* way of reading the papers. He wasn't like the average guy who'd just turn them over, he'd throw them away, read a page and it would just be thrown away. And Sunday morning he was outside the church. Oh, he was a *good* church-goer. Anyway, he'd go to Mass, have a chat with the auxiliary bishop, and he'd come then and sit on this bollard in the road by this newsagent's shop just beside a bridge. Well, he'd go in and bring out all the English papers and sit on that bollard and he'd go through all those papers and they'd be flying down Baggot Street as he read them. And after reading them he'd end up with nothing. It's *incredible*.

"Paddy used to be associated with *The Bell* and *The Irish Catholic* and all those magazines. He'd just get a bit of inspiration and write it down, a sort of feature story. Like I'll tell you a very funny story. This bloke, he was a painter, he'd a spray painting business. He'd go into the countryside and farmers would be fresh with their money from the crops and he'd tell them their farm and sheds needed a bit of a touch-up and he'd give them a price. So one summer they brought Kavanagh with them. And Kavanagh was having the life of Riley. They were away three whole weeks wining and dining and sitting in pubs and drinking the best and chatting all day long and Kavanagh *loved* it! Oh, he was a country man, you know . . . mad about it. So the lads gave him a great time. Now he came back home and there was a thing called the *Farmers Journal* which goes out to all farmers to tell them what's happening in the farming world. So he *writes an article* about the spray painting gang and all the hookey that went on when they put on one coat of paint when they *should* have put on three and all this. And there was *war*! 'Jesus, did you read that?', says yer man, 'look what Kavanagh done! He *ruined* us. Can't go into the country ever again.' He *exposed* them. But I explained to this man that he didn't do that for malice, he done it for the money, for a few quid. But there was *vengeance* for him. And the next thing was that Paddy had been in a pub and was leaning over the canal bridge and somebody comes up behind him and just tips him over into the canal. Just got him by the legs when he was leaning over—and he half-drunk—and tipped him up and he went head first into the canal. And, lucky enough, the canal water was very low and it was all muck. No one ever knew who did it but they said it was the men in the article that had sworn vengeance against him. Anyhow, Kavanagh was picked out of the canal and brought to the local hospital and washed and cleaned and put to bed. And on the Monday morning he comes into McDaid's with a whole new tweed suit—looking like a farmer—and I says, 'You look great.' *'You don't know what happened to me'*, he says, *'over the weekend. I'm a lucky man to be alive at all! Begod, it was only for that muck.'*

"I loved me life at that stage. *Loved* the job. Loved the crack. And when McDaid's was going up for sale I tried to buy it with another man. It was going for £78,000. We were going to halve it. Now Tuesday morning was the auction and comes [the previous] Friday evening and in came one of the auctioneers and says, 'Paddy, a bit of bad news for you. There's £80,000 offered for the house *before* the auction. It's a woman from London, they own a chain of pubs in London and a few pubs here in Ireland and they've got money to burn and she wants a literary pub.' So we says, 'We've come this far, we'll go to £80,000 too, what's another few thousand?' So the auction came and it went to £87,000! She kept bidding and bidding and bidding. So that was the end of me. And all the other city publicans having nothing to do with it and me thinking I have the whole field to meself . . . and then out of the blue.

"At first I was thinking of retiring cause I thought that it was all over. Kavanagh had died and Brendan was dead and so was Myles na gCopaleen and Pope Mahoney and a lot of people like that who *made up* the place. They were all gone, bit by bit they died. John Ryan was still around. What was coming in in their place was more the student type. The writers, really, had gone. But *still* it was an arty pub. Anyhow, Tommy [Smith], he used to frequent McDaid's a lot because he used to love this literary scene. So Tommy told me about this other pub [Grogan's] that was going for sale in the area. And he bought it and I come over. And *all McDaid's* people come right across! All the crowd moved across cause it was so near. So she never got her literary pub. It was the reverse. McDaid's fell asunder. She put in a barman who knew *no one*. And all the people were saying, 'Where's Paddy O'Brien?' And so they all came across looking for their pals.

"I loved the whole life at McDaid's. To *know* them they were *lovely* people. Often I'll be sitting in me home reading a book or a paper and I'll say to meself, 'There *never* will be a McDaid's again.' Cause I expect back in the age when you had music, you know, Mozart and his crowd, and the place gone mad with music . . . well, the same thing happened at McDaid's with writers and poets and artists. They all seemed to live in the *one time*. And they're *not there* any more, and there's no one taking their place. There's other people writing stuff but there's nobody as *big* as them or as prominent as them. Or writing such stuff. I loved me life at that stage. I *loved that*."

TOMMY SMITH—AGE 54

As a young man he did his drinking in McDaid's pub, attracted by the literary ambience. It was a quirk of fate that in 1972 he bought Grogan's pub on exactly the same day that McDaid's was sold. When he promptly installed his good friend Paddy O'Brien as manager the entire McDaid's literary crowd followed him. Today, with his shock of grey hair and gregarious manner he looks the part of publican in Dublin's only genuine literary pub. The social mix of writers, artists and musicians creates a discernible artistic-literary atmosphere. Tommy relishes his role and is proud to be carrying on the old McDaid's tradition.

"I was born in Cavan, from a small farming background. I came here to Dublin when I was 15 for economic reasons, it was the only job I could get. I got a job in McCauley's pub on the South Circular Road and I served a five-year apprenticeship. My wages were £3. 11. 10. I got digs and I paid £2.5s. And one of the first things I was told by my mother when I came to Dublin—and you're told a *lot* of things when you go to the large city—she told me to join the *library*. As you can gather, I had very little money to live on so to join the library was a very good idea and it appealed to me *anyway* because I had spent more time reading than I did at farm work—anything to avoid farm work. As a youngster I used to take out the newspaper and read it and my father would say to me, 'You'll blind yourself' or 'Books won't feed you.' So I read from early on and would have been familiar with Behan and Kavanagh and I read *The Borstal Boy* when it came out. And I loved *Tarry Flynn* and loved Kavanagh, that's one of the books that sticks in my memory because it comes from the same rural background that I had come from and I could identify every soul in it.

"Then I worked at a pub called Killane's on the corner of Gardiner Street and Parnell Street. It was a tough area. It was sometimes referred to as 'the four corners of hell'. You had Mick Scanlon's pub on the other corner and you had the Blue Lion and a pub called Healey and Fitzpatrick's on the other corner. I was there for five and a half years. It was working-class people and after a year you got to know everybody. Oh, but you were on trial. You knew you were going to be watched and on trial so they could see what you were like, whether you were soft or hard or whatever. They were *wonderful* people, very loyal, very kind. They were very much inter-married and committed to the community. And a lot of roughnecks, toughs, wandered in and honestly you would never have any trouble with them because you knew that there was always somebody in the pub who'd say, 'Didn't you hear what he [Tommy] said?' And they *went*. Oh, it was *their* pub. Oh, yeah. Oh, it was *their* house, it was their *home*. And men stood or sat in their own spots, *every one* of them and you could rely on them for their habits. Oh, it was part of their life. The slate was part of that, and a lot of honesty. For instance, there was one guy there who used to get the loan of about £3 off me, a fair bit of money then, every week. And it was *religiously* paid back when he got paid. And I knew one man there, he worked in a coalyard, and he found a purse with about £5 which would be the equivalent of £40 or £50 now. And do you know what he did? He had her address and he got on the bus out to Crumlin to deliver that purse to the woman. Oh, yes. That's the type of people they were.

"Now I had heard of McDaid's, it had a good reputation as a pub where you'd meet interesting literary people. Actually, I drank in McDaid's very early on in my drinking days. So I knew Paddy O'Brien quite well. Yes, I liked McDaid's and I liked the *atmosphere*. Though I have a limited education I'm quite interested in literature and I read quite a bit and I'm interested in the arts. So I was drawn to the atmosphere. And it was just a good functional drinking room with a high ceiling, nice counter, and you could sit back along the wall and have a pleasant conversation. You see, what makes a bar attractive is people, their *presence* in a pub. It had a *homely* atmosphere. And Paddy created that. Oh, the publican [or head barman] sets the tone of the place. It was an interesting, comfortable pub and I can well imagine people being inspired to write in it —and I can well imagine people spending *too much* time in it.

"Oh, it had a literary flavour, by all means. Anybody was liable to drop into it . . . university professors who drank too much, people who aspired to write, those who wrote very well, well-known actors and actresses, visiting American millionaires, the whole lot arrived. It was a human chemistry and the excellence of it. They were people with a very broad grasp. And quite a few people who spent a lot of time there had come out of prisons in England, IRA men and people like that. There were literary people, interested in literature, and were able to write literary pieces, like Des McNamara and Eddie Connell and Richard Timmons. And I knew some of the younger people who came on the scene like Aidan Murphy who ran a broadsheet and operated out of McDaid's. And some of the Dubliners started going to McDaid's in the middle sixties, Luke Kelly and all. And John Jordan was another great frequenter of McDaid's who [later] transferred his allegiance to Grogan's pub. He was a great literary person who was a wonderful literary critic and a wonderful agile mind. And John Ryan was a wonderful man. His interest in literature and the visual arts and the theatre was total. His presence would have been felt. And there was another very interesting man named Kevin Monaghan, an American who never went back home after the war, one of the GIs and a *very* interesting person. He was an aesthetic eccentric, a *dandy* dresser, you know, impeccable and whirly whiskers which he'd be waxing away. One of the pleasures of going into McDaid's was seeing him leaning against the bar. He was a friend of J. D. Salinger's, Kevin had served with him in the war. He was an artist, he painted and he dabbed a bit in antiques, a very cultured man and would *not* tolerate bullshit for *one* minute. Like he would just talk to people and then if they started bullshitting he'd just turn away and they didn't exist. They didn't exist. They could talk *at* him.

"And I knew Patrick Kavanagh and Brendan Behan. I went into McDaid's once about 5.00 and I called for a pint of stout and I was reading the evening paper and Kavanagh walked in and he sat down beside me and he looks at the paper and sees that it's the final and he whips it from under my arm and says 'the *late* one!' And he took my paper and went back to the racing page and he looked at it and then rolled it up into a ball and hands it back to me dishevelled and says to me 'Do you back them?' and I said 'No', and he said '*Better off*!' My *Herald* got the treatment.

"And I know the Behan family quite well. But when I met Brendan my impressions weren't great. Yes, he was an extremely talented man who tended to act a bit. Now even when I was a youngster I could see that he acted a bit. I remember him coming into the pub where I served my time and he was told to leave eventually, that he had had enough. This was a feature of the man. He never impressed me. He had an *extremely sharp* mind, you know, it's a great pity. Behan was extremely sharp, polished in 'Dublinese' terms, but probably an unhappy man to some degree. He probably couldn't write without drink and wrote then when he was drunk and he got involved in this business of being a showman. And he *liked* the show, liked the newspapers writing about him. Anybody could get drunk and disorderly but it was Brendan Behan that got the front of the newspapers and I think he fell in love with it. Oh, but it was a burden to him because he craved attention.

"Paddy O'Brien was a *wonderful* man and he's a very hard act to follow. Paddy created the atmosphere at McDaid's. There was great sadness at his death but death is part of life and the graveyards are full of people who couldn't be done without. But Paddy loved to get up in the morning, shave, wash and go to work. He *loved* it, this routine. Paddy *hopped* around at 72 years of age the day before he died. Paddy was an extraordinarily energetic man for his age. And his word was *law*, that's the type of respect he had. And he was very kind to a lot of people. Paddy had a very keen eye, he was watching all the time and he could spot trouble. Paddy's temper was really only a two-minute temper. If it rose it dropped very quickly. But he was a keen observer and he could spot some piece that didn't fit into the jigsaw and he would say, 'He shouldn't be there with them, he's not in that company and he'll cause trouble.' This kind of thing he could spot. And he could spot an intellectual basher, a guy who goes in to take them [literary figures] on. I've seen that happen. Like I remember having a drink with Ulick O'Connor and his book on Behan had just come out which suggested that he might have been homosexual. And in comes this guy and he came and said, 'Mr O'Connor, I don't think Brendan was queer.' And Ulick didn't lift his head, he just said, 'Did you read the book?' 'No, but I'm going to.' 'Well, when you do, come back.' And that was it.

"Any publican or barman would have to spot trouble coming, it's part of the job. What makes a pub—and I say this totally—is the people behind the bar. I like people, I like people a *lot*, and I like meeting people. And you don't know *who* you're going to meet today, you could have an *array* of people that would be interesting coming in one day, but then for a week you mightn't see anybody who would be of any interest. But you have to have a fair understanding of people, a respect for people. Like even a person who you would call a roughneck, a bowzie, you have to consider that they're human beings for a start. Like they *do* have something, you don't just abuse them totally, you have to treat them as human beings. We all have our defects of one sort or another and they're wearing their defects on their shoulder. You have to appeal to people rather than abuse them. Every time that door opens you have to make up your mind, 'Is this guy drunk? Is he liable to cause trouble?' And it's only folly to be other than diplomatic. You have the right to bar. It's a personal judgment. There are people who are barred for life because they've done something that's unpardonable such as throwing a glass. Somebody who's done that once is liable to do it again. You have to keep an orderly house. There's hardly a pub in Dublin that hasn't plenty of people barred.

"Up to the time McDaid's was sold it was still a literary pub. And we bought Grogan's at the very same time that McDaid's was sold. That was in 1972. Two of us were buying Grogan's, Paddy Kennedy and myself, and both of us still control it. So McDaid's went for sale and we were in the process of buying Grogan's at exactly the same time. Would you believe that the two houses exchanged hands on the same day! Which was *purely* a coincidence. The end of November it was. And I was talking to Paddy O'Brien and I said 'There'll be a job for you over with us if you want it.' And so Paddy came over as manager and most of the people from McDaid's, they all shifted to Grogan's. So Paddy was taken on and there he was until the day he died and that's the way he wanted it. He *loved* it. And he took the vast majority of the literary crowd with him. Ah, there was a lot of literary and artistic people still around at that stage. You had an array, like Aidan Murphy, Michael Hartness, Tony Cronin, McDara Woods and John Ryan came and Ben Kiely, and Liam O'Flaherty was an extremely frequent visitor to Grogan's in those days, sitting on his own drinking gin and tonics. They *all* shifted to Grogan's.

"Ah, Grogan's is a very cosmopolitan pub, you could meet *anybody* in it. They usually tend to talk about artistic things, about what's going on in the latest published book, like the wonderful book of poems by Michael Hartnett. And then Michael will come in and talk to them about it. Grogan's is very much like anyone's sitting room, it's not very well done up. But that's what the people *want*. A telly—no. A radio—no. Background music—no. If you want to *talk* you go there. So it *would* be a literary pub and there's quite a lot of the visual arts [people] drink in Grogan's now as well. Quite a lot of artists drink in Grogan's . . . and aspiring artists. I would see it as an artistic-literary pub. And I would like to see it continue. I myself am a member of the Council of Poetry of Ireland and I like to be associated with literature and if there's anything happening in literature I would love to see it happening *there*. And there's not as much serious drinking, a lot of the people who write today they don't drink in the same way. Like you would never recreate that phrase, 'heavy drinking literary people who should have wrote more'. But then I've seen people who gave up drink and gave up either being a writer or an artist, or stopped being a *good* artist. That happens. See, its a *madness*. It's an inspiration some of them get. It's a very uncertain existence.

"The publican is still well respected, he's part of the community. And in Ireland the pub is still the main social centre for the community. It's a *club* for a lot of people. And, by the way, when I talk about pubs—unfortunately—I would exclude a lot of these awfully big, huge, dreadful, horrible places with long bars and big lounges and *no* intimacy. It's just a money-making place. Like the vulgarity of the guy spending recently £1.5 million for a pub and then knocked down the premises and built a new one. To my way of thinking that's alien. To me, they don't count as pubs. They only understand money. You had a period in the trade in the sixties which was the 'formica age'. I have personally seen a pub where I worked, McCauley's, where the *finest* of mahogany fittings, the *finest* of marble tops and beautiful ornate counters were taken out and replaced by formica. Oh, what a *sin*! What a *disaster*! It made me *mad*, I couldn't believe it. Like that was alien to me because I'm a conservationist. It was a hatred of the old."

JACK CAGNEY—AGE 70

From behind the counter, he proclaims, 'I've seen the best in life and the worst in life.' At age 18, with a reference from his County Limerick parish priest, he got a job in the Oval Bar in Abbey Street. Years later he worked in the swank Doran's pub in Marlborough Street which had the first lounge in Dublin. He became a strong union man and was active in the "bitter" barmen's strike of 1955.

"I'm from a farming background in Limerick and I wanted to go to university for dairy science. But I failed the Irish test and I couldn't matriculate. And I happened to be in Dublin when I was 18 and that's how I got into the licensed trade. Now at that time all the top-class houses in Dublin were controlled by the union and you had to do an apprenticeship. At that time *all* the major public houses were between the two canals and Dublin was a small place, population about half a million. Everyone wanted to get as close as possible to O'Connell Street and the [Nelson's] Pillar was the *focal* point. You had the Scotch House, O'Meara's of the quay, Lloyd's and Madigan's and Mooney's. At that time 80 per cent of drinking in Dublin was done on O'Connell Street and off O'Connell Street. See, *everything* was in the centre of the city, that was *it*. You had Cleary's and Arnott's and the trams were still running and the cinemas were there. Now today it's the reverse, 80 per cent of the drinking is done in the suburbs. But back then everyone wanted to walk O'Connell Street on a Sunday morning. At that time the licensing laws on a Sunday were 2.00 to 5.00 and you had your Sunday stroll and everyone came into O'Connell Street to go window shopping, and to Grafton Street. Now on a Sunday outside Lloyd's pub and Madigan's and Mooney's there would be a *thousand* people waiting—it was thirst. Three thousand people every Sunday morning waiting for those three pubs to open. That's right. They'd take in a hell of a crowd.

"The best thing then was to get into a union house where you got good conditions and wages. If it wasn't a union house it was a family house or a small backstreet pub. Now I was told that there was a vacancy, an apprenticeship, at the Oval Bar on Middle Abbey Street. And I had to have a parish priest reference. Then I went down for an interview. It was *character* that they were looking for, and your appearance and elocution. I got a trial for six weeks and I started on 18 April 1941. Then I got a four-year contract. Twenty-five shillings a week and I had to pay for my digs at Gardiner Place and you had to get your laundry done. I had to have a certain standard of dress and appearance. Oh, a tie and properly shaved and your hands cleaned. And there was certainly an art to pulling a pint then. Slowness . . . not to rush . . . slow, slow, like a golf shot. Slow and let the pint settle. The pint at that time was about 90 per cent of your business and you *had* to be good. Oh, a barman had to have a reputation for drawing a good pint.

"At the Oval it was all business people. We used to attract an awful lot of journalists because the *Independent* was there and then we had the civil servants, shop assistants, chemists, drapers and the tradesmen. And stockbrokers and people in the legal profession. And Joe McGrath originally started the Irish Hospital Sweeps in the Oval Bar. The idea for the Sweeps originated in the Oval. And at that time all the film renters were in Abbey Street—RKO radio studios, Paramount Studios and Warner Brothers. They would be the people who would sell the films to the cinemas. They would be agents of the Hollywood studios. The top cinemas at that time was *the* thing for relaxation. You had the Savoy, Carlton, Adelphi. They were Americans and most of them Jewish and they were good customers, people with money at that time, and Scotch drinkers mostly. *All* business was done in pubs, all contracts were made. It didn't matter what deals, you'd come in and have a drink over it, that was *tradition*. Solicitors would do deals in pubs. And like now if you and I agree to rob a bank *we'd* meet in a pub! *All plans* were made in a pub.

"At that time the war was starting and things were pretty grim and all the drinks were rationed. We were on the quota system at that time. What Guinness did in the war years, instead of rationing they reduced the gravity of the drinks, the *strength* of the beer came down. The quality of the drinks came down so the prices were maintained all during the war years. But whiskey was very much rationed and only the major pubs had whiskey because they were whiskey bonders, they bought the whiskey raw and they bonded it. And pubs who had a big business with foreigners during the war had big quotas of Scotch. But if you were caught watering whiskey you were finished—the name of the house! *That* is the greatest sin you can commit in the licensed trade. Oh, the Corporation inspectors were going around. And if you lost your reputation you were gone!

"Then I was in Doran's pub on Marlborough Street from 1947 to 1954. The first lounge in Dublin was Doran's lounge in 1938, to compete against hotels. And right after the war they were *fantastic* years because the English people started to move and he advertised in America and people who would go to the Shelbourne and the Gresham, they would go to Doran's because that was the 'in' place at that time. There was a visitor's book there that was *that* high. It was all very plush, very modern seats and the toilets had to be immaculate. It was the only pub of its type in the city. See, Doran, he got New York experience and he would have any drink from any part of the world, he had it there. He was the first man to crack hotels, where he could give better service than a hotel.

"I reckon that Doran was fifty years ahead of his time and I'll tell you why. To be a barman in Doran's you had to be A-1. He was fantastic. He had a record there of your performance, for barmen, whether you were late or on time. He took all that down in writing and he could tell you all your faults and all your good points. He kept records on all the staff which was fantastic. There was twenty-six of us at that time. He was the *best* employer at the time and you were on bonuses. That's how a lot of publicans in Dublin were trained, in Doran's, at that time. You got the training and then you had a good reputation. Oh, very strict because that was an international bar. You had to be dressed immaculately and groomed properly. Now I was called at one time into the board room and when you were called you were kind of worried. That's where his office was, overhead in the building, and it was beautiful, the latest. And he says to me, 'Jack your hair is lovely groomed, your collar and tie is perfect, nice white coat, your trousers are beautifully pressed *but*', he says, 'you never polished your shoes this morning.' *That's* how meticulous he was.

"And you had to be a good listener and very discreet and not be interfering in people's conversations unless you were invited. Now in Doran's if you come in and want to light a cigar or cigarette and you were fumbling with the box of matches, well, I was supplied with a cigarette lighter and if I hadn't my lighter flat in your mouth before you could use your box of matches I was asleep on the job. And I had all the newspapers for you to read. I was trained in all these things, they were all gimmicks and you were anticipating the customer. And if you wanted a taxi, if you wanted to go to a race meeting, if you wanted a train or a bus or a plane, we had *all* the schedules there, that was part of it. Oh, *full alert* all the time. I reckon Doran's was the greatest thing as regards training assistants.

"But now there was a certain amount of jealousy [from other publicans] because Doran's attracted an awful lot of women in the lounge. If a young girl was seen coming into a lounge at that time she'd be looked upon as a kind of loose person. There was a bit of scandal, it wasn't the done thing. And if two women came in on their own and they accepted drink from two men and they were caught they must be barred. That was the way it would happen. If they accepted drinks from strangers, *out* the door. That was the rule of the house. There was a lot of propaganda about Doran's. The Pro-Cathedral was on one side there and they would say that Doran's was the 'pros' cathedral'—now that was trade jealousy. That was wrong. And then, you see, Dublin started to expand and then there was twenty or thirty Doran's [type] lounges all over. They all went into the game then, they copied him.

"And you had to keep proper hours, getting your customers out at a proper time because the police were very strict. You know, getting people out is hard because the last drink is the sweetest drink. Now with tourists, Americans or even English, the minute you rang the bell they're just out. But you can't get the Irish crowd out, they just won't rush a drink. They love the crack and the chat. And there's always a tradition with Irish pubs that if you have money you can drink all night. That's right, there was *speakeasies* and you could just get into these places that stayed open. There was a famous shebeen in North King Street, supposing to be serving coffee and tea but they were serving drink in there—Dolly Fawcett's. That was the famous one in my time. It was an old dive! But it was a famous place, a brothel. One of Dolly's sons was always coming into Doran's always reading a novel, a very intellectual fellow. They raided Dolly's now and again but they never closed it down. It was kind of an old restaurant. Ostensibly you'd go in there for coffee but there were spirits sold. It was well known that the aristocracy was going there too. They *all* went there. Everything was kept under cover in Dublin. You know, we were very *Catholic*, very close.

"In 1955 I went up to the Big Tree pub on Lower Dorset Street. They had a lounge there. Now in 1955 I fought in that strike. In 1955 things were *bad* at that time, the wages was poor, there wasn't a living for nobody. Everybody was low, it was a very depressed time. So the barmen went on strike, over wages. You couldn't live, couldn't exist, couldn't rear a family. And your unsocial hours. Our claim at that time was for a £1 increase every second Sunday. The strike lasted for five weeks. In previous strikes in the licensed trade the bosses always won. There was two major strikes before, one in 1922 and another one about 1927.

"This was a *bitter* strike. Emotions were very high, no doubt about it. Every pub was picketed where they had a trade union staff. What *amazed* the employers was they thought the customers would pass the pickets. But it was 99.9 per cent of the customers backed the barmen. There was more respect for the employees. And that's how the publicans lost out. Oh, a lot of them remained open and maybe the boss or his family worked or maybe he got in some non-union workers. If you passed a picket you were called a scab. And there was a few cases like that. But a lot of them just closed down the doors. Now quite a few pubs settled. And then the non-union pubs were open all the time, the backstreet pubs, and they done a *booming* business. Because people wanted to drink because it was one of the warmest months of July in records. It was up to 80 degrees. And there was quite a few scuffles outside. Like maybe a picketer might have a few drinks and maybe have words toward their boss. Then some of the bosses were very indiscreet too and they were antagonising the barmen on strike. A married man that was on strike got £4 a week from his union and a single man got £3.

"Negotiations were going on all the time but it broke down. And then Guinness's took an extraordinary line. See, Guinness's were your main suppliers for the trade, that was about 80 per cent of your turnover. And the employers that settled, that had no dispute, Guinness's only offered them the quota of the previous year plus 5 per cent. But these houses were doing *at least three times* their normal trade and would be quickly *sold out*. In other words, there weren't *sufficient* supplies going into the pubs that was open to keep the customers happy. In other words, Guinness's were backing the publicans and the Publicans' Association naturally supported Guinness's limited quota practice. Guinness's policy of not supplying the 'settled' houses with all the stout they needed favoured the publicans and angered the barmen who wanted Guinness's to supply all settled houses with their full requests. They felt that Guinness's policy was aimed at trying to break the strike.

"So the Barman's Executive Committee decided to march from number 20 Parnell Square to Guinness's Brewery—3,000 barmen! I was in that march myself led by our President, Mr Danny Gleeson. We marched eight deep down O'Connell Street shouting 'Guinness's the strike breakers!' and we marched down Westmoreland Street, College Green, Dame Street, Thomas Street and James's Street. And we went around the whole Guinness's block and we shouted 'Guinness's the strike breakers!' And there was a warning that if any of our lads broke the march or got into any trouble they got expelled immediately—it had to be done properly. Now we arrive back after three or four hours and everyone went back to their picket duties. And we got a ring from the general secretary of the workers of Guinness's, 'Why are you up shouting? We have no dispute with the barmen.' And we said, 'But *we* have a dispute with Guinness's.' And the question was put to them, '*Why* did you take sides in the dispute?' And Guinness's then said they would like to end the strike. See, after the demonstration Guinness's realised the strength of the union and solidarity and actually agreed to help mediate the strike. They volunteered one of their public relations men, a Sir Charles Harvey. Now he was a very prominent man and he was delegated as an assessor to the dispute. There were two assessors, the other one was a Mr O'Sullivan and the chairman was Father Kent. Negotiations really started then and after about ten days the strike was settled. Because Guinness's said if anyone was open for business they'd give them all the beer they wanted. So we were on the winning streak after five weeks and on the first week of August it was settled. As a result of that strike the price control was taken off the drink and they could charge their prices and then things started to look up.

So in the long term they gained from it too, it was good for business.

"Now my boss at the Big Tree said, 'We'll refuse to talk about it [the strike], Jack' and we opened that night. First of all, we needed to get supplies in. Now by virtue of having been very prominent in the strike I had a hot line to Guinness's and I had supplies in within six hours. He couldn't get over it! And I'll never forget his face when all his customers walked in. All the customers that were traditionally there, they all filled up the place that night. And the number of customers that had passed the picket was only four out of a possible thousand customers. They all came in that night and shook hands with the boss and shook hands with the staff at the Big Tree. He was embarrassed, naturally, and so were we. It was 'let bygones be bygones'."

JOHN O'DWYER—AGE 72

He started out at age 10 wearing short pants in his father's pub pulling pints and cleaning out filthy spittoons during the TB years. In the 1940s he worked at Lalor's pub in York Street in a real "rough and tumble" tenement area. Later he was employed at the Pearl Bar in Fleet Street where he served Dublin's most famous journalists and literary figures. In 1949 he bought his first pub and eventually owned several others including the Oval Bar in Abbey Street.

"My grandfather was a farmer and my father came to Dublin in 1898 from County Tipperary and started in the pub trade at age 13. I always felt that my father was a great man. He came up to Dublin with nothing and he made his life and his money and he worked very hard. In his era the pub time was 7.00 in the morning until 11.00 at night. They worked very hard for very little. He served his time off Parnell Street and served his juniorship up on Cork Street. Then he went to Ringsend to the Yacht pub and met my mother who was next door and they got married. Later my father had a pub in South Earl Street, just a corner pub, and that was where I was born. The whole family was living above the shop. Nine in the family, my four brothers and four sisters. Very crowded.

"Actually, I started working for my father when I was about 10. Oh, I used to go in and pull pints in short pants for about three years. If you were under the control of your father at that time it was overlooked and no one bothered. Then I left school at 13 and went into the pub. I was very keen on going to work. My apprenticeship was five years and two years' juniorship. At 13 my week's wages was two and sixpence. My first job in the morning was cleaning the spittoons. Take them out and get a kettle full of boiling water and clean them out with a little brush. It was a *horrible* job. It wasn't nice at all, especially during the TB epidemic here. Some barmen wouldn't do them, they refused to do them. Brasses cleaned *every* day and you had to clean the mirrors every week. And then, of course, you had your bottling. We wore blue aprons during the day when we'd be around the cellars cause they'd get soiled. Then at night we wore a white apron down to your ankles. But the strength of the booze would rot your shoes. It would just rot away from the beer dropping down on them when you were serving. Eat through the leather. The booze was very very strong then but as the years went on they reduced the strength of it.

"In my time the local pub was a part of the life of the people. The pub was *the* thing, very important in people's lives. It was part of a culture in its own right at that particular time cause *everything* that happened was all discussed in a pub. *That* was the place to be. From the time people were born up till the end, the centre of life was all in the pub at that time. At that time all life was related to going to Mass, going to the pub, going to work. In that order. And in some pubs there was no such thing as rings or darts, there was just *drink* and *conversation* and nothing else. But we always discouraged politics and religion in the pub cause there was always a bog-down in those. Anywhere I worked there was a rule that if conversations turned to politics and religion we could intervene and say, 'Listen, we don't entertain politics and religion in here.' Cause it always led to trouble, there was always a row at the end of the tunnel. Before it started we stopped it. See, in the thirties you were only after coming out of the twenties, you know. The Civil War was only over and talk about politics and religion it was very difficult because you wouldn't know *who* would be in the place. You'd have people coming back that were ex-British soldiers from the 1914–18 War, you'd have old-timers from the Boer War, and fellas from the IRA and then the Blue Shirts, all these fellas. It was impossible. It was a big powder keg. And the whole thing could explode because you wouldn't know who'd be there.

"Oh, back then they had great respect for publicans. They looked up to a man who had something and he was important. And they could confide in him. A publican was a man who, if there were difficulties in a family, maybe the people might call him outside and tell him that they were having terrible trouble at home and ask him [for advice] and he'd listen and give them guidance. Ah, he was next to the parish priest. And he used to sign for people for to buy furniture and stuff on the payment system when that came out in the late thirties. See, they had nothing they *owned* and had to get a guarantor. And the publican was the man who *christened* them, *married* them and *buried* them, the local people. When people were getting married the booze was given to them and then repaid later on a weekly or monthly basis. No extra charge, it was just a way of life. With christenings the same thing applied, to get a party. Same thing when somebody died. If somebody died and had no money for to bury them my father'd take over the burial and he'd organise the funeral and when it'd be all over the family would come along and pay him so much until the debt was cleared, normally about three years. *All* these things were celebrated, death was celebrated, christenings, and marriages, they were the big things in the family then, and the local publican he was *the man*, he was there for them. And my father *always* went to the funerals. Sometimes he'd go to maybe two or three funerals a week. One year I done 240 funerals meself! If you didn't attend a local funeral they'd go to the pub next door and you lost their trade. But if you attended a funeral they'd come back to your pub and they'd spend all their money. You had to respect them and be there.

"After my apprenticeship I worked in York Street at Kennedy and Lalor's public house, that was in the early forties. They had two pubs, they had another one down on the north quays and I worked in that one as well later. But York Street was a real rough-and-tumble area. On York Street they were rough, tough people. All tenement houses. They had *nothing*. One house on York Street had twenty-four families in it and only one toilet at the bottom of the yard. And there was always a row. Oh, *really* tough. And it was very difficult to bar people in that particular area because if you barred somebody there could be a family of ten or twelve or maybe their cousins as well and then they'd *all* leave. Back then if you barred one fella you were barring the whole family and the cousins and all would go cause they were all so closely related. But the fear of being barred was one of the greatest fears the customer had. And a man could be barred for *all time*. But he'd get plenty of warnings. And suddenly he'd be refused and sometimes we'd eject them ourselves. Two or three of us might do it. I've ejected many people myself, got into serious difficulties and got injured several times. And then you'd have pleas from the family to let him in. I used to have *petitions* for to let them in again. In one case I lost a family of sixteen, the whole sixteen went. And, see, if you changed your mind it'd mean that you'd have to let the ones that you'd barred previously back. And they'd say then that you were weak. You had to *rule* the thing or you didn't! And the people that worked for you wouldn't have the respect for you either. You *learned* to handle it, it came with the years.

"A lot of men when they finished work they never went home until the pub closed. Men had full control of the wages and they always had enough to drink. Always. But the women were *slaves*. Oh, sure, they were slaves. They had to be home *all* the time. They never went anywhere, never had the money to go any place. They dressed very poorly and never had any money for any incidentals. Women worked very hard and I don't know how they stood by the men. It was part of the *culture* at that particular time. And they had rows and a woman with a black eye was never allowed outside the house. Oh, but the neighbours would tell you all right. We'd *know* about it. We'd know what was going on because conversations always come back into the pub. *Whatever* happened in a tenement house would always drift back down into the pub. It was like a confession box.

"Where I was there were women dealers and they used to sell oranges and fish and so forth and a second business for them was moneylending. Oh, they'd come in and have their drinks. Oh, they had plenty of money, they had *loads* of money. It was all old women with their shawls on. They'd go into the snug. No women allowed in the bar at all, wouldn't go near the bar. Other women at that time they'd come in with the jug and they'd get a pint in the jug and the publican always had to put a tilly in, a drop extra. That was the way it was done. That was *all* on Sundays for Sunday dinner. The locals used to come up on Sundays and they queued with their jugs. Oh, yes, there was a special jug kept in every house, a delft jug, and always *beautifully* coloured, that'd hold a pint. And some of them had their little names on it or their initials.

"Now there was no darts in my time, it was all rings. Oh, very serious and there was championship matches and pubs in the north versus pubs in the south of the city. I played a lot of rings myself. Oh, yeah, you'd play for £5 and at that time it was a terrible lot of money. It'd be about two weeks' wages. In certain cases teams would play, six against six. Then there'd be individual championships. And there'd be bets on both sides. I played a match one time in a Hill Street pub and there was £150 worth of bets. This was about 1938, it was a fortune! And there was [supposed to be] no gambling in pubs in those days. If you were caught you'd lose your pub licence. Oh, but the place would be full, *packed*. Betting was all done between the customers. Some of them might take a book to back such and such a fella and he'd have his little price like maybe 2/1 or something like that. And you had to bring your own bodyguards in case you'd be robbed going home. Oh, yes. Sure I was robbed one night coming back from a ring competition. I played for Dublin against Waterford and we won and we were waylaid on the way home and all the money taken off us. Oh, it was somebody in the pub who was there watching the thing. So you never went anywhere alone.

"Then I worked down at Kennedy and Lalor's on the north quays. It was a complete docker area. It was a half-seven house in the morning. Dockers never strayed from the quays. Drink was the main diet. The dockers *lived* on that. They *lived for pints*, they had *nothing*. It was *food*—they used to *call* the pint the 'liquid food'. That's what they called it. And dockers were paid on the spot, every day, and they were all paid in the *pubs*! Oh, I saw it meself many times. That's the way it *was* in those days. See, cause they [stevedores] had to have a centre point to pay their men that was out of the rain. The pub was out of the rain so that's where they paid them. Oh, it was a terrible system. Sure, those dockers, half of them never brought any of it home. Oh, their wives and children were starving. I'm not saying *all* of them now because there were some very good people but there was a percentage that wouldn't dream of handing the wages over to the wife.

"From 1944 to 1945 I worked in the Pearl Bar on Fleet Street which was a literary pub. All the writers and journalists all assembled there. It was a *wonderful* place to be because there was a great cross-section of people. You had the likes of Lord Killanin and Lord Powerscourt and all these wonderful fellas. They *all* came in. It was one of the most interesting places I ever worked. I met all those fellas. I had the privilege of barring Paddy Kavanagh and Brendan Behan and Ulick O'Connor. And I knew Brian O'Nolan well and he was a brilliant man—they *all* were actually, they were brilliant people. But they were all alcoholics in my opinion. But Paddy Kavanagh wasn't. But he was terrible *mean* and had a filthy habit of spitting. Now when I owned the Oval Bar in Abbey Street in 1962 one of my first customers in was Paddy Kavanagh and he started spitting on the floor and I wouldn't serve him! And I didn't let Paddy Kavanagh come back. No, I wouldn't let him in at all. Had this terrible, filthy habit of spitting on the floor. Shocking! And people objected to him. And no matter how often you'd talk to him he wouldn't listen to you. And he never had any money.

"But Behan was the opposite. He was terrible generous altogether. Oh, if he walked into a pub he'd give the barman a few pounds and buy everybody in the place a drink. But Behan was always in trouble and he went completely haywire when he drank. He was brilliant in his way though with a marvellous wit and fantastic songs and a great way about him. But a certain pitch with booze and he was gone. You couldn't handle him. He'd have an answer for everything, for the police, *anybody*, made no difference. Oh, he was a colourful character. Without a drink he was a lovely human being. I remember going up to see him in the hospital shortly before he died.

"And I remember Brendan when he come out of Brixton [Jail] and he came into the Pearl Bar when I was working there and a fella by the name of George Smyllie was there and he was a famous editor of *The Irish Times* and Smyllie had seemingly wrote some [critical] article about Brendan being in prison. And the minute Behan got out of jail he travelled all the way across by boat and done all the pubs up along Westland Row and made *straight* for the Pearl to see Mr Smyllie. And I remember the scene and this sticks in my mind. It went like this: 'You're George Smyllie?', Behan says. 'I am.' 'Do you know who *I* am?' 'I don't.' 'I am Brendan Behan. You wrote filthy things about me in the paper and a lot of them were untrue.' And Smyllie says, '*Mr* Behan, we don't know where you have been but this is not the place for you to be seen.' And Brendan Behan says, 'Do you know what, Smyllie? First time I ever seen a man with a *dropped chest*.' Cause Smyllie went over with a big belly. That was Brendan's reply . . . the wit! Nothing happened, he went off then.

"I started as a publican in 1949. I started with £1,000. I bought the Welcome Inn in Kilmainham, paid £9,000 for it. My father secured the rest for me. I had it paid for in four years. Then I went downtown and I owned the Oval Bar in Abbey Street. Then two years later I bought the Plough in Abbey Street. Then I bought the Barge up in Richmond Street. I'm retired now since 1981. I retired at 58. There were three of my sons in the business but they've all gone out of it now. They didn't like the game. It very seldom goes into three generations, *very* seldom. Don't know why . . . it never goes past two generations . . . very, very seldom. But I *loved* my life in this business. Sure, I was never educated at all, anything I learned I learned from other people. You learned how to *love*, which is tolerance and understanding, compassion. I worked every day. Sure, the hard work you put to it you got out. I enjoyed the work even though the hours were unsociable. But to me it was a great cross-section of human beings that I met in my life and I never regretted that. I *never* regret being what I was. It's a way of life."

CON MURRAY—AGE 62

He was born over his father's pub in Sean McDermott Street where it was customary for tradesmen to hold their meetings. His father reserved a back room for carpenters who wore bowler hats and met monthly to drink, smoke, talk business, sing songs and say the rosary.

At age 13 Con was pulling pints for these tradesmen. He remembers some drinks with unusual names like a "pony", "tailor", "50-50" and "top-up".

"I was born in the thirties on Sean McDermott Street, born over the pub actually. My father started in the trade in 1913 and was apprenticed to a man called Tom Gaffney who owned a pub on Sean McDermott Street at the time. The traditional way it was if you were a good worker your boss would guarantee you at the bank. So in 1927 my father bought Phil Shanahan's pub down on Corporation Street and extinguished the licence and transferred it to a pub on Sean McDermott Street. My father's pub was just called Murray's but the local name on it was 'Black Mac's' cause a man named McEvoy started it. It was a large pub with fine rooms, a fine big house by comparison with the other pubs in the area, and it was the *busiest* house in the area.

"In those days we had a grocery counter with tea, sugar, that sort of thing. And there was a natural mix in the population and we had people like printers and carpenters and dockers. And women dealers that sold fish, they could come in to the front of the pub in snugs. Women drank a GP, a glass of plain. And when my father first opened the place he used to get a lot of farmers from the north county. Parnell Street was a very busy street then and they'd pull in on Sean McDermott Street and our pub had a great name for the *quality* of the drink so they'd come down there. And in bad weather my father used to prepare a hot whiskey and hot claret for them.

"In the pub different tradesmen would keep to themselves, especially the carpenters. They used to wear bowler hats and my father kept a room for them and they'd hold their meeting once a month. That was a *tradition* in Dublin to have a room in the pub for men like that who wanted to have a private drink. And they'd drink and sit around and chat and say their party piece, sing their songs. About twelve or fourteen men and generally the carpenters would drink stout. Then you had the working men's clubs and they had a room. They were just working men from the dairy, working on the docks and carrying things. My father rented them a room over the stable at the back of the public house. It was a big loft over the stable and they had a billiard table in it and they had a radio set up and they'd have a game of cards. The night would start with them saying the rosary and then they'd play billiards and you'd take your turn on the table.

"Most publicans were very conscientious, very decent men. They were responsible people and they were all mixed up then with the St Joseph's Young Priests Society. Publicans were patrons of that and their wives used to do a lot of work in that, raising funds. And my father was an agent for the Sick and Indigent Roomkeepers Society. He was a member of it and an agent. See, people then who were poor used to go to the Roomkeepers Society or the St Vincent de Paul Society if they were short and my father'd sign the paper for them and they'd get some money. And if some fella maybe had an accident or died without a shilling, well, the publican'd have a 'whip around' and collect coins in a brown sugar bag. And people'd have the publican sign the HP forms, the hire-purchase forms, like for to buy a bike.

"I started in the pub washing glasses at the age of 12. *Everything* was done by hand. And all cold water. You had a big tub which was the half of a very large [wooden] barrel and you put your bottles into that and you let them soak and that got rid of the old stuff in the bottle. Then they were put into a tub of clean water. Now washing the bottles you had little lead balls, called shot, like from a shotgun or a musket. So you put twenty or thirty small little shot into the bottle and let the water flow into maybe a third of the bottle and you put your thumb on the neck of the bottle and you shook it up and down and that scoured the inside of the bottle. But that was done away with when they found out about [the danger of] lead. Then you had corks for the bottles of stout and porter. The cork was from the bark of the cork trees and they came in big sacks and you scalded the corks in hot water in sacks and that'd keep the corks soft.

"The casks were in the cellar downstairs and you drew the beer with a pump into the tumbler through a lead pipe but that lead pipe was coated with the skin of the yeast which prevented the beer actually contacting the metal. Guinness was always the safest drink you could buy. It was originally made with the *purest* of natural materials. The actual hops came in compressed into big bales and the grain and barley was all grown here in Ireland. I think it's the only drink you could say is good for you. But during the Emergency Guinness's reduced the strength of the raw materials and they never restored it. And at that time we had plain porter and stout. Then you had a mixture of porter and stout, it was a 50-50 and they called it a '50'. Then you had a 'top-up', or a 'fill-up', that was half a pint of stout topped up by a bottle of stout and that was a hard drink to sell. Then there was a thing called a 'pony' of stout, that was an illegal measure. A pony of stout was simply a whiskey glass full of stout for a fella who wanted something to wash down his whiskey. Water was against the religion or something! And you had a 'tailor' which was a measure between a pint and a half-pint—about three-quarters of a pint—and that became illegal. A lot of those old measures and the glasses made for them had to be taken out. All those minor, in-between measures, had to be done away with and we were confined strictly to measured drinks.

"Now I was pulling a pint when I was 13. And a barman back then he was more developed on the right-hand side, the shoulders, from pulling the pumps and from using the cork drawer. See, the corks had to be drawn out of the bottles with a machine called a cork drawer on the counter of every pub. And the story was that a tailor could tell a publican or a barman because of the development on the right-hand side. But there was certain barmen that a man [customer] wouldn't let pull a pint for him cause they never got the art of it right. You had to have a *feeling* for what you were doing. Some fellas would just *pull* it and they got anything that came up. See, when you were using the pumps you had to know how to nip the tap to produce the pressure and this produced the froth. And you had to give that time to settle down. And when I started pulling a pint you had to learn to *blow* the froth off it. You held the glass at an angle away from you and blew across it and that hit the top head, the bubbly head, but underneath was the creamy head. And then 'technology' arrived and we were issued with scrapers. That was a development within the trade.

Somebody was travelling 'abroad', somewhere as far as Mullingar or somewhere, and saw these things. Our first scrapers were made out of metal, they were rather like a kitchen knife, and they were called a 'skimmer' and you skimmed off the top. Guinness then arrived with the plastic ones with 'Guinness' written on them. If you didn't cut down deeply enough with the scraper you didn't get a nice smooth pint.

"Now people on the northside, they liked a thin head, thin but creamy, but the people on the southside liked a heavier, thicker head. And the sign of a good pint was that it hung to the side of the glass and by counting the rings at everywhere he stopped you'd have a ring on the glass and you'd see whether he was drinking fast or sipping his pint. It would leave rings. But if you went to a strange pub you'd very often ask for bottled stout as opposed to a pint cause there was great stories about barmen using all the 'slops' as they called them. See, your beer overflowed into a pan and then there was beer left over in tumblers and then they'd shoot it all into the pan and that became known as the 'old man'. And a fella'd know the pump that belonged to the old man and he'd say to the barman, 'Keep off that!' He didn't mind waiting if he got a pure pint."

Fergus Newman—Age 81

At age 14 he worked in his aunt's country pub over a hundred hours a week for a measly ten shillings. In 1933 he became a barman at O'Neill's pub of Suffolk Street where his boss was a tough taskmaster. In those years pub staff were intimidated by imperious Guinness inspectors who strutted in to sample their stock. In later years he fought against Guinness's monopolistic practices and helped to change the old system. In 1956 he opened the Comet pub in Santry which does a thriving business.

"My father is Longford and my mother County Kildare but I was born in Dublin. I left school at 14 years of age and at that time you had no option, it was whatever your parents put you to and that's what you did. Now my mother had an identical twin and she married a publican and they had a public house down in County Kildare and I was shoved down to the bloody country with this aunt of mine and I hated the pub business because you were never off and you worked bank holidays. I reckoned that I worked 103 hours a week and my wages was ten shillings a month. I lived above the shop and was fed and kept there. Then after about twelve months I got browned off and I come home one day and I wouldn't go back. But eventually I was *sent* back. And when I went back she increased the wages from ten shillings a month to ten shillings a week.

"At that time you were three years an apprentice and two years a junior. And in their public house there was a grocery and provisions and selling every farm implement. I was never finished working. I had to be down there at half eight and sweep the whole place out and take down all the paraffin oil lamps. They were lovely lamps all right and I took every one of them down, cleaned the globe, pared the wick, filled them up with paraffin oil, put them back in place. *Every day* of our Lord! There was no such thing as unproductive hours in my young days. On Monday I weighed up a big chest of tea and weighed that out in quarter-pounds, half-pounds, and pounds. And you tied the packets up in twine. Tuesday I weighed up *two* sacks of sugar and there was two hundredweight of sugar in each sack and I often carried that sack of sugar on me bloody back and I wasn't 15 years of age. Then apart from that I was slicing bacon and you cut the rashers with a big knife. Then Wednesday I was weighing up flour and bran and all. And then on Friday we had a pony and trap and I'd go around to deliver coal, flour, bran and you bloody well name it and I done it.

"Now, as I said, I reckoned that I worked 103 hours a week. I had to be in at half eight in the morning and we closed at 10.00 at night. But when the pub closed all the bloody customers that came into the place went back to the kitchen. Where I worked was on the edge of the Curragh and there was all the racing crowd and people with racing stables so when the pub closed at 10.00 at night *all* the boys, the bloody customers, went into the kitchen at the back. See, it was really a family house and I was the only staff they had. And this aunt of mine was the biggest slave-driver in Europe! So all the customers were in the kitchen after hours and it was illegal. *Absolutely* illegal. I had to stay up and serve them till 3.00 every morning. And I was lucky if I got to bed at half three in the morning. Now you can work out yourself how many hours that was.

"And at this time it was only a six-day licence. In other words, it didn't open on Sunday—but Sunday was the *busiest* day of the week! The doors were closed and we'd have two fellas keeping an eye out for the guards. And the guards would occasionally come. But at the back of the pub we had a field and all the customers would be out and they'd disappear through this field. I remember this one chap, Billy, and he was well into his seventies, an old man he was. But this particular Sunday morning there was an unexpected raid and everybody had to scatter and *out the back* and through the pasture. And there was poor old Billy tearing along and there was a hedge and he wasn't able to get away . . . God help him.

"I finished my time in 1933 and then I came back to Dublin and got a job in O'Neill's of Suffolk Street. And O'Neill, he was a very shrewd man and if you worked at O'Neill's you could work *anywhere* because of the reputation he had as a terribly strict man on his staff. Very strict and he done things he shouldn't have done but in those days the trade union movement was only in its infancy. It was like this: because of the unemployment in those days if you got a job you kept your mouth shut and you done things that you shouldn't have done. Like we opened at 10.00 and the union said it was 10.00 we had to be there, but he insisted that we were in there at half past nine. And he'd be standing by the door and he had a gold watch and he'd take it out and say, 'You're two minutes late.' And we got only one half-day off in the week at that time. Now according to the [Barman's] Union we should have been off at 1.00 but O'Neill never let us. At that time there was the Holy Hour and you closed from half two to half three and when we closed at half two *that* was your half-day. We couldn't protest, we were afraid, because if you did we'd be *sacked*.

"O'Neill was a little bit imperious. Now I'll tell you, one day a customer came in and ordered a bottle of stout. So I got the bottle of stout and poured it out and put it before him. And O'Neill says, 'Fergus, what did that man ask for?' 'A bottle of stout, sir.' 'Well now, does he know it's a bottle of stout? When a man calls for a bottle of stout you pour it out and put the bottle in your left hand at the customer's right hand and you face the label *out* to him and in that way he can see that.' But he was bang on! He was dead right. He was a perfectionist. The same way a man comes in for a small whiskey. You put the small whiskey there and you put the water beside it at your left hand and the customer's right hand. And in my young days you addressed *everybody* as 'sir'. Oh, yes, absolutely. You'd never call him by his Christian name. And another thing, in O'Neill's you couldn't wear a watch. He wouldn't allow it and that was it. I couldn't tell you why, it's a thing you wouldn't question.

"Now O'Neill had two public houses at that time, in Suffolk Street and in Fleet Street, and I'd often be shifted down to Fleet Street if they were busy. So I happened to be shifted down this Saturday to Fleet Street and there was a big trap door behind the counter down to the cellar. And the trap door was very wide. Now the foreman, Mick, he was very interested in racing and he had the newspaper there and was talking to a customer who was also interested in racing. Now Mick was standing where the trap door was and I was going down into and cellar and I said, 'Now be careful, Mick, cause I'm going down.' 'That's OK', says he, cause he was reading the bloody paper. Well, I hardly had me coat off and the next I heard was 'boom'. And it was Mick fell down through the bloody trap door and finished up in a case of bottles. And Mick had to go to the hospital. Anyway, O'Neill comes down and *what he didn't say to me*! And, of course, I kept my bloody mouth shut and I took the blame for it because I couldn't say that I had told him and that he was studying the bloody racing form —which was a thing he *shouldn't* be doing. So I got a lacerating and if my memory serves me right this was 23 June and I didn't get a Sunday off till the following October! This is a fact. Punishment. And one day when I was working at O'Neill's I happened to break a glass and it was, 'Fergus, you broke a glass today.' 'Yes', I said, 'I did, and Michael [foreman] he broke two or three.' 'Don't be *impertinent*', he says to me. And so I told him I was leaving, quitting, and that was the happiest day of me life when I told him.

"Now there was another chap named Billy Fox who worked alongside me in O'Neill's and when Billy finished his time in O'Neill's he bought a public house at 194 Parnell Street. And Billy bought it for £950. *Nine hundred and fifty pounds*. Are you hearing me right now? This was around 1934. So I went over to work for Billy in Parnell Street. Then I went to Doran's on Marlborough Street and worked there right up to New Year's of 1949, all during the war. I was in charge of the cellar there all through the war years and done all the racking of whiskey and brandy and rum and gin. In those years we used to bond all our own whiskey. Now we used to import sherry and port and wine and I had to learn all about 'fining' that. See, you got in a hogshead of port and it would be like muck, very dirty . . . the sediments. You couldn't sell it like that. So what we had to do was 'fine' it, it was called 'fining'. Now to fine it you had to get the white of a half dozen of *perfectly* fresh eggs. The eggs must be fresh, fresh from the hen. And I used to have to get the fresh eggs. So I used to go out in the country to Mrs Bourke's farm specially to get the eggs. I used to go around with her and she'd pick the eggs out from under the hens, *hot*. Oh, that's right. Then you'd break the half dozen of eggs and just get the white of them. Then I'd get the six eggs into the tumbler and I'd put a drop of the wine in it and beat it all up with a fork. Then when you'd done that you'd tap the cask of wine and you took a bucket full. We had a stainless steel bucket. And we'd take about a gallon of the wine and pour the egg mixture into the bucket and stir that up as well. Then I'd pour it into the bung hole at the top of the cask and stir that around for about twenty minutes and that would form a big foam on top of the cask. Then you'd put the bung back in the cask and leave that there for about a fortnight, at least. I often left it there for months. This fining, that would solidify on the top of the cask. And then eventually it would gradually, gradually, gradually lower right down to the bottom. *Everything* that was in suspension was brought right down to the bottom of the cask. Then you'd draw a glass off it and it was perfectly clean and then you'd start bottling it.

"Now the publicans in my young days were *afraid of their bloody life* of Guinness's. See, at that time there were different breweries in Dublin, like there was Darcy's, Watkin's, McCardle's, Jameson and Pim's, Mountjoy Brewery and Guinness's. Now Guinness's, of course, was the tops. Oh, Guinness had 80 or 90 per cent of the trade. And, funny enough, in the old days Guinness's never advertised but they did give you stickers for your pub window and they said 'Guinness only sold here'. And at that time the Guinness bottle label would say 'Bottled by such a pub who sell no other brown stout in bottles.' That was on the label—'who sell *no other* stout'. So you'd keep other stout out of sight. Now Beamish Brewery of Cork, they opened up pubs in Dublin and they were what we called 'tied' houses and they were owned by the brewery to sell their products. But other publicans were absolutely afraid of Guinness's. For instance, Mountjoy Brewery was a bloody fine brewery and a lot of publicans sold it under the counter. I'm telling you trade secrets now! When I worked in Doran's we sold Mountjoy beer. I'll tell you why they sold it under the counter now. Going back to my friend Billy Fox now, he was only after starting up his business and Guinness's gave him no credit—but Mountjoy and the other breweries gave you credit. They were very generous because they were going mad for business. But you didn't want your customers to see you getting in products from other breweries so maybe you'd say to Mountjoy, 'Could you send me in six kilns of porter and two kilns of stout—but label them "ale".' Do you understand? And naturally they'd do that to sell their products. So when the ordinary Joe would see them going into the cellar he'd think they were ale. Publicans kept other stout out of sight because they were afraid of Guinness's. Oh, Guinness's were unfair, *very* unfair. Eventually, after years, we had an action against them and got that changed, through a free trade commission. Myself and others got that changed.

"Oh, at that time everybody'd be on their toes when Guinness's would come in. They had Guinness inspectors going around and they'd walk into your premises and you'd say, 'Oh, Jeez, it's Guinness!' They would tell you who they were and they'd call for a glass of stout. Guinness's was very temperamental about their product and in the summer you had to contend with the heat and then in the winter you had the other extreme. In the heat of summer it'd go high and be all bloody froth and then in the winter cold there'd be no head at all on it. You got the two extremes, so your cellar had to be a fairly even temperature. Now I'm going to tell you a story of what happened to me in Doran's. We used to sell Guinness but we also sold Mountjoy and McCardle's stout but it was in the cellar and when we pulled it nobody knew what the hell it was. And this Guinness inspector came in one day and he said to me 'A glass of stout.' And he used to have his little thermometer in his pocket and he'd put that in the glass of beer and leave it there for a few seconds and then he'd take it out and look at it and he'd taste a bit of it. And I says, 'Is everything all right?' 'Oh, it's grand', he says, 'but the head's a bit high.' But what he didn't bloody know—and I didn't make him any the wiser—was that what he was after sampling was a glass of *McCardle's* stout!

"Now there was a difference in price for porter and stout and some of the publicans, particularly fellas that were hard up, when they might be bottling a barrel of stout they'd get a kiln of porter and mix the two while they were bottling. And the customer never noticed that. Now that never happened where I was working. But some of them were *caught* by Guinness's. In fact, I know one man—and I won't mention his name—and he was caught. And Guinness made him put a *public apology* in the paper. Oh, that's right. In the 'special notices' in *The Irish Times* and the *Irish Independent*. I can't remember the exact wording of it but it was a fairly long apology obviously dictated by the brewery. Oh, there were several caught and they had to apologise to Arthur Guinness publicly and guarantee that no such practice would ever happen again. There was a whole bloody rigmarole—and it would hurt the reputation of the house. In my young days, the Guinness's of old, the way they treated the publicans, I didn't have any time for them.

"And in the old days the public house was even a morgue. Did you know that? It was a morgue in so far as if somebody was killed out in the road there, that corpse would be brought into my pub and left there and I could do nothing about it. They'd hold the inquest and all there in the pub. That was the *law* and it wasn't changed until 1960. Anyone that was killed out on the road he was brought into the first public house and his body was left there till after the inquest. As a matter of fact, there's a pub in Templeogue and it was always known as the 'Morgue' because in my young days there was a steam tram that used to run from Terenure out to County Wicklow and beyond Blessington. And in those days there was what was known as bonafides and there was *more bloody people* killed on that road going out to Blessington and the corpses were always brought into the pub. That's a fact, that's why it was called the 'Morgue'.

"Now my brother was a carpenter and we went in together and built the Comet pub in 1956. But you couldn't get a pub licence unless you extinguished another licence. In other words, the only way you could get a licence was to buy an old derelict pub licence like where the Corporation were knocking down a lot of old derelict buildings in the city and invariably there was always a pub or two in the area. In this particular case there was a pub in a place called Thorncastle Street in Ringsend and it was getting knocked down. And I bought this licence. So that licence was extinguished and we were issued with a new licence. And that procedure is *exactly* the same today. It's a good system in so far as you're not over-crowded with pubs and no one'd get a living out of it. But back then we had a bonafide up the road here, the Swiss Cottage they call it now, but that was Eugene O'Reilly's pub and that bonafide done *more bloody business* with all the locals around here. See, a bonafide traveller was supposed to be a traveller that came at least three miles by the shortest possible route from wherever he slept the night before. So the locals *shouldn't* have been served because they weren't bonafide. But on Sundays Eugene would be opened at 1.00 and I'd see all my customers up there outside waiting for him to open cause he opened a half an hour before us. Now I never realised how much business that cost us until the 1960 Act that done away with bonafides and then when we were all on the same hours *then* I realised it."

WILLIAM MULLALLY—AGE 76

He loved working as a barman at Donoghue's pub across from the Dublin fruit and vegetable markets because it drew a colourful mixture of feisty women dealers, broken millionaires, kind-hearted prostitutes, crooks, rogues, and country farmers who liked their hot spiced whiskies.

"I was 21 when I came to Dublin, from Kilkenny, a farming family. I went to an apprenticeship right off in Ryan's of Sandymount Green. The old trams used to come and stop right outside the door, that was the last stop. Ryan's was a fine big pub. There were very wealthy people all around there and they all bought their groceries there. My wages was £1 a month and you lived-in. Oh, I couldn't be out after eleven and I couldn't marry. First of all you were behind the counter and I wore a blue apron and the beer *rotted* your shoes. Then you were taught the art of pulling a pint. Some of the publicans used to pump the kegs themselves and they had a foot pump and they'd have like a valve of a car and they'd pump air with their foot. It was just an ordinary car pump, like pumping up a tyre. An old foot pump, that's what they were pumping the kegs with. It would go through a little valve, a tube of a car, and it'd go into the tap which meant that when you were pumping the air can't come back and it put pressure on, you see, for a *better head* on it. And then maybe this publican had the art of pumping the kegs better than the other publicans. But Guinness didn't approve, they said you could be pumping foul air into it.

"I went over to Donoghue's pub in Mary Street about 1953. We were right opposite the Dublin market gate and we opened at 7.00 in the morning. Country people would come in before 7.00. All the farmers, the market gardeners, they came from Rush on the market days and sold their vegetables. They had horses and carts and tractors. It'd be cold in the morning and they'd be on the road from maybe 5.00 and they'd be coming in having hot whiskey and coffee and lemon and sugar. Then we had the fish market as well there and all the fish filleters, they were all great customers. Oh, the characters! You could meet anything from a broken millionaire down to a man that never had a shilling in his life. Some jockeys used to come in that was broken down. And people who'd been out [all night] having 'a do', they'd be out all night at the parties and they'd come in and finish off at the 7.00 hour. *Anybody* could come in. Oh, never a dull moment. Crooks and everything that used to hang around the markets. One day near Christmas this old farmer came in from the country and enquired in the pub about the turkey market and the man had his turkeys outside all in bags. And this man in the pub went stealing his turkeys. We *knew* the fella that was after stealing the bags of turkeys but you could do nothing about it, you minded your own business. And he was selling the turkeys on Christmas Eve that he stole and he was getting money in so quick and he was buying drink so rapidly that he got drunk and had to be carried home.

"And there'd be these fellas that used to hang around the market and they'd be in the pub selling hot stuff. They'd be doing a deal with you where you'd pick up the stuff. Oh, it could be anything . . . parts of cars or boxes of oranges they'd be after stealing. Or boxes of fish. They'd be fellas that lived out of selling stuff that they'd stolen. They'd just come in and make their deal and go away. But I knew what was going on. And fellas would have bets between themselves on matches. There were fellas who used to make books in pubs, like taking bets on horses. Money would secretly change hands. Then during the war there was the black market with bicycle tyres, batteries, all these things. And they had all sorts of tricks, like they used to put sawdust in a bag and they'd put only a bit of tea on the top and sell you that for a bag of tea, to fool you. Oh, they'd sell that in the pub. And then they were gone! A 'fly-by-night' they used to call them.

"And the women dealers were great characters and they'd come in and have a few drops. They used to go on the beer. They used the snug. They'd drink a glass of stout. Oh, they loved their beer—and they could drink it. Oh, they could drink for a day there and they'd still be standing. They were great. Sometimes they'd have a bit of a skirmish over something and they were well able to give a lash with the tongue. But no toilets for women. There was a grating outside some pubs and they used to go out and just stand over the grating and that was it! They wore long skirts. Then there'd be women in the pub who had been 'out on the town' all night and they'd be in the pub in the morning. They called them 'unfortunate girls'. Very kind they were. It didn't mean because they were prostitutes that they were bad. They'd be operating around the city, like around Heuston Station. Some of them dressed flashy but more of them were a bit down-and-outish. They'd be around their thirties the majority of them. They turned to drink. They'd be drinking in the snugs and they'd be *known* to men. You would feel sorry for them, but they were quite happy in their way. But now every year the publican had to get his licence renewed and the police might be objecting to you if you had too many of those illegal girls in your pub. Your house might be of bad repute, like you could be running a brothel. You had to conduct your house properly.

"The pub where a lot of women used to drink was a pub called Crilly's on the quays, around Queen Street. He always had this wine and you'd go in there and he'd always give you some of this wine and fellas used to end up getting drunk in his pub. And all these women, prostitutes, used to frequent his pub and they'd be drinking the wine there too. And the men could meet them, pick them up there. That was considered to be a public house of ill repute. And now a shebeen was a house where they had drink and sold drink after hours, illegal. Dolly Fawcett, she was over in North King Street and girls used to hang around there. It was the Cafe Continental they called it and she'd have drink there, whiskey, and she had no licence. You called it a shebeen.

"But the local people respected publicans and they could get a few drinks on the slate. And he would help them out on different things, like a burial. He'd help them with the money. Oh, he was a very respected man he was. He would help men to get jobs too. He'd be a man of standing and a reference from him, well, you knew that he knew his people. And he maybe had a couple of sons priests and maybe a couple of daughters nuns as well. They all made priests and nuns and doctors out of their children, that went in the family. And customers maybe had sons or daughters away in America or maybe in England and they'd have to come in and get their letters read by the local publican. He'd read it for them. It was somebody they'd trust, you know. Any problems they'd have they'd ask him. Like a customer was *valued* in those days and husbands and wives and sons and cousins, they all drank in that pub.

"In 1955 I belonged to the union and we went out on strike. The sun blazed down and people were thirsty. The doors were open and the boss himself was inside but we were on picket duty outside. There were no people in the pub, they *honoured* the barmen's picket. During the strike I went to work in a Beamish house, a non-union house, in Parnell Street. They were from Cork, the two fellas that had that pub. It was a huge place. I was there for the whole strike and they weren't picketed. And during that month they made so much money! Oh, they came by the hundreds. I couldn't keep the pints pulled fast enough. And then we marched up to Guinness's and said 'strike breakers!' And Guinness's closed up their windows and all. They thought we were going to wreck the place. Yeah, they got terrified up there. It was a sunny day and you'd want to see them running and closing windows and doors. When you see a couple of thousand of men outside you don't know what . . . it only takes one to set the thing alight, you know."

LIAM HYNES—45

His Mulligan's pub in Stoneybatter Street is over two centuries old. Most of his customers are regulars as the pub serves as a sort of community hall for the neighbourhood menfolk. Some regulars staked out their stool and have been sipping pints in the same spot since 1930. Liam can tell the exact time of day by their arrival. Routines don't change much after half a century.

"This pub goes back to 1792. Oh, it's very much a part of the history of this area. When my father first bought this pub it was all cattlemen. We used to open at 6.00 in the morning. I was working here since I was 10, just collecting glasses and washing bottles, emptying ashtrays and sweeping the floor. It was what your father done and you stepped in line, you know. Now years ago when me father built up the business you wouldn't believe the sandwich he gave the people. Ham and cheese mostly. It would be thick as a doorstep. So the cattlemen used to come down from the market in the morning for their sandwich and he gave it away for nothing, to build up the business. Give them a mug of coffee and this sandwich for nothing. And he built up the business and it would be jammed at 6.00 in the morning. See, he was in competition with two other pubs, Hanlon's and the City Arms, which were nearer the cattle market than he was but they'd come down.

"The local pub means communication among people. It's part of the community. You know, it's like a *community hall*. About 75 per cent are regulars here and you could nearly put their drink on the counter at the right time. It's that type of regular basis. Some have their regular seats. There's a lad here now that's about 70 and he sits there all the time and if someone is sitting there when he comes in he'll sit there behind his back and haunt him till he goes—and then jump in. But people mix well, have a bit of a laugh and a bit of atmosphere. This fella here will be discussing sports and the fella in the middle will be discussing politics and this fella down here will be talking about his wife and problems. No one's coming in here with any hard feelings or hatred against anyone.

"You'd be surprised at the amount of problems you get and how they try helping people. They bring problems in here and discuss them and kind of go out and say, 'Well, I've got that solved.' Like one lad here, Ned, about two or three months ago lost his wife and he's only getting over it now and we're rubbing him back in, you know? Now he's been drinking here since 1930. He used to drink pints of plain here and his father used to drink with him, so it really goes back. Now since his wife died he doesn't like to stay in the house at all. He might have a sandwich and down back here again. The other lads understand how he feels and we don't really make him laugh but we just let him come back to himself. Ned will tell you that every time he comes in here he forgets all about it but when he goes home he's miserable. But when he comes in here he forgets it because he's cracking jokes. It's the atmosphere.

"And drink can change personalities. Some of them get aggressive, some of them get funnier. But you have to know who you're dealing with. We have one customer here who won't bet unless he's drunk and then he has big bets, hundred pound bets on favourites. He'll sit down there and drink about three pints and four large whiskies. He really gets jarred. And he's lost about £10,000 over three years! I've tried to talk him out of it, tried to talk sensibly to him when he's sober because once he gets drinking he just can't stop. And he admits that. 'Sure, when I'm sober I never bet . . . it's only when I'm drunk.' He *knows* his own problem, God help him, but it doesn't seem to help him. He's actually broke now.

"Now since I came here we haven't had one serious row, thank God. I can handle everyone here because I know them inside out. It's like a club, you know, and I know how they react when they get a few drinks in them. I know when to stop serving them and tell them to go home and get tea. But you have to be tactful. More psychology than bravado—discretion is better than valour. But when we bought this pub here there was two barmen left and there was a man, a customer, that was an epileptic. And he got upset one time and drove a truck through the front window. It's the way the barman handled him that made him do it. He came in here at 12.00 at night and there was no one left but the door was open and he just walked in and the barman says, 'I'm not serving you. Get out of here before I throw you out.' That attitude. So yer man kind of lit a fuse and he just went out and got the truck and drove straight through! He was an epileptic and he takes fits and a certain amount of drink drives him. It done terrible damage. There's a pole in the middle there and that was bent, but if that gave way the whole pub could have come down. He was arrested and got sixteen months suspended sentence.

"Years ago the snugs would give people privacy. Women'd use the snugs and people used to have little family meetings, little gatherings, there in snugs. Or if you wanted to see your local TD or do a bit of business you'd go in there. And I remember when we'd stay here until 2.00 in the morning and it was no problem. They'd pull down the shades and Paddy Mulligan himself would serve away and send the staff home. Ah, the guards didn't mind, they used to turn a blind eye. And the Holy Hour, it's done away with now, but one time there was eight of us in here one day at twenty past three and this big tall guard, a sergeant, knocks on the door and he walks in and says, 'Ah, drinks on the counter.' So he says, 'I'm not leaving now until everyone gets out of here.' So they all polished off their drink. Now a few weeks later in comes this copper [during Holy Hour] and says, 'Ah, not *again*, you're making an idiot out of me. Now this is going to cost you money.' So he gave me this sponsor thing [for charitable donations] and he says, 'If you fill that up I'll drop the charge.' And he says, 'If that's not filled up I'm going to have fines here galore.' So we left it down with the priest [to collect donations] and about twenty pounds came back to us. But your man wanted it for *himself* and he kept it. He was twisted."

FRANK O'DONNELL—AGE 83

At the age of 19 he got a job as junior barman at the swanky Scotch House which, he attests, was the top pub in Dublin at the time. It was strictly an upper-crust clientele to whom he served the finest whiskey. Men had to wear a coat and tie and no women were served. It was a sad day for him when the elegant Scotch House was demolished to make space for an office complex.

"I came to Dublin in 1926 from County Limerick and went to serve my time on Wexford Street at Peter Lalor's pub at 16 years of age. I lived indoors and worked fifty-six hours a week and got five shillings a week. Working behind the counter was hard on clothes and shoes. You'd spill stout on them. It was hard on shoes because it was inclined to rot the leather so you *had* to polish them every day. And sometimes if you wore the same trousers for the whole week behind the counter your trousers would become solidified at the end, sticky with stout.

"We had more labourers than anything else and porter was the principal drink at that time. Cuffe Street was all tenements and about eight families in a house and an average of seven children in the families. The one room would be their dining room and sitting room and the whole lot. *Cramped.* And the kids were all around fighting among themselves and the man'd say, 'I'll get out', and he'd go down to the pub to have a pint and chat with his friends. For the father the pub was an *escape* from home life, surely it was. The public house, 'twas the place for the social gathering. On Saturday night they got paid and Saturday night was the busiest night in the pub. And some would drink their wages. I saw that. As a matter of fact I remember where a woman went to the publican and she said, 'That man came home to me last Saturday night and he hadn't a shilling in his pocket, he spent it all in *here*. Would you not be a decent man and tell him, "You've gone far enough. I'll not serve you any more. Go home with whatever money you have left and give it to your wife."' And if you were a decent man you'd do that for her, but you'd have to do that *diplomatically* because the fella'd say, 'What the hell does that have to do with you? Mind your own business. That's my money and I can do what I like with it.'

"Heavy drinking and rows as well on Saturday nights. Oh, they'd fight. Fisticuffs. They'd be labourers. I remember one time one fella struck another and I said, 'That's enough.' So I told him to get out. And he said, 'No. Would you put me out?' And I said, 'I don't have to put you out, I'll go to the telephone.' And I went to the telephone to get the police and this policeman came in and I said, 'I want that man put out.' And he said, 'It's my place to *assist* you to remove him from the premises.' 'Does that mean', I said, 'that I have to handle the man?' 'Well', says he, 'put your hand on him anyway.' So I went over and put my hand on his shoulder and I said, 'You'll have to go', and the guard took over then and I didn't have to do a thing. Legal.

"You were advised *not* to give a reason when you barred a man because he would possibly dispute the reason and maybe bring you to court. According to the law you weren't bound to give a reason. So you just told him to go, and you didn't want him. No more than that—and he'd have to go. It could be for assaulting another customer, that was the principal reason. And if a fella was mooching you barred him too. Now in a pub on Leeson Street there was a publican and he had glass-topped tables and somebody banged one with a bottle and it cracked and he had to get it replaced. So he said, 'No more bottles on the table, just a glass of stout.' So this particular man, a civil servant, said, 'I want the bottle to take across to the table with me', and the publican said, 'I'm not allowing bottles on the tables any more', and he told him the reason. So the man says, 'I'm *entitled* to the bottle *and* the glass on the table', and he *insisted*. So the publican said, 'I'm barring you. I'm not serving you here any more.' And the man took the publican to court. And the district judge decided that the publican had the right to bar him. He said, 'The publican has the *same right* in his licensed premises as he has in his own private house and if he doesn't want you you're *out*, that's it!'

"Whiskey was very scarce because you were rationed during the war. But there was a distillery up in the Dundalk area and they had big stocks of whiskey and you could go up there and get it, illegally. I remember very well one time a publican at the Trinity Bar went up and brought back five gallons but it was young stock, that was the problem, because whiskey has to be *matured*. Whiskey was never sold less than seven years [old]. But this was raw and bitter and he'd sell it in his pub. Now I knew this fella that went into the Trinity Bar, his name was Billy, and he was a whiskey drinker. And he took a drink of the whiskey and says to the barman, 'I often had a whiskey that would take the paint off the door, but that stuff would take the God damned hinges off!' *Raw* and *bitter*. And poitin sometimes got into pubs in Dublin and they mixed it with good whiskey. It would knock you out, the poitin. If customers found out you wouldn't be trusted any more and you'd lose trade over it.

"I became a junior assistant when I was 19 and I went to the Scotch House. And I was lucky to get a job in the Scotch House on Burgh Quay, it was *the* best house in the city. We had a lounge and a bar and panelled walls of mahogany and the floor had expensive teak wood like they use on ballroom floors and it had to be polished every day. It was elegant. It was the most valuable public house in Dublin. Two men owned it at that time, Peter Foley and Davy Byrne. They went into partnership and bought it in 1924 for £24,500! And you could get a backstreet pub for £800 then. We had a very big staff, fifteen assistants, the biggest staff in Dublin. When I went in there as a junior assistant I got £3 a week, that was five shillings *over* the union rate. They treated you well because they gave you over the union rate. This was unofficially done and you weren't to talk about it to *anybody*. Even the man beside you didn't know what you were being paid. It was great and you were *delighted* to be living-out, Oh Lord, yes. And your aim all the time was to go on to be a publican. *That* was the reason that most fellas went into the trade, to become the *owner* of a public house yourself—and many of them did. As soon as you could you bought a pub. But a barman would have to get security from somebody cause he'd have maybe a fifth of the price of the pub. But if you were quite a few years with a publican and he liked you, well, you could ask him to go security for you. It was on a paper for the bank. Then, of course, if you failed he'd be *stuck*.

"At the Scotch House we had a grocery department in the front and we sold bacon, cooked hams, bread, tea, sugar. And we had a horse-drawn cart and we'd deliver to places like Rathmines and around. Because the good-class people lived out in these places, you know, and they came into the Scotch House and found out you had a delivery service and you could phone in the grocery department and give your order and it was delivered that day for you. We had a special man for that, he was a porter really, and he did the deliveries.

"At that time it was a great whiskey house. Mostly whiskey. There was gin and Vermouth. But we never sold porter there. Stout, yes. And no women were ever served at the Scotch House until the middle thirties when we organised a lounge upstairs. But the most respectable people came there to the Scotch House, professionals, solicitors, civil servants, shopkeepers, big drapers like Denis Guiney who owned Clery's in Talbot Street. Respectable people we got. And politicians. And we got Americans who came to Ireland on holiday and people from England. Then the Theatre Royal was opposite us there and the top-class artists would come in there, like Jimmy O'Dea. And a customer *had* to have a collar and tie. A fella couldn't come in with no collar, he wouldn't be served. There was a sign—it was understood. It would be slightly embarrassing but you had to carry out the rules of the house. And you were always advised to address the customer as Mr and you'd never call them by their full name, it was Mr K. for Kelly. The man didn't want it advertised that he was in a public house at all, you see. I remember one case, a man came and he was an agent for a couple of firms over in England and he'd come into the Scotch House. His name was Clarke and his friends called him 'Nobby'. So, anyway, he came into the Scotch House one day with a customer from England and this barman approached him and said, 'Hello, Nobby.' Oh, *terrible*! So the man passed no remarks. So when he got the opportunity he said to him, 'I'm with a customer—I'm *Mr Clarke—watch it!*' Oh, that was terrible altogether.

"It was full all day. We were busy and you sweated on Friday and Saturday night, going like blazes. You'd *trot* to serve the customers to keep up. Always on your toes. You always had to look pleasant, you put on a bright front always. Oh, they smoked cigars then and we sold about five different brands. And we kept plugs of tobacco. But there was no such thing as spittoons in the Scotch House. People there didn't spit. If they wanted to spit they went into the toilet. Quite a lot of them were uppity. Yes. Some of them wouldn't even say good day to you. Oh, yes. You accepted it, you knew that was to be expected from some people. And you never *obviously* listened to conversations between two customers outside the counter, that is bad manners. It was not done. But at Christmas time some of them'd give you a *present*, hand you a wrap-up present. Oh, yes. They knew I smoked a pipe so maybe it would be a tobacco or a fancy knife with a

scraper in it. Or a fountain pen or a tie. I'd say I'd get about twelve presents from
the real regulars.

"Davy Byrne died and Peter Foley bought Davy Byrne's interest in it and he
became the complete owner. Then later he decided that he would retire and he
sold the Scotch House and Doran's of Marlborough Street bought it. And then
later developers bought it and it's a block of offices that are there now. It was a
pity to see it go . . . but there was more money to be made out of it because it's
there near O'Connell Bridge. Barmen today, they just put up the drink and they
go away. That's it. But we had *good friends* at the other side of the counter when
I started. Oh, it was a great education . . . surely it was."

ALFRED MILLAR—AGE 70

*When he landed a job as barman in Mooney's at Doyle's Corner, a classy
establishment, he felt "seven foot tall". Years later he became manager of
North's pub in Ringsend which was a "real spittoon pub" of dockers and
seamen.*

"I started in the trade at 15 at the Red Bank restaurant on D'Olier Street. It was
a public house *and* a restaurant. It was a beautiful place, a lot of mahogany. At
that particular stage there was very few Dublin men as barmen, they were all
country. There was some prejudice or something. Then I worked at the Pearl Bar
for a year and I met quite a few very interesting people there, like the poet
Kavanagh and Myles na gCopaleen. I found them very nice, always talking about
literary stuff. For the next ten years I worked for Mooney's at Doyle's Corner in
Phibsborough. Do you know who got me into it? It was Myles na gCopaleen. He
knew somebody at Mooney's and he said, 'There's a job going up in
Phibsborough, would you like it?' And he gave me a letter and I had an interview
and I got the job. You had to be the best working at Mooney's, you had to be 'spot
on'. They had a certain standard Mooney's did. Oh, yes, it was very hard to get
in. I mean the fact that you got a job in Mooney's you were seven foot tall! Now
Mooney's never had a great name for their pints but they had plates of ham and
that. Oh, packed. I'd say you could have 300 people. A good crowd. But
sometimes a fella'd come in off the street and start messing and using bad
language and we'd just get the porters and they escorted him out the door.

"I was at Mooney's in the war years and we got six bottles of whiskey a day
[quota] and so you had to be very discreet in how you were going to let it out at
that time. You might give a man two or three glasses and he'd be satisfied with
that. There was a lot of rum drunk at that time and a lot of gin was sold too.
American soldiers came down in uniform from Belfast. Mostly whiskey they
drank. Oh, they seemed to have money to burn. They'd always leave their dollars
on the counter. And then maybe they'd have a chaser, a bottle of beer or bottle

of lager. Very well behaved, they didn't drink that much. They sort of stayed among themselves. They were totally accepted. Now watering of whiskey was done during the war years, to make it last a little bit longer. Oh, it *was* done, watering whiskey. And mixing porter with stout in bottling it. *Not* in Mooney's! You'd *never* water whiskey in Mooney's. Oh, but a few of them done it and they had to put an apology in the paper for at least a week. And then poitín would come into the city. Smuggled in I suppose. Oh, I got a couple of bottles of it myself. They'd say it was good for a cold but you'd want to take very, very little of it because it was first-shot whiskey, that means it was *raw* whiskey, unrefined whiskey. Oh, Good Lord, it would make you drunk. Oh, Christ, it was firewater!

"Then I went on to be a manager myself down in Ringsend in Peter North's pub for about eighteen years. It was 100 per cent dockers and seamen. A real spittoon pub. Very hard-working men. They all had nicknames and I knew them all. Ringsend people were people unto their own, if I can put it that way. Let me put it this way. If you didn't get on with them you might as well put on your coat and get on the bus and not come back! I got on extremely well with them. I was eighteen years with them. And you had to put it on the slate. I wasn't in favour of it because of the lessons I learned at Mooney's to give no credit, but you *had* to do it down there. You knew that you were going to get the money as soon as they got paid. And there was some great characters down there. There was one fella there and his wife brought over his dinner into North's pub and says, 'You won't come home so I'm bringing it over to you.' And he just laughed. Great characters, most of them all dead now. And it was *their* pub and they didn't want fellas coming in and messing about. Down in Ringsend they had their own crowd and if some fella'd come in off the street jarred and pick a row with somebody you hadn't to interfere yourself, *they* got them out of the pub for you. But sometimes now sailors, if they were storm bound, they'd come into the pub with boxes of fish, beautiful plaice and black sole, and they'd sell that to the dockers in the pub for maybe three or four bob. They'd sell it to get the drink. Ah, I'd have to start dishing out plenty of newspapers to cover up the fish and the dockers'd take that home.

"Dockers, they didn't seem to want to do anything else but be in their pub. They'd drink pints all day. They lived in very bad tenements and at home they'd have a meal and they were no time there and they'd be back again to the pub. They had a tremendous capacity for drinking. They had to work very *hard* at that time now on the coal boats. Their whole life seemed to be bent around Guinness. Ah, yes, porter. I often wondered how could they drink so much and *not* become alcoholics. They were the toughest men in all Dublin, couldn't get any tougher. They were *hard* men but very genial, very funny, a tremendous sense of humour. Now I did have to bar a few of the dockers for bad language, but I was very careful about using the word 'bar'. I'd just say, 'I'm going to send you on a holiday.' And they'd ask, 'How long is the holiday going to last?' and, says I, 'I'll spread the word around and some of your friends will tell you.' Ah, maybe it was two weeks. And then he'd have to apologise to whoever it was he insulted. Then he could come back if he'd be watching himself. But you had to be fair in Ringsend because they were like a clan. And I went to practically every funeral. Even for customers who didn't belong to me, funerals for the *other* public houses, we *always* made a point of going to their funerals as a show of respect."

DANNY GLEESON—AGE 83

He tended the bar in Cleary's pub in Amiens Street in the heyday of train passenger service. Cleary's had a great reputation for bonding its own whiskey and was always packed. He was the President of the Barman's Union during the contentious strike of 1955. Like a little general, he led 3,000 determined barmen through the streets of Dublin to protest outside the Guinness Brewery. At age 83 he feels a sense of pride in his historical role.

"I'm from Tipperary. My father, he was a farmer's son, and he was in the trade. He worked in Dublin here for some years and then went back home and bought a pub in Nenagh. Men came out of the rural districts to be barmen then. It was farmers' sons who saw no prospect of getting the farm and they came to Dublin and eventually bought public houses. At that time, in the 1930s, I would say that there were not six Dublin men working in licensed premises in Dublin as barmen. Oh, no, not at all. The Dublin lads wouldn't *work* the hours. They were virtually all country. Barmen *particularly* came from Tipperary and Cavan, they were the backbone of the barmen. In Cavan when a male child was born they'd slap it [on the bottom] and say, 'There's another Dublin publican.'

"I came to Dublin in 1930. A cousin of mine was working out in Dun Laoghaire and he told me that there was a vacancy going at Walters which was the outstanding public house. It was a good-class pub—but a non-union pub. You had very few non-union houses in Dublin then. I found out to my grief that virtually all the barmen in Dublin were all organised in the Barman's Union. There was a south against north city barmen's hurling team and I was selected but it was found out that I wasn't a member of the union so they wouldn't have me. They said, 'Sorry, Danny, we'd love to have you but as you know this is all union men.'

"Now I started there at Walter's on that dangerous date, 1 April—Fool's Day! Let me tell you of my experience the first morning I walked into that house. There was a public bar and a short small counter and then a little bit of a grocery in it. And there was a select hallway that you served through windows where ladies was. Now only a very few ladies used to go into pubs at that time. So there was three windows there and this was my very first service—I'll never forget it—and I was told, 'That's the bell for you and when that rings you serve that window.' See, women'd go in that hallway and they'd ring the bell. And I was only there maybe a half an hour after starting in the pub and the bell rings and 'A large sherry, please.' And then I turned around and wasn't there a trap door there which had been lifted and *down* I go with a bottle in one hand and a glass in the other! And the bottle hit the neck on the floor going down. Fortunately it was my rump that went down and took the bump. Now the old man that owned the place was very strict and I'll always remember that I'm sitting below on the floor with the glass in my hand and a sherry bottle with the neck knocked off it and he says, 'Are you all right?' 'I think so, sir.' 'Well, the customer is waiting!'

"After that then I started in Cleary's pub of Amiens Street. And Cleary's was non-union also. Mr Cleary had had some row with the union and he didn't want union and he was a bit thick over that. So it was one of the few non-union houses in Dublin and that's why I was able to get a job as a non-union man in town. But I had the same rate as all the union men. The wage for a senior barman at that time was about £3 a week. From 10.00 in the morning till 10.00 at night and compulsory living-in. In the thirties we were a very busy area because there was terrible traffic on the Amiens Street [railway] station which covered the North. Cleary's had a very mixed trade, a fair share of dockers, railway workers, people from the tenements, working-class people, some post office workers, and we also had a good clientele out of the custom's office right across the road. But we had some very solid, hard-working fellas off the quays and off the railway and I'll tell you they were there to stand by you when anything happened. I remember having to bar this one man because he was inclined to be rowdy and kicking up rows, always looking for arguments. And he came in and I said, 'Sorry, you know you're not served.' And he took up a glass and hit it on the edge of the counter but there was a couple of fellas seen him coming on and they took him and they dragged him and *fired* him out the door. They were customers, regulars.

"The railway men and dockers drank mostly porter, as opposed to stout. Porter was the main drink. In the thirties when a man came into a public house and asked for a pint you gave him a pint of porter. But you would never get porter sold in the country in a pub, 'twas always stout. In Cleary's when a man came in and called for a pint of stout you always said to yourself, 'I wonder what part of the country he's from?', because you'd *know* that he was country. In Cleary's at that time we'd do twenty to twenty-two barrels of porter during the week and we'd sell maybe two barrels of stout. It's the same kind of stuff except the porter was a lighter gravity than stout and it ran freer. Now the drink was very good at that time and the Dublin man was very *critical* of his pint. Some houses got a great name for a pint—and for not using the 'old man', as they used to say. See, there was a pan under the counter and there was four taps and a pan under that to catch the overflow. And that overflow was attached to the pumps. Now there was nothing wrong with it but that overflow cooled a bit and when you drew that out of the pan they didn't like that and they'd say to the publican, 'Don't give me the old man.' Oh, the customers knew well. The pint drinker was very selective, even more than a whiskey drinker. He knew where the pint was good. Like Mooney's was never noted for having a good pint, they were more concerned with wine and whiskey, and the average pint drinker wouldn't go there.

"We bonded our own whiskey. See, we bought new whiskey from Jameson's or Power's that was twelve months old and it would be bonded in a bonded store for you. Seven years was the standard. But during the start of the Second World War the whiskey was rationed. Definitely. But we had a good quota of whiskey, better than a fair share of houses even bigger than us. And you only had whiskey at certain hours of the day. It would be on from about 5.00 to half six or so. And it might be on again at 8.00 or 9.00 for an hour. And you kept a bottle of whiskey under the counter and you didn't display whiskey. Even the best customers came to know that whiskey was rationed. But there might be special men that you served in a private hallway of the pub and they would have more.

"Now I joined the union in 1931 and in 1955 I was very active in the union. I happened to be president of the union at the time of the strike. We had discussions among ourselves at meetings about a change in conditions of work and changes of hours. And better wages. We had only one Sunday off in four and that was particularly one of the things. And you had only a half day off in the week. We were working much longer hours than anyone else in shops, like grocery shops. We were working about fifty-six hours. There was around 3,000 of us in the union. So we had pickets out all the time and the great majority of customers stayed out. There was houses that opened with non-union men and a number of houses that did settle, so there was always a pub open for someone. The very big pubs in Dublin, like Mooney and those, were completely empty. But the backstreet pub, family houses, were entitled to get out of it what they could.

"After the five-week strike we did get a definite improvement and established that we were an organisation that had to be dealt with. We *won*, we got more money and time. And better hours. When the strike finished after five weeks we didn't hold it against them [publicans] even if they were bitter themselves. I was blamed by some of these men for the strike. Well, I didn't care, I was the president of the union and that was that. But I know myself that some of them liked to throw me into the Liffey. However, that didn't worry me."

Eugene O'Reilly—Age 84

When his parents died at a young age he was forced to seek work in the local pub-grocery. His apprenticeship was served under a strict uncle whom he likens, in jest, to Hitler for his dictatorial practices. Eventually he bought a pub in the notorious Monto district where he had to expel drunkards, bullies and prostitutes to make it a respectable pub. In 1948 he purchased a pub in Santry which became one of Dublin's most famous bonafides.

"My parents were teachers, in Leitrim. I got into the pub trade by accident, and necessity. My mother died at 39 and there were eight children. Then my father got ill and he died and that finished our education. I went to serve my time with my uncle at age 18 in the Windy Arbour pub in Dundrum. I asked him and he took me in. It was a neighbourhood local and we did some groceries besides, tea and bacon and all. And my uncle was very, very strict. Oh, God, he was strict in every way conceivable. I mean you had to be on time and you always had to be doing *something*. You got a half-day off in the week but he wouldn't let you know *which* day you were getting off. No, he didn't want you to be able to plan to have friends and companions. That was the most difficult time I ever had with anyone. But he could be nice, too, he had sort of a two-tone personality. But once you were behind the counter it was all business. I'll give you an example of it. This old lady, she was a very good customer and I suppose she was spending about £5 a week. She'd get groceries and get meal and all from us. Anyhow, she paid her bill and I marked it off but she left a ha'penny of a balance due. So I write down that Mrs Duffy paid. And he says to me, 'Did Mrs Duffy pay her bill?' 'Oh, yes, sir', says I. 'In full?' 'She owes a ha'penny', says I. So he gets the book and says, 'I don't observe it, I don't see it marked down.' Now he was a generous man in a good many ways and people told me that if they were sick or they were poor he was very generous but he had this *damned* idea of driving business into you. So he started telling me that two ha'pennies made a penny, twelve pennies made a shilling, twenty shillings made a pound. Oh, he was a tough man to work for. I was there with my uncle for three years. Afterwards, when I got out of his clutches, I told him that Hitler was around Dundrum incognito for about five years studying his [uncle's] way before setting up his system!

"Anyway, I graduated and 'escaped' from my uncle and went to Vaughan's public house of George's Street around 1930. I was living-in at Vaughan's but there was more freedom there than in with me uncle. But the boss was very ill, very emaciated and I had to go up and shave him with an open razor. And Vaughan had a bacon shop there as well and I had to take off the shoulder and the ham and split the belly from the back. Oh, I had to do that. And cut the rashers in the machine. So one day I was having a bit of a joke and I took off my apron and says [to the manager], 'That's it, that's enough. I'm leaving. I don't know whether I'm a barber or a butcher or a barman!' Cause I was shaving him and splitting the pig up.

"After that I went to Gaffney's pub at Fairview and then to Gill's pub on the North Circular Road right next to Russell Street where Brendan Behan was born and reared. I knew him as well as I know myself. He was still young at the time. Brendan and a crowd of kids would be playing hopscotch and Brendan would be letting out with four-letter words, as a young lad. Anyhow, I bought my first public house after I left Mr Gill's. It was on the corner of Talbot Street and Corporation Street. I bought it from an old fella called Byrne. This old fella Byrne was eighty-something and it was a rough place and he was doing nothing in business. I suppose he wasn't able to handle it. I lived above the shop and it was only my brother and myself and a porter. The area was a *fright* to the world! In every way. Very working class . . . and half of them not working at all. A lot of dockers and some factory workers. They were religious in their own contradictory way. But it was a rough time from morning till night cause you'd never know what was going to happen. A *rough* locality. I started going to Mass then to pray that I wouldn't be killed before night!

"Now the pub was only a few hundred yards down from the Monto. It had a reputation for brothels and Becky Cooper was the queen of the activities. They were called kips. Becky Cooper was a big towering woman, a madam. So I was within a few yards of the Monto and I knew about all the prostitutes, you know. I'm sure that I had plenty of them coming in but I didn't *know* that they were prostitutes. And the shawlies—the women who wore shawls—would come in all the time. See, it was a locality where every Monday morning you'd see them with their bundles into the pawnbroker's. Then on Saturday evening—cause they'd only get paid on a Saturday—they'd be back releasing them. That's the way they lived. No one thought of tomorrow at all. Well, they'd come in for a glass of porter. It was as natural now as to see a cow eating grass to see all of them in their natural environment in the snug in the pub. But the funerals were the best of all. They'd come in and the woman might be sitting in the snug there and she'd be saying 'poor John' and all this sort of thing. And they'd say to her, 'Well, you had a good life together', and then the next thing she'd be joining in with a bit of a song—two hours after the funeral. This is true.

"Back then droves and droves of these men were coming back from the war and all these unemployed men would be hanging outside my door there, standing around. 'Corner boys', we called them. They were all back over from England. These corner boys, they wouldn't look well and they were a deterrent to trade. Like if I was passing by a pub and saw anybody rough looking around the door I'd pass it by. You can't have these bowzie type of people mixing with the more sedate people coming in. So I was barring customers who would give trouble. Like I'd have no singing, no messing at all. I barred them, refused to serve them. I stood up to them. I kept a tight rein and I was very lucky. I nipped arguments in the bud right away and I put them outside. I had a couple of amazing experiences. For instance, I remember this one night when these two fellas were arguing. This one fella was a fine, big harmless wino and he was an ex-Irish guard and he was the most innocent fella you ever saw. And this other fella was called 'the Boxer' Dowling. But the two of them started arguing and I said, '*Get out now* and have it outside.' So the big fellow comes back in in a few minutes and I said, 'Where's Dowling?' and he says 'He's lying in the gutter. I beat him in a fair fight—I got a flat stone and got him in the side of the head with it, beat him in a fair fight.'

"And there were these two brothers and they were bowsies, terrible bowsies. Dangerous. Anyhow, I was there on a Saturday night and the glasses we had were very rough old glasses, you couldn't get good ones at all, you see. They were like jam jars. But didn't I see this one bowzie putting one of them into his pocket. And didn't one of his pals come up and say, 'Mr Eugene, he put that glass in his pocket.' And, of course, I had to look surprised. Now, having *told* me about it, if I hadn't taken action it would go like wildfire that I was *afraid* of him. So I went up to him and 'Give me that glass', says I. 'I've no glass.' 'It's in your left pocket, give it to me.' And he had his hand up with the glass to break it on the counter. And, God, it was instinct, I put my foot out and put him down [tripped him over backwards] and put me foot on his chest and I said, 'Now take him out.' And they thought I was *outstanding*. So I had a couple of instances like that where I sort of established myself. If you stood up to them they'd respect you.

"Another time there was a docker, a big strong fella, and he was coming home one Saturday night and he asked me for a large bottle of stout and he gave me £1. But he had just been paid after working on the boat and there was *two* new £1 notes that was stuck together. So I rang up the pint and brought him the change from £1—and I kept the other. Now Sunday morning he came in when we opened at 12.00 and I says, 'Billy, here's £1', and he says, 'What's that for?' and I said, 'You gave me two last night.' See, he had been fairly drunk last night and I said, 'That's the reason I didn't give it to you last night because you'd be drinking and it'd be all gone.' So then about three or four months afterwards the war was on and the Belfast crowds were coming down like hell, you see, and these three fellas was sitting at the counter and they were drinking. And Billy was sitting at the counter drinking his pint and he was a powerful big man. So this one Belfast fella says to me, 'I gave you a pound', and I said, 'You did not, you gave me ten shillings.' 'I gave you a so-and-so pound', he says. 'I'm telling you, you gave me ten shillings', says I. 'I gave you a pound and I *want me change.*' So the next thing big Billy the docker reaches over and grabs him by the shirt and says, 'Excuse me, but when I was coming home one Saturday night a few months ago I gave this man £2 and I thought it was only one and he handed it back to me the next morning—he's a very honest man. *Now* what do you think you gave him? Was it a pound or ten shillings?' 'Ten shillings.' 'Ah, that's better', says he.

"Then I went out to Santry and bought a pub in 1948. It was a bonafide. I called the house 'Eugene's', not O'Reilly's. It's now called the Swiss Cottage. But when I went there first the house had a very bad reputation and it was nearly empty. It was prostitutes getting into it, coming out in taxis and all. So I cleaned it out completely. I barred them and wouldn't let them in. And a couple of taximen came to me when I was only new there and I had no money and was in debt but I thought that a half-empty house would be better than this bad stuff. Anyway, this taxi fella says, 'Are you the new owner here?' 'I am', says me. 'Look after us taxi fellas and we'll look after you.' 'Oh, I *will*', says I, 'I'll surely look after you. Every time you come in here and behave yourselves I'll serve you with a drink, charge you the full price, give you good service, that's how I'll look after you. But don't bring me any of your clients because I don't need them.' So I got them out that way cause they were bringing out the girls. I cut it all out, you see.

"Now I could take in 300 or 400. Oh, it was a very big house. The people were coming out from the city in buses because cars were very scarce at that time. Many of them were half-drunk for a kick-off. *Nobody* wanted a drunk in the house, they're a nuisance, they're a *menace* and they can upset people. So at first I used to pay fellas to watch the door for me but they'd take the money and drink and let in the wrong fellas, so I had to do the door myself. I had a sixth sense and I'd be watching them getting off the bus and coming across and seeing how they were behaving and was there any sign of drink on them. I'd be strutting in and out between buses and it was a terrible rough time and people threatened to put me through the door if I wouldn't let them in.

"Now I was open *every* night of the week and they could stay till midnight and we had no Holy Hour at all. It was a hard job. But I was building up a reputation of being very strict. And I had great rapport with the guards and I ran the house well. For my bonafide it had to be three miles from where you last slept and I could not serve local people. No. But I knew damn well that many *were* local. But the guards gave me no trouble—and they were getting no backhands or anything. But there was a publican down in Drumcondra and he'd close at 5.00 on a Sunday evening down there and he'd be up to me and he had a crowd with him. And when we used to close on a Sunday evening they were singing outside my shop. So I went out and I said to them—and the publican among them—I said, 'Listen, lads, will you cut out the singing?' So this publican says to me, 'Listen, you can control your house inside the door but you can't control it outside.' 'That's the truth', I said, 'you're definitely right there. But I'll tell you something. I know you all and there's a lady at that corner in that cottage and she has young children and they're probably going to bed and she'll be up in the guards' barracks complaining about the noise. So you'll never stand in my house again, any one of you, if I hear you singing another song.' And then they went off. Oh, I earned my reputation . . . oh, I did."

FRANK FELL

A VIEW OF DUBLIN PUBS AND PUBLICANS

For the past eighteen years Frank Fell has served ably as the Executive Director of the Dublin Licensed Vintners' Association. He probably possesses a better overall perspective on Dublin pubs and publicans than anyone else associated with the trade. Apart from his official role, he has a genuine affinity for the history and evolution of Dublin's public houses. During his tenure he has witnessed some profound changes in the pub business, some of which he regards as unfortunate and sad. His following account provides an illuminating view of Dublin pubs and publicans.

"Basically I'm an economist by profession and most of my career was spent in the food industry in the dairy sector. At the end of 1978 the LVA was looking for a chief executive and my particular speciality in the dairy sector was pricing policies. And the licensed trade at the time was in a very bad way in the sense that the government had instituted a very tight system of price controls and for a number of years the trade was just not legally able to get any price increases. So they wanted somebody with the experience of lobbying government, dealing with the prices and other factors. And I had experience of pricing policy in a very sensitive area. We do a lot of lobbying government in relation to taxation because tax in Ireland is near to 50 per cent of the price of drink, one of the highest ratios in the world. There are only two countries in Europe that have higher rates of alcohol taxation than Ireland—Sweden and Denmark.

"I'm genuinely interested in pubs and I was interested in them long before I came to the Licensed Vintners Association. We have minute books here going back to 1862 with only a few gaps in them, and some minutes going back to the 1830s, so I'm pretty well familiar with the history of the trade and the way things developed over the years. In the main it was apprentices who became foremen who became publicans. They came from Tipperary and Cavan, they were the two counties, and a little bit of Limerick. Ultimately, they got the money to buy a pub and then he and his family lived over the pub. People living over their pubs now is almost non-existent. Then very often apprentices were nephews or relations of some sort. I think it bred a very honest type of barman and ultimately publican. A great sense of tradition—but it's dying.

"See, in Ireland the licensed trade is very close in its thinking process—or was —to farming. In the past, farmers saw farming as a way of life, they didn't necessarily see it as a business in Ireland. In the 1970s the Agricultural Institute here did a study on what farmers liked, what they got most satisfaction out of, and they found that the vast majority of older farmers said that they got their best enjoyment out of working their own land. In other words, they saw it as a *way of life* rather than anything else. Now the licensed trade is very much the same way. The ethos of it was very similar. The older publicans saw the pub trade as a way of life. And if you talked to them they very seldom had very much else to talk about other than the licensed trade. Nowadays it's changed an awful lot because the value of pub property in Dublin has escalated beyond all recognition. And that has changed the whole way of thinking about and seeing pubs. Pubs now in very many cases are just seen as simple business assets to be bought and sold.

"There's plenty of history in Dublin pubs. They used to stay in the family for three or four generations but that's gone now by and large. Now I know from the way that the families in the Dublin licensed trade developed that trade is probably responsible in the past for producing more of the professional classes in Ireland than any other sector with the possible exception of agriculture itself. You very often found that the publican would have possibly the eldest son in the pub but the other sons more likely than not would go for the *key* professions such as medicine or the law. Or the priesthood, that was the third one. You often find today that an awful lot of senior professional people in Dublin are descended backward to the licensed trade. Probably more so than any other background. In a way, the licensed trade helped to create a native Irish upper middle class from a professional sense. Now, strangely enough, you very seldom found that the sons of publicans went for the civil service. There were very few civil servants. But they *did* become a very large proportion of the professional classes.

"The status of publicans has always been very high in working-class areas of Dublin. Even still, with so many social changes. And there was always great respect for a publican. Now I've often wondered why this was, why they didn't have that great respect for the grocer. And I think to an extent one of the reasons why was that of *all* the retailing sectors the licensed trade was the only one that was actually *licensed*, the holder of a special licence. Whereas if I had a grocery shop on the quays any morning I could wake up and find that another grocery shop had moved in beside me. But the way the licensing laws work in Ireland it's virtually impossible for another *pub* to come in beside me. So pubs have always had a privileged role from that point of view.

"The background to this goes back into the history of the land war in Ireland in the 1880s when Parnell and all these guys were around. The situation was that in the 1880s, up to that stage, you had to have a licence but licences proliferated and the magistrates were the people who issued licences. And in the 1880s the land war happened and there were wholesale evictions, particularly in the west of Ireland. Many of the magistrates were Nationalists and when people were evicted they often applied to the magistrates for licences to sell drink and the magistrates rarely refused because it was one way of ensuring that the people had some kind of living if they had been evicted. In areas where there were wholesale evictions you tended to get a huge population of licences. And in 1902 there was a strong abstentionist feeling in the British House of Commons. There have always been total abstentionist movements from London and, of course, at that time we were governed from London. So in 1902 because of the proliferation of licences there was the belief that a reduction in the number of pub licences would reduce the level of drunkenness. So the 1902 Licensing Act for Ireland forbade the issuing of new licences. And from that date onwards licences had to be *transferred*.

"So new licences are not created any more, not since 1902. The result is that if I want to put up a pub here on Anglesea Road I'd have to go out and buy a licence from somebody, presuming that one was available. And the system is that in the transfer of licences from rural to urban areas that you have to buy *two* licences and extinguish those two whereupon another licence is created. There again, it's all part of the reduction process because you're buying two and you surrender the two licences to the authorities and then they give you a new licence. And the reduction in the number of pubs continues in the older areas of Dublin which are gradually cleared out and demolished and streets have been taken down for road widening.

"Now the Irish are a peculiar race in terms of their drinking habits because the Irish people either drink or they don't drink. The concept of moderation in drinking has never been a national strong point. Although the tendency is changing enormously and you are getting a lot of moderate drinking today. But there was a huge amount of drunkenness. I suspect that really wasn't due to the strength of the drink so much as it was to the poverty of the diet. Now one of the most interesting statistics today is that 94 per cent of all beer produced in the state is consumed *on* pub premises, not in the home. Now if you compare that with your American statistics you'll find that there's about 80 per cent of your beer consumed at home. And that [Irish figure] hasn't changed for years. The Irish people want to talk and drink at the one time. Now there are about 775 pubs in Dublin, so Dublin has only 7 per cent of all the pubs in the state but it has around 34 per cent of the total alcohol sold in Ireland in pubs. And all our market research shows that the pub rates as number one in terms of Irish people using it as a leisure facility. Above all kinds of other things. From anything to sports facilities to theatre to cinemas, *all* the other competing elements of the leisure sector *pale* beside the popularity of the pub as a place where Irish people get together to talk and to have fun.

"The LVA represents about 93 per cent of the publicans in the greater Dublin area. Now I would suspect that if you went out there and had a look to see what was going on right now you'd find that only about half of those members of ours would be what you would call 'traditional' publicans, people who served their time in the trade and built up their businesses over a long period of time. The tendency now is that you might have a professional manager but behind the business is possibly an accountant and a couple of businessmen and they really are the holders of the licence. So the traditional aspect of the trade is dying and it's been dying fairly quickly in the last ten or twelve years. They'd see themselves as professional business people who are employing a professional manager to run the pub on their behalf—they wouldn't even *declare* themselves to be publicans. So there's a big change in the business.

"The changes in pubs came very quickly. I think the thing that started it, the catalytic element in it, was the beginning of the 1960s when the Irish economy started to take off and when much more liberal views on how life should be led began to take over in Ireland. One of the first things to go—and publicans exploited it to the full, I'm glad to say—was the 'men only' pub. Bringing women into the pub *demanded* that the pub be done up and refurbished. So the sixties would be seen very much as a watershed in the sense that so many of the Dublin pubs that were around at that stage were Victorian buildings and had Victorian interiors and that period saw the vast majority of them being ripped out and being replaced by formica. It was really *unbelievable*. It was crazy! But it was the view of the time. That was to cater to the onset of women in the pubs. Instead of floorboards and sawdust on the floors you now introduced carpets and seating rather than stools and you had couches and all this kind of stuff. And that change was instituted by many traditional publicans themselves. I did a count here with a couple of experienced publicans who know the trade and we came down with a view that there are now less than twenty pubs out of the total population that have *authentic* Victorian interiors. That's all. So you're talking about probably 3 per cent of the total pub population that would have authentic Victorian interiors—97 per cent have everything else.

"I would say that the next wave of change then came in the 1970s and into the 1980s when there was an exodus of older publicans out and it started the business of people investing in the trade from outside. So I'd say that the mid-1970s would have been the starting point for *real* change in the way that people were investing in pubs. Very many people came in and bought pubs at that time who were not publicans at all. And this escalated in a huge way after 1985. So now you've got a large part of the trade that is non-traditional in its background. It's non-publican and therefore it's non-traditional.

"Now we've done some recent market research where we went out and polled 500 people on their attitudes to pubs in Dublin and one in seven in this survey noted that they had actually left their regular pub because it had been done up in a way they didn't like. They felt *so* strongly about it. And these refurbishments, the expenditure, can often be up to half a million pounds. And a lot of people have spent *more* than that doing up a pub. Some pubs have fetched huge prices in the last four years. The record is £1.9 million, that was for the Bayside pub in Sutton. And there's always somebody out there who wants a pub. The licence comes with the public house, you buy the two together. But if the pub is demolished and the licence stands on its own the licence is worth about £35,000. They're not particularly valuable when you consider that a licence plate for a taxi in Dublin would sell for around £45,000. That's an interesting sort of comparison. There are still cheap pubs available in some run-down working-class areas for about £200,000 or £250,000. But the price of entry into the trade has never been higher. And so one of the major changes in the trade has been that the ambitious barman would find it much harder to get his own pub now than he would have in the 1920s."

4

ORAL TESTIMONY OF PUB REGULARS AND OBSERVERS

FRANK WEAREN—AGE 93

At the age of 93 his life has spanned most of this century. As a young man he joined the IRA, carried a weapon, participated in actions and was imprisoned. He grew up around the Monto with its tawdry pubs, shebeens and kip houses. There were certain "safe" pubs run by publicans and curates who were in the Movement where he and his IRA compatriots could meet and plan. They had to be vigilant because the Black and Tans raided such public houses. He survived his early activist years to become one of Dublin's last lamplighters.

❝ I was born in Gloucester Street, around the Diamond, that's what they called it. They was all big tenement houses. I was 14 when I come out of school and I could hardly write me name and I couldn't spell 'Dublin'. That's no lie. First thing I done was went to work on a messenger boy bike for five shillings a week. Then I worked for a man called Connolly that used to own the Refuge pub. I went to work for him pushing a handcart with groceries and beer and what have you. Then I got mixed up in the boy scouts and I got transferred with two or three more boys into the IRA, into 'K' Company of the Second Battalion. I carried on with the Movement till the fight of 1922 and worked then with the IRA up to 1955 and I was discharged and put on reserve.

"When I was getting trained I was very active with the short Mauser rifle and it only held five [cartridges]. The Enfield rifle held eleven and it was 7 lb weight and I couldn't balance it accurate. But when I got the Mauser I could get the bullseye. So when I was active in the Movement I was known as 'Short Mauser', that was my rifle. I was getting trained when I was 18 and I seen a few actions. I'd a .38 [revolver] in my pocket. It was nice and light. The .45 was very big. Now the IRA always condemned drinking. Oh, yes, they didn't like drinking because you might take one or two over and wouldn't have the same knowledge in your brain. They liked a man that was silent. Most of them took a pint. I remember the pint being tuppence! Then it went up to fourpence and sixpence and up to eight pence. And look at it now!

"The Monto, that was the toughest part of Dublin. Scruff and poor and poverty-stricken people resided in it. All tenements. Monto was a flourishing place when I was a boy. There was always a story to be told about the Monto. Now Monto was flourishing up to 1916 and when we got the freedom in 1921 between the clergy and the local councillors they decided to abolish Monto, so they built flats there. But I remember when there was shebeens down in the Monto. There was thirty or forty of them. They were called kip houses. The girls would be out on the town walking on the path or sitting on a seat outside. Now 'brass nails', that was the name they had on them, instead of calling them prostitutes. And if they were a bit advanced [in age] they were called 'riggers', they were the cheap prostitutes. But the expensive prostitutes were always nice young girls dressed up and clean and spotless, attractive. Some of them would be only 18. Most of them from the country. They wore a white blouse to make themselves attractive and big earrings and maybe imitation bangles on their wrists. But they wouldn't let you stand to look at them. Oh, they'd give you a clap or chase you. But they used to call you to go for cigarettes for them and give you tuppence or thruppence when you came back. Soldiers and sailors and everything used to go in and a man looking for a brass nail would pick the best-looking one he could get. If you wanted an hour with her she might say five bob, or if it was a night she might say pounds.

"Now the owner of a kip house, she'd always have a bottle of whiskey or two hid so's if you wanted a drink or you wanted to treat your woman to a drink, well, she had the drink for you—and you paid the highest price for it. Now I remember a shebeen house in Gloucester Street and I often remember seeing her [the madam] go to the grate and opening it and taking out the large bottles of stout. She'd have them hid in the grate outside of the path, under the grill. She'd have bottles under that. And the police then got to know about it and when they were going into a shebeen, if they seen any drink inside they'd come out and they'd kneel down and put their hands down and pull up the grill and if there was stout in it you were summonsed and brought to court. Oh, yes, you'd be lagged for selling drink against the orders of the day.

"Now for meetings, for men in the Movement, we'd go into a certain pub where we had support, like a curate there was *in* the Movement and they'd make arrangements to hold the snug private for so many hours. There was one pub called O'Hagan's we used to be in, in the slum part of the city on Cumberland Street. It's now Scanlan's. Then we used to hold a meeting down in the Barrel pub on Benburb Street. Then we used to have another pub, it was Leech's of Drumcondra Bridge, and we had two IRA men working in there. There was another pub or two on Talbot Street and they used to assemble in those when all the football matches would be on. They'd meet all the men [in the Movement] from the different parts of the country and have their discussions there. Or maybe they'd meet in the Long Hall pub over in George's Street. They had various pubs to go into that were sure and secure. Like Paddy Clare's pub down at the corner of Foley Street, that was a rough pub, very rough. Now that man Clare was mixed up in the Movement too and he died a very poor man because he neglected his business and was always handing out money and taking in men that was on the run from the country and keeping them there a week or maybe three. They'd be living in the house *over* the pub. See, publicans had a spare room. They all had to take risks.

"See, an awful lot of curates in Dublin pubs was in the Movement. Oh, yes, and if he was a senior man he was actually running the pub for his boss. So if you were doing intelligence work for the IRA you always had certain pubs you could go into and leave information. And then the interrogating officers of the battalion or company would go there and *get* the information. See, they'd get to know you and knew they could *trust* you. But you had to *whisper* and you always kept in a corner to yourself where there'd be no ear-wigging people listening. The curates knew everyone going in and had their own code, had different signals. They knew everyone going in and knew their opinions. Like if there might be an ex-British Tommy that was living on wounds disability they'd make a sign like that [eye wink] so you'd know to keep away from him. Different signals. It might be by their faces or a movement or maybe they'd tap their cap or take it off, put it on again, or tap their right shoulder. The curates used to do all them tricks, they used to be trained to do it for protection. It was giving you information whether you were *safe* or not in the pub. And a curate, if you left a message on paper for him when he got that message if there was any danger he was to put it in his mouth and eat it, *swallow* it. It'd be a small note only that size. They had to do it because if that was captured you were gone!

"There was one publican, McEntee was his name, and he run a pub called the Cat and Cage up in Drumcondra and McEntee was raided one night and they captured a lot of stuff [arms] in the Cat and Cage and he was sentenced to a couple of years in prison and when the general amnesty was signed he was let out. But his pub was used by the Second Battalion and we knew the pub so well that we might crawl in there and have a conversation preparing for such a raid or such a thing. But there was a lot of informers here and there. Once they [IRA] got to know the informer was passing on information to the British they made arrangements to plug him. There was always a man or two appointed to watch him and at the first opportunity to *shoot him dead*! Oh, shoot him dead. Dead. One man named Pike, he was an informer and he was coming out of Fagan's pub on Botanic Avenue and when he come out with his wife and his wife's friend this man come up on a bike, threw his leg off the bike, walked over and pushed the two women that way and put two bullets into him. Shot him dead outside the pub in broad daylight.

"Oh, men'd bring guns in with them to the pub. The men that done these jobs [killings], they were special men. They were really the principal men in the Irish Republican Movement. Always had a gun with them. They were always prepared to shoot their way through. Keep the gun under their arm in a holster or maybe have a special pocket. And if they had it in their topcoat pocket they, of course, would shoot from their pocket if they were attacked, if they couldn't get a chance to get it out. They always patronised the pubs where there was a way in and a way out, they always had a side door. And if you had a good secret pub that was in the Movement he could hide a dump of stuff, maybe ammunition or maybe a gun or two. They'd hide them in the cellars. And when the IRA wanted them they could get them. Guns were always hid away in pubs where they wouldn't corrode or get rusty. Then if they wanted a gun or two immediately if they were there at that pub the curate would be able to go down to the cellar and roll them up in paper and come up behind the counter and say, 'There's a parcel that was left for you', and that'd be two guns.

"The Black and Tans did often come into the pubs and raid. Could be five or six of them and they'd *rush* right in with their guns and '*Hands up!*' Yes, everyone had their hands up. The Black and Tans, they'd scatter everybody in a pub, give you a battering and clattering on the face and order you out and ask you your name and all. They'd be searching for certain names. And if they couldn't make any progress they'd lose their tempers and might shove you around. Oh, everyone was afraid of the Black and Tans. Give you a box across the back of the neck or on the side of the head—for *nothing*. That was the sort they were. Oh, you couldn't get worse! These Black and Tans were all recruited out of the long-term prisons in England and all the bloody big jails, fellas in doing a life term or maybe ten or twelve years. Their trousers was a sort of black or dark green and then they had their jacket and that was khaki. And they were never sober! A pound a day was their wages, £7 a week. That was a terrible lot of money. They used to drink a lot in their barracks in Dublin. But the pubs wouldn't serve them in their uniform. No. They wouldn't be served dressed in leggin's and knickerbocker britches and a tunic. They might be able to slip into a snug privately, dressed as if they were going to the theatre or that. And the curates, they'd take note of different Black and Tans patronising their place and they'd tip off the IRA. And they'd be watching him and the first opportunity to get him and they'd wait till he come out of the pub or before he went into it and they'd shoot him. I don't remember any pub where anybody was shot *in* it. They always got you on the outside, on the path or on the road.

"There was always rows in pubs. In nearly every pub in Parnell Street, Summerhill, Gloucester Street, maybe on the quays. Certain pubs where there was always a rough element. Rows was mostly two men that'd fall out over football and fight over Gaelic—on the drink—and wouldn't agree and get into a hot argument and 'C'mon, we'll settle it outside!' The publican'd throw them out and the curates would jump over the counter and shove them out—'Fight *outside!*' Ah, yes, they'd push them out. Oh, cause they'd break up the place. In about five minutes the row'd be over and then they'd be all back in the pub again laughing and talking. And sometimes when they'd have a boxing match they'd come out in the morning to finish it. They would! Either apologise or come out and finish it, that's what they used to do.

"Parnell Street was very rough in my time. They were all working-class people and there was a lot of women dealers along the street selling fish and vegetables, and they all took their glass. *Every* pub had a snug for women. Women could drink maybe eight or nine glasses of porter and go home sober. And some would get a gill or two and get a baby Power's and bring it home with them. But during the day they'd hop into the pub and have a quick one. Now I seen women in scraps. I remember seeing two women one day and both of them had a hold of one another with their hair and another woman was trying to separate them and they wouldn't let go. They were two young women about 30 or so. People couldn't separate them and they wouldn't let go, screaming and trying to punish one another. And this man came along and took a scissors out of his pocket and cut the hair of one of them and she had to let go. I never forgot it.

"Publicans, they always lived on the premises and dressed in the best of navy blue serge and a beautiful stiff collar and tie and some of them would wear a bow. Well dressed. And if a customer died the publican supplied you with a couple of dozen of stout and a bottle of whiskey for the wake. And he'd go to the bloody funeral. And if there was a wedding he'd always throw in a good hand of whiskey. And some of the guards was fond of the pint, big strong hefty men, and they might hop in for a quick one, into the snug—and they might be two or three hours at it! And there was no such thing as bookie shops at that time so if you wanted a bookie you patronised a certain pub. Yes, and you'd be sitting down there taking a drink and the bookie would come into the pub and take your few bob and give you a docket. There was *always* a bookie in a busy pub and there'd be fellas going in backing two bob or five bob and so on. The bookie would always bring in a certain amount of money and he'd leave it with the publican. And he'd put it away in his till. And if you came in and you were owed and you won three to one or ten to one, if he hadn't the money loose in his pocket he'd just ask the publican. Oh, they were well dressed, some of them'd wear a big gold watch and chain and big rings on their fingers. You always knew the bookie, they were dressed in the *best* of style."

BERNIE SHEA—AGE 60

One of Moore Street's venerable dealers, she is known for her quick wit and tart tongue. She is a daily fixture at her stall directly in front of a dilapidated pub with no name identification on the exterior. Locals simply refer to it as the "Trader's Pub" but she prefers to call it the "Looney Bin" because of all the characters it draws. All day long she enjoys a steady stream of banter with the "boys" shuffling in and out of the dumpy pub.

"I'm on Moore Street selling for over forty years. My mother sold newspapers on O'Connell Street. It was all old tenement houses around then. This pub about forty years ago was Leahy's pub, then it was Bourke's and then it was O'Neill's Bar. When I was young the pub here was spotless clean and you could go in there and Mr Leahy would make us a cup of Bovril which was great. Ah, he was a nice gentleman, he really was. And when it was Leahy's you used to be able to go in there and he'd boil a kettle of water and you could go in with your old billy can and you could make tea and stand out here drinking it. And if a trader was ill she'd be brought into the pub for sitting down. So years ago as

children we'd go into the pub but then you had to go to Confession and you'd
say, 'Bless me, Father, I've gone into a pub.' And he'd say, 'You had *no* authority
to go there, do you know it's not a nice thing to do? Do you want to make Our
Lady happy? Keep out of the pub, you're only a child.' But now, of course,
they're breast-feeding babies in the pub! That's the gospel truth.

  "There used to be a side entrance to the pub there in O'Rahilly's Parade and
the women dealers would sit in the snug and they'd get a glass of stout. But they
wouldn't go in and mix where the men'd drink. *Not at all*, it wouldn't be allowed.
It'd be the talk of the *world*! They'd be frowned on. It'd be a *mortal sin*. Maybe
the poor unfortunate girls of the street from around the red light district, they
might venture in but they had no reputation to begin with. But the dealers would
be going in to get themselves a quick one. Their mothers done it before them and
their grandmothers. A lot of them'd slip in saying that they were only going to
the lavatory. They'd leave their baby with someone and say, 'Sure, I won't be
gone a minute, I'm only going into the pub to pass water.' And they'd go in and
just gobble it down and then they'd come back immediately. You had them that
controlled themselves but then you had them that'd be going in from morning at
half ten and they'd be nipping in and nipping out, getting themselves a quick
one. Not to the extent that they'd be maggoty, mouldy drunk because that'd be
bad for business. Do you know who used to often drink *on* the street? Rosie,
queen of Moore Street, up on the top. She's dead and gone now. She'd often have
a bottle of stout out standing but none of the other women'd do it.

  "Most of the traders here are buried in Glasnevin. The remains would be
buried and all and we'd say, 'Now we're going down to O'Neill's pub.' Now see
Grace [dealer friend] there? Well, her mother sold there all her life, Maggie, and
she died and it was her wish when she died that there'd be a couple of large
bottles buried with her. And this was her pub. So when she was going to be
buried the funeral came here and stopped, the hearse stopped where you're
standing. And they went into the pub and got two large bottles of Guinness and
they were given up to the hearse man and put into the hearse and they went off
to Glasnevin to bury Maggie. And the hole was dug and Maggie's coffin was put
down into the hole and the two large bottles of Guinness was put down on top of
her in the coffin cause she said 'Let me go out with a bang.' So Maggie was
buried, the Lord have mercy on her, and all the crowd come back here and they
danced and sung. That's the way she wanted it. It's a very joyous occasion
because you're going home to God, cause we Irish are a very religious people.
We're not like you Yanks. When you Yanks die you go to limbo and you's have
to wait to see if they're going to let you into Heaven or not. The Irish, we get to
go *straight* to Heaven, so it's rejoicement we're having that she's gone to Heaven.
She's nine years dead now and if you was to dig up Maggie's grave them two bottles
would still be down there . . . unless she got up and drank them, which I wouldn't
be a bit surprised if she did because she loved the bottle. She's entitled to it!

  "Now today we call this pub the 'Looney Bin'. Oh, all the people that drink
in there are mental. And the pint is very cheap compared with other places
because there's no carpet, practically no windows and things are all broke. It fell

by the wayside. As you can see, it's not in a notorious state. You get myxomatosis if you drink in there! There's no decorations in the place. A very simple pub but it's the real McCoy, a real traditional Irish pub. They all drink in there because the pint in that pub is the *best* pint you'll get in Ireland. *Any* pint drinker knows. It's word of mouth from grandad to son to grandson. The story is that they have a very good cellar and that's why they excel. So it'll always make money because it has the best pint in town.

"Years ago they used to put sawdust on the floor and there was rows here to beat the band. The men when they'd be fighting would strip to their waist. They'd kill one another there in the pub, it was a way of life. They'd be drunk in the first place and there'd be some grievance. Some of these men, they're non-stop every day, I'm looking at them going in and out morning, noon and night. They're like second kin to me. One routine day in and day out. They've no variety in their lives and it's an awful pity because there's more to life than drinking. It is a curse, drink. It's a drug and it's habitual. So today it's the 'Looney Bin' because all the madmen drink in there. Regulars. Wheeling and dealing at the Looney Bin. If you want to buy a grand piano go into that pub and say, 'If somebody gets me a grand piano I'll buy it', and I'll guarantee you, you count to ten and it'll be coming down the street here. They'll get it for you. *No* problem! They wouldn't get you a jet plane or anything like that but they would get you a motor car. But there'd be no problem getting you a helicopter!"

TOMMY O'NEILL—AGE 68

During the war years he plied the Dublin streets as a jarvey and haunted all the "horsy men" pubs around Smithfield. Some of the publicans were real rogues who watered their whiskey and clobbered unruly customers with a wooden mallet. He especially liked to hang around the Widow Reilly's pub which was famous for match-making. While sipping pints, he watched the finesse with which the good Widow brought couples together—for a fee, of course.

"I was born in Chicken Lane. My father was a jarvey and me grandfather was a jarvey, and an undertaker. Oh, yes, we were all jarveys and undertakers. There was twelve of us in the family. My father, being a jarvey, he'd bring them out to the cemetery and make sure they got the six foot under. And jarveys were the best drinkers in the world. My father could drink two or three bottles of whiskey a day and you wouldn't think he had it on him and he'd get in and drive a hearse. Now the jarveys after a funeral they'd all go to all the pubs going back and have a sing-song, like at Bush's [pub] in Phibsborough and Hedigan's. The jarveys would get the drink and they wouldn't have to pay for it. And jarveys could drink! Ah, they were seasoned to it. After a funeral they'd be inside the pub drinking, drinking. Some of them would be there till closing time that night —and the funeral crowd'd walk home!

"Jarveys were the best drinkers of the whole lot and terrible witty. The old jarveys were all great characters with hard hats and there were all nicknames for the jarveys. My uncle was called 'Kissing the Bottle', then another uncle was called 'Run Away with the Hearse' and then there was 'Blue Nose' and 'Lousy Cushion' and 'Redpole' and 'Banker'. I knew them all well. My uncle, Corny O'Neill, was crowned king of the jarveys in Dublin. Cause he was a character and he was six foot six. And always mad for a fight, he could fight any of them. Oh, jarveys would have rows. It'd start over one taking a fare off another. They'd use the chain that they used to put around their wheel so the horse wouldn't run away and they'd get it across the head. Indeed, I did see it. And my uncle, oh, he was a big man, Lord have mercy on him. Oh, my God, all he could do was drink, drink, drink. He drank himself into the grave.

"Now there was 'Daddy' Egan's pub there in Smithfield. I used to always be in there when I was a young man. At noon time he'd walk out with a rosary beads and you had to join in with the Angelus. That's true, inside the pub. He was a very religious man. Religious *mad*. He went to be a priest and failed. Oh, you'd have to kneel down and you'd be saying 'Hail Mary' and he'd be saying the 'Our Father'. Every day, if you were in there. But some days there'd be no one in there at noon and he'd lock the shop and you couldn't get in till the rosary was over. That's true, that's no lie. He was a lovely little man. He wasn't married, he was a bachelor. Something like Matt Talbot. But a *rogue*, a rogue in every way. He'd rob your change and everything. Oh, but you had to say the rosary! And he'd keep people in during the Holy Hour and there was police raids into the pub. When there was a police raid you could go out in the yard and over the wall. Sure, one fella fell through a hen house and broke his leg at the back of Daddy Egan's. He was caught and fined £12 and Daddy Egan was fined £50.

"Now there was two men who used to stand outside of Daddy Egan's and they used to be bouncers. He gave them a few drinks. They could handle themselves. Everyone knew these two men. If anyone cut up or broke up in Daddy Egan's they went in and ordered him out. One was 'Fisty' Carney and the other was 'Stealer' Gagan. One had an iron right hand and the other had an iron left hand. Gagan lost his hand in the 1914 War and he used to screw it on and off. And he always had a glove on it. And Carney had *another* iron hand. They were both in the army. It was just like the iron hall door knocker and when you got a belt of that! That's what they were there for.

"And Daddy Egan's, that's where all the deals was made years ago. They started out in Smithfield, all the horse dealers and knackers and the tinkers, like the Wards, the Cashs, the Joyces, all of them. Start out in the open and there would be horses and cattle and pigs and goats. So in Daddy Egan's pub there was what you called a middleman or a 'tangler' and he'd go into the snug with two men and then they'd do their deal. The tangler'd be dividing the money and he'd have to get a few pints and maybe ten bob at the time. You could buy *anything* in a pub, from a needle to an anchor. You could even get all the poitin you wanted years ago. It was all coming down from Cavan and Monaghan and all. It was in little jam jars. Everybody'd buy it around Christmas. Oh, it'd kill you. And they'd even bring a horse into Daddy Egan's, bring a horse right in. It was just for devilment. They used to do it to *torment* Daddy Egan. One time a horse went in and he fell through the floor. That's true, he went through the floor. A big heavy horse. Went down and broke the boards.

"Old Daddy Egan, he sold Red Biddy, bad wine, to the tinkers. He'd let a few in and the other itinerants they'd all sit outside the door. And they'd drink the Red Biddy. Big bottles. It was one and six a bottle at that time and they'd get drunk on that and hell would break loose. Then the tinkers would fight with their sticks, the ashplants, and they had hobnail boots. Oh, the best fights in the world used to be in Smithfield. Oh, five or six clans fighting. And the Wards and the Joyces would be all in bandages. The women'd tear with their nails. They never got their nails cut. That's why I got me nails cut so short because my mother made sure we got our nails cut short and she used to say, 'You're going around like tinkers'. Oh, the women'd tear you. When you got one tear off them you got about ten or twelve stitches in the side of your face. That's how all them old itinerants were all so ugly looking, all their faces cut and ripped. Now the [Richmond] hospital was only up Red Cow Lane and the police used to have an old push cart at that time during the war, sort of an ambulance with two big wheels, and the guards would run it down and pick them up and I seen tinkers getting pushed into the cart and taken off to the hospital.

"Then Mike Horan's pub was at the far side of Smithfield, but Mike Horan was after dirtying his bib. He was another Daddy Egan. Something went wrong with the barmaid, this was around 1952. He was after sacking the barmaid and she had been with him for about five or six years and didn't she report him to the guards! What was he doing? He had the girl up all night filling shell cocoa and he was selling it for stout! They were mixing the shell cocoa with stout and *selling* it. She'd boil the shell cocoa and him and his barman was bottling it. And all the heavy drinkers going in and thinking they were drinking the best stout in Ireland—and it was shell cocoa. They caught him. And he served at every Mass in church for years, he was even an old altar boy!

"Then you had Matt Lynch [publican] on Church Street. Oh, he was a rough man, a fine big man. No messing! Oh, he was a contrary bugger. Not everybody'd he'd serve. If you were in there with drink on you, you got thrown out. You didn't go out, you were *carried* out. See, a publican always kept a mallet, a tapper, for tapping the barrels. You only had to get a tap and *you* had to be buried. You were carried out. He got fined one time for hitting a man with the mallet and had to pay a couple of thousand pounds. Then you had Crilly's pub down by Smithfield. That was a terrible pub, that was a brothel. It was a dump. All the trash of the town would go and drink in it and the police would be standing outside waiting for them to come out. Crilly's was the lowest down pub around there. Oh, the roughest and the toughest would go into it. All the knockabouts drank in it. He had a fire to keep them warm. When you went in you got a drink of this stuff, the Red Biddy, and then you got another glass and you were seeing rainbows.

"Now Hanlon's pub, that was all a cattleman's pub and for the jarveys, they had a hazard, a stand, at Hanlon's. All the Englishmen [cattle buyers] used to be in there. Oh, Hanlon's sold the most whiskey in Ireland! Oh, yes. All the Englishmen went in there and when they'd be going back to the boat they'd have big trenchcoats on them and had bottles of whiskey in their pockets to a band playing! Cattlemen were all whiskey drinkers. Drovers would just stand outside Hanlon's with a stick and cattlemen'd pick a few of them out. Then they'd meet back in the pub and the cattlemen paid the drovers in the pub. And then they'd have a couple of pounds and they'd drink it. Pay them in the pub and maybe give them a pint. That's all drovers did. Drink. That's what killed them.

"And at Hanlon's pub there was two little nuns and they'd be outside with a big bag [collecting donations]. And one fella, he'd tell them he was putting in money but he could do it so fast that he'd let on to put one in but he'd *take out two* half-crowns. He'd be watching what'd be going in and then it was, 'How are you, Sister?' and then the hand would be going in. And there was buskers at Hanlon's. You had this man with a melodeon and he could only play one tune, 'It's a Long, Long Way to Tipperary'. His name was Stoney and he'd go around and play in all the pubs and he'd get a good few drinks and a few shillings. And there was a small little woman at Hanlon's and she had a bad leg, a short leg, and she had a melodeon and she could *play* that melodeon and she'd sing all the songs of the day. And the famous Margaret Barry used to be up there. Oh, she was. She had a guitar and she'd play all the great songs. Now women weren't served then but these buskers were known and they were brought into the pub and given bottles of stout. Yeah, drink till the cows come home.

"I knew Dolly Fawcett well. Cause we had a pig yard at the back of Dolly's. It was a brothel but she got away with it. I often had a drink in it. There was a bar and she had no end to the whiskey down in the cellars. Our yard was on back of the Cozy Kitchen and then she had the Cafe Continental. Sailors and all would come up there and the men'd have to buy the women drinks. And when they'd be finished with the condoms they used to throw the condoms into our pig yard. And the pigs, the sows, was eating the condoms—and the little pigs was born with rubber coats on them! But the girls were all country girls. Ah, nice looking. Dolly, she used to always dress in red and when she was going up to the chapel on Dominick Street her six girls all wore red coats. But you had to buy them drinks and they'd rob you as well! Oh, they were all deep-handed, they'd rob you. Many a cattleman went down there with wallets of money and come out with nothing. See, they'd meet the woman and go around with her in horse cabs. And they'd be in the cab carrying on. He'd [customer] tell you [jarvey] to just keep going around and looking steady [ahead]. And then maybe when he'd be finished he'd just be out the f——ing door and you got no fare off them! You'd have been maybe driving around for half an hour and maybe an hour and you'd look around and the two of them gone. Jumped out.

"And I knew the Widow Reilly well, up in Phibsborough. Knew her *well*. She was twenty stone. And if she told you to get out, you went out! Or she'd scruff you out. Kate Gilligan was her maiden name but she was known as the Widow

Reilly. Now her husband had a pub in James's Street and he always wore spats. And he never spoke to her. And she *hated* him! And when he died everyone then got free drink for three days. But she done time for black market during the war. Selling black market tea and sugar. She sold sawdust and half tea. She sold it direct from her old grocery store. When she bought that pub out in Phibsborough she done well in it. She dressed very old fashioned, big old black hat and an old shawl and a long black coat. And pulled a pint herself. Oh, she was a *tough* woman. But she ran a marriage bureau out there in the pub. Yeah, a marriage bureau. You could go in there if you wanted to get married, in her pub. Match-making! You'd go in there and you had to pay her so much. Had to pay her a fee. So you went into her, she had a special compartment of her own, and she'd take all the particulars. Oh, she'd write it all down. And you'd meet them [women] then in the pub. It was like going to the cattle market and buying a cow. That's true. That was good for her business. You'd go in there and it was packed with women, like a big dance hall, and she had a fella playing the accordion and a great accordion player he was too. Oh, it'd be *packed* and she'd make a match. She'd get you fixed up, get you married. They got married out of it! And then she'd give you a wedding present if you got married."

JOHN GREENHALGH—AGE 82

As a young Ringsend lad he would go to Fagan's pub to fetch a few bottles of stout for his granny and stand fascinated watching the barman seal them with wax to comply with the law. At that time Ringsend pubs were famed for their rings competitions. And it was always great entertainment to watch the "hoggers" lapping up beer from discarded barrels and coming away looking like clowns with red raddle on their faces.

"When I was a kid about 10 or 11 my grandmother'd say, 'Go to John in Fagan's and get me two bottles of stout.' Now listen carefully—it was six old pence a bottle it was. So I'd go up for the two bottles of stout and with me being under age the barman he'd put the two bottles on the counter and do you know the sealing wax that used to be used in post offices years ago? Well, he'd light the sealing wax and seal the old-fashioned corks on the two bottles. That was to comply with the law. Once it was sealed it was legal. What fascinated me as a kid was he was so skilful at dropping the wax onto the cork. But if you went out with those two bottles of Guinness not sealed and a copper seen me he could go back and summons yer man.

"There was five or six pubs here in Ringsend. Pubs had sawdust all along the side of the counter [on the floor]. Guys made a living out of that. They'd have an old horse and cart and they'd go to the sawmills, gather up the sawdust in sacks and sell the sacks to the publican. It was to keep the floor clean. What they used to say was, 'Where are you off to now?' and he'd say, 'Oh, I'm going over to spit in the sawdust . . . I'll be over at the pub.' And over on Bridge Street there

52

The Bleeding Horse in Camden Street was a prosperous inn during the eighteenth century.

53

Maureen Grant of the Olympia Theatre is Dublin's most famous barmaid.

54

The Oarsman pub in Ringsend has long been the local for seamen and dockers.

55

The Royal Oak Tavern in Parkgate Street was established in 1742.

56

Unloading Guinness's metal casks at Mulligan's pub of Poolbeg Street.
These also became known as "iron lungs" or "depth charges".

57
O'Neill's pub of Suffolk Street was known for its fine whiskey and high-class clientele.

58
The Glimmer Man pub in Stoneybatter Street.

59
Pintman Paddy Losty. Some of Dublin's great pintmen have been known to put away thirty pints or more in a day.

60
The Long Hall in Great George's Street was the local for painters and other tradesmen.

61

*Mulligan's pub of Stoneybatter, established in 1792,
still retains its grocer's sign.*

62

The Old Stand in Exchequer Street, 1970s.

63

The Brazen Head's proud claim.

64

Publican Thomas O'Dowd of Grangegorman Street.

65

Horse being led out the door of Broggy's pub in James's Street after being given a pint of stout. This is an old custom around Smithfield and the Liberties on horse fair day.

66

Cleary's pub in Amiens Street has long been noted for its fine whiskey and railway passenger trade.

67

The pub as a tranquil haven, removed from the turmoil of the outside world.
(Courtesy of John Woodfull)

68

The Shakespeare pub in Parnell Street.

69
*Pub regular Tony
Morris of O'Dowd's
in Grangegorman
Street.*

70
O'Neill's pub in Pearse Street displaying colourful hanging plants and flowers.

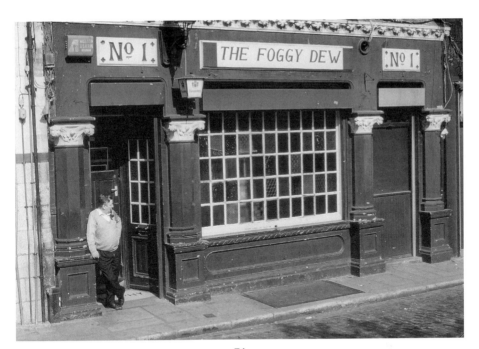

71

The Foggy Dew in Fownes Street.

72

*Hill 16 pub in Gardiner Street noted for its
"soccer-mad" regulars.*

73

Float laden with old Guinness casks on the cobblestones of Smithfield advertising the Glimmer Man pub.

74

Legendary barman Paddy O'Brien of McDaid's who later moved to Grogan's pub taking the literary set with him.

75
*Publican Tommy
Smith, heir to
Paddy O'Brien,
presides over
Grogan's which
is Dublin's last
authentic literary
pub. (Courtesy of
John Woodfull)*

76
*Grogan's pub of South William Street drew away the literary crowd from
McDaid's in 1972.*

77

Publican Tommy Smith of Grogan's doing cellar duty.
(Courtesy of John Woodfull)

78

Bowe's of Fleet Street with its striking exterior.

79

Jolly pintmen in the doorway of a pub at the lower end of Moore Street, variously known as the "No-Name pub", "Trader's pub" or "Looney Bin".

80

Splendid solitude of the pub sanctuary. (Courtesy of John Woodfull)

was a pork shop there and they used to boil the pig's feet. And say there was four guys together drinking in the pub, well, they'd say, 'It's your turn to go down and get four pig's feet' from the woman that owned the shop. Oh, bring it down in a sheet of paper and eat it out of their hand *in* the pub. And there'd be more pig's feet bones! And then the next guy in the company would be sent down and it was, 'Get tripe this time.' And, I'll tell you, the poor guy that'd go down for the tripe, he'd have a half-pint [left] and he'd leave it when he was gone and they'd drop a bone from the pig into his pint. A bit of a joke. It was always fun. But TV finished the lot. No conversation, no nothing any more. It's 'Shhh, I don't want to miss this programme.' That's a shame. It's the greatest curse ever invented.

"The pub, it was really a working man's club. If you wanted to meet anyone that's where you met them. There was *always* a pub that was the meeting place. See, if you wanted to see someone you knew the pub they drank in and *that's* where you went. You *knew* you'd see them there. And there was a lot of business carried out in the pubs. Like if you were out of work and, say, there was a building job going and you had an idea of where the guy that takes on the men drank, well, you'd go in there and ask him, 'Any use, is it worthwhile going in the morning?' And, oh, many a lad going for a job the publican would write him a reference and put it in an envelope. The publican was respected. And everyone was told by the publican that there was two subjects not to be mentioned —religion and politics. Leave that to the pulpit and the recruiting man! And they had a slate years back. There was 'put it on the slate' for regulars. They made progress from the slate and chalk to a little cash book and he'd mark it down. And if you died for a couple of pints you'd go in and you'd just give him a nod or wink and he'd pull up the pints. He was very, very rarely let down. Because you *knew* [if you didn't pay] that you were only hurting yourself and losing your mates because you couldn't go into that shop any more.

"Back then Guinness had their own fleet and when their ships would come back from Liverpool and other parts of England with their empty hogsheads, the big casks, well, that's how 'hoggers' got their name. See, Guinness'd throw all them empties up on the quayside and stand them up in rows all along the quay. And there might be a half a pint of booze, porter, in one. And one that was empty that's what they called a 'dead man'. So the hoggers'd come along and pick one hogshead and there might be a pint in that and they'd tip that. And they'd say, 'time to have a sup.' But they'd clean the top first, make sure it's nice and clean. Then they'd put the peak of their cap to one side of their head and sup it up. And they had the red raddle on their nose and their forehead. Oh, there was no need to have a circus—no Hollywood make-up! Oh, it was a regular thing, you seen it every day when you were a kid, it was just a way of life.

"In those days if a woman wanted her husband out of the pub she might be walking the street and she'd see some man she knows and she'd say, 'Mick, tell Michael I want him.' Well, that man'd go into the pub and he'd just side up to the man and just whisper to him, 'The missus wants to see you outside.' Oh, she daren't go near the pub for him. Oh, it'd be murder. Cause all the guys would be saying, 'Oh, your missus is going in after you!' So if it was an urgent message she'd see someone she knew and he'd go in. Now if a woman *went* to the pub she had to go into the snug. It was a sort of *religion* among the men that a woman wouldn't be seen in the bar. And they might have a bottle of Guinness, that was their favourite. They'd come in with the shawl around them and go into the snug and the publican'd know what they wanted. But there was no ladies' toilets at that time. It was a terrible thing, all right, no toilets for women. But this publican in Ringsend, he had the first toilet for ladies. How did he manage it? Well, I'll have to tell you. He got a Jacob's biscuit tin, half filled it with sawdust, and put it in the snug for the ladies. Half filled it with sawdust, that was the silencer! The Niagara Falls! That's true.

"This was a real town for rings. Oh, a lot of money gambled on rings in pubs. Oh, yeah. There'd be bets put on the counter. You might see a fiver and that was a lot of money then. They used to have competitions. A ring team from Ringsend would play a team out in Dun Laoghaire in a pub. And then they'd have a competition in another pub, say in Finglas. Used to travel around just like football teams. The publican liked that because the followers, the supporters, would go with them. And it was always on a week night that'd be a slack night and, well, he'd have a full house in his pub that night. Win or lose there'd be cash spent. And there were some great ring pitchers. They'd have their pint on the ledge there and take a sip out of it now and again and put it down. There was one man, Bass Byrne, and he could twiddle the ring, get the ring and he'd *spin* it all the way over onto number 13. He had that touch, it was marvellous to look at him. Oh, he was a local hero.

"The pubs of the present day, we often feel sad about it . . . it's not the same. Not the same fun or sing-songs the way we had it. Every fella would sing in his turn and sometimes you'd get a fella with an old melodeon. And they'd play the spoons. And the fella that'd play the melodeon for the night, well, he'd go around with his old hat and they'd throw a few coppers into it, that made *him* happy. And he was getting a free pint in between from the barman. And some fella'd always come along with a joke, there were some great comedians. All for fun, everything was for fun. It'd all be in order and they'd have an MC. The MC, well, you know the old mop they'd use for mopping up the pub, he'd get a cigarette pack and put it on the top of the mop handle and use it as a microphone. And every pub put up Christmas decorations. There'd be paper chains the publican would put up about two weeks before Christmas. And a Christmas box, that was a custom. Once the publican knew you were a regular there you might go in and he'd put up the pint of Guinness and a glass of whiskey beside it and 'Happy Christmas!' And the pub'd be in *uproar* with 'I'm Dreaming of a White Christmas' . . . it's not the same."

BILLY SULLIVAN—AGE 80

He made so much money during the war years skinning rabbits that he could drink in Donoghue's pub every day of the week. At another pub he and his mates used to secretly

siphon off whiskey from barrels and end up in a sing-song. He also frequented
some of the rougher singing houses where he served as an MC for a few free pints.

"I was born in 1914 in Mary's Abbey. My father had a pony and cart for hire and people'd buy their vegetables and bags of potatoes and he'd deliver them. He got a few shillings. I spent thirty years in the two markets, the fruit and the fish market. I worked mostly casual, it was 'where the wind blew, you blew'. Ah, I drank at 14 years of age. I could drink me fair share of pints. Now in my time porter was eight pence and stout was ten pence. You couldn't drink a pound's worth in my time! And I was working for Carton's skinning rabbits for three shillings a hundred. It was piecework. And I got a shilling for skinning a badger and a shilling for skinning a fox. Rabbits were exported during the war to keep England in food. Oh, yes, *thousands*. I'd do a hundred an hour. Oh, we had to be fast, like lightning. You'd think we were skinning bananas! At that time building labourers had £3 wages [weekly] and we were earning £8 and £10 doing the skinning. And you'd be *drinking every day* of the week. I went to Donoghue's pub, it was at the corner of Arran Street and Mary's Abbey. He had a great pint in there years ago.

"I remember the Black and Tans, seen them coming up Capel Street when I was only a kid. Coming up and shooting every window along the street. Oh, the Tans were all ex-convicts out of the prisons in England. When curfew was on they'd knock the pubs down going into them. They'd break into the pubs and come out stupid drunk. Oh, a bunch of bowzies. But the British Tommies were all right. They could drink in a public house. But there were parts of Dublin where they couldn't go into a public house, like the Monto, cause they'd beat them up. Oh, just give him a hiding and they'd throw him out.

"Now there was five public houses around the markets that had a 7.00 [morning] licence. There was three in Arran Street: there was Donoghue's and Roberts's and Corbett's. Now this is going back to the twenties. And the Daisy Market dealers, they'd drink in Corbett's public house at the corner of Little Mary Street, next to Many Penny Yard. He'd serve women, no problem. They'd wear shawls. They'd have a glass of porter, a gill, and a baby Power's and that was one and eight pence. Oh, some of them'd drink you under the table! Now you've heard about Dicey Reilly? She was just a knockabout, very fond of the drink and she had a little tricolour and she'd come into the market in the morning and wave it and start going 'Up De Valera!' cause the Civil War wasn't very far gone in the twenties. And she'd get a few bob and, as the song goes, 'Dicey went for another little one.' The women dealers were the most wittiest people in Ireland. Terrible, terrible witty. And on a funeral day they'd go and make an excursion out of it. They'd bury the corpse first and *then* to the pub. And they'd be in that public house all day then. And now there was this one dealer in the market, Maggie, and she'd faint, playing possum. And a crowd would congregate around her and she'd say, 'Ah, me poor old heart!' Always outside a public house she'd do this and someone who didn't know the act would go in and get a half a whiskey. Pretend she was sick and there was nothing wrong with her at all. And it was an *act*. Cause she'd get a half a whiskey! Always done this outside the boozer . . . and then Maggie'd do her act again.

"Around the market the pubs opened at 7.00 in the morning and it'd be *packed*. They'd even be waiting outside for them to open. And you could get a cup of Bovril and a bun. And Gilson's pub in Church Street, it sold pig's feet and there'd be bones all over the place. But it was mostly dockers and drovers [who] were the best pint drinkers in this town. They used to have a competition down on the docks to see who was the champion pint drinker. And some of the houses had a *great* pint, but more of the houses hadn't. I could never understand that. Maybe it was the pumps wouldn't be so very clean, that could have been the cause of it. You could get a bad pint. Oh, a bad pint and you'd be going to the toilet all night. And, see, there were fellas that when they'd go into a pub at 2.00 on a Sunday they wouldn't be the first in, they'd wait for someone else to go in because yer man would have pints lying maybe from the previous night that was left behind and he'd just top them up. That's how you'd get a bad pint.

"Market pubs was always packed and one time I seen Jack Doyle coming in with two girls after being out all night at a dance, in a dress suit. And I often seen Brendan Behan and he was terrible boisterous then. Now in the market there was a great friend of mine, 'Bubbles' Fagan was his name. And Ronnie Drew of the Dubliners would come into the market and bring Bubbles out for a gargle in the pub because Bubbles knew songs that *nobody* knew. And there was another man who if he got a few drinks on him he'd get up on the floor and he'd give out 'Dangerous Dan McGrew'. And he'd give the accent and all. Oh, he was great. He'd recite that. Oh, we'd be quiet listening.

"Now if you got drink on the slate and, say, you owed for six or eight pints the barman might say you owed *ten*. And you couldn't contradict him. If you did, you wouldn't get in again. So you had to pay him. Some of these bartenders opened up their public houses in a few years. Oh, it was on the fiddle. Definitely. They'd be lifting money out of the cash register. They *did* that. And I'll tell you, policemen were on the take. A very good friend of mine, Sean Kennedy, he had a public house in Capel Street. And a sergeant and an ordinary guard came in, you see, and they ordered a drink and so Sean put up the drink and said, 'That'll be five shillings', and the sergeant says, 'That'll be all right' [meaning he wouldn't have to pay], and Sean says 'No, that'll be five shillings.' So the sergeant *paid* him. And now for nights after that he'd be raiding the place to catch the customers drinking after hours. And Sean would always have the clock a *half an hour fast* to make sure they got out, so he wouldn't be caught when yer man come to raid the place. He'd raid cause he was angry that Sean wouldn't give it to him for nothing, because he could probably get it off another publican for nothing.

"Now in the 1920s there was a publican named Peter Murray on Little Green Street. Now it was a legitimate public house but he served some queer characters, they were pimps and prostitutes. Now this is the funny thing, he *died* and he was waked in the public house and anybody could go up, pimps, prostitutes, *anyone*. Now in the history of Dublin when a publican died here he went back to his own county, to Cavan and Wexford. But he was waked *here* in the house. And usually a publican's house was strictly private and you wouldn't get in to see a publican dead. Oh, not at all! But *everybody* went up to the pub to see him. He was the best but he was always getting criticised from the church. The church was criticising him because he was running kind of a notorious house, serving drink to the 'ladies of the night'. But he left all his money when he died to the church! Ah, he was a good man.

"The singing houses were rough. The only recognised thing in a public house was a piano and the publican would pay the piano player a few bob. Ah, there was some great singers in the public houses. I used to do the MC in one of the singing houses and you'd name a fella to come up and I got a few free pints for doing it and then you might get a fella that'd give you a pint for to let him sing. But maybe there'd be three or four other fellas and they'd say, '*I'm* next, or else!' And you had better call them up next or they'd give you a bang with a bottle on their way out. But I seen a pub wrecked from fighting. *Wrecked*. It was Lalor's on the quays, a singing house. Cause you'd get different types coming into a singing house and a fella'd get a few drinks and he'd want to sing and there'd be some *other* fella coming up and *he'd* want to sing. They were messers. And there'd be murder. But this fight come up and the place was wrecked. Must have been sixty or eighty fighting. Could have been a hundred in it. Oh, everything was flying. Anything that was in it. All wrecked.

"Now old Mick Keating, a publican, when there was a funeral around the place he'd go to the funeral of the customer and then he'd come back and anyone that was in the pub he'd give them two pints of porter. Then he left his assistant there at the bar and he'd go upstairs and say the rosary for the deceased. He was from Wexford. And now in Keating's they used to have their own whiskey and they had two big barrels in the shop. And did you ever hear of an old bed key? Well, a bed key years ago when you put up the sides of the bed you could tighten it with this. But this could open *barrels*. See, it was square, the same as the thing on the barrels. So a few of us used to go in, sit down, and we'd loosen the thing on the whiskey barrel with the bed key and let the whiskey run into our pint tumblers. And then close it up again. It was just a small pub and you'd be sitting in a seat along there and the barrels were in back of you and old Mick would be serving down there away from you. So we'd put our pint under the whiskey and you'd be drinking all night . . . and in about an hour's time you'd be all singing."

Mary Corbally—Age 74

Born in a tenement in Corporation Street, the second eldest of fifteen children, she went on to give birth to twenty-one of her own. She grew up in the Monto next to Phil Shanahan's and Paddy Clare's pubs, both of which were famous IRA havens. She was very accepting of the many shebeens and kip houses around her and found the prostitutes kind and generous. She recalls with amusement how one madam would hide the stout bottles down the gramophone when there was a police raid.

"I don't feel any shame in coming from the Monto. The reputation was there cause of the girls. In them years they was called the 'unfortunate girls' but we never heard the word 'whores' or 'prostitutes'. You heard your mother say, 'Oh, the girls are down there', around the gas lamp at Jack Maher's pub. His pub was a kind of figurehead going into the Monto. Oh, the girls used to drink in there. And there was Paddy Clare's pub on Corporation Street and then facing that was the famous Phil Shanahan's pub on the corner of Foley Street. Everything that happened was always connected to the pub, from wakes, weddings and hooleys. The pub was the mainstay. Oh, there was never a dull moment. I can still picture meself looking out the window on 54 Corporation Street cause you could see into Paddy Clare's when the gas light would be on and you could see who was in the pub. And as kids we used to sit outside Paddy Clare's and Phil Shanahan's on the steps and we'd make a concert. I'd be 13 or 14 years of age. You'd get up and dance or do your turn and the men'd come out of the pub and be looking and clapping and then they'd throw a penny to us.

"You never seen women at the counter. Women would go into little snugs that'd hold about three people, *confession boxes* we'd call them. Funny thing, I can never remember seeing young women. Of course, in them years young women looked older because they wore long skirts and shawls and had their hair tied in a bun. But they'd have a gill. The way the women used to do it was there was a shop on our street there and the women used to sit in the front of the shop. It used to sell penny sweets and turf and coal. They'd be sitting there and they'd 'stand in' and give tuppence or a penny or thruppence and they'd put it together and they'd go over to the pub for two gills or three gills. It was never more than three gills because the jug didn't hold any more. I often went meself for it [for them]. I was about 8. I done this for me mother and the older women. This one woman had particularly lovely jugs, jugs with all the famous men on them. She'd one jug with Robert Emmet on it, I remember that. I used to love going with it cause the people'd look at it and call you over and then maybe you'd get a ha'penny off them. You'd go to the counter and put the jug up and I remember that the publican'd come out the door with you and *he'd* carry the jug and he'd look up and down the street and then say, 'Go on, straight down.' I think at that time they were trying to stop children going into pubs.

"To me, publicans was all country men and they always seemed to be better educated. I can't remember a Dublin man being a publican. And they used to sell sugar and tea and Kerry tin milk and tobacco. They had a thing like a spade and they cut the tobacco with that. Men used to chew it. And there was sawdust on the floor about a foot wide under the counter because the men with their pints would be spitting. Some of the pubs had gas lighting and some only had an open fire. But publicans were wealthy. They must have been wealthy because all the rooms over the pub and you never seen tenants in them. And *all* the publicans helped with burials. They were very good. See, we grew up with them and they were kind of figureheads to us. When people'd be in financial trouble they could always go to them. Jack Maher, you could go over to him in the middle of the night—*any* hour of the night—and knock at the door if you had a sick child or if any of the family would be sick and you might want a sup of whiskey or a sup of brandy. You'd run to him and knock at the door and he'd give you the little baby Power's with a sup of whiskey in it. They were very generous like that.

"And we used to love Christmas Eve because publicans had baskets and you'd see the porter with the basket on his shoulder bringing up your order. See, sometimes the pub had a club up and you'd pay so much into it every week. You'd pay sixpence or a shilling whenever you'd have it, say from August to Christmas. Whatever few bob you had you'd put in. It was a porter club for the drink and you'd order it and then he'd bring it up. He might bring a dozen of bottles, large bottles that was a pint, and a sup of whiskey. And then he'd stand at the door and you'd open one of the bottles for him and give it to the pub porter for bringing it up. And he'd drink it on the spot there and you'd wish him a merry Christmas and off he'd go. Then the porter had to come back and collect the bottles but we used to run away with them and sell them. You'd get a ha'penny each on them. But there were bottles that you could feel the raised stamp on the glass and you got a penny on them.

"Phil Shanahan was a very famous man, you know, in the Movement, and there's a big monument down in Tipperary to him. His pub was facing Paddy Clare's and they were great companions the two of them. But Phil Shanahan was always on his own, a very lonely man he was. He'd have company in the pub but upstairs he only lived on his own. He had something to do with the Movement and he was very silent. No one knew his business, he was always very close to himself. He always gave me the impression that he was terribly lonely. When he'd be in the pub he never served much, he was always leaning on the counter and never had an awful lot to say. But he was a terrible nice man. He had a big pot belly and he could never stoop to tie his laces. We lived facing him and we'd always stand at the door and watch him and he'd motion us to come over and tie his shoes for him and six or seven of us would go over and he'd give you a penny to tie his laces. He couldn't get down to tie them.

"Jack Maher's pub used to be called the 'queer house' because all the girls, the prostitutes, they were at the gas lamp post outside the pub. They used to stand there. See, that was called at that time a 'red lamp' district. That was the Monto. The girls used to drink in the pub there and the men used to come mostly off the boats. Most of the girls now that I can remember were from the country. It was for the money, just to keep themselves going. Oh, they were gorgeous. And they were always clean. Their shawls used to be lovely. Our shawls were black with fringes on them but they used to get the Galway shawls, big grey shawls with flowers. We were very innocent in them times, like I didn't know really the meaning of a prostitute. And there was a lot of them that turned real religious.

"Now Jack Maher's pub was troublesome. Used to be a lot of trouble there. Always fighting. *Always* fighting at Jack Maher's. Saturday nights—hell open for sinners! It was a six-day week so most of them got paid on a Saturday. Then they'd be fighting. Always to do with drink. They used to get out and boxed on the road. They used to strip off or roll up their sleeves. And all would stand around in a ring when they'd be boxing. Then the policemen used to pull the men's arms around them and drag them off and their toes would be getting dragged along. Now 'Doddler' O'Leary was a hard man, a docker. He was *always* out boxing. He'd be on the drink. His drinking day couldn't end without a fight. He was a fine big man Doddler was and he had ginger hair. And boisterous, very boisterous. He was always bellowing out. When the fight'd be over they'd shake hands and go into the pub. And then maybe the same two fellas would start again that night! Sometimes he'd come out the worse for wear but he was always at it. Up till he died he never would change.

"So at Jack Maher's pub there was always fighting but now Paddy Clare, he wouldn't tolerate it. Paddy Clare reminds me of Ian Paisley. True as God. He'd real steel white hair and the big broad shoulders, real severe looking. And he had that tone of voice. It'd be the *sound* of the voice and you'd run. And if he seen you doing anything out of the way in his pub you were *out*. And you didn't have to get out, he just lifted you and *put* you outside. If you were barred you couldn't show your face near him the next day. Someone'd have to go and talk for you then, like you were on probation. But if there was a funeral you could walk in and have your drink even if you were barred. But after the day of the funeral you were back out again.

"One woman, Mary, I'll never forget her. She was a little woman and a real Republican, a real '16 woman, and she'd start fighting in Paddy Clare's pub. Like she wouldn't stop, you'd have to put your hand into her mouth to make her stop, during the drink. So she'd be lifted up and landed outside of the door. And she'd *still* be giving out! He used to put her out of the hall door on the street and he'd shut the door and put the bolt on each door. And she'd be *banging* his door down and all. I remember one time she said, 'I'm after leaving a glass of stout behind me and don't think I'm letting you away with that—I want me glass of stout!' So he said, 'Wait there and I'll get it for you.' And do you know what he done? He came out with the glass of stout and he *threw* it into her face. And I needn't tell you what she said. And she went for him again but he locked the door on her. And it was all dripping out of her and her banging the door down.

"Then there was a lot of shebeens and kip houses, houses that they call brothels now. See, a 'kip' meant going for a sleep or a rest. Some lovely places they had. There was one particular family that had a kip in Railway Street and I went into it every week cause it belonged to my mother's landlord and I used to bring around the rent. But you'd *love* going because the halls was all lino and always a vision of red, red lino with big flowers on it and then you went into a sitting room and it was the same and red velvet cloth on the table and a big standing lamp. Some of the girls lived there. The women'd bring the men in. It was a regular routine, they knew where to go and what to do. We never called them sailors, they were 'seafaring' men. And sometimes the women'd be sitting out on the steps in coats with a fur collar on them.

"Now the girls had madams. I knew the women by name. One of them was our landlord's mother. She had a big house on Railway Street and me mother used to work in it, used to scrub for her. Now we didn't call them 'madams', we called them 'kip keepers'. Now Becky Cooper's was a famous kip in Railway Street. She was a big stout woman, a lovely woman, and a very generous woman. She was always dressed in black and always a big rope of beads on her neck, like pearly. And you had to call her Ma'am. And there was another madam, May Oblong, and you had to call her Ma'am. May was a huge woman too. She'd grey hair and up on top had a big comb in it. And jewellery. Boney hands but loads of jewellery, big diamond rings and diamond brooches. And always wore a big white stiff apron and a shawl. She had two big tenement houses together in Railway Street. Now these kip houses, they sold beer. And they used to hide bottles of whiskey. Cause the police would raid the place and if they found the drink they were summonsed. So the kip keepers used to have to hide it. And do you know the gramophones with the big horns on them? Well, I remember them putting their bottles down the horn of the gramophone!"

TOMMY MURRAY—AGE 75

As a docker back in the 1930s his local pub was Walsh's on City Quay where you were "real family". Regulars had their own stools and tankards and shared life's problems with their mates. His fondest memory is of the annual summer "buck excursion". Mr Walsh would hire a bus and provide about twenty-eight cases of beer for as many men as they headed out into the countryside for a day of drinking and merrymaking. He shows a visible nostalgia for those bygone days.

"I was reared in Lime Street and I worked in a fertiliser factory for years. Oh, it was the hardest job in Europe. You had wheelbarrows with big iron wheels and carried up to 350 lb and you had to plough through the ground. You'd strain yourself. Oh, yes, and sometimes the acid would affect your skin. One fella says 'This is worse than a concentration camp.' Then I got into dock work after that. Dock work was very hard and I done it for fifteen shillings a day. You were paid every day then and at half seven in the morning certain pubs on the quays here opened. And the pubs were always open over in the Dublin market early. Oh, I often went over. Like after being out all night doing a ship and then you could go and have a few pints and go home and have a sleep.

"I drank in one well-known pub, Walsh's on City Quay. It used to be known as the Sugar Loaf and then it became Walsh's in the forties. Oh, it was a real docker's pub. It was a *fantastic* pub. One of the best pubs in the twenty-six counties. It was such a friendly pub, real natural people. You were a *family*. In Walsh's you always had your own place and some of them had their own old-fashioned tumblers. They were pewter tankards and they had their names on them. And always shooting tobacco into the spittoon. It was the greatest friendships I ever had in my life in that public house. The pub was an escape I'd say from the pressure of married life in the tenements. And it was the *conversation*. To get out and speak to another person, that's the thing I loved about it. And if a fella could help another fella that was always done. Like for a communion and even for a funeral if they didn't have enough money to bury the person. When you had problems you just put your cards on the table and you knew who you were talking to. It was 'my troubles were your troubles', *that* is the way we were and it was handed down. We were all the *one* crowd.

"The Walsh brothers were good publicans, nature-wise and civility-wise. The publicans then, they were a whole different breed from publicans today. It was just their nature. The publican today thinks he can't get enough money but the publican years ago was satisfied he was earning a living. And they were always living above the place. They were part and parcel of the community. If someone died they'd come to you and say, 'How are you fixed?' They'd help the family out, they always did. *Always* did. Walsh's was known for it. And at a funeral the publicans always shut their doors and pulled down their blinds and the hearse'd stop outside the pub for a while. Then there'd be an excursion to certain pubs like the Punch Bowl, that was a stopping place and they mightn't come home till 6.00 in the night, singing. For women it was more or less a type of holiday for them because they were out of the home. For them it was always a glass of porter or a bottle of stout. There was some famous ones from around here who could drink. There was 'Battling' Sue and Biddy Mitten, they were two famous ones and they'd always sit on their own. They could drink as good as any man. Battling Sue, she was a battler. Oh, Sue was a huge woman, about twenty stone weight, and she lived in a big tenement. And could she drink her beer! From morning till night she'd sit there, no trouble.

"And Dooley's, that was one of the most famous pubs around when I started drinking, about 1935. Dooley sent a parcel to each and every one at Christmas in that neighbourhood. There was always a baby Power's and a half dozen of stout for each family. That was regular. *All* the neighbours in the street got it. That's as true as I'm sitting here. *Ah*, he was a gentleman, and the family after him. There was two daughters, Cozy and May, and the son Joe he was in charge. And I'm not codding you, you wouldn't find such nice people. And Cozy, she was always cold, she was known for it, and she was always rubbing her hands. We used to have a bit of a crack about it. Cozy and May, they were as good as *any* barman ever in this country pulling the pint. Now there was plenty more pubs along the quay but *that* pint, I'll tell you, it was always perfect. In Dooley's. Oh, what a drink! They had one of the best cellars in Dublin and it kept a certain temperature and they had the barometer [thermometer] always in the front of the shop and the first thing you'd do, you'd look at it and you'd know the pint was going to be all right. It was like a tube going down. Oh, they was *noted* for their pint. And *no rush*. If you sat down it might take ten minutes to bring it to a head, the creme, and it'd take you some time to lift it off the counter it was so strong. You could *feel* the substance of it. See, at that time it was pulled from the barrel down below and when they'd finish it off naturally the leavings come down alongside the class and it'd *stick*. Oh, lovely. And I'll tell you, you could drink about twenty of them in a night and the next morning you'd be like a two-year old, there'd be no hangover. When I was a single man and I was working very hard I could consume around twenty-five to thirty pints over the day, in two sessions. Yes, sir.

"Every public house had their own singers. Everyone had to sing in turn. Oh, you sang in turn, only one voice. It was something that went with the drink, you know, with the company. We used to have a great old character and he was a great man with the tap dancing. He worked in the coalyards and Terry Lynch was his name, a *great* dancer. Ah, you'd want to see him, he was great with the reels and jigs. Especially Saturday night and Sunday night they were noted for the sing-song and Terry'd then be called up and he'd hold the floor for nearly an hour. And he was a lovely singer. How he used to keep going with the dancing and singing I do not know. But you should have seen him dance, he was fantastic. And they'd have to have a chair there cause always when he done a tap dance he'd always finish up with his leg up on the chair. And he got a few pints.

"There were some great characters around. There was one and we used to call him 'Jingle Bells'. He was a small man, he was a newspaper seller. We used to get great crack with him in Walsh's pub. See, when he come in one of the barmen would say, 'Would you not give us a song?' And Jingle Bells would sing a bit of a song. And then it was, 'Sing another song.' And he'd be singing songs all night. And the barman would keep giving him a half whiskey. And he'd start staggering. And here's the best part of it—the *best part* of the whole lot—he'd be singing and do you know what it was all the time? It was lemonade with water in it! It was always, 'Sing a song for us and you'll get your half whiskey.' And he *really thought* he was drunk. Thought it was whiskey and he had to have a tumbler of water beside it. True as Heaven. We used to look forward to that. That was the greatest laugh. I hope he's in Heaven, he's years dead now.

"And rings, that was the dockers' game. There were teams in all the different pubs and they had rooms for them. Oh, there was some fantastic ring men. They weren't just dockers alone, they were tradesmen, builders, labourers. They were some of the greatest pitchers you ever saw. It was all money. Sure, there used to be bookies in the pubs then. Oh, it wasn't legal, betting on the spot, but there'd be fellas laying bets in there. And they always had a great following, you see, because they came from north and south. There'd be a cup or trophy competition and they'd run a money competition and give so much to the winner. There was one pub here, the College Bar, and that was one of the most famous of the ring houses. And the Tara Bar. That's where all the betting was done. I'd say there could be a lot of money lost. Even if they only put up a tenner, it was a lot of money at that time. Some of the ring men were very famous and, oh, they always had their money, always had their beer. Then there was those you couldn't trust. See, cause they could *throw* a game. They made *more* money that way than they did the other way. Oh, that's the truth. *You* didn't know about it, it was only after that you'd be told about it. That happened. I know for a fact they did that. I never backed a man in a ring match cause I never trusted them.

"At Walsh's we used to have an excursion on the first Sunday in every August. To Arklow. It was what we called a 'buck excursion', only men'd go. Anything from twenty-five to thirty men. Some pubs had an 'off' [irregular] one but ours was regular for years and years. I'd say it went on for over twenty years. And Mr Walsh, he'd supply all the beer free. Could be up to thirty of us men and you'd want to see the beer that was going! Ah, he always had a bus and there'd be up to twenty-eight cases of beer. Oh, and you'd want to see the beer *before* we'd go! Cause he'd always open the pub early and you'd have a few pints and he'd always have a 'watcher', someone watching in case there was a policeman. So before you went to Arklow you had your pints and then you'd drink it going down on the bus and then you got outside the city and you stopped and went out into a field and took out the cases of stout and sat down and had your drinks. And there was nothing, only drink. See, you'd pull off the road and you'd just get out there and you could be out there for four or five hours drinking beer. And then you'd drink it coming home on the bus. And when you were coming home then in the night you'd tell the driver to stop and the driver'd pick a spot and you'd finish off all the beer then and come home about three in the morning. But you'd always have a cure for the morning, you'd have about four or five bottles in your pocket. We did that every August.

"Oh, I'd love to see Walsh's there again, or Dooley's. And, a funny thing, there's a few of us still alive who drank there and we still can't get it out of our memories when we meet. When the lads meet we still talk about it ourselves . . . can't get it out of our heads. We were neighbours, very loyal, grew up with one another and we knew one another's complaints. You might as well be living under the one roof, no secrets, no secrets whatsoever. You couldn't *hide* a secret if you tried to. And on New Year's [Eve] people'd come outside the pubs and bring about a half a dozen bottles with them and have a drink outside and the police wouldn't interfere. At each pub along the quay there'd be a crowd of men shaking hands and singing and dancing and an old accordion and the boats [horns] would be going. You'd get kind of a chill through you. It was a special time. I know that cause I'm fifty-seven years drinking and if I don't know it *nobody* knows it."

James Higgins—Age 70

As a regular at O'Dowd's pub in Stoneybatter he feels that the local pub is like the "pulse" of the neighbourhood. It is the centre for socialising, news, gossip and provides men with a safety valve in times of domestic stress. Here he and his mates meet daily to enjoy companionship and sort out life's problems.

"I've been coming to this pub now since 1958. This is my local. I like coming up here for a very good reason, there's no television here. So you can talk. A pub is a place where you can assemble and there's always an invitation there. Go in and have a drink, meet somebody, exchange pleasantries of the day with them. It's an experience that adds to life. You see, a local pub like here, it's like a *pulse* of the neighbourhood. You can gauge how the area is going. As you go through life you develop friendships and you share the trials and tribulations of life and the joys as well. I mean if somebody won a few quid they'd set up a few drinks for the people that were there. One night a fella come in and he'd won a lot of money gambling on the dogs and he bought a drink for *everybody* in the place. We share the good times and the bad. Like my mother died and my friends here, as a mark of their respect, they got a Mass said from the church and they sent a wreath and the card read 'from the staff and customers of O'Dowd's public house'. They knew that my mother had died and they sympathised and that's how they showed it. And they appeared at the church that evening and the Mass the next morning. When you experience grief it can be very supportive when you have people like that. So we share the good times and the bad.

"Now what makes a good publican in my book is the presentation of the drink and the personality of the man behind the counter. A man who will listen, not pry, sympathise, not pity. You want a person to show genuine interest, not be falling over you. For instance, my young lad had a bit of an accident yesterday and had an eye operation last night. And I come down here at 10.00, which was closing hour, and I gave a tap at the window, got in and had a drink and Tom [publican] says, 'Sorry about that, Jim, don't rush it. Needn't rush the drink.' That's what I mean. As I said, sympathy without pity and a sense of friendliness without throwing his arms around me. A good man, a decent man and he's one of them. He keeps a good pub. And now you can measure a pub by the toilet. That's a very odd thing to say. It's spotless how he cleans that toilet.

"Now if strangers come into this pub and if you got one or two unruly animals they'd immediately sense that there was a crowd of fellas here that were local and if they were haggling for a row this is the last place they'd pick. They'd be out the door! For instance, this pub was raided some time ago by two young hoodlums and the customers beat the hell out of them. They had come in to rob it. They had a bar and a stick. And a number of men here physically hammered them. Ah, you have to stand up and be counted. Ah, those two hoodlums who came in here that night, they won't come back here any more. No way.

"I can remember back now to the year of the [Eucharistic] Congress, that's 1932, and it was almost unknown for a woman to go into a pub on her own. It was *verboten*. Wouldn't be done. If a woman did that she was frowned upon by her neighbours. The pub is different now when there's women involved. I think that women have a place in a lounge to come in and enjoy themselves. Now I don't mean to be offensive but a pub, the bar, is a man's refuge and men feel a little bit put off or apprehensive if women are present. It's a bit awkward. Being a little bit old fashioned myself I think that a pub is a man's domain. Like sometimes men express themselves rather vulgarly and very outspoken and they'd *never* do that if their wives were here. See, basically the man is working all day and he comes home, is weary maybe, has a meal, talks to his wife. But then in the evening hours he wants relaxation and he comes up here and has a drink. It's just like a *safety valve*. She understands his needs. She understands that he's not going out gallivanting. She knows where he is and if he has a few drinks too many somebody'll drop him at the door and that's it. But if I overstayed here my wife would let me know her displeasure. Now I have seen where a woman came into the pub and said to her husband, 'You come home. Your dinner is ready on the table and that's it.' And he was shamed to leave the pub. And he wasn't seen in that pub for two or three weeks then. He wouldn't come back because he felt he'd been shamed by his wife coming in.

"There's been a few characters in the place here. We have a man called the 'dead man', he's a patient up in the Gorman [St Brendan's Hospital] and he says he's dead and that he just comes up now and again to have a drink. And he *looks* dead. He's dreadful looking. His face is a dreadful colour and he has a mouth of bad teeth. But he's harmless. But he's *convinced* he's dead. He's a character and he'll come in and look for a drink off anybody. Then we have 'Paddy Carwash' who washes cars for want of something better to do. Again, he's a patient. He's a day patient, in and out, you know. Lads will get him a pint for washing their car or he'll charge them a pound or two and then he'll drink that up. And Paddy, on a good day, he'll drink twenty pints. Now Paddy Carwash won our Christmas draw last year. See, the pub always runs a draw and a ticket would cost you £1 and if you're lucky enough to win you can go back with a magnificent prize. You'd get a turkey, a ham, tins of biscuits, a bottle of brandy, bottle of port, bottle of gin, bottle of vodka, maybe two or three dozen beer. Paddy won it and put it on his credit then and he took so much each day."

NOEL HUGHES—AGE 60

A well-known local amateur historian, he probably knows as much about northside pub life as any Dubliner. He knew personally the most famous publicans, barmen, madams and pub prostitutes of his time. As a young man, he frequented all the local speakeasies and shebeens, taking in all the action and recording it in his remarkable memory bank. As he tells it, the meanest and "lowest" pub in all Dublin was Tom Crilly's pub on Sarsfield Quay. It was a dangerous hive of haggard prostitutes, muggers, bowzies and brawlers—but a great setting in which to learn about life and human behaviour.

"I was born in a tenement house in North King Street. Life was hard in the tenements. If a man had the price of a pint the pub was an escape from those old tenement houses. See, he was in a room where there was maybe six children and the wife and himself and the *pressure* was there. And then the wife might be angry and the children crying. So there was hardship and he was delighted on a Saturday night that he'd have maybe three shillings and he'd go in and get a couple of pints. That kind of took the pressure off him. The pub was the place where they met, where you met your pals. It was a place to discuss your problems. But any man who drank the money on his wife was an outcast. Oh, they'd know. And he was an outcast and nobody wanted to drink with him. It was, 'F—- off, you're not a man, what you do.' You'd hear that expression. They had their own set of morals.

"In those days there was very little furniture in a pub, it was all sitting up at the bar. Hard stools. And at the back of the pub there'd be a shelf facing the counter, along the wall, and there'd be more stools or maybe they'd stand up and drink their pint off that. All the pubs in Dublin had a spread of sawdust and some pubs had no heating at all. In those days they had such a hard time of it that they didn't bother with the cold. It was eight pence a pint in my time and one and three pence for a half a whiskey. And if you went into the pub and you'd say to a fella, 'What are you having?', he might say, 'If I have a mouthful I'll be satisfied with it.' A 'mouthful' means a pint. Drovers of the cattle they'd come in and get a pint and, oh, they were good drinkers. But the best drinkers of the whole lot were the dockers. You see, they used to work so hard on the coal boats and the drink didn't take an effect on them. They were known to drink ten or twelve pints in a session. And in pubs the drovers and the dockers, they'd cling together, kept to their own kind, because back then if a fella had a trade he was reckoned to be above someone else. Back then it was, 'Oh, he's a carpenter, he's a bricklayer, he's a tradesman.'

"Oh, an awful lot of dealing was done in pubs. For instance, the Connellys, the carriers, might want a couple of men. Well, old Martin Connelly would be in the pub and he'd say, 'Be down in the yard in the morning.' And the Coopers [horse dealing family] would go into one of the pubs around Queen Street and they'd get a few halves of whiskey [with a buyer] and then the deal would be made and they shook hands. They'd say, 'Okay, I'm taking them twelve horses at £20 apiece.' They'd make the deal in the old snug at one end of the bar. And I seen an awful lot of that dealing with the pig trade in pubs. You'd hear the pig men arguing over the price in the pub. I seen hundreds of pounds [changing hands] in the pub with pig men. Going back to my father's time I often seen him selling pigs and he'd be paid in the pub. A bad employer would pay his men in a pub. That was a dirty thing with employers cause the man would have to buy him a couple of drinks back out of it. They *had* to buy him a couple of pints back. The employer'd say, 'I have no money on me now, I'll see you over in the pub', and the poor unfortunate man would go over and he'd be forced to buy him a couple of pints. They were penalised that way. He was known as a bad employer.

"Ah, years back pubs were the most important places of IRA men, the Flying Columns and all. The public houses gave the biggest help, very important, because a lot of the information was passed on there. See, the owner of the pub would be an IRA man, the publican or the curate. So they were 'safe' houses. There'd be one man trusted and it was *his* job to watch who was going into that pub. They always spotted a stranger because all those public houses had their own local people. There might be three IRA men involved in a conversation and they'd be whispering, it was so secret. And if a stranger went in the curate or the publican would give a sign, like tap their head or something, or pull their nose or touch their ear, something to that effect. Now the Black and Tans raided many a pub and some were led to their death. They'd pull up in their Crossley tender and when they'd come out of the pub the door would be locked immediately and the firing then would start right into the Black and Tans. It was a set up, an ambush, and the pub door would be locked as soon as the last Tan'd be out.

"There was a pub known as the Seven Stars in Parnell Street and that was a well-known IRA pub. Then you had Phil Ennis's public house, too, in Parnell Street and that was another known pub. The men, they'd meet there and their officers would meet there and they'd leave messages. Now one thing that the IRA men was told, that they weren't to overdo it [drinking]. You know, a couple of pints. Oh, they had to keep their mind clear and keep themselves ready for a quick exit. And then there was always some IRA men on the run and they'd be hidden up in the bedrooms above the pub. A pub called Backhand that was in Coleraine Street, that was a pub where they hid an awful lot of IRA men, where they slept. And Macken's pub on Church Street was another of them. Then there was Big Macken's pub on North King Street, that was another one. And then you had Walsh's in Stoneybatter, that was a *notorious* public house for IRA men to sleep in when they were on the run.

"Oh, and an awful lot of public houses were used for hiding guns and ammunition. In cellars. IRA men, they often got weapons in pubs to go out and use them. And, see, when they would run out of ammunition they would know where to go, to what pubs to pick up a recharge of ammunition. McGowan's pub on Francis Street, that was a pub where ammunition was stored. *Dynamite* would be wrapped well in those wooden kegs to keep it dry. It was a perfect place. There were secret barrels. It'd be broken into sections, they'd divide the barrel and they'd have their stuff down in the barrel in the middle, safely hidden in there, and there was beer at each end of it. But the ammunition would be in the middle. And maybe the pump handle that they'd pull the pint with, there'd be a dummy one and that'd be screwed off and the stuff would be put in that. And there'd be false downspouts and that's where hand grenades were wrapped and stored. They'd divert the water to go down the next downspout on the roof. So if the rain came it was a safe place. And women of Cumann na mBan, they'd come into a pub with a baby in their arms with a shawl around them and they'd deliver stuff, maybe explosives, revolvers, ammunition, bullets. She'd have it wrapped in something and then she'd be in the snug and the stuff was passed on that way, just hand the publican a parcel.

"On a Saturday night the pubs closed at half ten and you were always sure of a row, in a pub or outside of a pub. Two fellas would come out and fight. It'd be a fair fight and next thing one fella might go in with his head, give the other fella a butt with his head. But they were mostly fair fights. Ah, I had a few of them myself. Oh, I did . . . quite a few fights. Some simple bloody thing would start it and maybe there'd be a digging match in the pub. But you'd go outside to finish it. They'd say, 'All right now, *out*!' And they'd let them have a go at it. I seen meself with thirteen stitches in me, then shaking hands with the fella and going back in to have a pint with him. And I remember being in a pub one night and I had a fight with a policeman. The two of us were drinking and an argument arose about football and he criticised Dublin and I criticised *him*. He wasn't a Dublin man. And the next thing we belted each other and we were on the floor belting each other. And somebody says, 'Jesus, if we get the police we'll all be put out.' See, they couldn't afford to get the police because it was a *speakeasy*, it was a pub that served drinks after hours. You'd just give a knock on the door and he'd open the door and you'd go in and there'd be a man on the lookout. And I remember another day being in a fight in a pub when the Holy Hour was on. See, you used to *stay* in the pub and the door would be locked. But a fight arose in the pub and yer man [publican] couldn't do anything about it, you see, he couldn't bring the police. And the women was screaming and all in the pub and the doors closed. And he got a clatter himself! Yeah, I hit *him*, the owner of the pub. See, he got into the fight as well. He still couldn't call the police.

"The tinkers, the gypsies, there was the Wards and the Joyces and they were served in the pubs around there [Smithfield] because they were great spenders. They were all horsy men. And they'd bring a pony into the pub for devilment, a joke. See, the pony would come in and someone'd say, 'Will you get that bloody thing out!' 'Ah, he only come in for a drink.' And some fella'd say to the pony, 'Will you have a pint?' and maybe the pony'd wag his head. I remember a pony coming into a pub and he done his droppings in the pub! And another one come in and he done his wee in the pub. They barred him [the owner] for life! And the fella come back in and says, 'I thought it was the pony you were barring, not me—*I* didn't do it!'

"The tinkers used to go into a pub right on the corner of Red Cow Lane and Neelan's pub was on the far side and they used to go in there. But they fought among themselves and they were told, 'Here, *out*! Get out *there* and fight. You're not fighting in *here*.' So they'd go out on the cobblestones there at Smithfield and have a fight. Dozens of times. There might be five or six men on both sides fighting. Kicking 'em in the head and all that business. Then they'd shake hands and *back* into the pub for a few drinks. And some tinker women were very dangerous when they'd get a few halves of whiskey on them. I seen Mary Ward with a scissors and she was sticking it into another woman, into another gypsy. I seen that in Smithfield when I was only a boy.

"But I was delighted to see many blokes getting barred. Cause some blokes asked to get barred. A nuisance. If they raised a fight in a pub, or tormenting. By tormenting I mean being a scrounger. Going in and saying, 'Give me a pint.' I know blokes that was barred indefinite, for life. There's a fella now, Danny, and he's barred in the Orbit public house on North King Street. See, he had broke the publican's window and he was barred. For *life*. He was barred back when the Bradys owned that pub and then when the Reillys took over the pub he was barred for as long as *they* had it. See, the customers told the new publican behind the counter, 'See him? Well, we're not staying in this public house if you're serving Danny. He can't be trusted.' They tell the new publican who's bad and who's not. See, it's usually passed on from the customers. It's *their* public house.

"And there was characters in pubs. Like there was a fella called 'Baby' Nugent and he painted his horse *pink* and he got on his back and rode him into the pub. He opened the door of the pub and come in with the horse. *Rode* that horse into the pub. Just for devilment! Now another truthful story—a man had a mule and 'Magso' Leonard was the name of the man. And Magso was an awful man for drinking. And what did he do, he went out and got stupid drunk and in he come to his tenement room. So we took the wheels off his cart, carried the cart into his room, brought in the wheels, put the wheels back on it, brought up the mule, yoked it up, put the harness on it, and tied it to the bed. And Magso lying in the bed bloody drunk and never minded. And the next morning Magso woke up and he's wondering how he got the mule in . . . didn't know. For the rest of his life he wondered about that.

"Paddy Reilly's pub at the corner of Henrietta Street was a well-known speakeasy, a pub known for drinking after hours and on a Sunday morning. A *really* well-known speakeasy. Now Paddy Reilly would allow *anyone* in and you got your change in candle light or by match light. On Sunday night the closing time was 7.00 and the lights were blacked out. And you had to keep the noise down. And you might say, 'Speak easy, there's a policeman outside.' Now in behind the counter he had a candle and he'd be pulling your pint for you and he had a box of matches and he struck a match while giving you your change. But you'd have to watch him cause he'd fiddle you. Oh, he'd fiddle you! And Paddy Reilly was a bugger for watering the whiskey. And there was even policemen drinking in that speakeasy. And it was raided a few times. On Sunday morning I was there at ten to eight drinking when a heavy rap come to the door and I said, 'Oh, this is it.' And who comes in only a *superintendent* and a sergeant with him and they were going off duty. So the two of them come in to have a drink.

"Dan Griffith's pub was at the corner of North Anne Street and that was my favourite drinking shop. It was the most local drinking shop in the neighbourhood. Your *father* was in it before you and your *grandfather* was in it before you and your *great grandfather* was in it before you. And in that same public house in 1916 the British Army shot four innocent men in the cellar. It was a honky-tonk looking shop, small and friendly, and back then there was an art to pulling a pint and Dan Griffith was very, very good at it. See, he had a mountain cellar. It was called a mountain cellar because the breeze used to blow across from the Dublin hills, what you called the mountains, and it'd blow up through North Anne Street and go down in that cellar and that's how it was always cool. At that time he had the tap in the barrel and temperature was important. You'd go into another pub and it'd be lukewarm, but his was always cool. I remember it well when you'd put the pint down on the counter after a minute you'd go to pick it up and you could feel a kind of glue, it was so powerful, so good. Oh, it was a lovely pint. So that was my local shop but Dan Griffith, he was religious mad. If you cursed in his pub you were barred. And when the bell would ring for the Angelus he'd put the towel over the taps and he'd make the sign of the cross and he'd say the Angelus. And you'd want to *answer* him. But it was a *lovely* shop and always a bit of a laugh in it. I curse the day it closed up about seven years ago.

"Now Griffith was an old terrier, an IRA man. I remember this occasion when somebody started cursing in the shop—'For the love of Jesus', somebody said —and he says, 'When you drink that pint you get out.' And this bloke made a jump at him and he hit the fella with a big old wooden mallet that was for tapping the barrels. Gave him a bang with that mallet. And now if there was a fight with customers Griffith, he'd take off his apron and would come outside the counter and fight himself as well. Griffith loved to fight. He was around 60 but he could fight like a young fella. He was so strong and he was boney. So strong. Cauliflower ears he had and a broken nose, that was old Dan Griffith.

"But there was a trick done to him one time when two fellas started an argument in the pub and then went outside to fight. All the fellas went outside to watch the fight and Griffith run out and locked the door. But what did this geezer do, didn't he hide in the toilet! It was a fella called 'Turkey Hole' O'Hara, that's his nickname. And Turkey Hole hid in the pub in the toilet when the fellas was out fighting. See, it was an *arranged* thing amongst them. They set it up. And didn't yer man take the money! But he was cute, he didn't take *all* the money out of the till. So when the fight was over the publican opened the door and the whole lot of them was let back in and Griffith never minded. He didn't know.

"Then you had two very well-known places that were a shebeen for the drink and they were also known as brothels. One was called the Cozy Kitchen and that was in North King Street and the other one was the Cafe Continental on Bolton Street. They were two places you went to for to have a drink and you got your whiskey in a cup and there were prostitutes. A place where you went in to either pick up a girl or have a drink. They were run by Dolly Fawcett. She could be described as a madam but she was a married woman and had two sons. Dolly, when I knew her, was in her seventies. Oh, she was a fine looking woman, the appearance of a woman that was very good looking in her youth. The prostitutes, they were mostly country girls. From 17 into their thirties. Oh, very good looking. And a prostitute was a very kind-hearted person.

"So the girls would be around the place at the counter and a man would start chatting her up. The whole neighbourhood knew of this—the whole of *Dublin* knew about it—because the sailors off the ships used to go in there an awful lot. Men, they'd come from all over, and from the docks. Oh, the police raided it a couple of times but they got backhands. There was backhands going on at that time, paying policemen off. Now the girls weren't high-class prostitutes or anything like that, they were just ordinary commoners. I suppose they charged maybe ten shillings or a pound. And a lot of their business went on around in the back in the lane off Capel Street. The lane was dark. Oh, but the men didn't care—'You're not looking at the mantelpiece when you're poking the fire!'

"I remember an instance in June 1954 and I was drinking in the Cafe

Continental when a knock come on the door and who was it, me mother! She was looking for a taxi driver, the cabbie, to bring her daughter-in-law to the Rotunda Hospital to have a baby. But I thought somebody was after seeing me going in and they went for me mother. I was down at the back and I recognised me mother's voice and the cup fell out of me hand with the fright. So Fawcett, the son, pushed me under the table. Oh, the hair stood up on me head and the sweat run out of me! Frightened the living daylights out of me. I nearly took a heart attack.

"Down in Dan Cleary's pub on Green Street, that used to serve shady ladies, street women. That wasn't a brothel but it was where these girls used to go into and fellas used to pick them up. It was like the pubs around the Gloucester Diamond where the girls were out in the open. But the offence wasn't committed on the premises, they just met there. Now Crilly's pub on Sarsfield Quay, that was the *lowest* of *all* the public houses. It was a shop where there was down-and-out prostitutes who had gone *beyond* the age and who were diseased. Crilly's was a well-known pub throughout the world wherever there was sailors cause they used to tell one another about it abroad. It was an old-time pub and it wasn't very clean. Crilly lived above the shop. He was heavy and very bald headed and round faced. He had a big baldy head on him, as bald as a child's behind. It was supposed to be that Tom Crilly seen the devil, but that's all a fantasy I'd say.

"Now I was in Crilly's on many occasions but not for the purpose of women, just for a curiosity as a young fella. It *was* a house of prostitution. Men would go to meet them in there. See, he didn't publicise it as a brothel but if you wanted to go in and have a drink with a girl and take her out of the pub that was none of his affair. He was getting a lot of custom with these crowds going into the shop. Actually, a lot of it went on in the hallway which was called a snug. It was dark in the hallway and there was more prostitutes seduced in that snug than anywhere else. And then around back of the pub between the quay and Benburb Street there was a laneway there and that's where a lot of the activity took place. I knew a lot of the women and they were old and haggard. It was maybe five shillings, ten shillings they got. And there was more fellas got a dose of the 'pox' out of it than any other place that was known. Gonorrhoea! And syphilis. They got that out of it.

"There was a lot of fellas mugged in Crilly's and he held a lot of the money that was robbed. And when strangers used to go into the pub they used to maybe get a pint or a whiskey and he'd give them a small sup of this wine and it was more of a drug than it was a wine. And it was called 'chat'. It was a kind of wine affair and it would make you drowsy. Oh, the police often came into the pub all right after fellas complained that they'd been robbed but the police didn't give a damn cause the police knew that anyone that went in there knew what they were going in for. They had no sympathy. Now I know one fella in particular and he went in with some toilet paper rolled up in his pocket *pretending* that he had a roll of money. And he was mugged. He put his hand there and he felt it was gone out of his pocket. One of the prostitutes took it off him and she thought she had a wad of notes and he says, 'You can wipe your behind with that now.' Oh, he was wise."

STEPHEN MOONEY—AGE 68

In his early days tradesmen had their own favourite pubs where they regularly met and conducted much business. He found that carpenters, plasterers and bricklayers preferred to drink with their own ilk. As a member of the painter's trade, he and his mates hung out at the Long Hall and Peter's pub while tobacco workers preferred the Widow Donoghue's pub. There was as much politicking and hiring done in the local pub as in the tradesmen's union halls—and plenty of bribing.

"The publican, he was the money man in the area. If there was a funeral he'd supply the families that had been his customers down through the years. Actually, five publicans paid for me uncle Christy's funeral cause he drank in five pubs, like Ryan's around the corner. I recall being with me mother and she was sitting there and she was crying and I didn't know what she was crying about. And there was a knock on the door and Mr Ryan brought up five bottles of whiskey and he sent a couple of dozen of pint bottles of porter later in the evening. This was to help with the function of waking the dead. And publicans, they'd recommend you if you wanted to get a job. And, of course, that was as good as conversing with the bishop. Oh, yeah. Then they were good financers for the political parties and so they had an input there. And nearly every publican would have a son a priest.

"If you were leaving the day's job to go for a drink you just went with the people that were your norm. The tradesmen broke up. Like plasterers wouldn't drink with painters or bricklayers. Oh, yes, they were 'above'. Plasterers and carpenters were the meanest men in the building trade, they kept their distance in a very close social sense. They all drank together all right. And some of the unions that these fellas belonged to had [favourite] pubs and that's where they'd sooner be because it was at these pubs that they'd get jobs. Like the tobacco workers used to go into the Widow Donoghue's pub and there was a lot of plotting and planning there. That also applied to painters. Now we had a pub called the Long Hall in George's Street and that was primarily a painters' pub. Our union hall was at the top of Aungier Street and so you had painters drinking over there in the Long Hall. And you'd get a job *quicker* in the Long Hall than you would in the union! See, if the fellas knew there was a job vacant, well, they went off to get their mates, so whichever mate got there to the pub first usually got the job. That was common practice. That was the way the whole building trades operated.

"So the painting crowd would go to the Long Hall or to Peter's pub which was around facing the Mercer Hospital. And a section of the elite of the trade union used to sit in Peter's pub drinking and using their position in order to get drink from the fellas coming in that they'd gotten jobs for. Stephen Behan spent a lot of time in Peter's pub. He was the president of the union and he *did* get work for fellas and, of course, he was paid in kind with drink. Oh, yeah. The same thing applied to the general secretaries of *all* these unions. Yeah, they had their own cliques. It'd be wheeling and dealing for drink, for jobs *and* drink for the positions that would be going. And in order to win votes for positions in the union it was necessary for to drink with people, to socialise with them, and get into their ear and 'I'll rub your back if you rub mine . . . you need *this*, I need *that*.'

"And in my time down on the docks if you got a job through the stevedore you had to *pay* the stevedore. When I was working on the docks the stevedore'd say, 'Are you coming into the pub?' and if you said no you wouldn't get a job there again. So you went into the pub and you'd just send a pint down for him and he'd say, 'Ah, thanks very much.' That suited him cause he'd get twelve, thirteen pints in a night. That's all they were fit for was drinking. Some others used to do it in a different fashion in order not to lose their dignity. They'd hand the stevedore a box of matches with ten shillings in it and he'd take that and put it in his pocket. Yeah, that was a bribe, that was the procedure.

"Then Hanlon's pub on Hanlon's Corner, that was the pub where the cattle market was and the farmers and the buyers would all retire there to fix their deals up. Thursday was cattle market day and there was wheeling and dealing in Hanlon's pub there and a deal was finalised with a spit and a slap of the hand. Sometimes before it ever got to the auctioneer's they'd sell their cattle there in the pub. I used to see it as a kid cause I'd go up and milk the cows because the cows would be full of milk and you could drink the milk then and some other kids would sell the milk for fourpence a bucket. It was a lovely pub and it looked the part with lovely wooden counters . . . but the drovers stank to high heaven!

"There was speakeasies around. Johnny Curran's up on Meath Street was a speakeasy. It was on the corner of Engine Alley. Now the itinerants, we called them gypsies, there was a lot of pubs that wouldn't allow them in to drink but Johnny Curran would let them in. He would allow them in there and there was fights between the itinerants. The tinkers would spend a lot more money in the last hour and then they'd be all sprawled outside drunk, *really* drunk, outside the pub. That corner of Engine Alley, it was a *rough* place, *really* rough. Then the police at night shoved the tinkers down to their caravans. So Johnny Curran used to throw a *lot* [of money] into the police station for different funds, like the policeman's ball and all that, because he made a good business out of these tinkers.

"Pubs all had sawdust on the floor because there'd be fights and there'd be blood and other occasions where people'd get sick and that had to be cleaned out and replenished. If there was trouble the publican would say, 'Take it outside the door.' The irony of it was that in those days men didn't like to be called a coward and so it was, 'I'll have you outside.' That was the usual remark. 'Why don't you ask him outside if you're so tough?' And that got things away from the pub. They fought it out on the road and when they were finished they all went back into the pub to drink. And many a time covered with blood. I seen a fight I'll never forget, it was when Murphy fought Keaton, two fine big men. They started this row and the two fellas had to meet and they got out and they *beat* themselves practically unconscious, total exertion so that they couldn't lift their hands. And everybody said, 'They're *both* men.' And everyone went back into the pub and the men had little or no shirts left on them and they were *smothered* in blood from their noses and their ears and cuts on their hands. Yeah, it was a fierce fight. You talk about John Wayne and Randolph Scott, well, we had our own spoilers. They'd fight it out and then retire to the pub. And the publican always put up the drink for them, *free* drink."

TESS RYAN—AGE 65

She is a third generation Iveagh Market dealer who had twenty children. As a child, all the older women dealers snuck off to the local pub for their glass of plain porter. In Doyle's pub the grannies were hidden beneath a huge wooden staircase to have their beer on the sly. They were grand old days, says Tess, who still spends a few days each week selling clothes in the market.

"Me mother was in this business all her life and her mother before her. She was here in the Iveagh and I used to come in with her when I was a child. We had a room in a tenement house and there was eight children and I was the oldest and I used to have to bring the stuff up on little carts to the market. Me mother sold all clothing from people in the big [suburban] houses and she could get them very cheap. Oh, me mother was a lovely person. She was the pick of the market here, she stood out in appearance and she was very happy, always had a laugh and a joke. And me mother always dressed up here and she had a black lace parasol umbrella and a hat with ostrich feathers on it. She'd be going around like that dressed up to entertain them and she was a lovely singer. That's the way they used to be in here years ago. Always happy. I was in here from 4 and 5 years old in a pram and from then on I started. It's me whole life in it. I had twenty children, fourteen living children. I worked all me life, worked *hard*. I love the market. It's the memories that it holds for you. By God, I've seen a lot of lovely old women here.

"The market was *alive* with people. Now years ago in here all the tuggers would meet at the gate there and they'd decide themselves that they'd split up and take different areas. They all had their own territory. They were out in all classes of weather. Then they'd all come back with their clothes and the dealers here would auction them off. And the old women after getting a few bob would go into the pub and they'd get a few drinks, get a glass of porter. So the dealers went into the snug but their children wouldn't be let in, they'd be left outside and maybe the publican'd give them a glass of raspberry and a little package of biscuits. And at a funeral the women'd all go off and make a day of it at

Glasnevin or Mount Jerome. They'd go into a pub and spend whatever they had drinking. It was just an excuse to go off and get drunk. After a few drinks they'd be all singing and, oh, they'd come back in good spirits. And at that time the countrymen would come up to the market and they'd say, 'I'll bring you up some poitin if you want it.' They used it here for a cure to rub on themselves, for rheumatism and that. They'd say, 'Rub poitin into you', just over the skin. And women used to say that a sup of stout killed the worms in a child. And some of the women'd keep the small porter bottle and use them for a baby bottle, to feed the baby. And maybe the tit would fall off the top of the bottle cause the top wouldn't grip and all of a sudden the tit would go up in the air and the baby would be drowned.

"The old women would go into McAuley's pub and they'd get a few drinks in the snug. There were two McAuley brothers and very blocky, Paddy and Charlie. I think they were from Mayo and they were both fond of the drink. They had a kitchen upstairs and a big iron kettle on the range and they'd let you get boiling water and you'd make your own brew of tea. It was only the women dealers that got the privilege. And they had a sister named Kate and she had a pub up on New Street. It was called Kate McAuley's and she had a nephew there, Johnny, and a niece there, Mary, and they lived with her. She never married. Oh, she worked behind the bar pulling pints and her niece and nephew too. To me, she never got old looking, do you know that type of person? She always dressed in a navy serge costume. She lived above the pub and she was very wary of people, always very protective. She never let strangers in, they were always the one regular crowd from the local area. And she gave a good drink. It was very drab and dark but they didn't mind because they were getting good drink. My father used to drink in it. She was happy just to keep things going. And you had to knock at the window for her to open and then the people were there till all hours of the morning. The police even used to be there till all hours of the morning! Sure, the police would get in there at the side door.

"And the women dealers here in the market, if they got a few bob they'd all set out to Frank Doyle's pub here at the corner and they'd go into the snug. He had a separate little snug under the stairs and there was a marble table like you see in garden furniture and three or four of the women'd be under the stairs drinking. It was a real old staircase with a lovely bannister and it was private under the stairs going up to his living accommodations. They could be under there hiding on their husbands taking a drink and he wouldn't know where they'd be. That would be the last place he'd think! Mary Warren would drink there and Tesso Lynch, she's over 90 now, and my grandmother used to call her the 'Little Flower' because she collected on a Saturday night with the poor box for the Little Flower. She was a dealer here. So Mary Warren and Tesso and my grandmother used to drink together there after their week's work. Great pals all their life and they'd drink together under the stairs. Always porter. They'd spend half their day under the stairs. And Mary Warren she used the snuff all the time. There was white and brown snuff and she'd have it in a mustard tin. Oh, there was nothing wrong with the women years ago that used snuff, they were all fine healthy women. It used to be a grand laugh here. This market was really alive."

JOE MURPHY—AGE 66

As one of Dublin's last shipwrights he has lived his life around dockland pubs. As a young lad, his grandmother used to send him down to "Baldy" Fagan's pub to fetch her gill in an enamel jug. Then she would stick a red hot poker into it to mull it. His grandfather once stomped out of his lifelong local pub when the price of a pint was raised from seven to eight pence. Two weeks later the publican came to his house and begged him to return.

"I was born in Ringsend and me father and me grandfather and me great grandfather were all shipwrights. And I'm the last of them. It was a little community, a very close-knitted type of people. Oh, and Ringsend was riddled with pubs. In my time Par North's was the leading pub down at the end of Thorncastle Street. And his brother Peter North owned a pub up at the *top* of the street near the chapel. Then you had the Yacht Tavern and 'Baldy' Fagan's. My grandmother, she used to send me over to Baldy Fagan's for her gill in an enamel jug that held about a gallon and you put this thing on the counter. And you carried this gill back for your grandmother and she'd have the fire roaring red and she'd take this poker out about two foot long and it'd be red with sparks flying and she'd stick it into this jug and the *smell* off it! I used to run out the door. It mulled the beer by putting this hot poker in it and then she drank it when it was lukewarm.

"Now the shipwrights and the dockers were thick as thieves. I always admired the Dublin dockers, they were great men. They had it tough, they must have been made of flint. When I used to go into the pub for my grandmother for her gill I used to see their shovels, you'd see this shiny thing like a sheet of armour. Each docker had his own shovel and dare you go near it! They'd take them *into* the pub alongside them and they had their names carved into the handles. The dockers, by God, they were terrible hard-working men. And after working coal boats when they went to the pub all you'd see was their white eyes and white teeth and red lips and red tongue, but the rest of them was *black*. And when they'd spit into the sawdust it would be black. And dockers mostly kept to the one pub because they used to have this thing called the slate. It was a book. And when days were bad you went in for a pint and put it on the slate. And this stroke went into the book against your name. Whenever he got paid he probably owed for two or three pints. And you must remember that the pint in those days will never be seen again, it was a *different* type of drink. It was mostly porter in those days and then Guinness came in with a 'fifty-fifty', half stout and half porter. And the dockers would knock back anything from ten to fourteen pints in a shot. Oh, God, yes. On their way home from the boat they'd go *straight* into the pub before they'd go home and they knocked back pints hand over fist.

Guinness was a *food*—at least we called it food. And anybody that was sick or invalid they used to have a Treble 'X' stout in bottles and there was always three X's on it and that was the superior Guinness's drink of the whole lot. If you drank that you'd live forever!

"On Ringsend was a lively village and hooleys in pubs was mostly Saturday nights, all sing-songs. And on a Saturday night there was tripe and pig's feet, crubeens, you know. Oh, God, yer man would come into the pub with a white enamel bucket full of cooked pig's feet or mussels or prawns and they'd eat them with their porter. And men had handkerchiefs then and they used to be red and they'd stretch them out on the counter and put the pig's feet on top of it. And then they'd spit the bones out on their handkerchief.

"Now for references it was the publican and the parish priest and the local constable. But the publican, he was *the* man, he was the lord and master. And if he didn't come across to a destitute family he was in a bad way because the people wouldn't go into his pub. Oh, no. He'd give them money or something. Mostly with burials he used to help them out. And in Ringsend now for a funeral the whole village would come to a standstill. Shops, *everything* would shut down. Blinds down on everything, pubs, grocers, hairdressers, the whole works just shut down dead. And then they'd go back to the pub after the funeral and 'sympathise', they used to call it, and they'd get *scutted drunk*.

"Par North had one pub and his brother Peter had a far superior pub and they hardly spoke to each other, although they were brothers. They lived above their pubs and they were never married, an oddity. And when the new church was getting built down there they poured money into it hand over fist. Now a lot of the dockers and shipwrights used to go into Par North's but other people like carpenters and painters and plumbers and plasterers, they used to go into the other North's. See, in Ringsend in the pubs everyone had something in *common* to talk about, their work and all. Tradesmen mostly drank with themselves. If a docker went up to the other pub they're in there talking about bricklaying and the docker doesn't want to hear about bricklaying so he doesn't go into that pub, he goes down to hear the bullshit in his *own* pub.

"The cheapest that I remember the pint in Ringsend was seven pence. And I remember that Par North put it up to eight pence and my grandfather used to go in the same time every day and he went in and here's his pint of stout standing in front of him and the grandfather, God be good to him, put up his seven pence and he was just going to put his hand on his pint and Par says, 'You owe me another penny'. And my grandfather says, 'For what?' And he says, 'For the pint, it's gone up a penny'. And me grandfather says, 'Well, you can keep it!' and he walked out the door. Yeah. And do you know that Par North came into our kitchen about two weeks later and asked my grandfather to come back and drink in the pub. See, he drank in there for donkey's years before that. So Par came over and me grandmother opened the door and she says, 'Peter, Mr North wants to see you', and he said, 'Well, send him in to me.' But he didn't get up. And he comes in and the grandfather says, 'You might as well sit down. What's on your mind?' Old Par North, I can even see him now coming in the door, he was a big man, and he says to my grandfather, 'Peter, what's wrong? What's happened between us?' 'God damn you, you put the penny on that pint', he says in bitter language, 'you're not getting it off *me*, you robber. You'll see hell before you see heaven.' And so Par said he'd give him an extra week at the seven pence. That's true."

SENAN FINUCANE—AGE 75

He came to Dublin from County Clare in 1939 to join the Garda. On his Liberties beat were many rough pubs frequented by animal gangs and brawling tinkers. Some publicans were crafty about serving drink after hours but he learned how to crack their secret code to gain entry for a lightning raid. Amidst the ensuing panic, customers scrambled out the back door and over rear walls to escape being fined.

"I'm from Clare, from a farming family. I left in 1939 and came to Dublin and I was never in the city before. We lived in the barracks, about fifty of us, in Kevin Street. Oh, it was like the army. Up at 7.00 in morning for drill and boots shining and we had the brass buttons to shine. My first impression of the Liberties was, of course, the tenements. Oh, there'd be nine or ten or twelve children. There was only one toilet downstairs and then they used slop buckets. There was a lot of hardship then. You'd see barefoot children and on Thomas Street there were street dealers going around selling fish. Down on Francis Street and Bride Street and on the Coombe, they were the *worst* tenements in Dublin.

"There was what was known as 'Red Biddy', that was a cheap wine that was a favourite drink of the down-and-outs then. *Cheap* wine. It was only a few shillings per bottle and that was a drink of the poorer classes and especially the women. And you'd get *so drunk* on it that they could be operated on without an anaesthetic! Cause they wouldn't feel the pain, those drunks on the street. We'd get them off the street in the prison van but they'd be so drunk that you could operate on them and they'd feel *no* pain. They'd just go unconscious with the drink after a pint of cheap wine and they'd be sleeping in the lobby of the tenements. And there was prostitution in Engine Alley. The women were out in the street, anything from 25 to 45 years of age. Oh, they were dressed pretty well. Very good looking they were. And they might say to a man, 'Hello, anything good on your mind?' Then they'd go off to a side street in the dark. And sometimes they'd make use of the air raid shelters. A lot of times the door would be broke and they could get in.

"The working man loved his pint and he loved to go into the pub for a chat with his workmates. Pubs had their own regular crowd and the regulars had their own seat. And the pub was a mine of information where you'd get loads of news, *all* sorts of news. In pubs you could hear a lot about robberies and who was selling the stuff. It was where everyone congregated. The publicans were respected because they were of a good class, most of them. Most publicans lived over the premises. The publican had jurisdiction over his house and he *had* to run a fairly good house, otherwise it got a bad name. The grannies used to send children down to the pub with their jugs for pints but the drink was supposed to go in a corked and sealed vessel. Sometimes the publican would just tell them to fill it up and go off quick. It was *illegal*. Oh, we'd take him back to the publican and warn him that that was not to happen again. And if it was a regular occurrence we'd prosecute him for supplying drink to persons under age. And occasionally you would be called into a pub if there was somebody kicking up a row. Some pubs we would go into pretty often now, sometimes two or three times in the one night. There was often a few blows struck and a few tables turned upside down and a few glasses broken. They were told to get out and sometimes they'd be arrested.

"The animal gangs was a factor at that time. Pubs would serve them because they'd be *afraid* to refuse them because they might produce a knife. Ash Street was pretty tough there and Meath Street. If a pub was rough the good average man would avoid that. Oh, but the animal gangs were very strong then. They'd only fight among themselves, like rival gangs. You had a southside gang and a northside gang. They'd travel two or three miles over to the other side of the city and a row would start. Sometimes they'd get transport there, maybe taxis or cabs, and go to the other side *just to have a row*. There could be twenty to forty to fifty in a gang, many of them unemployed. All ages, 20 to 50, would fight. They'd no guns, just maybe bottles and chains and usually their fists. But there were knives and bottles. Our orders, of course, were to deal with them as best we could. And to get *help* as soon as possible. You just had to go and get help, you couldn't go into ten or twenty fellas fighting each other. And then there'd be those supporting the gang, they had supporters. Like even the *fathers* and *mothers*, if the other gang was fighting there [in their neighbourhood] they'd go out and help their sons. Oh, yes. Oh, yes, I saw women throwing stuff *out the window*! In a big row you'd often see maybe 200 people in the streets and running in all directions. And maybe one chasing two or three that had no weapon, you know, that kind of thing. And we only carried a baton. Oh, I often had to use that. If there was a baton charge to disperse an unruly crowd. Oh, there *would* be a baton charge. But we would only draw the baton as a last resort against an animal gang, or there could be other types of fighting as well.

"And we always had to check at the pubs for after hours trading. There was always a few publicans around the Liberties that would take advantage of the after hours trade. A couple of them were noted for that and we had to keep a watch on those. We would check because other publicans would complain if they were doing after hours trade, keeping them drinking inside. Or their wives would complain too. We were in plain clothes and we were on bikes fairly fast and you'd come quick and they wouldn't expect you. So you'd go in as quick as you could and if we saw any irregularities we'd say, 'It's closing time, get them out.' We'd get their names and tell the publican to clean his house and then the publican would be prosecuted for keeping his premises open. If he had a couple of convictions his licence could be lost. And some of the customers would give you the wrong names and addresses, but we'd know some of the people who would be there. It was very awkward. And they could be prosecuted for being on the premises during prohibited hours and they might be fined a pound or two.

"Now certain places didn't keep the Holy Hour and we'd often be out there on special duty in plain clothes, maybe a sergeant and a guard, to see that the Holy Hour was observed. But people could be *sneaky* in keeping out of sight and there could be thirty or forty people inside the public house during the Holy Hour. Cause they'd usually have a watch out to see were the guards coming in uniform. It's amazing how quiet they could be. We got seventeen in a public house one day and we couldn't hear a *thing* outside until we knocked on the door. And, see, they'd always have a code knock for the door or the window or so many rings on the bell. Oh, they had a code. And they'd change the code. It might be three knocks, a single one, and two more. Or it could be three and two or one. The publican always had code knocks so they could get in. But we used to break the code! We often got in just the same. Oh, yes. One time we went in there with the right code, just knocked and went in, and to their *great surprise*. We could hear *nothing* outside but when we went in they were *jumping* all over the place, out the back door and over the wall. We were there another time and we thought that there was nothing doing and we saw a fella coming out and there were *sixty* in there. All drinking and not a *word*—hush up! There'd be not a *move*. Then some of them would run out the back and over the wall. Oh, yes, maybe a dozen of them made an escape. Great excitement!"

TONY MORRIS—AGE 50

He is the quintessential pub "regular" in O'Dowd's pub in Stoneybatter, unfailing in his daily drinking ritual and loyal to his mates. O'Dowd's is truly his home away from home. A gifted conversationalist, he has his own stool where he likes to hold court with his cronies. Life's problems, he feels, are best shared and resolved over drink with friends. He visits the pub twice a day and can put away a full bottle of whiskey in two sessions and walk out the door perfectly lucid.

"I took my first drink in here on 5 June 1965. It was the day I started work in St Brendan's Hospital as a psychiatric nurse. This is my regular pub now. I come in normally twice a day, fourteen times a week. It would be fair to say that I spend a good portion of my life here. You'll always meet someone you know here, there's always someone to talk to. We normally drink with the same fellas. About six of us join together. Some days there could be fifteen of us altogether. See, this isn't really a pub as such, it's more of a club. Some of us have our own stools or chair. That's my spot there on that counter. Now if I walk in and there's somebody sitting in it I'll just move down another spot. But there's one or two fellas who come in and we'll actually give them their spot. One man, 'Uncle Joe' we call him, well, I've often sat in his seat and he'll come in and I'll say, 'Oh, sorry, Joe, here you are' and I'll stand up and give him the seat. He wouldn't ask me for it but I'll give it up to him cause that's *his* seat. So I usually come in seven days a week but if I didn't come down for four or five days somebody would be coming up to the house to see if I was sick. It's a nice feeling to know that you're wanted.

"We talk about all sorts of things. Could be something from the news. Or it could be something that happened at work. You can hear the same thing over and over but with a different slant on it. I don't know how many times we've fought World War II down here. You know, if Churchill had done this and such and such had done that. It's all bull but it gets rid of all your tensions, you just get rid of pent-up energy, you know. But there's always a bit of fun on a regular basis. Like there's two pensioners in our group and a couple of fellas around 22. You enjoy this more because if they were all your own age you wouldn't have too much to talk about. Young lads now talk about girls they go out with and the dances they were at the night before and we're telling them what it was like in *our* times, and then the pensioners are telling me what it was like in *their* time. It makes for fun. You're hearing something new, something different. And I hate television in a pub. See, if you're in company sitting at the bar you're going to be half looking at the television and half listening to the conversation. Your attention is divided. You look up and see something funny happening while somebody is telling you some deep thought of his. So you're insulting your partner in the conversation.

"We actually *start* arguments here just to get an argument going, just for fun. Some Americans that I brought in here once, they couldn't understand it all. They thought there was going to be a row, though we're about to hit one another. Your countrymen couldn't understand it. We were just arguing away. And an awful lot of bull is spoken. But you won't have much bull if you have no drink because you'll think of what you say first. But when you drink you just don't care and you can tell the biggest lies under the sun and you know everybody doesn't believe you but you still keep telling them. Now during Lent I never drink but I still come in here. I'll drink a lemonade and chat away with the lads. And I was standing at that bar there one day listening to the fellas talking and I remember saying to myself 'That's the greatest load of bull I've ever heard spoken in my life.' Cause I was *sober*, you see. And I said to myself, 'If I was drinking I'd be in the middle of it and I'd be worse than any of them!'

"I find that if you have a problem it is very easy to talk about it over a beer. Among the four or five of us that drink regularly we'd discuss our problems. Some fella has a problem and he thinks that one of us can help him out with it. Maybe he'll tell us about it and we could figure out some way of fixing it up. Like if there's a problem with the wife or one of the kids is sick. Now the last problem I heard was when one of our lads' kids was making their First Holy Communion and he hadn't enough money to buy the dress. And we just said,

'That's no problem', and we just dressed out the kid. We just dipped into our pockets and threw a few quid on the counter and said, 'If that's not enough come back to us.' And the first time I went on strike my youngster was christened that morning and I had a party that night. Now the normal thing when a child is born is you throw a pound into the pram so that the child will never grow up poor, you see. At least that's the custom in this neighbourhood anyway. But it was £10 notes that went into the crib that night because I was out of work. Cause I was on strike and God knows when I would get paid again. It wasn't really for the kid that they were giving it, it was for me. £10 at that time was an awful lot of money because my take-home pay was £28 for a fortnight. You remember it for the rest of your life if somebody does a good turn for you.

"A publican and the barman make a pub. You can have the nicest decor and everything else that you want in it but it mightn't necessarily be a good pub as far as the customers are concerned. It depends on the publican and the barman because they know everyone's business who comes in. Some publicans are the cream of the country. Tom [O'Dowd] is actually a brilliant publican. I remember one night I was sitting there, about broke, nursing two drinks and Tom knew from the way I was drinking that I was broke. And a couple of pals come in that I hadn't seen for years and without even batting an eyelid he comes over and puts down three drinks and gave me the change for a £20 note—never said, 'You owe me that.' He *knew* that I knew that I owed it to him. He's a very good publican. He's a fella who can mind his business when it had to be minded and mind your business when it should be minded. Like if he knows that I don't want my wife to know that I'm here and she rings on the phone he'll say I'm not here. He's one of the best publicans I've ever come across.

"There was never a row in this pub because Tom's quick enough to notice that there was a row in the making. And I never heard him giving out to anyone. He'd just say, 'Now you've had enough, go home and get something to eat and come back.' When a fella treats you that way you *have* to go home, even though you probably want another drink. So normally the publican will come out and stop a row before it starts. And even if there is a row in a local pub it's usually over in two seconds because the locals themselves want to keep their pub clean. Like if it ever happened in this pub I'd jump in immediately and so would all the rest of the customers—because this is *our* pub. I mean, the publican only *thinks* he owns the pub but it's *our* pub as such. This is where we come to drink, this is where we come for our social life. So we want to keep it nice and clean.

"Here's the way I feel. *If alcohol wasn't discovered*—suppose there was no such thing as drink and it was discovered tomorrow—it would be the wonder drug of the century. Because it keeps more people out of mental hospitals, it really does. OK, it put a few in, you have a few alcoholics, but if you compare the number of alcoholics to the fellas it keeps out! Like a fella comes home and the wife starts giving out to him. He'll go down to the pub, have a few drinks, get a bit jarred, and then if she starts giving out to him he's half jarred so he doesn't mind. So you go up to your bed, get up the next morning feeling sick but you feel good because the row is over."

JOHN-JOE KENNEDY—AGE 75

As a young Liberties lad he worked as a lowly pub porter in a rat-infested cellar. In the 1940s he joined the local animal gang that hung out at tough pubs where there was always "blood spilling". When the pubs closed he and his mates would bring out bottles of stout and have a great sing-song on the corner until the wee hours of the morning.

"I was born up the road in Engine Alley. Oh, Engine Alley was all tenements. All big families and there was poverty, *really* poverty in them times. There wasn't much money but now I remember when I started drinking a pint was eight pence, that's old pennies. It was plain porter then. You'd have ten bob in your pocket and you'd go home drunk and you'd *still* have money to get up. The pubs around the locality [Liberties] they were all like the real cowboy saloons. There was sawdust and men chewed tobacco and they spit in the sawdust—they could nearly blind you with it! Sure, a fella rode in on a horse to the pub on the corner there on Meath Street. Come in on a horse. He was jarred. And pubs sold provisions, tea, sugar, oats for animals, tobacco, cigarettes. Cigarettes wasn't exposed the way they are now. No, they were all in drawers. You could go into the pub and ask for a cigarette and a match. A ha'penny for a cigarette and a match. There was no such thing as 'Give me twenty or thirty cigarettes.' Oh, we all smoked.

"Now I was a porter in a pub when I was 18 years of age, that was in 1940, and I worked in the cellar. An old blue apron we used to wear. I got thirty bob a week and I worked from 10.00 in the morning till nearly 1.00 in the morning. I got annoyed with that all right. Clean the brasses and clean all the mirrors, clean all the tumblers. And you had to do the toilets. You had a fire in the cellar but it was always very damp and alive with rats. The beer used to draw the rats, the smell of the malt. Washing the bottles was desperate especially if you put your hand in and there was a broken one and you got a real cut. Only an ordinary wooden tub with four or five dozen bottles. Cold water. We used wire brushes inside each bottle. I used to get sick of it. Your hands were like ice and as red as a cherry. The only thing I liked was bottling the beer cause you used to have to suck the taps to get the beer going. I had to do all the bottling and it was in all wooden barrels at that time and I had to keep the temperature right. I had a coal fire and a thermometer. Then put on Guinness's labels with paste and cork them.

"You *stuck* to your local. The way it was, you made one pub your local and you were part of the furniture then. You were a stranger if you went anywhere else, you know. That was *our* local. I often drank twenty-two pints, in two sessions. I seen men up at the pub where I go and I seen them there from 10.00 in the morning till nearly 12.00 at night and they'd walk out of that pub like they never had a drink. That's a fact. The stuff is not in the drink now at all. Beer was better altogether back then. I mean years ago you put down a pint and you couldn't lift it up, it was the yeast. When it'd overflow the yeast would stick to the counter. It's all *chemicals* now, all forced. Years ago you drank eight pints of plain and you *knew* you were drinking eight pints of plain. Because you were either drunk or merry! You'd start singing or you'd start fighting, one or the other! But when I had whiskey I used to get terrible ratty. I'd be drinking a few pints and then you'd feel yourself getting filled up and, 'Ah, give me a small one', and you'd turn on to whiskey and you'd get drunk *then*. And years ago men believed that for a hangover it was a mug of cabbage water on a Sunday morning. See, when the people around here would do the corned beef they'd put the cabbage in the water and boil it. And you could take your mug of cabbage water out of that in the morning. Oh, I always had it. And break up the bread and plenty of pepper on it. It used to be great. And then you could go down and drink some more pints after that.

"It was rare to see a woman in the pub in them times. Women'd send around to the pub with a can or a jug for a glass of plain. They'd have to call out a man and ask that man to get it for her. She had to wait outside and then it'd go under her shawl and no one'd see it. The only place a woman could go into was the snug and then it was only a chosen few that went into the snug. All older women, married women. You wouldn't see a single woman in it. They'd have a glass of plain, it was all porter. And the women all in shawls. Never wore nothing else, only a shawl. And you'd see them puffing, maybe a pipe. A little bit of a pipe. You'd never see them *openly* smoking. It'd be underneath their shawl. A small clay pipe, a 'scutch' they called them. It was cut down to a little small thing they could hold in their hand. And no toilets for women. They'd have to go out in the street. Yes, in the open street. Out in the street over the railings [grates] by the pub. They wore skirts down to their ankles and they didn't wear any underwear. When we were kids it used to be a laugh, you know.

"There was a shebeen over there across the bridge. It was called Dolly Fawcett's. A shebeen, that was illegal. It was a kip house as well. Dolly Fawcett's was famous, known all over the world. They were coming from all over the world to Dolly's. She was a madam. She was an elderly woman but she started very young. She had girls there regular, they lived in Dolly's. There was a restaurant there but that was only an excuse. The women used to be there and you'd pay for your drink—*pay dearly* for your drink. She served wine, whiskey. All country girls and you wouldn't see film stars like them. Ah, they were beautiful. The [local] women themselves used to stand looking at them when they used to go out dressed. Do you remember these black and white two-piece suits? Now they wore them. One would wear a black one with white dots and the other would wear a yellow one with black dots. The clothes they used to wear used to be *fabulous*. Some of them was brazen. But if you done them a favour they'd never stop paying you. And very kind to children. The ones that used to go with the well-to-do people, they used to be paid well, we'd say a fiver or a tenner. That was a terrible lot of money at that time. And police used to go into it. They got the backhand off Dolly, you know. But the police used to raid it regular and you'd go up over the wall and wait. But she was in with the police. Even when a new inspector would come along he'd be led into Dolly Fawcett's and that was it—on the take.

"Now I was in the local animal gang and we hung out at Johnny Curran's pub at the corner there. There was about twenty-five of us together. You went in there and if you'd no money you'd just say, 'Give us a pint, see you at the weekend.' You know. And he'd give you the pint. He'd give you a couple of pints and he'd put it down in his book. Then at the end of the week he'd say, 'That's your little bill.' If you didn't pay you got *no more*. And if you raised a row that was a thing you'd be barred for. But you mightn't be barred, he might tell you to get out and 'Go on, go home, steady up and you can come back in the morning.' Then you'd have to go back in the morning and tell him that you were sorry. Oh, you'd have to *apologise*. But many a publican got an awful banging years ago. Ah, yes. If you got impudent he might turn around and say, 'You're barred, get out of here!' Next thing the man might take up a tumbler and 'bang', bash him. In the pub they'd do it. But one thing about publicans, they never called the police.

"There was always blood flowing in the pub at that time. Always. Especially when the racing mob would start fighting among themselves, when money was missing. Like if you made so much money spinning the wheel or the three-card trick or if you picked pockets [at the races], well, there might be a man that might try to fiddle them. They were after coming back from a race meeting and they were in the pub dividing the money and one fella says, 'Hey, wait a minute, there *must* be more money than this.' And then there was *blood* spilling. Might be five of them from the racing crowd that got into it. Kicking and belts with bottles and everything. When they finished up they all went and had a drink! But there was always terrible rows in pubs, dirty rows. An argument and there'd be digs and lashing and 'bang' in the pub. The worst row I ever saw in a pub was with this fella and he was an awful head case. It was all over a ha'penny and he took up the stool and it was a round one with them long legs and he was swinging it at a young apprentice behind the counter. And this fella says, 'You dirty so-and-so!' and the young fella [apprentice] bent down lucky enough and yer man took up the stool, and I'm not codding you, he *split* the counter in two with the belt of the stool. He'd have killed the young fella stone cold if he'd have caught him. But it hit the counter and split it in two. And he was told, '*Out*, you're *barred*!' So he goes outside the pub and broke *every* pane of glass in the pub.

"Tinkers were allowed into the pubs in them times and they were great spenders. The tinkers used to mix with us in the pubs, have a bit of crack with us. Most of them was chimney sweeps, like the Wards. We used to love to see them fight. And it was all bare knuckle. Sometimes it was two families. But it would all be fair fighting. You'd just watch it, you wouldn't interfere. The women, they'd start a row with another woman and you'd see blood then! Oh, the women were *better* than the men. They used to live up here in caravans and I seen two women boxing and the men made a ring for them. And they fought like men. They didn't pull hair, no hair pulling. And one of the women, God help her, she was pregnant and yer [other] woman *beat* her around the place. And her husband kept saying, '*Get up* or I'll kick this and I'll kick that out of you. Get up and *fight*.' Oh, it was terrible.

"We used to go into the pub and we'd come out after the public house had closed and we'd be well jarred and you'd have a great sing-song outside the pub. There'd be a sing-song on the street second to none. You could bring a half a dozen bottles out with you and you could open them up if you wanted on the street. So we'd come out of the pub and we'd just all stand around the corner and they used to be sitting in the tenement windows waiting for the pubs to close for the sing-song. It'd carry all over the place and people all looking out the windows. It used to be terrific. There was one fella and Al Jolson had nothing on him. And there was a girl there, Lizzy, and she used to have an old melodeon and there'd be a sing-song and a dance outside the pub till maybe 2.00 or 3.00 in the morning. It used to be *great*. Nearly everyone up around Engine Alley would be there from the tenements and looking out the windows and listening. We'd be out there singing like a nightingale! Them nights that we used to have, they were great nights . . . summer or winter.

"Then we used to go to the bonafides. You had to be three miles outside the limit to be bonafide. We'd go to the Red Cow out on the Naas Road. Oh, they'd check you at the door and ask where you were from and we'd say Ringsend and they'd say, 'Go ahead.' That was it. We went out on horse and cart. And another place we'd go, the 'Dead Man' Murray's, you could stay there all night. They'd serve up till 12.00 and then put you out at 12.00 and you could stand outside the pub door till a minute past 12.00—and then you could go back in again. Once it went after 12.00 you could go back into the pub. See, they had a twenty-four hour licence. And then if you wanted to stay there all night they'd stand there serving you. But if you went to sleep they'd put you out. You'd have to keep buying. And then you'd be going home bedsheets!

"The publicans would all come up here to Dublin from the country and they all had land back home. Oh, you wouldn't see a Dublin man owning a public house. They used to come up here and started off as a barman and then started fiddling in the 'Jack and Jill'—fiddling in the till! Oh, yeah. The till, that was the 'Jack and Jill'. Generally, when a man was made a manager he'd own his own pub in about two or three years' time. Fiddling the till. *Everyone* done it. The boss done it *himself*, so he knew. The manager'd check the till and put it away in the safe but he'd take out his own whack out of it. There was no such thing as a man going out straight and buying a pub, they were *all* barmen first, every *one* of them. At that time the top price for a public house [in the Liberties] was £3,000. Yeah. And the pub beside the chapel on Meath Street, that went for £1,800. And some of the publicans then used to water the whiskey. Oh, yeah. Especially if a fella got half way canned and he didn't know what he was drinking. I seen a fella getting drunk on water one time!

"Now only one man in our local pub had his own spot, a blind man. The blind man and his wife used to be allowed to sit in the bar together, Mickey and Mary Ann. And Mary Ann sat there with her shank of a pipe. She was 70-odd, wore a shawl and one of them Mother Reilly hats. She smoked the clay pipe in the pub there, under her shawl. She was his eyes. They used to go up and beg at the cattle market and he'd come back and he'd get a pint. And he was able to sip so many sips of his pint and he'd know how many mouthfuls he'd taken. Well, a couple of fellas used to go behind him and take up the pint and take a mouthful out of it. Well, he *knew* that someone was after drinking that pint and he'd get up his stick and he'd start *swinging* the stick all around. And his language used to be *unhuman*."

Mairin Johnston—Age 60

As a young girl growing up in the Liberties she found the dark, drab pubs with their spitting men, soiled sawdust and stench of smoke and drink to be "disgusting" dens. It is her sad recollection that many men in those days drank away their paltry wages and beat their wives. Many a bruise and black eye she saw on neighbourhood women after the man's drinking binge. Her insightful perspective on old pub life provides a valuable woman's view on the social institution.

"Public houses were so much a part of the scene because there were so *many* public houses around. Your first impression was that pubs were *horrible* and there was sawdust all over the place and the men just spit everywhere and they'd urinate everywhere. There was no hygiene at all. And the *smell* of smoke and the smell of tobacco! An awful lot of men smoked clay pipes and they also chewed tobacco, so when they weren't drinking they were spitting. I remember this spitting so well . . . *nobody* seemed to think that was wrong. But I used to be horrified with it, I mean it was *disgusting*. And TB then was really rampant and there were notices 'No spitting allowed'. One of my granduncles worked in Judd's hide and skin yards down on Hendrick Street and the people who worked in skin yards they *stank* to high heaven! The *smell* was just incredible! And they went to their own pubs that would let them in, usually around the area where the skin yards were.

"By and large, women didn't go into public houses, unless you were one of 'those'. You know. Women who went into public houses were looked down upon. I mean going into a pub you were like a prostitute, really. Around Pimlico you just *didn't*. Except the older women did go and they would go into the snugs. Grannies could go in because they were beyond sin. But they wouldn't be served a pint, they'd drink a bottle or they'd get the baby Power's if they were hard drinkers. Now my granny just drank a bottle of stout and never *ever* did I see her drunk. She might meet a crony and they'd go in and have a little jar in the snug. And my granny, if she was in the pub and my mother was looking for her, I'd run around the corner and say, 'Granny, your dinner is ready.' And granny'd be sitting there with her cloak and bonnet with the glass of stout in front of her with all the yeast on the top and she'd say, 'Come over here and have a bit' and you always got the froth. Oh, that was supposed to be the *best* thing in the world for your health. It tasted gorgeous. So children could go in and they always got the froth cause the old women thought that this was as good as mother's milk. In fact, nursing mothers in the Coombe Hospital, they always got a bottle of Guinness. It was felt to be beneficial for milk.

"There was Mr O'Connor's pub on the Coombe and he ran a *very* respectable house. And he was a *very* respectable gentleman. He'd a lovely face and a lovely moustache and he wore a white coat and an apron and a wide-brimmed hat. Now I had a friend who was the twenty-first child in her family and her mother *rarely* got out of the bed—which is one of the reasons why she had the twenty-one children! And both of her parents were very fond of the jar. And when we were young we'd come from school to her house and her mother'd shout, 'Is that you, Dina? I want you to go down to Mr O'Connor's.' And we'd get the jug and Dina would have to put the jug under her coat and we'd go down to Mr O'Connor's. And it didn't matter what time we went down, even if the pub was shut. Mr O'Connor didn't always open to the opening hours, he was open whenever he felt like it because he lived there and he didn't give a hoot, you see. So if the public house was shut we'd just knock on the side door and Mr O'Connor would look up and down the street to see if there was any sign of the garda. And he'd bring the two of us in and he'd fill up the jug with porter and it'd go on the slate, no money changed hands, and Dina'd put it under her coat. Now to give us that drink, it was illegal for him to do that, but he used to give us kids the drink to bring up to her mother who was drinking it in the privacy of her bedroom. So he was a very respectable man—but he *still* gave it to us.

"The public house was where you went to chat and talk and meet people. I mean, if anybody came to visit you, if a family came, cousins and uncles and all, on a Sunday, the minute the men could come in it was *around to the pub*. They'd leave the women then to chatter and backbite and they'd go off. The pub was to get away from screaming kids and nagging wives and to get into the company of other men. Because there was always this camaraderie with other men, you know, that they wanted to be together—the 'boys'. I mean, being stuck with a woman all the time once you'd married her, that was it. I mean, you had her whenever you wanted in the bed! But your friends were your friends. And a man who was kept from the pub, other women would look down on his wife, that she wouldn't let him go around even to have a drink . . . 'The poor unfortunate fella, she won't let him out', you know. And I have to say, unfortunately, that an awful lot of women regarded it that their men going around to the pub that they were *men*, they were macho. That made them macho. I remember, actually there was a little weaver who lived over us and he was one of the last of the weavers and he didn't drink and he didn't smoke. My mother said that he didn't even shave! And because he didn't go to the pub he was considered to be a 'Nancy boy'. It was kind of effeminate, 'Nancy' being the name.

"Men got their wages on a Saturday and they'd go off into the pubs and wouldn't come home with the wages. Sometimes they were paid *in* pubs, so they'd have to go into the pub. Dockers might be paid in the local pub and hide and skin workers as well. See, it was just left over from the times that Jim Larkin fought against and he was a great temperance man, he detested drinking. He *insisted* that men got paid their wages outside of pubs. But on a Saturday their wives and their children would be looking for them. And the mother'd be sending the kids down to the pub, 'Tell your daddy I've no money for the shopping.' Or the woman would be waiting outside the pub for him to come out —and if she went in he might *hit* her. And it demeaned her because she didn't want people to know that her husband wasn't giving her the money. They had their pride. So maybe she'd tell another fella who would be sympathetic towards her and understand that he was a drunkard and he might go in and say, 'Would you not go out and give Lizzy a few ha'pennies?'

"*Every* Saturday night there was a row. There was a pub at the corner of Meath Street, it was Johnny Curran's, and it was a *real* rough house. Oh, the rows and the boxing matches! And some of the older women who went to pubs, they would fight just as much as the men. A lot of them would have been dealers. Oh, God, that was the weekend entertainment! It might start inside the pub and then they'd be thrown out, 'Get out', you know, and they were thrown out onto the road. The minute you'd see this happening you'd run all around and say, 'There's a ruggy-up at the corner!' And if you intervened you might end up with the two of them attacking *you*. I mean, that was always a danger. They couldn't fight with the shawl on so they'd throw off their shawls and underneath they had cross-over bibs as we used to call them, with no sleeves, just two holes, and they had pockets. Oh, they'd be tumbling on the ground and kicking each other. And then they would do what we used to describe as 'reef' themselves. It meant that they would *tear* each other to pieces. And the women in those days used to wear their hair up in buns with little pins in them and when they'd tear their hair down they'd have this great big length of hair and they'd 'streel' [drag] each other along. That's another term. And another expression somebody'd say was, 'She scrobbed the face off her.' I think that's an old English word, 'scrob', to scratch. And it would *tear* the skin down. And *ferocious* language. And they could hold the bitterness.

"A funny thing about fighting was that if a man who had been drinking was beating his wife the police *never* came! *Never* interfered. For the police to come along was interfering in a domestic quarrel. A man had a *right* to beat his wife. That was *absolute*. Now the women around here, whether they were related or not, they were always very supportive of women who were beaten. Absolutely. In those days when there was such a close-knit community this acted like counselling and help. And grannies might throw the man out. Oh, yeah, throw him out of his own room. And then very often the man would break the door in. So you might as well leave him in. Sometimes you'd see the wives black and blue and maybe even with a broken arm. I mean they would beat them something terrible. And the awful thing was that they'd beat them when they were *pregnant*. I mean there were so many women beaten and so many women miscarried as a result of the men's brutality. Really, the wife was there in those days for one thing and one thing only, to administer to the man's needs in every way. Rape! And if you went to the priest and said that your husband had beaten you and you wanted to get away from him and you maybe had a miscarriage and you didn't want anything more to do with him, the priest would tell you that it was your *duty*! It was your *duty* to stay with your husband and it was his right to exercise whatever punishment he wanted on you.

"Years ago you depended on the publican if you were having a funeral or a hooley or a wedding. You went down and said you wanted so much drink and you *got* it. They didn't ask you for the money straight away. It was put on the slate. And you could go into a public house for political collections. Republicanism was held in very high esteem then and if a local Republican died, a man who had fought at some stage, there'd be a collection in the pub. They'd all go into the pub on the night of the funeral and there'd be a 'whip-around' for his wife and kids. 'Whip-around' means you'd go around with a cap, pass it around. The publican didn't mind that. And the same with any charity, you could go into the public houses. In fact, that's where people collected most of the money for charities, in the public houses. And people selling political papers. There was *always* political papers every Saturday night in pubs. In every pub. Every few minutes there'd be somebody coming in with a box or papers or pamphlets. And the ballad singers with their ballad sheets. They'd sing the song outside the pub to let you know what the song sounded like and then they went into the pub with their leaflets and went around and sold them for a penny. Now in some pubs they could sing, like in Johnny Curran's. The old ballad singer, John Wilson, he used to go into Johnny Curran's and sing inside the pub and he'd be plied with drink. Oh, yes. And shellfish were hawked in the public house then. They used to go around selling cockles and mussels just like Molly Malone with the big baskets and they'd go into the pubs. And the men'd eat them in the pub with their Guinness.

"Publicans had a better lifestyle and they had a prominent place in the church and they were also well in with the priests. Because they contributed a lot of money to the church. So they were looked upon as pillars of the community. And the funny thing about publicans is that they always had sons who were priests or bishops. And my mother always used to say, 'How could they equate this with sending unfortunate men out stoned, blind drunk, who would go home and beat their wives or their children would be starving?' My mother always said that the priests and the bishops got educated on the backs of the people. She always said that the 'road to hell is paved with priests and bishops' because they *always* drank and they always bet on horses. Oh, the priests drank. Yes, they did. They might go to a hotel to drink, that was a very respectable place, and they'd sit in the foyer and be having their whiskey. But *numerous* priests were drunkards. And my mother'd say, 'Sure, why wouldn't they be, didn't they come out of a public house? Wasn't their father a publican?'"

Timmy Kirwan—Age 75

He was born and reared in the famed Monto red light district surrounded by tawdry pubs, shebeens and kip houses. He knew all the shrewd madams who hid their stout and whiskey bottles under street grates and in the sewers beneath manhole covers. As a young lad, house-bound prostitutes used to lower cans on a string and ask Timmy and his pals to have them filled with porter at the local pub. In reward he got a few pennies for the picture show.

"I was born and reared in a tenement on Corporation Street. There was ten of us sleeping in one room not three-quarters the size of this. Eight or nine families in a tenement and one toilet in the yard. Now it was a red light district in them days and the whole area was called 'Monto' and the English was here at that time. It was all pubs and kip houses and shebeens. And the children, their father used to send them down for a jug of beer, plain porter, and you had to put it under your coat because if the police seen you coming out he'd be charged for serving you under age. And before they'd come back to their father with the pint of beer they half drank it and some of them'd put water in it. And back then they'd give a sup of stout to the babies to kill the maggots inside of him, to kill the worms. Yes, that was a cure. That's what they used to say.

"I worked as a docker down there for thirty years. All mates of mine down there. Dockers were the best pint drinkers in the world. They'd drink at 7.00 in the morning and half twelve at night time without a bother. They'd drink about five pints before they'd go to work and come out at beero hour, that's 10.00 in the morning, take off for a break and down to the pub again. Two or three more pints and back off to work again. Then at dinner hour some of them wouldn't go home—*straight* into the pub again! This was their life. The crack was great. But now I'll tell you, the tradesmen never classed us. See, they were the 'gentlemen' of the trades. The tradesmen would drink together. Snobbery. But most publicans was very good, I'll say that. If a person died and you had no money you'd get a sugar bag and you'd go into the pubs and make a collection and the publican would help you. And if a person was being put out over rent —an eviction—they'd do the same, make a collection as well for them people. They often did that at that time.

"Now Phil Shanahan [publican] was a great leader of the IRA at that time. A stout man, a Tipperary man. And the cellar in his pub and Paddy Clare's pub across the road used to lead for *miles* underground. Tunnels would go right into O'Connell Street where the GPO is and down to the Liffey River. The lads were able to go down there and do their business and hide from the British soldiers in them cellars. There was some vicious soldiers went into Shanahan's shop. But when the British army would come to raid them the lads would go down there and they were *gone*. All underneath the ground. Oh, yes. They used to get away from the British that way. One of them pubs is still there but the cellars is all blocked off.

"I knew all the madams in the Monto. I knew them well because I lived among them. They had their kips there in the tenements on Pudding Street, Railway Street. There was Becky Cooper's, Polly Butler's and May Oblong. Joyce's books and all had their names in there. They were red light houses. The madams were around here from the nineteenth century. Now where they came from I don't know but they used to speak with a Dublin accent. The best kip you had was Becky Cooper's. Becky Cooper, she was 83 when she died, a lovely woman. She was six foot three. Now May Oblong, she lived beside me and she was over six foot. And she used to wear rings on every finger. She had a big heart. See, the madams, they were the best in the world for helping the poor. Oh, yes, if you wanted money for food or anything. Now May Oblong, if you hadn't any food she'd give it to you on the slate but she wouldn't charge you a lot of money for it. She'd give it to you instead of [you] going to these other moneylenders. She'd see you down-and-out and she'd help you. And a lot of poor people worked for the madams, they *had* to do it. They had the old people in the neighbourhood working for them cleaning the delft and collecting glasses and giving them a few bob. My mother worked for the madams, cleaning up for them to make a few bob for the family. She done a lot of scrubbing and washing the house and all the delft. Now the tenement house we lived in was owned by a man who owned kips. He was the landlord and you had to pay him so much a week, the rent. He made his money out of all that and his family was sent to Scotland for a college education. Oh, they were able to do that for their families.

"The madams kept girls there in the kip houses. Madams had seven or eight girls. They were lovely girls, mostly country girls. Some were beautiful. And they dressed very well. See, the madams dressed them and looked after them, made sure they were washed and cleaned and all. They were about 20 or 24, around that age. And the girls were very decent, very good natured. Local people didn't mind them at all. Because the prostitute on the corner of the street, these country girls, they'd take children in their bare feet and buy them shoes and boots. That's *right*. Or you'd be going by with your baby in your arms and they'd take the baby out of your arms and take them around to Talbot Street here up to the clothes shop and *dress* the child for you! Yes, they *did* that. They were called 'unfortunate girls' but they were kind people.

"Well, them country girls was locked up in the night time and all day long in the kip houses and they couldn't get out of the house. No, the madams would lock them up. This was around Montgomery Street and Railway Street. And when we'd be going to school in the morning and we were all in our bare feet because it was a really poor place we used to see them roaring out the windows and they'd let down a can with a string on it and the money'd be in the can to get them cigarettes and matches. And then coming back from school, you'd go down the same way again and they'd let down the can again with the string on it to go off and get them a gargle at the pub, to get the stout in the pub and hand the can up again and they'd tell you to keep the change for the pictures.

"The girls were there at night time and the men went into the houses. Oh, there were sailor men and gentlemen. Norwegians, Chinamen, the Frenchmen,

Americans now and again, coming off their ships, they'd go into these places. And the well-off people, they went to the houses. Oh, yes, some of them big-shots. They were gentlemen and lords and everything else. They'd come in on a hackney cab, a horse and cab. They'd come in covered-in cabs and they used to hide inside them cause you could pull the curtain over them and they'd say to the driver, 'Go to number 9 . . . or number 12.' It was night time and nobody'd see them and they'd open the door and go into the house and the cabby'd wait up the road a bit till two or three in the morning cause they'd be drinking. See, at that time when the men were put out of the pubs after hours they went to these places, the kip houses or what were called shebeens. And the girls were working there. And there was a bouncer there and the lady looking after the girls. So after you were put out of the pubs you'd go over to these places and ask for a drink. See, back then you had these people selling porter and drink after hours. And the girls there. And they were *hiding* the drink in the manholes. They'd go out and lift up the manhole and take up the porter or whiskey or whatever was there and bring it in for whatever the men ordered. See, they used to hide the drink in the manholes, in the sewers. There was a woman who sent all her sons off to the States and to Canada to be educated out of the money she made off of drink after hours.

"Now you had *policemen* in these places drinking all night as well! They were from Store Street [station]. I knew most of them. All these police was Mayo men, all big men. And they were 'on the take'—or them places wouldn't have been *open at all*! They should have been closed up but they closed their eyes and they got *that* [money in their hand] every night. They were able to sit in them places *all* night. See, they'd come on duty at 4.00 and they'd go up in the neighbourhood and slip into one of these places then for the night. They'd be drinking there all night and they'd get their backhand then the next morning before they'd go out. Then there was fights outside the kip houses and shebeens at 9.00 in the morning when they'd all be coming out, all stupid drunk. Ah, the police drunk as well, never sober. See, maybe you'd be sitting there next to them drinking and the police, they'd get cranky and you'd have an argument. And the bouncers would throw them out. Ah, they were *fighting* men. They had them bouncers in the pubs as well around here. Big fine lads who could use themselves. So maybe a policeman and another fella'd be giving out and the bouncers, they'd have to get them out of the house. So they'd go outside here in the lane or in the road and they'd have a go, the men and the police together. They'd strip off, no weapons, and it was hand to hand. It'd be a fair fight. And we'd be going to school in the morning and we'd see all this. Sometimes they'd just go out and it'd be 'bang, bang' and it'd be all over in a minute. Knock him out and then the women'd wash them up. But if the two of them were fighting the policeman could go back the next night looking for that man and he'd have four or five policemen *with him*. And he'd lag him out and give him a hiding."

Michael Gill—Age 66

*Born above his father's pub in the Liberties, he went into the trade at age
17. He got to know well most of the famous publicans of this century, such
as Davy Byrne, John McDaid and Pat Conway. To him, these "old chappies"
were great men and delightful characters. He later worked for the Dublin
Licensed Vintners Association where he developed a keen sense of Dublin pub
history.*

"I was born in 1927 and we had the pub in the Liberties then, at 86 Bride Street.
Originally it was all a tenement area and some were a tough bunch of rowdies.
We were at the south corner of Golden Lane and there were two other pubs
directly opposite us. It was called the 'four corners of hell'. Now my grandfather
had a pub up on North King Street and he had a market licence and could open
at 6.00 in the morning. All the vegetables came in from north County Dublin.
And about 6.00 on a frosty morning the farmers'd be coming down Drumcondra
Road and my grandfather had a big brass muller which he filled with claret—but
some of them referred to it as mulled brandy—and he put it on to boil and they
say the horse could smell it and he'd start to trot! It was sixpence a glass and that
did a huge business. Now one real snowy morning about 7.00 around Christmas
time there was a DMP man [policeman] outside my grandfather's door and he
felt sorry for him and he gives him a couple of glasses of this hot claret and his
sergeant came along and found him and he lost his early morning licence. Oh,
they were very strict at that time if you were serving a DMP man.

"I was 17 when I started in my father's pub on the North Circular. The people
there were rough in the sense that they were coarse and maybe took an odd
wallop at each other but I never found them difficult. In those working-class
areas they were so uneducated that it was common that they wouldn't read or
write. And I'd see my father at the end of the counter and the old dears would
come in and say, 'I got a letter from me daughter in Australia, Mr Gill. Would you
ever read it for me?' And we'd write letters of reference. I remember the first one
I wrote and I think he was going off to England or somewhere. So I got busy and
I wrote a very flowery letter about the background of his people and all this sort
of thing and I read it to him. And he says, 'Mr Gill, that's of no use at all. I want
you to just say that he's sober, honest, and industrious.' Then we got these old
fellas and they were largely illiterate and they'd get a pint on the slate. These old
chaps, they'd just have this string on their belt and every time they got a pint on
the slate they'd put a knot on the string, to keep track.

"There was a big jug trade there, as they called it. When the tenements were
really full in Summerhill there were 800 people to the acre and there were all
sorts of grandfathers and grandmothers bed-ridden and couldn't face the stairs.
So there was an awful lot of drinking done from the jugs and cans. Whatever
little nipper would be around the place would be sent running down to the local

pub for a can of porter. The legality was very doubtful but it would have been all right if he had sealed the can. The publican owned the cans and on a Monday morning the can boys, as they used to call them, went off up to the tenement rooms to collect them. He had a pole a bit longer than a brush handle and he went off to the rooms and put all these cans on the pole. And there was this rattling around Summerhill on a Monday with twelve or fourteen of these fellas collecting all these cans.

"Now the dockers, they drank a great deal. It'd take a calculator to find out how many pints they had. But he *needed* it, every one of them. And the dirt! The dockers'd go down ladders into this dark hole on the ship and it was pure black with the coal dust. And there was nowhere on the quays where they could get a shower. There was one fella that I was very fond of and he used to come into our pub on the North Circular Road and you'd see these white eyes coming in shining and you could *sweep* the coal dust off the floor when he'd be gone. But he was out sick one time and he was washed coming out of the hospital and he came in for a pack of cigarettes and I *didn't know* him without the coal. I hadn't a clue that I'd ever seen him before.

"Most of the old publicans back then had come up to Dublin from the country at the age of 13 or 14 to work as apprentices and a lot of them hadn't quite got familiar with shoes and they had their little tin box and whatever spare shirts they had and a half-crown. And they strove to improve themselves. They'd nowhere to go, only up. And if you think back now the opening hours for some pubs were from 7.00 to 11.00 and you lived-in. Get up around 6.00 and they were slow closing and a kid wouldn't get to bed till half-twelve and up again at 6.00. It was tough. They had to stay in the house up to 1936. And with the better publicans they all sat around for a meal together and the publican would be at the head of the table and the staff down along. And the publican would be laying it on for them whatever subject interested them. Like my father, for instance, he was fond of poetry and the poor apprentice that didn't know any poetry had better just get a book and learn it. Of course, some publicans thought of nothing but football and hurling.

"Years ago you used to loosely refer to the 'big five' pubs, but when anyone was ever asked to count them there was always seven or eight of them. There was Madigan's of Earl Street, there was the Tower in Henry Street, then there was Peter Foley with the Scotch House and then Davy Byrne's and the Palace was a well thought of pub, and James Browne had the Oval. It was all Tipperary and Cavan men back then. Tipperary men probably formed 50 per cent of the Dublin trade at that time and Cavan was next. There was a certain snobbery in it too. The Tipperary lads came from bigger holdings, they were better off generally than the Cavan lads. They used to say that the Dublin man was too cute to be a publican, there were easier ways of working!

"But the old publicans, the old chappies, were great. Like James Browne of the Oval, he was a great publican and he always wore a hat behind the counter. It wasn't respectable to go uncovered. A bowler hat was always worn by the boss and a soft hat by the foreman, *on* the job. Some wore top hats, the stovepipes.

That went right back to the 1780s and 1790s. And Peter Foley in the Scotch House was a great character. He was a sporting man and his knowledge of sport was great and he was an expert on dogs. At the Palace there was a man named Ryan there, a most dignified old soul, and he was a great man for blending whiskies. In the Palace Bar old George Smyllie, the editor of *The Irish Times*, sat over in his corner and there were all the leading literary types of the times and you had your standing in that circle. You couldn't sit too close—you could be accepted, but stay on the outer ring of the circle. Now McDaid's was quite the opposite, it was an easy going pub. John McDaid was a lovable old character, a big tall Donegal man, very quiet and always trying to be helpful. And you take Davy Byrne, a most extraordinary man. Davy held court in his own place. And the story goes that he was making out his will and was asked, 'Did you make all that money filling pints?' 'No, *not* filling them!'

"Now Pat Conway, on Parnell Street, he was one of the great characters. All through the 1920s and 1930s Pat sort of led the trade society. He always wanted to bring up Tipperary men and they were so nicely trained and turned out. Pat was one of the most successful publicans and he kept on the tradition of helping the lads out. Like if he was a good lad [barman] he'd lend them a thousand or two to get started [buying their own pub]. And Pat Conway told me that when they'd get up on Sunday morning they were polished and brushed out and shined and everything else and they'd march up to Mass, the staff, and he handed each of them a penny on their way up to put on the plate. Now the collection was outside at the time. And they'd all practise the business with their thumb and forefinger so that they could hit the plate and retain the penny! Then they used to get out on a Sunday for a walk or to play hurling or whatever. Then they used to walk to Carthy's pub of Drumcondra—it's now the Cat and Cage —and they got a butt of stout each for their pennies. A butt was a little bit better than a half-pint. There was a lot of odd measures in those days.

"Another funny thing, a law, is that if someone is killed the police are entitled to take the body and put it into the local pub. And the pub on the Templeogue Road was known as the 'Morgue' because of all the accidents and the dead bodies. And the body was kept there until it was disposed of to the relatives. During the war the police resurrected the law and quite a number of pubs as near as Howth they brought bodies into that were washed up at sea. Brought them into the pub and it upset the publican no end, especially since some of these bodies had been a month or two in the ocean. And another silly law was that you couldn't fly a flag from a public house. It went back to a row down in Bantry between the United Irish League and the Redmondites, the Home Rule Party. There was a split and each pub had its own flag and they organised all the parties and they fought it out and cracked heads all over the place and there was such a ruggy that there was an amendment put through some finance bill that you're not supposed to fly a flag on a public house."

TOM BYRNE—AGE 80

Growing up around the docks, he knew all the local pubs firsthand. The Killarney House was the most famous speakeasy in the neighbourhood. When the pub was raided the publican provided a secret escape hatch for scurrying customers. His favourite publican was a grey-haired gentleman with a red rose in his suit coat who, when a fight erupted in his pub, delighted in bolting over the counter and knocking men out cold with his bare fists.

"I was born off Oriel Street on Canning Street. My father was a seaman all his life and his father was the skipper of a schooner. There was nine children including the first set of triplets born under the Free State Government. The triplet sisters were born and the captain of my father's ship said, 'If it had been me I'd be drunk for a week!' I started as a messenger boy as a young lad and then I worked in a brushmaker's, it was Varian's on Talbot Street. I went to sea then for about eleven months and then I went into warehousing on the docks.

"There were *all* dockers' pubs along the quays. And dockers, they used to consume a *terrific* amount of drink. You know, sweating you're getting rid of the fluids so you've plenty of room for fluid and it was porter mostly. One fella, Charlie, a docker, they used to refer to him as 'Thirteen Pints'. The old slate was always there, it was an established practice, and they'd go in and even get cigarettes on the slate. You had to pay it back or you were finished in other pubs as well. Yeah, your record went ahead of you if you were a 'bad pay'. Dockers were paid each day and the bulk of it was spent in the pubs. And stevedores used to go into the pubs to pay them. Then they'd buy the stevedore a drink. This was ingratiating themselves with the stevedore. It was an unprincipled way for him to act. Stevedores made a practice of this but Jim Larkin did away with that and they couldn't be paid in a pub.

"Now the Killarney House pub down our way on Oriel Street it was owned by a Kerry man named Donoghue. I have vivid memories of it. A white marble counter and all sorts of shipyard workers, dockers and cattle jobbers. They used to sprinkle the sawdust and fellas used to say, 'Did you see so and so? and they'd say, 'Oh, yeah, he was down spitting in the sawdust.' That means he was in the pub. No spittoons. No, they'd be a weapon when a row starts! They actually used to call that pub the 'blood pan', that was the nickname for it. See, at the weekends *continually* there would be a row outside of it. The argument would start inside over politics or trade unionism, particularly those two, and then it'd be 'outside on the road!' See, trade unionism and politics used to be discussed on a very *high* level in pubs.

"Pubs then had 'chuckers out', you'd call them bouncers now, that's a nice name for it. They were mostly fellas who were handy with their hands and they'd be employed as 'can boys' around the pub. It originates from when people used to get cans of drink brought to them, like billy cans of porter. They'd bring around a few cans so they used to say, 'He's a can boy.' And then others used to be referred to as 'counter jumpers'. A counter jumper, he was a barman or a porter, and he'd be pulling a pint inside the counter and was handy with his hands and when a row would start he'd *jump over* the counter and 'ding, ding' —[knock] out. And some of the fellas who owned the pubs were very handy with their hands too. As kids we used to be watching this and we'd say, 'Oh, there's a row up at Donoghue's' and all the kids would take off to see this. There was very good fights, not like today with the stabbing business. A fair fight. The coats would be taken off and if one fella put the other fella down he'd step back and let him get up. We used to be watching this.

"The clergy was trying to cut down on the drink and stop the pubs from opening after hours. They referred to them as 'speakeasies', like the Killarney House pub. The pubs closed and the blinds came down and they had Players cigarette cartons and they made a hole in it and stuck a couple of pieces of string in there and put it up on the ceiling [over the light] and this would be hanging [like a lamp] like what you'd see in billiards saloons over the tables. The carton would hang down and there was only a square of light down on the counter and the other lights were all put out. The light went straight down on to the counter and there was a little light sufficient then to see and they'd be sitting around on barrels and talking in the dark and it was 'Shhh . . . be quiet!' This is how speakeasies was.

"So what they'd do then, the police, they'd have an odd raid and they used to come around in the open cars like what you see in some of those early gangster pictures like Al Capone. And nearly all had trench coats on them, plain clothes. Trench coats on them and soft hats. And they'd *whiz* down and there'd be four or five or six of them in these cars and they'd *pile* out and bang, bang, bang on the door and then they'd run in and you'd see fellas getting thrown out after they got their names and addresses. But there was this one pub that'd be open after hours but when the police'd go down to raid the pub it would have been cleared out. What it was, the publican was *related* to someone in the police station, desk sergeant or someone else, and they used to *ring* from the station and tell him to clear the house. That was going on for a long time.

"The Killarney House changed hands and the fella that took it over, he had a tenement house next door to the pub. And he had a big wardrobe in the living accommodation above the pub along the wall there and *another* big wardrobe in the tenement next door along the wall. And they backed on to one another. And there was a door broken open in it [through the wall] and he was hanging clothes in it. And when there was going to be a raid it was, 'Everybody upstairs!' And they went upstairs and *out* through the wardrobe and the door closed and slide the clothes back on the rack. The police came in and raided the place —nobody there. Then the police got the idea that they were going out over the back [wall]. So the police encircled the place on a couple of occasions and got no one! Most ingenious it was. So it was one of these can boys who spilled the beans, years after, when he had a falling out with the management. They blamed him for it.

"The 'hoggers' used to be up around the Custom House and I knew some of them. They were mostly down-and-outers, fellas who had fallen by the wayside for one reason or another. They were a harmless crowd but it was pretty funny to see them. There'd be some drink left in some of the barrels and they weren't fully empty and there'd be maybe a couple of gallons left in it, stout. They used to rock the barrels and listen and you could hear it swishing backwards and forwards. Then they'd get a bung out of it and they used to lift it up onto another barrel and tilt it and pour it onto the head of the other barrel. It was most unhygienic, you know. There was red raddle around the edges and one fella'd rub the raddle off with his cloth cap and blow the dust off it and then that was looked on as sufficient cleaning. Then they'd sup it up and you'd see the red on their mouths. And one fella was like the foreman and he'd see that one fella didn't hog too much.

"The word 'alcoholic', I didn't know what that meant until I was middle aged. A man was just a 'drunkard' and that was it, a fella who drank too much. And there was the height of sympathy for the way some of them treated the women. Oh, it was dreadful then. Oh, God, yeah. You could see the dire poverty. And most of these pubs then were known for having *bad* whiskey. Yeah, you'd get 'Johnny jump-up' as they used to say. It was rough stuff. It'd be cheap whiskey. See, the bottle would be under the counter. Now the regulars, of course, would be aware of it and they wouldn't get it. It was like paraffin oil! And then there was an awful lot of country people around and they'd bring some poitin in and give it to their relations and then their relations would be doling it out. They'd go into the pub and they'd be doling it out, but the publicans wouldn't know. It was like vodka, there was no colour in it. It was more like water—but it'd drive you *mad*. I saw one incident there and it was awful. One fella walked straight off the loading platform, walked straight out into a heap of broken glass and stuff. From the bad poitin. The blood was running out of him and he couldn't stand. And this fella was a good drinker! Oh, it was deadly stuff.

"There used to be hooleys in the tenements when we were young. In pubs then they had a kind of grey-brown paper bags that they used to give you out the drink in, for someone who had drink going home. And some of the publicans used to have a basket upstairs above the pub and what they used to do if somebody came [after hours] and wanted some drink, if there was going to be a hooley, they wouldn't open the door. They had a bit of lashing on the basket and they'd just lower it down from the window with whatever drink they wanted and that was it. Ah, yes. Lower it down in the basket and they wouldn't have to open the door. And *then* they could always say in court: 'The door was closed at dead on ten thirty!' But at the hooley they'd be singing all these wartime songs and emigrant songs and it'd be lovely listening outside and you'd hear them all laughing inside and the *clouds* of cigarette smoke coming out over the top of the windows. They were smoking like generals inside. And when there were hooleys there was this one pub and a stevedore used to own it and they had a piano and I think that they were the only one that had a piano on the street. But when there'd be a hooley they'd get a loan of the piano and they'd stick like a couple of spade handles through the piano and carry it down the street and bring it into the house where the hooley was going to be.

"Now by the Five Lamps there was these two pubs, Maguire's on one side and Humphrey's on the other. And there had been an argument that developed in Maguire's and somebody told this fella, the 'Mooch', that someone had hit a friend of his in the pub. Now I should tell you that his father and uncle were in the British Army during the war and they brought home as souvenirs two dress swords and they were crossed above the fireplace. Well, when this argument started in Maguire's pub the fella was a big fella that was after hitting his friend, so Mooch went home and got one of the swords down off the wall and he put it down in his overcoat and he went into Maguire's looking for the fella and somebody said, 'He's not here, he's over in Humphrey's.' So he run over to Humphrey's. Now I should tell you that Mr Humphrey was a lovely man, a lovely looking man. He was the publican and he used to wear steel grey suits and he stood out and he had a white apron on him tied at the back and a red flower in his buttonhole. He *always* had a red flower. And when a row would start in Humphrey's pub Humphrey had the can boys trained and he'd shout and the can boys would run and *bolt* the doors and he'd keep everybody in. Yeah, he wouldn't let them out. And he'd jump out and he'd go around and 'ding, ding, ding' and there'd be about six or eight fellas lying on the floor. He was round about his forties and he knocked 'em cold! Knocked them out. And that was it. He used to *love it*! Oh, he was a tough customer . . . and a lovely looking man. Then open the doors and throw 'em out. *So*, in comes yer man with the sword. See, he was after this big fella cause his friend wasn't very robust and he was going to sort this out. The sword, this was the leveller, you know? So this night when Mooch went in with the sword and it was 'swoosh'—*out* with the sword and 'You so and so!' He whipped it out and it must be six foot long. There would have been about fifteen heads rolling around. He frightened the *life* out of them and the next thing the place was empty—*including* Humphrey who was out on the path. And the police were looking for the sword afterwards, but they didn't pursue it."

MAY HANAPHY—AGE 87

She grew up around the turn of the century in the poorest tenements of Golden Lane which was known as the "Four Corners of Hell" for its rough pubs and fierce fighting resulting from drink. In those poverty-stricken times drink was an awful curse, feels May. She was especially distressed to see drunken men battering women. Perched at her tenement window she also watched street trading families after drunken binges battle one another with pokers, hammers and even hatchets. But it was great "entertainment".

"I was born and reared in Golden Lane. We were just real poor and it was very old tenements. Our lane was called the 'Four Corners of Hell' because there was a pub at each corner and a pub in the middle as well. There was a lot of drunkenness at that time and there were fights every Saturday night and

Sunday. My father was a painter and after work it was straight into the Chinaman pub. And he died in the Chinaman! It was a heart attack. My father was only 39 when he died and my mother had to go out to work for the five of us children. She just *slaved* for us. And my mother had to bring me wrapped up to the Poor Creche on Meath Street. You see, Kevin, *everyone* was very poor.

"Now I remember the pubs myself. We were allowed to go into them—not to drink now—but because they sold everything from a needle to an anchor. They sold pepper, salt, sugar, meal. As a child my mother'd say to me, 'I have no sugar, go over to Conway's.' And when you went in there was a big counter and little snugs about the size of a toilet. The family lived above the pub and the publicans dressed better and they had a pony and trap and anyone that had a pony and trap was rich. Their children had bonnets and little dresses but they weren't pompous about it. But pubs then were full of sawdust for the spitting around. And dogs would be at the men's feet and one dog had his beer! You know the big spittoons, they'd often pour a bottle of stout into it for the dog, especially in the summer when it'd be so warm. And the cockles and mussels man would go into the pub selling with his basket and the men'd open them with one of the pennies. Then we had the organ grinder man on the street with their monkey and they'd go into the pub. If you had a penny he'd play the organ for you. Lovely tunes they were. Oh, I remember dancing around the organ and we'd be *delighted*. But he'd go into the pub and the monkey would wear a little hat on him and the monkey had fortunes in little packets and you'd pay a penny for your fortune in pink, green and blue packets.

"Porter was tuppence a pint and the women went down with the jugs for a gill of beer. They were lovely jugs. They were *absolutely* out of this world. You'd see them now in antique shops, those old jugs. My friend, Kitty, her mother was a great drinker and she had a pair of jugs with a Japanese girl illustration on the jug and a Japanese boy on the other side and decorated all in these *beautiful* flowers and colours. Now a small white jug we had and in the quiet hours of the afternoon me mother'd say to me, 'May, would you go down and get me porter? And now don't forget to ask for a tilly.' They were not supposed to sell it to you if you were under age. They would be fined. But we went in and Mr Murphy knew us all, but it was a risk cause the DMP were harsh in their own way. And I'd say, 'My mother wants a gill', and mother used to give us a little cloth, like a little doily, to put over the jug when we'd bring it back. Then Ma would have it in the afternoon and she'd put it in a glass. And Ma liked a little baby Power's. That was nine pence. So when I was working at 14 in Jacob's [biscuit factory] I got eleven shillings a week and I'd go into Murphy's pub and get the usual little baby Power's for Mammy. I'd buy it for her. She'd put it in her tea and now that'd do her for the whole week. My mother was very thin and she drank that I think just to give her a little bit of energy.

"At that time when we were young the men they were nearly all big drinkers. Drink was terribly cheap and so they made hay! That's how rows would start, like the husband would come home drunk. Some men were very nasty in drink. Drink was a *big* problem. Then the wife was beat up. Ah, you'd see black eyes every day of the week. Oh, I remember all the women in our lane had black eyes.

My Ma said what a woman got from a man was a tub of washing and plenty of babies. You had no women's rights at all. Definitely. And the poor wives never got much money. But, oh, the men then were the best drinkers in the world. My brother, George, could hold forty pints! He could take *any* drink. Oh, he'd be in the pub all day. They always called it a 'session'. There was often a competition in pubs then, drinking. George would say, 'Now who'll beat me?' And the challenge would be taken up by another fella. George always said, 'You're never drunk till you fall on the floor'—and, by Janie, he fell on the floor all right!

"Pubs were very popular and always packed. See, there was nothing but the pub in them years. It was a man's world then. The pub was a way of life for them, there was *no other* life for them. But the old pubs, they weren't fit for women, they weren't nice. Oh, a woman'd be *murdered* if she was caught in a pub. It was a *disgrace* for a woman. But for men the pub was their friendship, entertainment. It was his world, his *whole* world. They hadn't the money to cross the sea and they hadn't the influence to get them up in a white collar job. There was no one to give them a life. In the pub they could have love, in a fashion like, among the men themselves.

"Now on Golden Lane there was the Swan pub and there was Murphy's and Conway's pub and the Circle pub. It was the 'Four Corners of Hell' cause there was rows on the street through drink. It would start in the pub and the publican would throw them out and they'd finish it in the street. *Always* after drink. We saw the fights, we saw them out the window or you could go down to the tenement hall door. And we'd enjoy them as well. About 10.00 at night time Mammy'd say, 'Oh, there's a row', and we'd say, 'Ruggy up! Ruggy up!' Oh, it was *entertainment*, indeed it was, Kevin. So they would have been having a quarrel first in the pub and it'd end up in the street. Maybe a family feud between one another. Like there were the Connors and the Ellises and they were dealers in fruit and they were related, say cousins. They were all intermarried and there was great enmity between them, there was friction. Anyway, when I'd be about 14 my mother'd say, 'There's going to be murder tonight between the Connors and the Ellises.' On a Sunday or Saturday. Particularly on Saturday night. In each family there was about seven or eight and it'd be murder. *Murder!* They'd come out in the street and they'd fight with pokers and big sticks and hatchets. Oh, yes, especially hatchets. Big hatchets and hammers and there'd be hair pulling, women's style. Men and women both. The husbands would fight, they'd box, and then maybe someone'd hand them a hammer or a poker and then everyone'd scream, 'He has that hammer!' And the women'd be fighting and they wore the big skirts and shawls and great big red petticoats underneath and they were tumbling around. Women in *particular* now would have it in for the other person's wife. Oh, there'd be a crowd and you'd all look at this fight. I remember it well. Oh, there was always fighting, it was *wonderful!* 'Oh, there'd be a good few casualties and some would have to go to the hospital. But there'd be no deaths, funny enough. The Lord have mercy on the Connors and Ellises . . . they're all gone now.

"And when there was a row they'd say 'Ruggy up! Ruggy up! Here's the police', and the police had whistles and once you heard the whistle blew you blew too! See, if the row got hot somebody'd send for the DMP—that's the British police —and they were very hard on the men. I saw this myself from out the window. When they'd get anyone that was drunk and helpless they were frog-marched into the old police station on Chancery Lane. They would make them walk on their hands and they'd hold up their feet and frog-march them. Very painful. And the men'd scream and shout. I saw them myself passing our window. And we'd throw pebbles and then run. They were a bit wicked the DMP. And if the men were drunk and couldn't walk they'd pick them up like a sack of flour and throw them into the cell.

"After the 1914 War was over there were a lot of shell-shocked soldiers and they had a small pension. But to make a few bob for drink they'd sing out in the streets. Two of the fellas were 'Tosser' and 'Win the War' and they'd sing outside Conway's pub. I remember it very well. And the fellas in the pub might give them a penny or tuppence. And then another fella whose poor old head was gone, he used to always stand outside of Conway's and he had a little paddle in his hand and he'd stand for *hours* outside the pub, trying to make a few bob. He'd say, 'Now send out all the flies, one by one, and I'll kill them and you won't have a fly . . . and I won't take much money off you.' See, there were millions of bluebottles and they'd bring disease. And he'd say, 'I'll kill all your flies but send them out one by one and I'll only take a few coppers off you!' He was a character. Ah, he was harmless. The aftermath of war was cruel."

Charlie Dillon—Age 75

His local is the Blue Lion pub in Parnell Street where his mother and father drank before him. He recalls women street dealers going in for a glass of porter and breast-feeding their babies in the snug. As a thirsty docker, he secretly spent many Sunday mornings in Sorohan's speakeasy in Corporation Street. His own granny even ran a shebeen out of her tiny vegetable shop to make a few bob on the sly.

"Now the Parnell Bar, that was an IRA pub. It was raided a few times and there was papers and guns found there. Yeah, there was an underground tunnel and there was secret stairs they found underneath and guns was down there. There was a false wall and the tunnel going straight through under Moore Street. I *seen* it. That pub, it's gone now, the ILAC is up there now. But the Blue Lion pub was there on Parnell Street when I was born and it's still the Blue Lion. Me mother and me father drank in it and Mr Fagan was the man who owned it. The Blue Lion had a good pint, straight out of the barrel. And you'd wait about a quarter of an hour before you'd get a head on it and drink it. That was the best pint. It was seven pence at that time, that was before the war. Plenty of hooleys in the pub and on Saturday night people would send down for a half-pound of tripe and the women'd go home and do the pig's feet and send them on to the men in the pub and they'd be eating the bones and everything. Pig's feet and tripe used to be great. And rings, there was plenty of betting on that. Con Martin was the champion. A man in the pub was like a bookie and he'd hold the bets and he'd get a few drinks then for holding the money. And the ring players, they'd bet on themselves against other fellas. Plenty of betting, like a bookie shop.

"All the old dealers along Parnell Street, about thirty women with long skirts and shawls, used to go into the Blue Lion. The women'd sit along the wall and they'd say, 'Give us a gill of porter.' Oh, and bring their babies in their arms with a wrap around them and you wouldn't know it was a baby and the child would be taking the breast, *inside the pub*. If they had a few extra bob they'd have a whiskey. Oh, they could hold their drink. Me own mother, God bless her, she could hold it there all day, drink all day and go home and have a sing-song on the way home. She'd be coming along singing a song and they'd be all out listening to her. But if the women dealers went on the beer there might be jealousy and then there'd be a row between them. Oh, there was always rows on a Saturday night. Me mother was a dealer and she'd be fighting two or three of them. Pulling the hair out of one another! Women'd get a grip, like a dead person's grip, and it was very hard to get out of it. And kicking and all. The women was *better* than the men. Oh, the language!

"And me own granny done a shebeen. She was a Wexford woman. Just around the corner here, where Kennedy's Bakery was, she used to sell cabbage and potatoes and for a Sunday morning she'd get a few crates of beer in and people'd go in and when they were buying the cabbage and potatoes they'd buy the stout off her. See, the pubs would all be shut and they'd say to her, 'Give us a half dozen of stout.' She'd sell it for about tuppence dearer and then you had to buy the cabbage and potatoes and walk out. She used to get it wholesale off the wholesale fellas and then she'd make a few bob. Oh, it was a shebeen.

"If someone died there was a wake and they'd be up all the night getting bottles of stout. A good wake and then a hooley after the funeral. It was all horse cabs and the jarvey'd pull into some pub coming from Glasnevin, like the Brian Boru. All the horses would line up there and all the jarveys would come in. Oh, they [funeral party] looked after the jarveys. He wouldn't buy a drink for anyone but *he'd* be getting all the drink all the time. Everyone called for a round and he'd be on it. See, he'd get his beer *free*. Oh, the jarveys could match the dockers in drinking. Cause they were going to funerals every day. Every time they were booked for a funeral they were off on the beer. And the jarvey'd be drunk driving the horses. Sure the horse would bring them home! The horse knew the road, just only hold the reins, that's all.

"Sorohan's pub down on Corporation Street, it used to be open early at 10.00 on a Sunday morning and you could *sneak* in and drink. You had to go in through the laneway there beside the convent and he'd have a watcher outside, a fella watching for the police, and he'd say, 'All right, go ahead.' The watchman he'd have to know you and then he'd let you in. Get about twenty or thirty in. And no talking . . . talk easy. Bring your own mug in and have a few pints but you had to go into the cellar part, you couldn't go into the bar. And then the watcher might say, 'Here's the police!' and we'd be all out the back way and up the other side of the lane. You had to get out. And then *back in* again when the cop goes. Oh, you could be fined about fifteen shillings. Yeah, they'd send for the van and bring you down and take your name and you had to go to court next day. So if the police came you'd run down the lane and over the wall and maybe leave your coat behind. And the police'd know that you'd have to get your coat back and so you'd have to go to the police station to get your coat and you'd get fined. Sorohan, he was lucky that he didn't lose his licence a few times. All the police were backhanded, all backhanded. Yeah. The policeman used to come in and he wanted to get the people out and *he'd* be having *his* drink then—clear everyone out and the barman'd look after him then!"

James Slein—Age 65

Now a distinguished Dublin physician, he grew up above his father's pub in North King Street. From his window he could look directly across at the notorious Dolly Fawcett's shebeen-brothel. He came to know and respect her as a kind and charitable woman. In fact, he professes that his spiritual growth was profoundly affected by a conversation he had with Dolly just a few days before she died. After he completed his medical degree he set up his first practice above his father's pub.

"Both my parents were from County Roscommon. My father left the farm because of lack of opportunity and he went to work in a pub in the local town. And when he was 16 he went to London to work for Mooney's. He came back then to take over the managership of the pub opposite McDaid's off Grafton Street. Then he was given a managership in Belfast and I was born in Belfast. Then we came to Dublin when I was aged 8 and he bought the pub in North King Street in 1935 and it became Slein's pub. He paid £800—complete with stock! And it was a hotel also, it was quite a high building. Our family moved in to live there and I grew up in that area. I remember the sign over the door, 'Tea Merchant and Whiskey Bonder'. I started—illegally—at age 13 serving pints. Oh, I worked there until the night before I graduated.

"They were all local people, working people. At that time you had a big jam and fruit factory on the corner, William and Woods. And a Tobler chocolate factory was there too. And there was a lot of working with horses at that time. Then the local women dealers would come in and my father welcomed them in a neighbourly fashion. We had one snug that said 'private' on the door, for women. And on Thursday that was the police pay day and our pub was a popular house for them. The police would fill *half* of our pub on a Thursday. So we had a very good relationship with the community and the police. And I know that my father was very respected. He had a sympathy and an empathy for the locals. I know of a few cases of mothers where if he heard they'd become pregnant and they had very large families he would tell our milkman to give them an extra bottle of milk every morning. And he would be asked to sign references and so on. Looking back on it I can see how depending on the publican would have a very *stabilising* effect on the local community.

"They were all neighbours and they were all welcome—with one exception! He was nicknamed 'Fish'. He was charged with pick-pocketing. Now he had one rather unique sentence passed upon him by a judge in the criminal court. If he was found in a public place and was not wearing gloves he was to be put in jail for a couple of months. This is absolutely true. He was such a chronic pick-pocket and a lovable gangster and all the judges knew him and they said, 'If you're caught in a public place without gloves you're in for two months.' My memory of him was that he was being ordered out of my father's pub. He was barred. I know that Fish was barred in several pubs around the place. But he was a kind of lovable rogue. And then you had 'Messy' Larkin. Did you ever hear of him? He was a 'messer', he'd interfere and he was very impulsive and he'd start a row. And I remember a priest, Father Flash Kavanagh, coming in. 'Flash', because he said Mass in a flash. The only man I ever saw saying Mass in four minutes!'

"As far back in my life as I can remember in Dublin I remember Fawcett's. I could look across the road from my bedroom window or from the window of the pub and you saw the Cafe Continental. Dolly Fawcett, she was a *notorious* person; not that she did anything dishonourable that I know of, but she was notorious because she ran a brothel. I was working in our pub from an early age and serving men in their thirties, forties and fifties who had *no* inhibitions about talking about it, so I'd hear things. I figured it out. But Dolly, though she ran a shebeen or a brothel and there were prostitutes working for her, she was part of the community. Dolly was regarded as a neighbour. Now there were two sons. Vincent was the older and more responsible and there was Eugene. And Dolly was married to Bob Fawcett. Her husband was a fine person. My father's pub was their local. But I never remember Dolly getting into a session of drinking for more than a half an hour. A gin and orange was her drink and she had only one. She kept her eye on her own business.

"I don't know exactly where Dolly was from, I think she was from Wicklow. But she was *known*, I think, all over the country because after Monto was closed by the Legion of Mary back in the thirties it was the only brothel that I know of in the north inner city. She was very lady-like. She was educated by the world itself. Dolly was an attractive, very intelligent lady and certainly well dressed for her time, in Dublin. You would notice her being distinctively well dressed. Her husband Bob, he was an officer in the DMP [Dublin Metropolitan Police] which was taken over by the Free State in 1921. He was from Newry, County Down. He was drummed out of the police here because he married Dolly—now this is the story as I was told it. 'So, right', he said, 'I love the woman and I'm going to marry her.' So Bob ran the place with Dolly. He did all the cooking, he was sort of the chef. They lived above the Cafe Continental and it was just across the road from where Vincent, the second son, opened the Cozy Kitchen. Both were shebeens. See, it was a cafe and you could go in there and have a meal but then they served whiskey, watered down, in cups. I know that my father sold them a fair amount of drink. She used to get the bottles of brandy and she sold it diluted in cups.

"The girls were in their twenties and they lived there. Oh, they'd come over to the pub to buy cigarettes. I can only remember three girls there at any one time. My memories of these girls was that they were dressed like French waitresses, black dress with the white apron. They didn't speak any better [than local women] but they were dressed better. The girls always looked a little bit anaemic, though they weren't underfed. They were probably better fed than girls of their own age in the community who were working in sweatshops and factories. But they always looked a little bit tired and in that way you'd feel sorry for them. Now the men, they were anything but locals. The men were lawyers, politicians, businessmen visiting the city, American troops down from Belfast during the war years. They'd arrive in taxis and cars. Some nights I'd just sit at the window, just gaze across, and it was quite interesting seeing the chaps going in until two or three or four in the morning. And as I remember it was very common for them to go down Bolton Lane [for sexual activity] and any dark spot at all. And they wouldn't close until business ceased.

"As I grew up I had the feeling that the powers that be were a little bit frightened of Dolly Fawcett because of the *knowledge* that she may have had about them. But she never kissed and told, that I know of. Like I know that a few barristers used to come in to her for a drink after the pubs closed. Quite often they'd leave our place when we closed and just go over to Dolly's and have a couple of jars there and drink on until maybe 2.00 or 3.00 in the morning. This was a common practice for professional people, those who liked their drink. It was harmless enough and the police regarded it as not a very evil thing as long as they kept law and order in the place. It was tolerated. Of course, the law said that it shouldn't be there but the police tolerated it. So the local police turned a blind eye and some of them even *patronised* her.

"Now the Cozy Kitchen was opened as a 'branch of the main office' thirty yards away, just across the street. And the reason for that was that the Bridewell police station boundary came right up the middle of Capel Street to Bolton Street and on up. So the Cafe Continental was in Fitzgibbon Street police district and the Cozy Kitchen in North King Street was actually in the Bridewell district. See, before the Cozy Kitchen opened there was solely the Cafe Continental. Then an inspector named Kingston was appointed superintendent in Fitzgibbon Street. That put him in command of the area in which the Cafe Continental was situated. Now he was a very puritanical man. He was a Dublin Protestant who had made his way up through the ranks of the police and he was a great man for purity and virtue and it became a kind of 'cause' that he was going to *shut up* and close down Dolly Fawcett's and there could be no sin in *his* district! So he began to raid it a couple of times a week and this became intolerable for poor Dolly and her benighted husband. So very shrewdly they moved the new business just across the road into the Bridewell police district and that became the Cozy Kitchen. Then things went swimmingly. Then

Kingston was transferred to the Bridewell station! And then the raids began again on the Cozy Kitchen, but at least they had some relief in the Cafe Continental. Oh, we all knew the motives behind these rules and what it was all about.

"As I got to know Dolly better in my twenties she was an *extraordinary* person. She was a *big* person, I mean a big-*minded* person. Now I do know—I've *seen* it myself—if Dolly heard of any old widowed or single lady living on her own who had become ill, you'd see one of the girls leaving the Cafe Continental with a tray covered with a tray cloth and bringing a hot meal up to that poor sick old person. And if Dolly was worried about her she would get the doctor and pay the doctor from her own purse. Oh, yes, she was an extremely charitable lady. Even though it was a brothel the people who knew her were non-judgmental. I can't remember anybody speaking badly about Dolly, even the more puritan people. Even the more narrow-minded people wouldn't condemn her. They might say tut tut if her name was mentioned but never anything bad about her.

"Dolly's places were there up to the time of her death. Bob, her husband, outlived her by about ten or fifteen years and he carried on at the Cafe Continental. She died in St Anne's Hospital. Now the last time I saw her I was jogging down towards O'Connell Street to get a bus and Dolly was dying and she stopped me outside Arnott's in Henry Street and although I was in a hurry I stopped because I hadn't seen her in some weeks. She told me that this was her last day out [of the hospital], that she would be dead within two weeks. She had cancer of the throat. And, funny enough, she could speak well all right. Told me that morning that she'd be dead in two weeks. And she said that she was just going around to some of the old spots for one last drink and she said she had been in to the old Metropole and she was going down to see my father. Then she said, 'Before I go I want you to make a solemn promise and do it before 6.00 p.m.', and I said, 'Sure.' And she said, 'Say three Hail Marys for my throat. They count. You may wonder at that but you're too young to have committed *serious* sin *yet* and God will listen to your prayer much quicker than he will listen to me.' And I was very touched by that. And I couldn't put her out of my mind all day. Even to this day when I look back on Dolly Fawcett she had an *extraordinary* effect on my attitude toward prayer. She was a stepping stone in my spiritual development because of what she did on that particular day. It was an enlightenment to me. My *mature* spiritual growth started at that moment. I *wept* at the bus stop. That was the very last time that I said goodbye to her. Poor Dolly, she was a good soul . . . she was one of us."

CHRISTY "DILLER" DELANEY—AGE 68

He's an old cattle drover who started drinking hard cider with his mates at age 16. Back then when drovers and dockers mixed in the same pub there were often bloody clashes. Much of his youth was spent in a Smithfield pub owned by "Daddy" Egan, an eccentric, religious fanatic. For sheer devilment men would bring a horse into his pub and give it a bucket full of porter. When the tinkers would start brawling out on the cobblestones men would stream out of the pubs to watch the free show.

"Now I'm fifty-five years drinking in this pub. Fifty-five years! I was born up the road in Blackhall Street and my father was a drover at the cattle market. My mother wore a shawl, fed pigs and sold vegetables up around Oxmanstown. Most drovers' families was born in one tenement room like meself. It was a difficult life. As a boy at age 11 I'd go out in the fields with me father in the night time in the dark. I was reared up to it. We walked about three miles in the dark and you'd have maybe 300 or 400 cattle in the field and maybe 500 sheep. So you'd do your night's work bringing in the sheep and the cattle to the market and all the pubs opened at 6.00 in the morning. It was a special licence.

"After the cattle'd be tied up the drovers would go over and have a few pints at Hanlon's. But children couldn't even stand in the doorway at Hanlon's, you couldn't even *look in* if you were looking for your father. Even on a cold day the doors would be pinned back open. And always sawdust on the floor. Oh, *thick* with sawdust, especially if it was a wet day and the man'd be throwing down the sawdust all the time, keep it fresh. You'd meet the sawdust coming out the door! But your father might get you a creme cracker and a cup of Bovril and sneak it out to you. And Hanlon's was the [cattle] buyer's pub, the Englishman's pub. The Englishmen would drink whiskey. Oh, good whiskey. Hanlon's had their own barrels down under. They done the flat pint whiskey bottles and they bottled *dozens* and *dozens* of them for every Thursday morning. And the Englishmen brought them back home with them in their dustcoats, their trench coats. They had terrific big pockets in them and they'd have at least a dozen going back to England. And the *weight* of them.

"But drovers were pint drinkers. Now the drovers that drank whiskey were always known as 'mad men'. Oh, he was a bad one. Cause he couldn't hold it. He was weary with the strain of hard work and it'd be the hunger. Now I also worked with the dockers on the salt boats and cement boats and all the dockers were great drinkers but the dockers were better grubbers. The dockers, they had better grub and they were big hardy fellas. But the drover was more of a poor empty stomach man. So porter, it was an enrichment and the glass would overflow and it'd stick to the big marble counter. It was so thick that you couldn't get it up, you'd have to draw it to the edge. You don't see that now. Droving was recognised as a very poor job and if you got a day's work it was twenty-six shillings and they'd drink their twenty-six shillings. Drovers were *all* very heavy drinkers. They'd all get drunk at the end of the day. There was Thursdays when we went in and drank thirty-eight pints of Guinness. One time I drank forty-two! That's no lie.

"Now 'John-Eye' Reilly's pub in Prussia Street, that was a great drovers' pub. It was John-Eye because he had something wrong with his eye. It's Hynes's pub today. But that was a gougers' pub where all the fights were. No fighting in

Hanlon's, John-Eye's was the famous pub for fighting. A fight could start over a simple little thing, maybe someone after stealing your pint. Yeah. Oh, if you were caught doing that! And a *good few* of them done it. They were 'pint snatchers'. See, there'd be so *many* people in the pub, it'd be *packed*, and you'd be leaving the pints on the ledges and all and you'd have maybe one pint there and another pint there and another pint there. And it'd disappear. Even the drovers were pint snatchers. We knew the fellas that done it. If they got caught it was a vicious thing. There'd be a dig and the fella'd say, 'C'mon, I'll have you outside', and they'd have the fight outside. Sometimes they'd have to drag him out, the fella that robbed the pint. The ash stick was a very vicious thing and they'd fight with that. They'd give it to you across the head and you'd be lucky if you got up. And they'd have to stop another fella from beating him. I was a little devil, I was a great one to stop a fight. I'd just get in between them and throw them back. I was even known for it in the market. I often wonder how many men would be dead if it wasn't only for me in the market—and I was only a little skimp.

"Between dockers and drovers there was jealousy. Bitter. See, the dockers, they were drovers too for loading the cattle into the boats—but we couldn't do that. So we were the drovers for the market but they come up from the docks to be drovers, coming up to take *our* work, with the result that there was many a fight down in the pubs. See, they could come up here as drovers in the market but we couldn't load the cattle on boats down *there*. That was what the dispute was over. But we [both] loaded all the cattle at the trains in Amiens Street and on Railway Street there was the Railway Bar and on a Thursday there'd be *slaughters*! Cause the drovers'd go over into it for a drink and the dockers'd be in it. The docker'd get his couple of pints, about seven or eight pints, and he'd get burly. And we had rough drovers as well and, oh, there'd be *murder* . . . through the windows and all they'd go. Oh, the frames of the windows and all would go out into the street. You had to be tough to be a drover down there, to have a drink down there. They'd come out of the pub and you'd make a ring and you'd let them fight. There could be three or four of us in it, maybe five of us, and it'd be all ash sticks going. See, the drover always carried his stick home. You always carried your stick and all the drovers had a prod on their stick and that'd rip you open. That's the only thing that beat the dockers, they got plenty of pounding with the stick. The Railway Bar was eventually closed up over fighting. It became the worst, it did.

"The publican was a very powerful man and a very respected man and they could bar a man for *life*. Very seldom would you get back in when you got barred. I see today now in the pubs you can get back in. But back then it was for life. For fighting, or for throwing a pint. Sometimes you'd throw a pint. I done it once. I was insulted and I threw it and [he threw a pint] and the two pints clashed! That happened. Clashed together. And we got barred for life. Never got served in there. Even with *new owners* we never got served. A note would be left on the shelf. And it's *still* carried out in pubs. Like a man across the road there, now he had only come from a grocery shop and he bought that pub and these lads come in that were barred and he told them, 'No service.'

Now he had never owned a pub in his life, he never even was a barman. But there was a note left there [behind the counter] that they were not to be served. Oh, that still goes on.

"Daddy Egan's pub, he was a very religious man. He'd give you a holy medal when you'd go in. Oh, he had bags of medals. And in Egan's when the Angelus would come it was off with the hats. Hats would *have* to come off. And in Daddy Egan's you didn't curse—and drovers were terrible cursers. Even the tinkers didn't curse in it. Couldn't even raise your voice. Oh, he was a very religious man. Now the tinkers drank at Daddy Egan's and they drove *horses* in. Oh, Daddy Egan, he let the horses in. See, they were big wide doors in the pub. Bring the horses into the pub and give the horses a pint! The tinkers would do that. Give the horse a full bucket of porter. Every Thursday the horse fair was there in Smithfield and the horse'd go in. A horse'd go in and maybe another one'd follow behind him and the men'd just stand back out of the way. And then some man'd just hit him with a stick and *out!* If they knocked down a chair, broke it, the tinker he'd pay for it. They loved to do it, you know. There was no harm.

"Then the tinkers would fight, always after drinking. Oh, there was *killing!* There was the Joyces and the Wards and they'd start off drinking in Daddy Egan's. He was the only one that'd serve them. First they'd fight with fists. Happened *every* Thursday. Big crowds. And when the fighting would get really rough they'd draw their sally sticks, big long seasoned sally sticks roughly ten feet long. See, they were all chimney sweeps and tinsmiths. They used the sticks for chimney sweeping. So they'd end up with their sally sticks and there'd be ten, twelve, fifteen of them all lying around Smithfield in bits. *Bleeding* bits! And up Red Cow Lane. And with any type of carts you'd have you'd take them up there to the old Richmond Hospital. Just throw them on the steps and the nurses and doctors would carry them up. Every Thursday.

"Next door to Egan's there was once an IRA pub, Murray's. Oh, Murray, he was a big shot in the Provos. Very respected. Oh, he had a great funeral. But that was a great IRA meeting place in Murray's and we could even get in there on a St Patrick's Day. Now there was a stables in the yard next door and there was three horse cabs lined up and there was spikes put on the back of the horse cabs to stop scutting, cause we used to scut them. So we were there in Murray's one Patrick's Day and didn't the guards come in! Two big fellas with their bikes. They used to handcuff you to them. Knocked on the door and the door was opened and in they come. So the wall out there was about twelve feet high and there was Guinness barrels put there and up on the barrels we went and over the wall and they'd jump down into the yard. And everyone was up and I was the last and I jumped down *right* on the spike, right up through the sole of the shoe, right up through me foot. I'll never forget it. I was only about 17. Oh, right up to the Richmond Hospital.

"Then we'd go into Dunne's pub, this was 1941, and he sold a lot of cider that was called 'Willie Woodpecker'. Oh, very strong. Bulmer made it and Willie Woodpecker was on the label. And, see, you got your big bottles of cider at that time, two and a half pints in it. Now we were only 16 or 17. He sold a lot of it. *Very* strong. Oh, after a few pints of that you'd go out and the path would come up and hit you in the face. After about ten pints. We'd drink it in a session. But he had two daughters who served there and one was terrible fond of the bookies across the road. So she'd leave the shop on its own and she'd go across to the bookies to back a horse and she'd tell us to put our empties at the back of the counter. And when she'd be gone we'd go around back with our bottles and we'd take two more *full* ones. And you wouldn't pay for it. Innocent really. Then come about 7.00 we'd start mixing cider with pints of plain and that was like port wine now. And, oh, when you'd go out then you'd beat your head off the wall and everything, the path would come up and hit you. I often found myself many times with complete black eyes, the cider was so strong at that time.

"Back then women wouldn't be served at all. They'd have the old billy can right under their shawl and they'd call a man out of the pub and just give him the can to be filled with porter. Then right back under the shawl and no one'd ever see it. These were women mostly from Queen Street cause it was a big tenement street. They'd put it under an old cover [when they got it home] so the children wouldn't see it. They wouldn't drink in front of the children. And for a cold they'd put a hot poker into it to mull it. Oh, some of the old women could hold it, like Biddy McCann in Queen Street. She was twenty-six stone weight! And she had about three pig's cheeks a day. Even when she died there was the bones of the pig's cheeks under her bed at number 14 Queen Street. She'd drink pints straight from the billy can, a great drinker, her and another old lady named Nanny Norton. They were the two best drinking women on Queen Street. And then you had Mary Snade, she was a great horse woman and she drank her pints over in Daddy Egan's—the only woman who was ever served and only on the day of the horse fair. They'd let her in and she'd have a pint. She wore hobnail boots on her. There was a little secret passageway there and a staircase and it went out in the back yard where they fed pigs. And she'd come in through the back and she'd sit on the bottom of the stairs . . . but she wasn't *really* let in.

"Now 'Dead Man' Murray's pub out in Lucan, we'd go out there. It was a bonafide. And then we'd walk the road from Lucan back into Dublin, singing! No fighting. We tried to walk along the tram tracks and we'd be drunk, fall off it, and get back up on it. Ah, we'd get home at maybe four or five in the morning —daylight. On Sundays we'd go. Then you had bonafides at Blanchardstown, Palmerston. And then you had what they called an unidentified one, cause it was so much out of the way—but talk about police drinking in it! It was called the Twelfth Lock cause it was down in the canal. A bonafide. It was very good. It was at the twelfth lock where they'd let the boats in. It was only a big shed converted to a pub, hidden down out of the way. And the police—there was an old police station in Clondalkin—and they drank in it. Come down on their bikes and walk down to it. And great singing there. There was no toilets, no nothing in it. You'd just go out and piss in the canal. We used to come out of the Twelfth Lock stupid drunk and dive into the can, winter and summer. Freezing."

Paddy Casey—Age 68

He was a policeman on the toughest northside beat a half-century ago. Back then pubs were working-men's clubs for the poor of the inner city. Around the cattle and vegetable markets pubs opened at 7.00 in the morning and were filled with country men and drovers.

"I spent thirteen years in the Bridewell station. I was around Capel Street, Queen Street, the quays, Dominick Street. One man walking the beat then. That was a poor area. I saw severe hardship. All old Georgian tenements, a mother and father and maybe ten children sleeping in the one room. Pawnshops were doing a booming trade. And the poor then were inclined to go to the pubs and come home then and there'd be family rows. In those days men were quite prone to drinking quite a lot. It was a hard home environment and it was the attitude of Irish people to drink at that time. But the men'd come home and they'd be drunk and the wife would start giving out, arguing, and it would involve a fight then.

"In those days I always regarded a public house as a cow or horse stables, you know, where men went in and they'd have *stalls*. Now I don't know if you know very much about farming but when you bring in cattle or horses, strangely enough, and put maybe twenty of them in a big barn for some reason every one of them had their *own* place and they'll never go any place else. They'll always know where to go. Well, it's similar with men when they'd go drinking. They went into their own place and if you were an outsider and went in and would take up one of those spaces you weren't very welcome. That was *their* territory. It was a peculiar attitude.

"The publican then was the lord and master and what he said was *law*. They weren't supposed to give credit but, of course, invariably he put it on the slate. He couldn't do business without it. And a guard could only go into a pub if you were called in by the publican to eject a man. And first you would ask *him* to eject him. It would only be if he wasn't able to eject him that you'd want to do that. There were particular pubs where that sort of problem arose. Generally, publicans were reasonably strict upon the attitude of people getting drunk on the premises and they'd say, '*Out*, you've had enough!' And he'd throw him out. For some reason public houses were sacred ground and they just didn't [usually] fight in the pub. Invariably where the fighting took place was on the street outside the pub. They'd come out and it was a *civilised* fight, if you could call it that. Just punching and the best man wins and shake hands and go home. Oh, I've seen fellas with their shirts off banging away at each other. It's rather frightening when you see two men like that. Generally, when the uniformed presence of a guard came in those days they sort of growled at each other and stopped.

"We had a different law around where I was because we had the vegetable markets and the cattle market and the pubs opened at 7.00 in the morning for the drovers and the vegetable men coming in from the country. And there was the

Holy Hour then. It's amazing now but at that time public houses had to close a full day on St Patrick's Day, on Christmas day and Good Friday. They were the three black days of the publican's year. Now for *some reason* it was quite difficult to enforce that. On those days we were *invariably* going to catch somebody in a pub, particularly Good Friday for some reason, I don't know why. Christmas day you never did. St Patrick's Day and Good Friday were the days. The pub was always shut and the doors closed but there'd be people inside that he'd let in. Always a few people inside having a drink. And that drink, I think, was better than any drink they had that year!"

Mickey Guy—Age 70

In his early days around the Liberties many publicans watered their whiskey, tolerated moneylenders on the premises, and served cheap booze to brawling tinkers. He especially liked spending time in the Widow Reilly's speakeasy where, dressed as a man in coat and tie, she intimidated the toughest patrons if they got too loud.

"The local crowd in them years used Doyle's, Dillon's, Connor's and Clarke's public houses. And McAuley's. When I was about 21 years of age I drank in Doyle's pub. It's now called the Liberty Belle. Only *locals* at Doyle's, there were no outsiders. Everybody knew everybody. And they all socialised with one another. The pub, that was life. It's for the company's sake. And in my days the publican was very important in the locality. Publicans were the *main* people at that time. Go to the publican for a loan of money, get it off him and pay him back so much a week. Oh, that's perfectly right. He was the *only* man that was your security. Or go to him to get a recommendation for a job. Go to the local publican cause he knows the people and the families in the locality. And if there was a death in the family they always depended on one person—go to the publican for a loan of money for the funeral. And *always* after a burial there was a good session. I remember in 1942 me granny died and it was me granny's dying wishes that we go to the pub and with the piano going all the time. She wanted us to have a good time and a good drink off her.

"The old women'd send down for the gill in a jug. They sent one of the family for it. Take it home and mull it on the side of the hob. They'd get the jug and pour it into a glass and they'd redden the poker iron on the fire and put it in and heat it and a big, big head would come on it. It was mulling it. It was great for sickness they'd say. It was plain porter at that time. Then after that came the 'fifty-fifty' which was half porter and half stout. Then the fifty-fifty went off the market and there was just the pint of stout. And the old women lived for a baby Power's if they had the price of it. The price at that time was one and eight pence. And the head place of all was Ryan's pub on Thomas Street. Ryan was an old man and he had all the baby Power's hanging up there with coloured paper around them. It was a pink paper always around it and a screw on top of it. And it was always fresh and beautiful.

"And now years ago publicans watered their whiskey. They *all* done it, Kevin, they all done it. That went on for years. Now this publican, Connor, he watered his whiskey one time and he was a general communion man in Francis Street chapel. But, still, they caught up with him. The inspectors going around tasting the whiskey caught him. They'd take away a sample and seal it. They didn't fine him but he had to put an apology to the public in the evening paper, for watering his whiskey. And they'd judge him from that and he'd get a slagging. People'd say, 'There's a great man, going to holy communion every morning —and he watered the whiskey raw barefaced on the public.'

"There was speakeasies, like I remember one run by Kate Gilligan on Thomas Street. And her husband was another publican at the top of Francis Street. Previous to that they had a public house in James's Street and they broke up and he bought a shop at the corner of Francis Street. Her married name was Reilly and she then was the 'Widow Reilly' because her husband threw himself out of the window. She was a big heavy woman with collar and tie. A man's tie, genuine. And she run a speakeasy. Served after hours. She'd close the doors at 10.00 but keep people inside and some would come knocking on her door and she'd say, 'Who's that?', and she'd let them in. It'd be 'shhh'. She was a tough woman, very tough, like someone that'd be in a jail in charge over the girls. Like that, real rough and ready. As long as you had the money she'd keep you there. And she had friends in the police.

"Up the street was McAuley's public house. It was what was called a market house cause the Iveagh Market was next door and they got the market crowd, the stall holders. There was two brothers owned it, Paddy McAuley and Charlie McAuley and they were very hard on the gargle all the time. Years ago two of the old women were waiting for the public house to open at 10.00 in the morning and they went knocking on the door and so Paddy opened the door and 'What's wrong?' 'Are you not open?', says the woman. 'We bought this f— public house for *ourselves*, not for you!' And I'll tell you about McAuley's public house. He had a glass case and they sold jam and sardines. A public house that sold fish! And there was a woman named Mary Kelly and she was a moneylender and she was married to a man named 'Cruiser' Kelly and he was a moneylender and he never worked. And they'd be sitting in the public house lending money. And Paddy McAuley was there drinking with Mary Kelly the moneylender and Cruiser Kelly all day. Now McAuley's was just old snugs and partitions and there was no ladies' toilet at that time. And women had long skirts at that time. So they come out of the shop and just stand over the grating—and there might be a poor fella down below bottling!

"Now the tinker crowd, they used to sell horses over in Smithfield on a Thursday when there was the market there and they'd all finish in McAuley's and they'd park all their horses and carts outside the pub there. They wouldn't be served in Smithfield pubs cause they'd be too troublesome. But McAuley's would serve them all right. And there'd be a row. There'd be boxing and all that. Ah, the women was worse than the men, fighting and tearing the face off one another. Oh, Jesus, it was fierce. And the policeman'd have to come with his baton. And the policeman with the baton would go bop, bop [on their heads] and leave them there under the pub window. Hitting them with his baton. And in them times they'd drag a man down [to the station] by his legs no matter how drunk he was. Drag him all the way down by his legs, be it a woman or a man. But with the tinker crowd there was too many. Oh, there could be as many as fourteen men and fourteen women. So the policeman would be dragging them under the front window of the public house and then he'd shout to us kids, 'Go down and get the squad car.' So we'd run down to the police station—it was in Chancery Lane at that time—and we'd say, 'The policeman on Francis Street wants the squad car.' And he'd say, 'What's your name?' and he'd write your name in a book. And there'd be four or five other kids messing saying, 'He sent *me* for him, mister.' But he'd only put the first name in. And then he'd get a bunch of keys and he'd open the side gate and he'd give you a trolley with six wheels, something like what you go into an operation with, something like what's in the hospital. It had six small little wheels and just two handles on top. We used to jump on it as kids and you just pushed that. And me and me mates, we're all jumping on one another bringing the car up to the policeman. And there'd be all big men standing around at the pub looking and the policeman'd say, 'Here, give us a hand', and he'd put them on one, two, three, hanging right across the car and he'd wheel them all down to Chancery Lane. He had four men on that, hanging right across it. They called it the squad car. And when he went in us kids went in and we'd be saying, '*I* brought down the squad car. *I* brought down the squad car.' And he'd have you sign your name and we got twelve pennies off him for helping out."

CLARA GILL—AGE 65

She was born above her father's pub on the North Circular Road. Her father, a Gaelic sports devotee, bought the pub because it was just up the road from Croke Park. On busy match days young Clara helped out by collecting stout bottles scattered outside the pub. She knew most of the famous publicans of her time and found them to be pillars of the community.

"My father bought this pub in 1930. I was born here. We *always* lived above the shop. My father absolutely adored football and hurling, Gaelic, and he always tried to get down to Croke Park. This is why he bought this pub, to be close to Croke Park. Even when he was not fit he walked in his slippers down to the hurling and football matches. He loved that.

"A good publican was like the father of the community. There was great poverty and my father, he had a great sense of dedication to the people, a sense of responsibility to help anyone he could. For example, my dad used to write notes for people after a funeral and would okay them to the undertaker so that there'd be no problem. He'd know them inside and out and he'd say that they would pay back regularly. He'd be a go-between very often and get them credit. And very regularly my father wrote letters of reference for people. They were character references. Up to his death he did that. And people all the time asked him for advice. See, whenever people had a problem they'd always go to the local pub and talk it out. To settle whatever problems you have. Oh, family problems. My father helped people and they said that he should have been a judge because he was so good at weighing up the sides of a story. He even helped people to make up wills.

"And all sorts of characters among the publicans. This was around the 1930s. I remember there was one very religious character, a publican, who used to walk around with a cross. And one day a garda came in because he was after hours trading and he said, 'I'll have to summons you because there are people in the bar.' 'Oh, that's all right', he said, 'wait now till I get the holy water', and he sprinkled him with the holy water and the garda got confused and put away his book and he didn't summons him. And my father used to talk about this other publican that'd go on the beer sometimes and he'd be stark naked behind the counter with a bowler hat—nothing else on. All sorts of characters in those days. Like we had a customer called Cromwell and my dad was very nationalistic and we had a cat and the cat bit Cromwell. It was very funny. My dad probably loved it. But he got money [settlement] out of that, but it wouldn't have been very much.

"In the 1930s I remember the women in their own place to the right-hand side and there'd be about four or five of them. A lot of pubs didn't want to serve women. In my time many of the older ladies wore these little black straw hats and a cape and long black clothes. And some of them might be selling fruit and that sort of thing. But we had a snug, a special snug for women who didn't want to be in public and they used to annoy my father, all the women chatting. I remember one day he said to them, 'You're like a hedge full of sparrows.' And we had a Protestant lady, a customer, who was a marvellous attender and they used to say they'd give her a medal for good attendance. She came in *every* single day and she used to be upset for weeks that we wouldn't be open for at least a *few* hours on Christmas day.

"Publicans had an awful lot in common, they were very much like an extended family. In fact, the way we were reared all our friends nearly were publicans. They all came up from the country and there was a certain set. There was groups, cliques, like the Cavan group and the Tipperary group. Groups of people who came from the same place. And very strict loyalty. Friendship. All our friends were the same *type* of people who came up from the country without a penny from big families and fought their way up and who had a very homogenous type of culture. They were the people who *didn't* emigrate. They were the people who stayed at home and fought and built this state. And they were very proud of the city and things like the Phoenix Park and they had great civic pride and civic responsibility. And they had great respect for education and literature. My parents were very keen that we would go to the ballet and to the opera. And daddy used to lecture the customers about the Famine, preaching

to the customers about history. And *all* publicans—or a good lot of them—used
to go after Mass on a Sunday morning and bring their families, and they all had
six or seven children, up to Phoenix Park. So we'd all meet walking up to the
Monument, a long walk, the publicans and their families. They had an awful lot
in common.

"Publicans were important people and *proud* of their status, and good church-
going people. And all the publicans were very fond of the Franciscans down on
Merchants Quay and Church Street. They were great Gaelic men. And some of
the publicans used to make up a parcel *every* week and bring it to them. Food.
Tea and sugar and that type of thing for them. And the publicans used to joke
about it and they used to call it their 'fire insurance'—that they wouldn't go to
hell. Most of the publicans were charitable and religious—genuinely. We always
had collection boxes there in the pub for the blind and such. Like there was a
blind man and my father never raised the price of brandy for him, he always gave
it to him at the old price. And that went on for years and then one day somebody
complained and the blind man said, 'Well, I'd prefer to pay the right price.' So
sometimes you try to do a good thing and it doesn't work out.

"Publicans have to *like* people. They enjoyed people and had reasonably good
personalities. And the publicans would ring each other up at night and they'd
be *roaring* laughing and joking about all the funny incidents that happened.
They had a great sense of humour and enjoyed all the oddities of human nature.
Like we had a very funny lady, Granny Robinson, one of these ladies who
always had a little shawl and wore a black dress down to her toes. She used to
come in to help clean up, a sort of charwoman. And I remember my dad
dancing, waltzing with her. A great gas. They all had their funny stories. Now I
had an uncle who was a very wealthy man, Jim Madigan, and he had eventually
about twenty-five pubs and a few in London. Jim Madigan had this funny story
about how he had a row with a shawlie, a lady selling potatoes. I don't know
what he did to her but she came into his pub with an apron full of potatoes and
pelted him with the potatoes and he had to duck behind glasses and everything
to avoid the potatoes.

"Oh, Brendan Behan, he was one of the crowd here. Brendan lived here on this
street [Russell]. Brendan said that this was the perfect street and he'd never leave
it because we had a pub in it, a bookies, and a post office and there was the canal
for swimming. Brendan used to come in a lot and he wrote lovely short pieces
often about the customers here. He had a great ear for conversation. Brendan had
a great love of humanity, a great understanding of people, you'd see it in his
plays. He was quite a character and a marvellous humour. He wrote excellent
funny stories for the *Irish Press* and often wrote them in here. I met him often
and he was always very respectful and polite and nice. But he always said it
wasn't a disgrace to be drunk, it was a privilege. You know, it was a great
achievement. And now my father was very strict about bad language, *couldn't
stand* bad language, taking the holy name in vain. There was the White Star
League, a thing against bad language, and my dad had a little star on him and
he used to tell off the customers for bad language. And they used to say, 'I didn't

say a f——— word, Mr Gill.' Cause they were so *used* to it. And this is the funny thing, Brendan *never* used bad language in front of people he respected. My mother now, who was a very strict Catholic, said, 'I never heard a wrong word from Brendan Behan. I don't know what they're talking about.' And she *didn't*. With people he respected he didn't use it. I never heard a bad word from him either."

PADDY "LYRICS" MURPHY—AGE 83

A Ringsend man, one of his favourite pubs was "Smokey Joe's" where old fishermen and bottle blowers from the local factory would sit puffing clouds of smoke from their clay pipes. Ringsend pubs had their own rowing clubs and when the home team won the proud publican might ply them with free drink for a whole week in celebration.

"I'm from Ringsend and I was born in a tenement. My father was a fisherman all his life. He used to fish on boats that had sails on the ocean cause they had no other energy then. I came out of school at 14 as a messenger boy in the butcher's shop. I carried a basket, got six shillings a week. On a Saturday you'd go in at 8.00 and you wouldn't finish till nearly 12.00 at night. I stuck that for a year and a half. Then I went to the fishing. Now the first time I went into a pub the first drink I had was Devonshire cider, it's alcoholic. I was after being fishing for salmon that day and I got £1 and that was the first £1 I ever earned. I was about 15. I was with the crew that I was fishing with and I got the £1 in the pub on the quay. I felt like a real man, getting a £1 note, do you know what I mean? Oh, a *lot* of money. But most of me life I worked at the Irish Glass Bottle Company. The bottles would come down the shoot and you'd pick them up and place them. I got thirty shillings a week. Oh, hot! Tremendous heat coming out of it. And the bottle makers were big drinkers, it was a thirsty job you know. I often drank ten, eleven pints meself, no bother.

"There were six or seven pubs around Ringsend. Now money was very scarce then and the pubs used to close at 10.00 and maybe you'd see the fishermen going in at half nine and maybe having two pints at the most. They hadn't the money. For most of the men down here it was just recreation for the mind, they went over to have a chat with their friends and they'd hang over a pint for maybe an hour. And they loved the sing-songs, especially on a Saturday night. I remember a pub down the street here and if you didn't sing the owner would take up, '*Now*, lads, what about a sing-song?', and he'd turn off the wireless. And you'd have an MC there and he'd be calling on different fellas that'd have a bit of a voice and there'd be a fella with an old melodeon. But a lot of fellas when they'd build up a slate they'd go to another pub and the publicans didn't like that. But he'd be welcomed back by paying what he owed. And back then there were moneylenders in the pub and there was a blind eye to it. A couple of men in Ringsend used to lend money and it was five shillings interest to the pound and you'd have to pay it back. And then fishermen would go into the pubs and look for hands to go to sea. And they'd give them plenty of drink and then shanghai them! Oh, yes. Fill them full of drink and carry them down and put them aboard the ship and they'd be away for Tombouctou!

"Peter North's pub, we used to call it 'Smokey Joe's' because all the old fishermen and bottle blowers always had pipes in their mouth. Especially the old clay pipe and they'd break the stem off it and they used to call them jaw warmers. The bowl of the pipe'd be stuck up against their jaw and they'd be always spitting into the sawdust. These bottle blowers were very aloof, stayed with their own kind in a pub. And they'd walk on the opposite side of the road with gold chains hanging out of their waistcoat and gold watches. Now there was very few women frequented pubs then but they'd be in the snugs over there at Smokey Joe's. Wearing shawls. They'd get a gill. I remember these three women used to drink there and Guinness's had three boats and they were nicknamed after the three boats, the Clare Island, the Clare Castle and the Carradore. And they'd say, 'There's the Clare Island going up to the pub.'

"Ringsend pubs had their own rings clubs and they'd go out to some other pub in the city to play them and they'd return the compliment and come down here. Oh, some of them was very good with the rings. And we had skip clubs down here, the rowing, and they'd pick a crew for rowing out of the pubs. Each pub had their own rowing crew. And some pubs from Irishtown, so maybe seven or eight pubs would be rowing against one another. It was a public house race. And we won it. I rowed for Fitzharris's pub, around 1940. I was asked to row for them and we won the race and they had us six to one. And there was bookies down there and all and we put a lot of money on our pub. I don't know how we won it, honestly. And there was a hooley going on for a whole week in the pub, no transactions with money . . . loads of drink. Drink on the house for a whole week!"

PADDY MOONEY—AGE 75

He grew up in the Liberties where you could get into the "Yank" Reynolds's speakeasy if you knew the secret knock on the door. Some unscrupulous publicans watered their whiskey and had ingenious methods of reducing the amount of whiskey served. Even worse were those devious publicans who would serve the "slops" to unknowing customers

"I first tasted beer at 4 or 5 years of age. The occasion was when me father used to come in he'd bring in the large bottles and he always gave us a small wine glass of stout. I'd say my father gave it to us for health purposes because it was always held that Guinness stout was good to counteract worms. And then graduating from that when my father died I went to live with uncles and they always had hooleys on Saturday and Sunday night and I always had a drink for meself but nobody noticed. This was starting at 10 years of age. It was porter.

Now the first pub that I was in was in Castleknock with this friend of mine Tom Kierney and we had been out swimming. We were about 16 years of age and we had a few shillings because we had started work and we said we'd go in and have a drink. And we went into this pub and we weren't refused. And I remember that we had three small bottles of stout each and, oh, our heads were going around cause that was an awful lot of drink for us. But we felt very *happy*. You felt great. What it meant was that you were *initiated*.

"When we lived in Pimlico there was Ryan's pub at the corner, that was the nearest one to us. Public houses were all very small and wooden tables and sawdust on the floor cause men at that time were constantly spitting. They were mostly labouring people in Ryan's. They'd work on construction jobs and maybe in some of the small factories and in the skin yards. And there were some tradesmen in the pub and they would drink stout rather than porter and they'd wear their collar and tie. They'd talk to the labourers but there was an expression at that time: 'I was with him but I wasn't in his company.' Meaning that you would talk with each other but you wouldn't buy drink for each other. And very few women went into public houses but it didn't mean that women didn't drink. Like Biddy, baskets of bottles used to go into her place but she never stood in a public house in her life. She lived opposite to us in Pimlico and the porter from the pub used to carry the beer in baskets for her. Never stood in a public house but she was semi-drunk for the best part of her life!

"The 'Yank' Reynolds's pub was a speakeasy, up in Marrowbone Lane. Oh, it was a regular licensed pub but then after hours he'd close the doors. This even happened in the daytime when there was the Holy Hour. The barman'd come along and say, 'We're closing now, anybody want to get out? Last chance, anybody want to get out? Okay, you're locked in.' And the bolts and the lock would be put on the door and you were locked in so you just kept on drinking. Then to get in after that you had to know the knock on the door. And at the Yank Reynolds's you had to be *known*. So the door was closed and you could stay in there but if you were boisterous in any way *out* you'd go. Even when I was a kid it was called a speakeasy.

"Now barmen fiddling with the till, that was a common practice in most public houses. It was known as 'fiddling on the till'. It'd be done during the day. I remember a man, Johnny Curran, and he was a Tipperary man and he had a pub at the corner of Engine Alley. And Johnny had the shakes, there was something wrong with him, but it wasn't from drink. But he decided to give up the pub and he said he'd sell the pub. And as soon as he said he'd sell the pub his foreman says, 'I'll buy if off you.' And the foreman *did* buy the pub and Johnny himself had to say, 'I know I gave him good wages but, Christ Almighty, *where* did he get the money for to buy the pub?' Everybody said that. He did it behind the counter because he was on the *fiddle*! It was being done time out of number all over the place. Everywhere you'd go you'd see foremen buying public houses. Unless they had some rich uncles in America! And I don't think there's that many rich uncles in America.

"And watering down whiskey was done in a couple of places. But instead of watering down the whiskey what some of the barmen used to do was to use the little measure for measuring out the whiskey and they'd put a coin at the [bottom] end. You had to get a coin that would fit, a coin that sticks, and you had to press it in. So you fill out the whiskey and you throw it into the glass and you hand it up. But that coin, as small as it is, has taken so much whiskey out of the amount of whiskey that you were supposed to get.

"And now I've often gotten bad pints. A bad pint can maybe be from a barman not knowing his stuff or how to top it up. Or it could be the cooling system that they have. Or maybe the pumps not properly washed out. But I got bad pints and, my God, my stomach would be in an awful state and I'd say, 'What's wrong with this drink?' So this happened to me at this pub once—then it happened to me twice. And so I went again and *this* time instead of facing the barman I went down to the *end* of the bar and looked up where he was pulling the pints. Well, there was at least a dozen pint glasses, some of them half full, some of them a quarter full, some with a little drop in it. And sure he was pulling pints out of all these *slops* and he was giving me the slops. It was beer that was left over from the other people who didn't finish their drink. Now that's supposed to be thrown out. But some publicans have got it down to a fine art that all those slops are given up as drink and, of course, they're saving on that.

"But there were great characters in a public house. Like in McGraw's public house. It was a pub that I liked because it was in *bits*. Oh, talk about a working-class pub! It was gone a hundred years beyond when it should have been redecorated. Now there was this fella Sylvester and Sylvester was an innocent sort of a fella and so they'd say, 'Ah, Sylvester, would you give us a bit of a song?' And he was the worst singer in the world! So he'd start singing and you couldn't hear him, you wouldn't hear him behind a sheet of toilet paper. They would always be seeing how they could project his voice and he'd be standing on tables and he *still* couldn't sing. It was just having a bit of fun with him. They were simple characters. Like 'Professor' Murphy, for instance. Now Professor Murphy was as thick as a bus. He knew nothing. He did nothing, only listen, until you had your argument and then they'd all get it up for Professor Murphy and they'd say, 'Ah, we're not getting anywhere in this argument, we'll have to go to Professor Murphy.' And there'd be Professor Murphy sitting there. He *lived* at the pub. So they'd say, 'Now what do you think of this, Professor?' And it didn't matter *what* you were talking about, politics, art, science, literature, music, drama, you could name the whole lot and he was an *authority* on it. And it was great to listen to him because he'd say, 'Well, he's right in what he says, but then what he said was right.' And then at the latter end you had to go by what Professor Murphy thought. Didn't matter what it was. And he knew *nothing*! But he was the last word. See, fellas would get into an argument themselves in order to get him going cause he'd always be sitting back listening to you. They were all simple sort of fellas that they'd make a bit of fun out of, but there was no malice there. It was a bit of entertainment for them at the time.

"Sometimes there'd be rows in pubs. Anything could spark it off. Could be football, could be horses, that some fella'd know more about horses than the other fella. And everybody's personality changes with drink. Now I remember Paddy Murphy and his son and they had an argument in Ryan's pub and it was on a Sunday. There was a *terrible* argument between the Murphys, father and son, and they were both fighting men they were. But it was getting very, very hot inside the pub and so they said, 'C'mon outside and we'll finish this.' And they went outside and the father and son fought each other and all the friends that was with the father and son, they all formed a ring. And the son eventually made bits of the father but it was after a tough fight. It lasted twenty minutes. And you'd want to see that old fella, he came into the pub the following day and he was as proud as punch and he says, 'The *only man* around the Liberties that can beat me was me own son.' He said that. *Proud* of it! Proud that his own son was able to beat him up—but nobody *else* could do it."

JOHN PRESTON—AGE 67

At age 17 he was drinking in Sorohan's speakeasy gulping down jam jars of stout at sixpence each while a lookout was posted at the door to keep watch for a police raid. In later years he frequented a pub in Parnell Street where Father "Flash" Kavanagh could be seen still wearing his red vestments while putting away pints and small whiskies.

"As a child you daren't put your nose inside of a public house. My granny used to send me for a gill in a jug and I'd have to wait until someone going in or coming out would get it for me and you'd have to hide it under a sheet of paper so no one could see it. But if you walked into a public house you'd get a box and they didn't care who you were. And when we were kids and we were going to a funeral they'd put you up on the dickey of the horse-drawn cab beside the driver. And he'd put a rug over you on a cold day and then you had to *stay* there when they went into a pub. For a woman it was a day's outing and they'd stay in the pub for the rest of the day and maybe have a sing-song. They'd bring you out a glass of raspberry and a package of biscuits. I remember going to a funeral with me mother and father—I was only 9 or 10 at the time and I remember it as if it were yesterday—and I think we were going to Dean's Grange and there was a bit of a hill and the horse that was pulling us dropped dead. The driver had to stay there till the knackers came and took the horse away.

"Now I used to drink in Sorohan's at 17 years of age. It was an off-licence and you weren't allowed to drink in it, not by law, only unofficially. See, it was a shop *not* for customers to drink, just to take away. I used to get in the side door and pay sixpence for a stout and we used to have to drink it out of a jam jar. A fella named 'Ski Heaps', that was his nickname, he was the doorman. I don't know how he got his nickname cause there's not much snow here! It was three knocks to get in. Ski would come out first and he'd look up and down the street to see if there was any of the law. Then he'd let you in. It wasn't in the shop now, there was a yard with a roof on it out in the back. Ah, he'd get twenty fellas in.

But the police, they'd raid occasionally. Oh, yeah, often done a raid. Raid in uniform. Bang on the door and everybody'd scatter in the back. And if the police raided it they used to jump up over the wall and some of them'd even bring their drink with them. You know, destroy the evidence! And they'd run in their house and get under their mother's bed. If they came to your door your mother'd go to the door and you'd be hiding under the bed. That's the truth now.

"Nearly all the pubs along the quays were dockers' pubs. You had the Liverpool Bar and the Wharf Tavern and Campion's and Connor's. And on the south side you had Kennedy's, Walsh's and Kelly's and the Lighthouse Bar down at Ringsend. Then you had the shebeens after hours. Like you had one down in Seville Place and you could get in there at night time. It was a drinking place, but illegal. And I remember Becky Cooper's kip house on Railway Street. I knew her personally. A big woman. And she had plenty of jewellery around her neck. I was in there one day supposed to be drinking coffee and there must have been something else in the coffee because it made me very happy. It was probably brandy or poitín. Anyway, I often sold sawdust to these pubs. I got it from the sawmills. I brought it on an old two-wheel boxcart. I got sixpence for that. They put sawdust there to keep it clean, for spilling drink. And for spitting as well. They'd sweep that up twice a day, like when they'd close at half two for the Holy Hour. Fellas would mostly stomp on it when they'd put their cigarettes out but you would get an odd one that'd leave the thing lighted in the sawdust and it would start to smoulder.

"I was a docker and dockers then used to get paid every night and that's how the publicans used to do well. You'd get a fella that'd only have one pint and go straight home and hand over his few bob to his wife, but then you'd get the other fella that'd go into the pub and he'd come out and have nothing left for his wife. I can mention one man, Sherlock, he's dead and buried now. He was a docker. That fella could *drink*. He brought me into this pub once and let me cover the first drink. And he kept watching me and he didn't touch his drink and I went down to nearly half. And he hadn't even touched his pint. And we called for two more pints and he picked up his pint and threw it down in one act. He put his pint out of sight in one gulp! That's the way he drank. *One* sip! That's the gospel truth. I'd say he could put away at least thirty in a day. At *least* thirty. And still be standing on his two feet. He was a huge man. But sometimes we used to give the publican a hand washing glasses behind the counter. And this fella Sherlock, he'd come in and he'd stand right at the trays where the fellas'd be pulling the pints and putting them there to settle and then to top them off. So Sherlock used to give me the wink and he'd wait till they were nearly settled and he'd put one away in one gulp and then throw the glass over to me. *One* gulp. This is gospel. And the barman'd say, 'Wait a minute, what's going on here? There were four pints there a minute ago and now there's only one!' And I had to keep washing the glasses to take the onus off him. Gulped it down and put the empty glass back. He could do that all day.

"Now Noctor's pub down in Sheriff Street, that's been there for donkey's years, over a hundred years. The Noctors are all dead and gone now. Noctor's son was a priest and he used to be behind the bar as well. When he'd come home on holidays and there was a crowd in the shop I used to see him behind the bar in his collar pulling pints. Of course, he learned to pull a pint in the pub before he became a priest. Noctor's was always a good pub, a good neighbourly crowd drank in it, but the snugs, they were for women. That reminds me of these two old women who had a few drinks in Doran's pub in Marlborough Street a couple of days before Christmas and they were passing the Pro-Cathedral and one says, 'I'm going to Confession, I might see you later on.' So she went into the confession box and she sat down on the little seat and she was waiting there and then she dozed off and the priest pulls back the slide and says, 'Yes?' and she says, 'Give me two more bottles and put the f ——— light on in the snug.'

"Rings were very popular in my time. You'd bet in public houses for pints. I used to do MC for the rings up in the Sligo Bar. All the top dogs there. I used to take the rings off the board and hand them back to them. And I just made sure they toed the line. And I had to keep the order for them as well, keep order for the men that was pitching. They played from one to thirteen and from thirteen back to one. Twenty-six numbers. Oh, you want to see the money that was changing hands! Some were playing for £20 and £30 a time. This would be in the late fifties now. Have the money in their hands. The two men that's playing would bet and, see, it was a two-horse race and so other fellas'd back the winner. I got a few bob off them for being MC and the man behind the counter used to look after me regards to drink.

"The Sligo Bar was on Parnell Street and there was this fella named 'Hurler' who lived in Summerhill. He was a great character in the pub, a great sense of humour he had. He was like Charlie Chaplin, had the moustache and a trilby hat and all. And he had a stick and he used to *walk* like him and all. Great crack and jokes and he'd really make you laugh. And in the war years you got American soldiers, the Yanks. They'd be welcome in the pubs. But they wouldn't be able to drink a pint. A glass of ale, that'd be their drink and they'd hang over it for the night. They just wouldn't be able for stout. They were interested in women only. And the kids used to chase them all around the city saying, 'Any gum chum?'

"Brendan Behan used to be in Paddy Clare's pub—he was in *every* pub in the neighbourhood. That's where he used to get most of his material. He used to go into the snug and he'd listen to all the chatter and that's how he got all his material, in public houses. A robust fella and a lovable rogue. Well, he was lovable and he was *un*lovable. He'd go out bumming in the heel of his days, when he was nearly finished. He'd come into a pub on Moore Street where all the dealers sell and he'd be very shabby looking and he'd ask you for a drink. I pitied him. And yer man refused him and he had to walk out. I felt sorry for him, you know. But Clare's was a great old shop, it was more of a club than a pub. They all met there. Ah, they done some terrible things there. They had a ring room there and there was a fella named 'Hen' Mahoney. His name was Henry but they called him Hen. Now they had a ring room and there was a big sofa in it. Well, Hen got very drunk one night and they brought him in and put him on the sofa and they joined his hands and they got a sheet and they put it over him and they put a black cross on it. And they got a little table inside and put a saucer of holy water and a feather in it. And a saucer of pepper. And Hen was sleeping away and he woke up and he sees this and he thinks he's f——— dead. That's the gospel truth. That happened! I think he went off the drink for a while.

"And Father Flash Kavanagh, he'd drink in the pub called the Deer's Head in Parnell Street. Used to drink there in the mornings and you'd see him locked [drunk]. You'd see him in there with his red vestments and he'd go right through the bar to a little back snug there and that's where he used to be and that was his berth. Nearly every day he was there. He used to do 10.00 Mass because the pubs opened at half ten and he'd be in there then at half ten—in a flash. That was him, 'Flash' Kavanagh. He'd drink pints and small ones [whiskies]—all according to the collection that morning!"

Appendix

Dublin's Historic Pubs

Genuine Victorian Pubs

The Palace Bar	Fleet Street
Toner's	Baggot Street
Doheny & Nesbitt	Baggot Street
The Swan	Aungier Street
Conway's	Parnell Street
Regan's	Tara Street
The Long Hall	South Great George's Street
Slattery's	Capel Street
The Stag's Head	Dame Street
Ryan's	Parkgate Street
The International Bar	Wicklow Street
Gaffney's	Fairview
The Hut	Phibsboro
Bowe's	Fleet Street
Kehoe's	South Anne Street
Sorrento House	Dalkey
Cassidy's	Camden Street
The Norseman	East Essex Street

Pubs Retaining Strong Characteristics of Victorian Age but not Classically Victorian

Mulligan's	Poolbeg Street
Mulligan's	Stoneybatter
Hanlon's	North Circular Road
Kavanagh's	Aughrim Street
The Gravedigger's	Glasnevin
McDaid's	Harry Street
The Lord Edward	Christ Church Place
The Portobello	Rathmines
Slattery's	Rathmines
The Brazen Head	Bridge Street

The Wig & Pen	Capel Street
Searson's	Baggot Street
Sandyford House	
& Public Bar	Sandyford
Bambrick's	South Richmond Street
Alfie Byrne's	Chancery Place
Clarke's	Irishtown

PUBS OFTEN REGARDED AS VICTORIAN BUT WHICH ARE CLASSIC EDWARDIAN

O'Neill's	Suffolk Street
Neary's	Chatham Street

(*Source*: Mr Frank Fell, Director, Licensed Vintners' Association, Dublin, 1995)

NOTES

INTRODUCTION (pp 1–7)

1. Barnaby Rich, *A New Description of Ireland* (London: Thomas Adams, 1610) p. 70.
2. Elizabeth Malcolm, *'Ireland Sober, Ireland Free', Drink and Intemperance in Nineteenth-Century Ireland* (Syracuse: Syracuse University Press, 1986) p. 12.
3. John O'Donovan, *Life by the Liffey* (Dublin: Gill & Macmillan Ltd, 1986) p. 16.
4. Samuel A. Ossory Fitzpatrick, *Dublin: A Historical and Topographical Account of the City* (London: Methuen & Co. Ltd, 1907) p. 206.
5. O'Donovan, op. cit., note 3, p. 31.
6. Desmond Clarke, *Dublin* (London: B. T. Batsford Ltd, 1977) p. 92.
7. P. T. Winskill, *The Temperance Movement and Its Workers* (London: Blackie & Son Ltd, 1891) Vol. I, p. 47.
8. Reverend James Whitelaw, *An Essay on the Population of Dublin* (Dublin: Graisberry and Campbell, 1808) p. 62.
9. Father Myles V. Ronan, *An Apostle of Catholic Dublin* (Dublin: Browne and Nolan Ltd, 1944) p. 190.
10. Sir Charles A. Cameron, *How the Poor Live* (Private printing in 1904 and presented to the National Library of Ireland, 8 May 1905) p. 14.
11. H. A. Monckton, *A History of the English Public House* (London: The Bodley Head, 1969) p. 9.
12. Maurice Gorham and H. Dunnett, *Inside the Pub* (Ipswich: W. S. Cowell Ltd, 1950) p. 40.
13. Mass-Observation (Study Group) *The Pub and the People* (London: Victor Gollancz Ltd, 1943) p. 18.
14. Thomas Burke, *Will Someone Lead Me to a Pub?* (London: Routledge, 1936) p. 3
15. Michael A. Smith, 'Social Uses of the Public Drinking House: Changing Aspects of Class and Leisure', *The British Journal of Sociology*, Vol. XXXIV, No. 3, 1983, p. 384.
16. Liam Blake and David Pritchard, *Irish Pubs* (Bray: Real Ireland Press, 1985) no pagination.
17. Monckton, op. cit., note 11, p. 7.
18. Marshall B. Clinard, 'The Public Drinking House and Society', in David J. Pittman and Charles R. Snyder (eds) *Society, Culture and Drinking Patterns* (New York: John Wiley, 1962) p. 270.
19. Mass-Observation, op. cit., note 13, p. 10.
20. Vincent Caprani, *Rowdy Rhymes and 'Rec-im-itations'* (Dublin: M. C. Caprani, 1982) no pagination; and Maurice Gorham, 'The Pub

Tradition', in Roy Boulson (ed.) *Irish Pubs of Character* (Dublin: Bruce Spicer Ltd, 1969) p. 11.

21.   Personal interview with Frank Fell, Director of the Dublin Licensed Vintners' Association. This figure is based on a calculation made by senior publicans in the association.

CHAPTER 1. *HISTORY AND EVOLUTION OF DUBLIN PUBLIC HOUSES* (pp 8–26)

1.   Kevin Danaher, *In Ireland Long Ago* (Dublin: Mercier Press, 1962) p. 51.

2.   David J. Pittman and Charles R. Snyder, *Society, Culture and Drinking Patterns* (New York: John Wiley, 1962) p. 176.

3.   James R. Barrett, 'Why Paddy Drank: The Social Importance of Whiskey in Pre-Famine Ireland', *Journal of Popular Culture*, No. 1, 1977, p. 161.

4.   P. T. Winskill, *The Temperance Movement and Its Workers* (London: Blackie and Son Ltd, Vol. I, 1891) p. 48.

5.   ibid., p. 48.

6.   A. Peter, *Dublin Fragments* (Dublin: Hodges, Figgis & Co., 1928) p. 92.

7.   Elizabeth Malcolm, *'Ireland Sober, Ireland Free', Drink and Temperance in Nineteenth-Century Ireland* (Syracuse: Syracuse University Press, 1986) p. 12.

8.   Barnaby Rich, *A New Description of Ireland* (London: Thomas Adams, 1610) p. 70.

9.   John O'Donovan, *Life by the Liffey* (Dublin: Gill & Macmillan Ltd, 1986) p. 16.

10.   ibid., p. 31.

11.   ibid., p. 31.

12.   D. A. Chart, *The Story of Dublin* (London: J. M. Dent & Sons, 1931) p. 139.

13.   Edward MacLysaght, *Irish Life in the Seventeenth Century* (Dublin: The Talbot Press, 1939) p. 199.

14.   Samuel A. Ossory Fitzpatrick, *Dublin: A Historical and Topographical Account of the City* (London: Methuen & Co. Ltd, 1907) p. 206.

15.   Malcolm, op. cit., note 7, p. 25.

16.   Nicholas O'Hare, 'Early Brewing Days in Ireland', *Irish Licensing World*, December 1967, p. 36.

17.   Desmond Clarke, *Dublin* (London: B. T. Batsford Ltd, 1977) p. 92.

18.   Malcolm, op. cit., note 7, p. 51.

19.   John Gamble, *Sketches of Dublin* (London: Baldwin, Cradock and Joy, 1826) p. 82.

20.   Deirdre Linsay, *Dublin's Oldest Charity* (Dublin: The Anniversary Press, 1991) p. 17.

21.   J. W. Hammond, 'When "Hell" was the Name of a Tavern in John's Lane', *Irish Licensing World*, April 1968, p. 8.

22.   Winskill, op. cit., note 4, p. 47.

23.   Reverend James Whitelaw, *An Essay on the Population of Dublin* (Dublin: Graisberry and Campbell, 1805) p. 50.

24. Malcolm, op. cit., note 7, p. 46.
25. Clarke, op. cit., note 17, p. 102.
26. John Rutty, *Natural History of Dublin* (Dublin: no publisher cited, 1772) p. 12.
27. G. C. Lewis, *Observations on the Habits of the Labouring Classes in Ireland* (Dublin: Miliken & Son, 1836) p. 20.
28. O'Donovan, op. cit., note 9, p. 31.
29. Sir John T. Gilbert, *The Streets of Dublin* (Dublin: no publisher cited, 1852) p. 333.
30. Ossory, op. cit., note 14, p. 206.
31. Malachy Magee, *1000 Years of Irish Whiskey* (Dublin: O'Brien Press, 1980) p. 76.
32. ibid., p. 75.
33. *Report From the Select Committee of the House of Lords on Intemperance*, Vol. XIV (London: House of Commons, 1878) p. 340.
34. *Report From the Select Committee on Sale of Intoxicating Liquors on Sunday (Ireland) Bill*, Vol. XVI, 1877 (London: House of Commons, 1877) p. 104.
35. *Report From the Select Committee of the House of Lords on Intemperance*, 1878, op. cit., note 33, p. 332.
36. *Report From the Select Committee on Sale of Intoxicating Liquors on Sunday (Ireland) Bill*, 1877, op. cit., note 34, p. 122.
37. *Report From the Select Committee of the House of Lords on Intemperance*, 1878, op. cit., note 33, p. 351.
38. *Report From the Select Committee on Sale of Intoxicating Liquors on Sunday (Ireland) Bill*, 1877, op. cit., note 34, p. 121.
39. *Report From the Select Committee on Sale of Intoxicating Liquors on Sunday (Ireland) Bill*, 1877, op. cit., note 34, p. 122.
40. *Report From the Select Committee on Sale of Intoxicating Liquors on Sunday (Ireland) Bill*, 1877, op. cit., note 34, p. 121.
41. Michael Gill, 'A Room in Ship Street in 1817', *Licensed Vintner's Magazine*, June 1967, p. 19.
42. Michael Gill, 'Modern Links with the Old Traditional Irish Pub', *Licensed Vintner's Magazine*, June 1967, p. 19.
43. Malcolm, op. cit., note 7, p. 207.
44. *Report From the Select Committee on Sale of Intoxicating Liquors on Sunday (Ireland) Bill*, 1877, op. cit., note 34, p. 95.
45. *Report From the Select Committee of the House of Lords on Intemperance*, 1878, op. cit., note 34, p. 95.
46. Winskill, op. cit., note 4, p. 48.
47. Malcolm, op. cit., note 7, p. 68.
48. Whitelaw, op. cit., note 23, p. 62.
49. Father Henry Young, *A Short Essay on the Grievous Crime of Drunkenness*, (Dublin: no publication data, 1823).
50. Malcolm, op. cit., note 7, p. 69.
51. Joseph O'Brien, *Dear, Dirty Dublin* (Berkeley: University of California Press, 1982) p. 188.

52. Norman Longmate, *The Waterdrinkers* (London: Hamish Hamilton, 1968) p. 120.

53. Winskill, op. cit., note 4, p. 99.

54. *Report From the Select Committee on Sale of Intoxicating Liquors on Sunday (Ireland) Bill*, 1877, note 34, p. 54.

55. Longmate, op. cit., note 52, p. 119.

56. A. J. Nowlan, 'Phoenix Park Public Meetings', *Dublin Historical Record*, Vol. XIV, No. 4, 1958, p. 108.

57. *Report From the Select Committee of the House of Lords on Intemperance*, 1878, op. cit., note 33, p. 15.

58. *Report From the Select Committee of the House of Lords on Intemperance*, 1878, op. cit., note 33, p. 15.

59. *Report From the Select Committee on Sale of Intoxicating Liquors on Sunday (Ireland) Bill*, 1877, note 34, p. 16.

60. *Special Report From the Select Committee on Sale of Intoxicating Liquors on Sunday (Ireland) Bill*, Vol. XIV (London: House of Commons, 1867–68) p. 62.

61. *Special Report From the Select Committee on Sale of Intoxicating Liquors on Sunday (Ireland) Bill*, 1867–8, op. cit., note 60, p. 115.

62. *Report From the Select Committee on Sale of Intoxicating Liquors on Sunday (Ireland) Bill*, 1877, op. cit., note 34, p. 72.

63. *Report From the Select Committee on Sale of Intoxicating Liquors on Sunday (Ireland) Bill*, 1877, op. cit., note 34, p. 107.

64. *Report From the Select Committee on Sale of Intoxicating Liquors on Sunday (Ireland) Bill*, 1877, op. cit., note 34, p. 73.

65. Charles A. Cameron, *How the Poor Live* (Dublin: private printing in 1904 and presented to the National Library of Ireland, 8 May 1905) p. 14.

66. *Report From the Select Committee on Sale of Intoxicating Liquors on Sunday (Ireland) Bill*, 1877, op. cit., note 34, p. 102.

67. *Report From the Select Committee of the House of Lords on Intemperance*, 1878, op. cit., note 33, p. 369.

68. *Special Report From the Select Committee on Sale of Intoxicating Liquors on Sunday (Ireland) Bill*, 1867–68, op. cit., note 60, p. 106.

69. H. A. Monckton, *A History of the English Public House* (London: The Bodley Head, 1969) p. 9.

70. Alice Hoffman, 'Reliability and Validity in Oral History', in Willa K. Baum and David D. Dunaway (eds) *Oral History: An Interdisciplinary Anthology* (Nashville, Tennessee: American Association for State and Local History, 1984) p. 68.

71. John D. Brewer, *The Royal Irish Constabulary: An Oral History* (Belfast: Institute of Irish Studies, Queen's University, 1990) p. 14.

72. Richard Dorson, 'The Oral Historian and the Folklorist', in Willa K. Baum and David K. Dunaway (eds) *Oral History: An Interdisciplinary Anthology* (Nashville, Tennessee: American Association for State and Local History, 1984) p. 295.

73.   Charles T. Morrissey, 'Introduction', in Willa K. Baum and David K. Dunaway (eds) *Oral History: An Interdisciplinary Anthology* (Nashville, Tennessee: American Association for State and Local History, 1984) p. xxi.

74.   Paul Thompson, 'History and Community', in Willa K. Baum and David K. Dunaway (eds) *Oral History: An Interdisciplinary Anthology* (Nashville, Tennessee: American Association for State and Local History, 1984) p. 41.

75.   Hoffman, op. cit., note 70, p. 72.

76.   Ellis Brady, *All In! All In!* (Dublin: Comhairle Bheadloideas Éireann, University College, Belfield, 1984) Frontispiece.

77.   Mary Maloney, 'Dublin—Before All is Lost', *Evening Press*, 17 May 1980, p. 9.

CHAPTER 2. *DUBLIN PUB CULTURE AND SOCIAL LIFE* (pp 27–89)

1.   Maurice Gorham and H. Dunnett, *Inside the Pub* (Ipswich: W. S. Cowell Ltd, 1950) p. 40.

2.   Mass-Observation (Study Group), *The Pub and the People* (London: Victor Gollancz Ltd, 1943) p. 18.

3.   ibid., p. 218.

4.   ibid., p. 218.

5.   Thomas Burke, *Will Someone Lead Me to a Pub?* (London: Routledge, 1936) p. 3.

6.   Michael A. Smith, 'Social Uses of the Public Drinking House: Changing Aspects of Class and Leisure', *The British Journal of Sociology*, Vol. XXXIV, No. 3, 1983, p. 384.

7.   Ernest Selley, *The English Public House as It Is* (London: Longman, Green and Co. Ltd, 1927) p. 20.

8.   Peter Clark, *The English Alehouse* (London: Longman Publishers, 1983) p. 205.

9.   Burke, op. cit., note 5, p. 50.

10.   'Conversation as an Asset', *Irish Licensing World*, July 1968, p. 15.

11.   'The Perfect Publican', *Irish Licensing World*, December 1957, p. 60.

12.   ibid., p. 60.

13.   Brinsley MacNamara, 'The Ideal Publican', *Irish Licensing World*, June 1950, p. 228.

14.   Lar Redmond, *Show Us the Moon* (Dingle: Brandon Books, 1988) p. 56.

15.   John B. Keane, *Letters of an Irish Publican* (Dublin: Mercier Press, 1974) p. 32.

16.   'The Licensee and the Law', *Irish Licensing World*, July 1961, p. 226.

17.   'Pity the Publican', *Irish Licensing World*, July 1956, p. 242.

18.   Pete St John, *Jaysus Wept!* (Midland Tribune, 1984) p. 5.

19.   Tom Corkery, *Tom Corkery's Dublin* (Dublin: Anvil Books, 1980) p. 16.

20.   Stephen Potter, 'Pubmanship', in Angus McGill (ed.) *The Pub—A Celebration* (London: Longman, Green & Co. Ltd, 1969) p. 73.

21. Maurice Gorham, *The Local* (London: Cassell & Co. Ltd, 1939) p. 3.

22. Vincent Caprani, *Rowdy Rhymes and 'Rec-im-itations'* (Dublin: M. C. Caprani, no pagination, 1982) poem printed with permission of author.

23. Ethel Mannin, 'Women in Bars?', *Irish Licensing World*, Vol. 1, No. 1, 1947, p. 16.

24. ibid., p. 17.

25. Corkery, op. cit., note 9, p. 18.

26. Corkery, op. cit., note 9, p. 16.

27. John D. Sheridan, 'Yer Pint-Man', *Irish Licensing World*, December 1952, p. 22.

28. St John, op. cit., note 8, p. 30.

29. John B. Keane, 'Pint of Porter', *Irish Licensing World*, December 1964, p. 38.

30. Sheridan, op. cit., note 27, p. 22.

31. Corkery, op. cit., note 9, p. 17.

32. Corkery, op. cit., note 9, p. 18.

33. Brian Cleeve, *A View of the Irish* (London: Buchan & Enright, 1983) p. 104.

34. Tony Gray, *The Irish Answer* (London: Heinemann, 1966) p. 309.

35. Keane, op. cit., note 29, p. 38.

36. Keane, op. cit., note 29, p. 38.

37. John D. Sheridan, 'Only Wives and Policemen Use the Word', *Irish Licensing World*, December 1951, p. 20.

38. *Irish Licensing World*, December 1958, p. 8.

39. St John, op. cit., note 8, p. 5.

40. Michael Geoghegan, 'The Pledge in Practice—The Difficulties That Beset It—The Help to Keep it', *Irish Ecclesiastical Record*, March 1890, p. 212.

41. John Ryan, *Remembering How We Stood* (Dublin: Lilliput Press, 1987) p. 26.

42. 'The Bonafide Lark', *Irish Licensing World*, April 1960, p. 161.

43. St John, op. cit., note 8, p. 50.

44. Eric Whelpton, *The Book of Dublin* (London: Rockliffe Press, 1948) p. 165.

45. John D Sheridan, 'The Singing Pubs of Dublin', *Irish Licensing World*, December 1962, p. 29.

46. Corkery, op. cit., note 9, p. 75.

47. Sheridan, op. cit., note 45, p. 29.

48. Corkery, op. cit., note 9, page 45.

49. Desmond Clarke, *Dublin* (London: B. T. Batsford Ltd, 1977) p. 97.

50. Page L. Dickinson, *The Dublin of Yesterday* (London: Methuen & Co., 1929) p. 73.

51. ibid., p. 73.

52. ibid., p. 73.

53. June Dwyer, 'A Drop Taken: The Role of Drinking in the Fiction and Drama of the Irish Literary Revival', *Contemporary Drug Problems*, Vol. 13, No. 2, 1986, p. 276.

54. ibid., p. 276.
55. ibid., p. 281.
56. Peter Walsh, *Dublin's Heritage of Pubs* (Dublin: Guinness Museum, no pagination, 1988).
57. Corkery, op. cit., note 9, p. 125.
58. Anthony Cronin, *Dead as Doornails* (Dublin: Poolbeg Press, 1976) p. 3.
59. Ryan, op. cit., note 41, p. 42.
60. Ryan, op. cit., note 41, p. 42.
61. Bernard Neary, *North of the Liffey* (Dublin: Lenhar Publications, 1984) p. 55.
62. Bill Kelly, *Me Darlin' Dublin's Dead and Gone* (Dublin: Ward River Press, 1983) p. 20.
63. 'The Strike', *Irish Licensing World*, July 1955, p. 239.
64. ibid., p. 239.
65. 'Death of Jim Downey Fails to End World's Longest Strike', *Irish Licensing World*, June 1963, p. 166.
66. ibid., p. 166.
67. Myles na gCopaleen, 'Some Side-Shows', *Irish Licensing World*, April 1965, p. 17; also 'One in Ten Dublin Bars has T.V.', *Irish Licensing World*, April 1956, p. 16.
68. 'Talking About Pubs', *Irish Licensing World*, June 1968, p. 15.
69. Gorham, op. cit., note 11, p. 4.
70. Angus McGill, *The Pub—A Celebration* (London: Longman, Green & Co., 1969) p. 216.

BIBLIOGRAPHY

Barrett, James R., 'Why Paddy Drank: The Social Importance of Whiskey in Pre-Famine Ireland', *Journal of Popular Culture*, No. 1, 1977, pp 155–66.

Barrington, Sir Jonah, *Personal Sketches of His Own Times* (London: Rutledge & Sons, 1869).

'Beer Drinkers Put Pub Life Before Love Life', *Irish Licensing World*, May 1968, p. 3.

Blake, Liam, and Pritchard, David, *Irish Pubs* (Bray: Real Ireland Press, 1985).

'The Bonafide Lark', *Irish Licensing World*, April 1960, p. 161.

'Bonafide Travellers', *Irish Licensing World*, January 1950, p. 88.

Brewer, John D., *The Royal Irish Constabulary: An Oral History* (Belfast: Institute of Irish Studies, Queen's University, 1990).

Burke, Thomas, *Will Someone Lead Me to a Pub?* (London: Routledge, 1936).

Burns, Dawson, *Temperance in the Victorian Age* (London: The Ideal Publishing Union, 1897).

Cameron, Charles A., *How the Poor Live* (Dublin: Private printing in 1904 and presented to the National Library of Ireland, 8 May 1905).

Cameron, Charles A., *Reminiscences of Sir Charles A. Cameron* (Dublin: Hodges, Figgis Ltd, 1913).

Caprani, Vincent, *Rowdy Rhymes and 'Rec-im-itations'* (Dublin: M. C. Caprani, 1982).

Carmichael, Rev. F. F., *Dublin—A Lecture* (Dublin: Hodges, Figgis & Co., 1907).

Chart, D. A., *The Story of Dublin* (London: J. M. Dent & Son, 1932).

Clark, Peter, *The English Alehouse* (London: Longman Publishers, 1983).

Clarke, Desmond, *Dublin* (London: B. T. Batsford Ltd, 1977).

Clinard, Marshall B., 'The Public Drinking House and Society', in David J. Pittman and Charles R. Snyder (eds) *Society, Culture and Drinking Patterns* (New York: John Wiley, 1962).

Connery, Donald S., *The Irish* (London: Eyre & Spottiswoode, 1968).

'Conversation As An Asset', *Irish Licensing World*, July 1968, p. 15.

Corkery, Tom, *Tom Corkery's Dublin* (Dublin: Anvil Books, 1980).

Cronin, Anthony, *Dead as Doornails* (Dublin: Poolbeg Press, 1976).

Daly, Mary E., *Dublin—The Deposed Capital* (Cork: Cork University Press, 1984).

Danaher, Kevin, *In Ireland Long Ago* (Dublin: Mercier Press, 1962).

Dawson, Timothy, 'The Brazen Head Re-Visited', *Dublin Historical Record*, Vol. XXVI, No. 2, 1973, pp 42–50.

'Death of Jim Downey Fails to End World's Longest Strike', *Irish Licensing World*, June 1953, p. 166.

Dickinson, Page L., *The Dublin of Yesterday* (London: Methuen & Co., 1929).

Dorson, Richard, 'The Oral Historian and the Folklorist', in Willa K. Baum and David K. Dunaway (eds) *Oral History: An Interdisciplinary Anthology* (Nashville, Tennessee: American Association for State and Local History, 1984).

Dublin Explorations and Reflections, written by an anonymous Englishman (Dublin: Maunsel & Co., 1917).

Dwyer, June, 'A Drop Taken: The Role of Drinking in the Fiction and Drama of the Irish Literary Revival', *Contemporary Drug Problems*, Vol. 13, No. 2, 1986, pp 273–85.

Fair, T. Wilson, 'The Dublin Total Abstinence Society', in Frederick Sherlock (ed.) *Fifty Years Ago: Or Erin's Temperance Jubilee* (Belfast: no publisher cited, 1879) pp 74–9.

Farson, Daniel, 'How Not to Run a Pub!', in Angus McGill (ed.) *The Pub—A Celebration* (London: Longman, Green & Co., 1969) pp 87–92.

Fitzpatrick, Samual A., *Dublin: A Historical and Topographical Account of the City* (London: Methuen & Co. Ltd, 1907).

Fourth Report From the Select Committee of the House of Lords on Intemperance, Vol. XIV (London: House of Commons, 1878).

Gamble, John, *Sketches of Dublin* (London: Baldwin, Cradock and Joy, 1826).

Geoghegan, Michael, 'The Pledge in Practice—The Difficulties That Beset It —The Helps to Keep It', *Irish Ecclesiastical Record*, March 1890, pp 217–21.

Gilbert, Sir John T., *The Streets of Dublin* (Dublin: no publisher cited, 1852).

Gill, Michael, 'Modern Links with the Old Traditional Irish Pub', *Licensed Vintner's Magazine*, June 1967, p. 19.

Gill, Michael, 'A Room in Ship Street, 1817', *Licensed Vintner's Magazine*, June 1967, pp 9–13.

Gorham, Maurice, *The Local* (London: Cassell & Co., 1939).

Gorham, Maurice, 'The Pub Tradition', in Roy Boulson (ed.) *Irish Pubs of Character* (Dublin: Bruce Spicer Ltd, 1969).

Gwynn, Stephen, *Dublin Old and New* (Dublin: Browne and Nolan Ltd, 1938).

Hammond, J. W., 'When "Hell" was the Name of a Tavern in John's Lane', *Irish Licensing World*, 1968, pp 8–9.

Hanley, David, 'The Battle for the Waterloo Pub', *The Colour Tribune*, 26 October 1986, pp 10–11.

Harrison, Brian, *Drink and the Victorians* (London: Faber & Faber Ltd, 1971).

Henchy, Deirdre, 'Dublin 80 Years Ago', *Dublin Historical Record*, Vol. XXVI, No. 1, 1972, pp 18–34.

Hoffman, Alice, 'Reliability and Validity in Oral History', in Willa K. Baum and David K. Dunaway (eds) *Oral History: An Interdisciplinary Anthology* (Nashville, Tennessee: American Association for State and Local History, 1984).

Hunt, G. P., and Saterlee, S., 'The Pub, the Village and the People', *Human Organization*, Vol. 45, No. 1, 1986, pp 62–74.

'The Irish Pub', *Irish Licensing World*, April 1973, p. 3.

Johnston, Mairin, *Around the Banks of Pimlico* (Dublin: The Attic Press, 1985).

Keane, John B., *Letters of An Irish Publican* (Dublin: Mercier Press, 1974).

Keane, John B., 'Pint of Porter', *Irish Licensing World*, December 1964, p. 38.

Kearns, Kevin C., *Dublin Street Life and Lore: An Oral History* (Dublin: Glendale Press, 1991).

Kearns, Kevin C., *Dublin Tenement Life: An Oral History* (Dublin: Gill & Macmillan Ltd, 1994).

Kearns, Kevin C., *Stoneybatter: Dublin's Inner-Urban Village* (Dublin: Glendale Press, 1989).

Kelly, Bill, *Me Darlin' Dublin's Dead and Gone* (Dublin: Ward River Press, 1983).

'The Laminated Plastic Disease!', *Irish Licensing World*, July 1973, p. 28.

Lewis, G. C., *Observations on the Habits of the Labouring Classes in Ireland* (Dublin: Miliken & Son, 1836).

'The Licensee and the Law', *Irish Licensing World*, July 1961, p. 226.

Liddy, Pat, 'Brazen Head Inn', *The Irish Times*, 2 March 1983, p. 8.

'Lifting of Barmen Must Stop', *Irish Licensing World*, June 1955, p. 215.

Longford, Christine, *A Biography of Dublin* (London: Methuen & Co. Ltd, 1936).

Longmate, Norman, *The Waterdrinkers* (London: Hamish-Hamilton, 1968).

Lynch, Patrick, and Vaizey, John, *Guinness's Brewery in the Irish Economy, 1759–1876* (Cambridge: Cambridge University Press, 1960).

McGill, Angus, *The Pub—A Celebration* (London: Longman, Green & Co., 1969).

MacLysaght, Edward, *Irish Life in the Seventeenth Century* (Dublin: The Talbot Press, 1939).

MacNamara, Brinsley, 'The Ideal Publican', *Irish Licensing World*, June 1950, p. 228.

MacThomais, Eamonn, *Me Jewel and Darlin' Dublin* (Dublin: O'Brien Press, 1974).

Magee, Malachy, *1000 Years of Irish Whiskey* (Dublin: O'Brien Press, 1980).

Malcolm, Elizabeth, 'Ireland Sober, Ireland Free', *Drink and Temperance in Nineteenth-Century Ireland* (Syracuse, N.Y.: Syracuse University Press, 1986).

Maloney, Mary, 'Dublin—Before All is Lost', *Evening Press*, 17 May 1980, p. 9.

Mannin, Ethel, 'Women in Bars?', *Irish Licensing World*, Vol. 1, No. 1., 1947, pp 16–17.

Mass-Observation (Study Group), *The Pub and the People* (London: Victor Gollancz, 1943).

'Modern Irish Public Houses', *Irish Licensing World*, June 1966, p. 16.

Monckton, H. A., *A History of the English Public House* (London: The Bodley Head, 1969).

Morrissey, Charles T., 'Introduction', in Willa K. Baum and David K. Dunaway (eds) *Oral History: An Interdisciplinary Anthology* (Nashville, Tennessee: American Association for State and Local History, 1984).

na gCopaleen, Myles, 'Some Side-Shows', *Irish Licensing World*, April 1965, p. 17.

Neary, Bernard, *North of the Liffey* (Dublin: Lenhar Publications, 1984).

Nowlan, A. J., 'Phoenix Park Public Meetings', *Dublin Historical Record*, Vol. XIV, No. 4, 1958, pp 102–112.

O'Brien, Joseph V., *'Dear, Dirty Dublin'* (Berkeley: University of California Press, 1982).

O'Donovan, John, *Life by the Liffey* (Dublin: Gill & Macmillan Ltd, 1986).

O'Gorman, Andrew, 'Barman's Union has a Century of History', *Irish Licensing World*, March 1974, pp 17–19.

O'Hare, Nicholas, 'Early Brewing Days in Ireland', *Irish Licensing World*, December 1967, pp 36–7.

'One in Ten Dublin Bars Has T.V.', *Irish Licensing World*, April 1956, p. 161.

Oram, Hugh, 'The Traditional Irish Pub', *Inside Ireland*, No. 68, February 1995, pp 8–9.

Orpen, Sir William, *Stories of Old Dublin and Myself* (London: Williams and Norgate Ltd, 1924).

Pender, Brendan, 'The Potcheen Industry is Booming', *Irish Licensing World*, November 1955, p. 40.

'The Perfect Publican', *Irish Licensing World*, December 1957, p. 60.

Peter, A., *Dublin Fragments* (Dublin: Hodges, Figgis & Co., 1928).

Pittman, David J., and Snyder, Charles R., *Society, Culture and Drinking Patterns* (New York: John Wiley, 1962).

'Pity the Publican', *Irish Licensing World*, July 1956, p. 242.

'Potcheen by Helicopter', *Irish Licensing World*, January 1967, p. 16.

Potter, Stephen, 'Pubmanship', in Angus McGill (ed.) *The Pub—A Celebration* (London: Longman, Green & Co., 1969) pp 73–8.

'Pub of Men Who Wield the Pen', *Irish Independent*, 28 September 1972, p. 17.

'The Publican's Lot', *Irish Licensing World*, December 1962, p. 3.

Redmond, Lar, *Show Us the Moon* (Dingle: Brandon Books, 1988).

Reed, Sir Andrew, *The Liquor Licensing Laws of Ireland* (Dublin: Alex Thom & Co., 1907).

'Re-Opening of the Bailey', *Irish Licensing World*, January 1967, p. 4.

Report From the Select Committee on Sale of Intoxicating Liquors on Sunday (Ireland) Bill, 1877, Vol. XVI (London: House of Commons, 1877).

Rich, Barnaby, *A New Description of Ireland* (London: Thomas Adams, 1610).

Ronan, Father Myles V., *An Apostle of Catholic Dublin* (Dublin: Browne and Nolan Ltd, 1944).

Rutty, John, *Natural History of Ireland* (Dublin: no publisher cited, 1772).

Ryan, John, *Remembering How We Stood* (Dublin: Lilliput Press, 1987).

Selley, Ernest, *The English Public House as It Is* (London: Longman, Green and Co. Ltd, 1927).

Shaw, George Bernard, 'Drink', *Irish Licensing World*, Vol. 1, No. 1, 1947, p. 48.

Sheridan, John D., 'Only Wives and Policemen Use the Word', *Irish Licensing World*, December 1951, p. 20.

Sheridan, John D., 'The Singing Pubs of Dublin', *Irish Licensing World*, December 1962, p. 29.

Sheridan, John D., 'Yer Pint-Man', *Irish Licensing World*, December 1952, p. 22.

'The Slum Evil', *The Daily Nation*, 7 September 1898, p. 5.

Smith, Michael A., 'Social Usages of the Public Drinking House: Changing Aspects of Class and Leisure', *The British Journal of Sociology*, Vol. XXXIV, No. 3, 1983, pp 367–85.

Smyllie, Pat, 'Traditions of a Famous Dublin Pub', *Irish Press*, 2 April 1971, p. 13.

Somerville-Large, Peter, *Dublin* (London: Hamish-Hamilton, 1979).

Special Report From the Select Committee on the Sale of Liquors on Sunday (Ireland) Bill, Vol. XIV (London: House of Commons, 1867–1868).

Stivers, Richard, *A Hair of the Dog* (University Park, Pennsylvania: Pennsylvania State University Press, 1976).

St John, Pete, *Jaysus Wept!* (Midland Tribune, 1984).

'The Strike', *Irish Licensing World*, July 1955, p. 239.

'Talking About Pubs', *Irish Licensing World*, June 1968, p. 15.

Thompson, Paul, 'History and Community', in Willa K. Baum and David K. Dunaway (eds) *Oral History: An Interdisciplinary Anthology* (Nashville, Tennessee: American Association for State and Local History, 1984).

Vasey, Daniel E., *The Pub and English Social Change* (New York: AMS Press, 1990).

Walsh, John Edward, *Ireland Sixty Years Ago* (Dublin: M. H. Gill & Son Ltd, 1911).

Walsh, Maurice, 'My Ideal Pub', *Irish Licensing World*, March 1948, p. 124.

Walsh, Peter, *Dublin's Heritage of Pubs* (Dublin: Guinness Museum, 1988).

Whelpton, Eric, *The Book of Dublin* (London: Rockliffe Press, 1948).

Whitelaw, Rev. James, *An Essay on the Population of Dublin* (Dublin: Graisberry and Campbell, 1805).

Wilson, George B., *Alcohol and the Nation* (London: Nicholson and Watson, 1940).

Winskill, P. T., *The Temperance Movement and Its Workers* (London: Blackie and Son Ltd, 1891, Vol. I).

Winskill, P. T., *The Temperance Movement and Its Workers* (London: Blackie and Son Ltd, 1891, Vol. II).

INDEX

Numbers in bold refer to photograph caption numbers